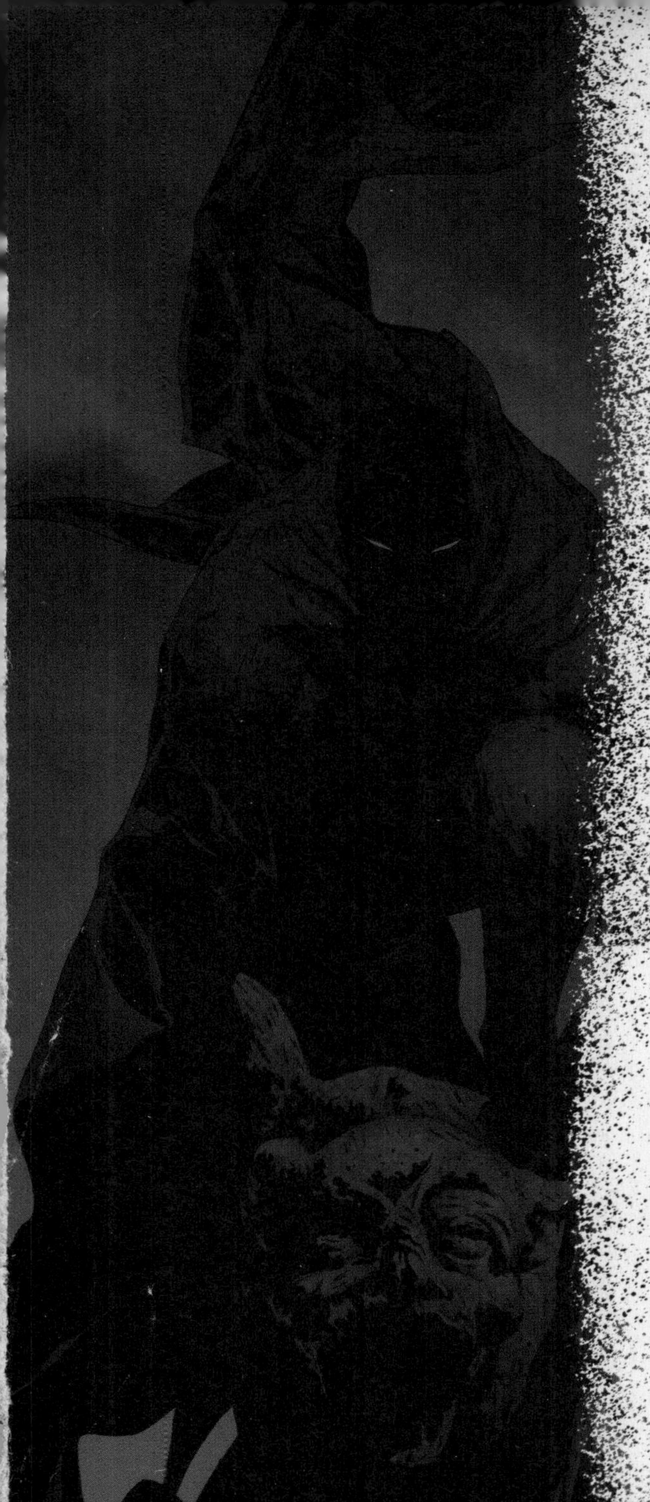

BATMAN WAR GAMES

ACT TWO TIDES

BATMAN WAR GAMES ACT 2

Published by DC Comics. Cover, introduction and compilation
copyright © 2005 DC Comics. All Rights Reserved.

Originally published in single magazine form as BATGIRL 56,
BATMAN 632, BATMAN: GOTHAM KNIGHTS 57, BATMAN: LEGENDS
OF THE DARK KNIGHT 183, CATWOMAN 35, DETECTIVE COMICS
798, NIGHTWING 97, ROBIN 130. Copyright © 2004 DC Comics.
All Rights Reserved. All characters, their distinctive likenesses
and related elements featured in this publication are trademarks
of DC Comics.
The stories, characters and incidents featured in this publication
are entirely fictional.
DC Comics, 1700 Broadway, New York, NY 10019
A Warner Bros. Entertainment Company
Printed in Canada. First Printing.
ISBN: 1-4012-0429-5
Cover illustration by James Jean

ED BRUBAKER
ANDERSEN GABRYCH
DEVIN GRAYSON
DYLAN HORROCKS
A.J. LIEBERMAN
BILL WILLINGHAM
WRITERS

RAMON BACHS
AL BARRIONUEVO
PAUL GULACY
MIKE HUDDLESTON
KINSUN
MIKE LILLY
JON PROCTOR
BRAD WALKER
PENCILLERS

ROBERT CAMPANELLA
JESSE DELPERDANG
TROY NIXEY
ANDY OWENS
JIMMY PALMIOTTI
FRANCIS PORTELLA
RODNEY RAMOS
AARON SOWD
CAM SMITH
INKERS

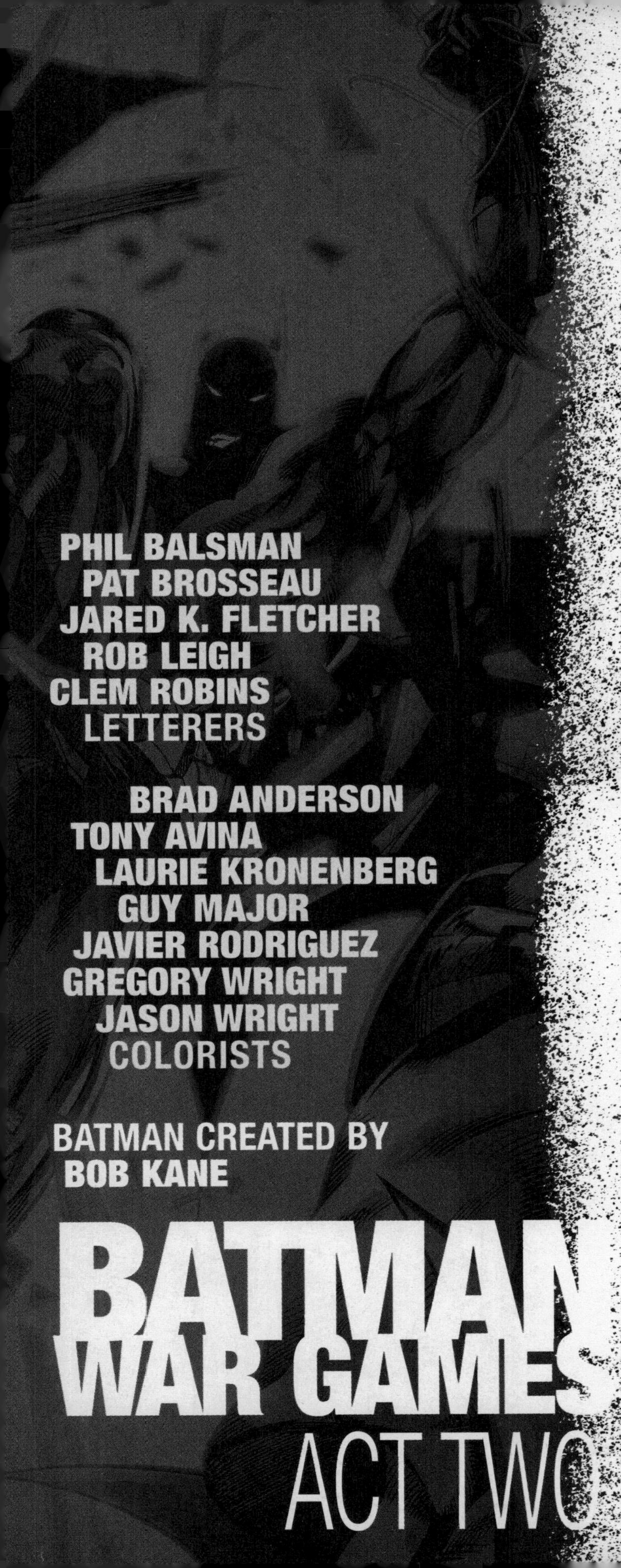

PHIL BALSMAN
PAT BROSSEAU
JARED K. FLETCHER
ROB LEIGH
CLEM ROBINS
LETTERERS

BRAD ANDERSON
TONY AVINA
LAURIE KRONENBERG
GUY MAJOR
JAVIER RODRIGUEZ
GREGORY WRIGHT
JASON WRIGHT
COLORISTS

BATMAN CREATED BY
BOB KANE

BATMAN
WAR GAMES
ACT TWO

WHAT HAS GONE BEFORE

Gotham's crime families respond to a mysterious invitation to a summit. Fueled by mutual suspicion, all the representatives bring along high-powered bodyguards including notable villains the NKVDemon, Silver Monkey, Zeiss, Deadshot, and Hellhound. All, that is, except the Burnley Town Massive's Crown, who is the first to pull a weapon. A meeting quickly becomes a shooting gallery, before the mysterious host makes an appearance.

Witnessing the bloodbath are Stephanie Brown, a.k.a Spoiler, recently fired by Batman as the latest Robin, and the Catwoman.

As the fighting among gang members spreads across the city, Batman finds he must rely on a dwindling number of allies. Nightwing arrives from Blüdhaven along with the new Tarantula, whose methods aren't necessarily Batman-approved; Batgirl eagerly wades into the fray, and Oracle remains as a coordinating force although she chafes as Batman uses her as more switchboard operator than ally. Tim Drake, the former Robin, honors his promise to his family, refusing to suit up.

As the various crime captains begin targeting rival leaders' families, the violence reaches Tim's high school. Tim does his best to protect the students and faculty. His efforts aren't enough, though, and the target, Darla Aquista, is mortally wounded. Batman, Nightwing, and Batgirl arrive in time to put an end to multiple threats but too late for Darla. As Batman emerges from the school, in daylight, the media record his arrival, the girl's lifeless body in his arms. They quickly conclude he was responsible for her death, but he's gone before either they or the police can get answers.

As the feline fatale ushers Stephanie, back in her Spoiler guise, out of danger, the teen admits she is responsible for the war gripping Gotham. She took and executed one of Batman's war game scenarios — a daring plan that would unite the city's underworld under his control. But acting as she has without complete knowledge of the Caped Crusader's plans, Stephanie does not merely fail to earn the hero's approval; she has exposed as reality the urban legend of The Batman and is responsible for a mind-numbing body count . . . a body count that continues to grow.

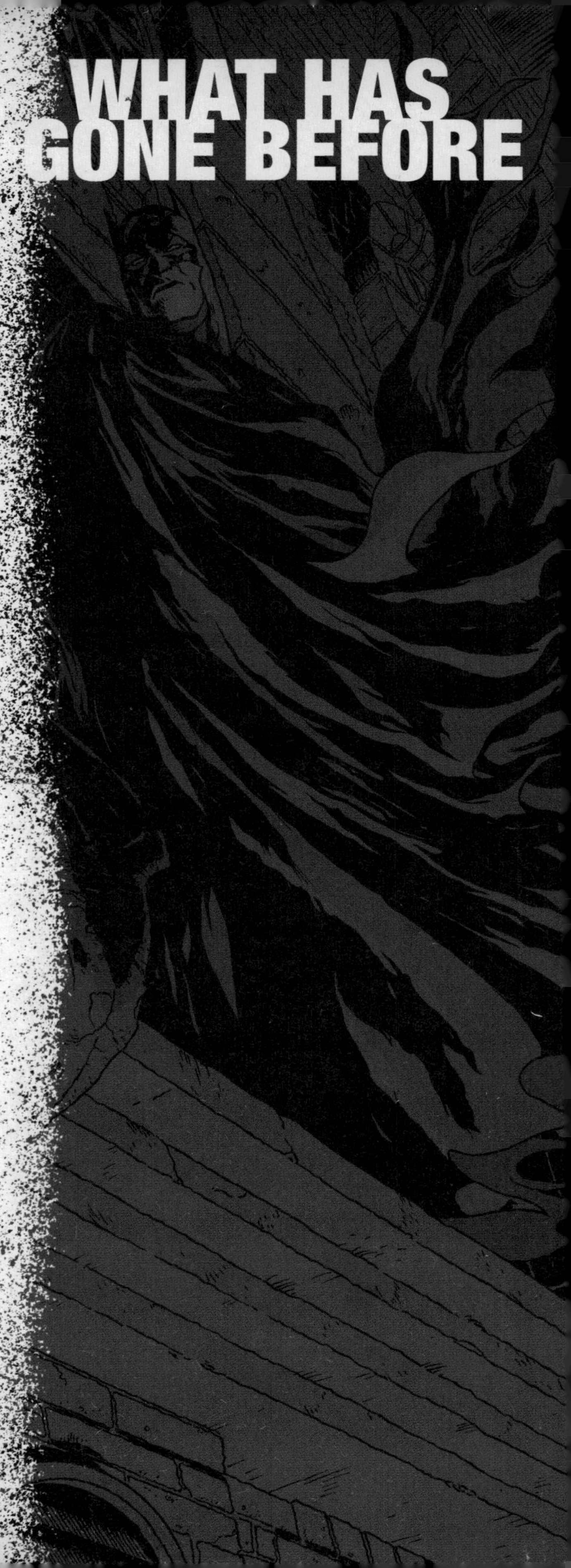

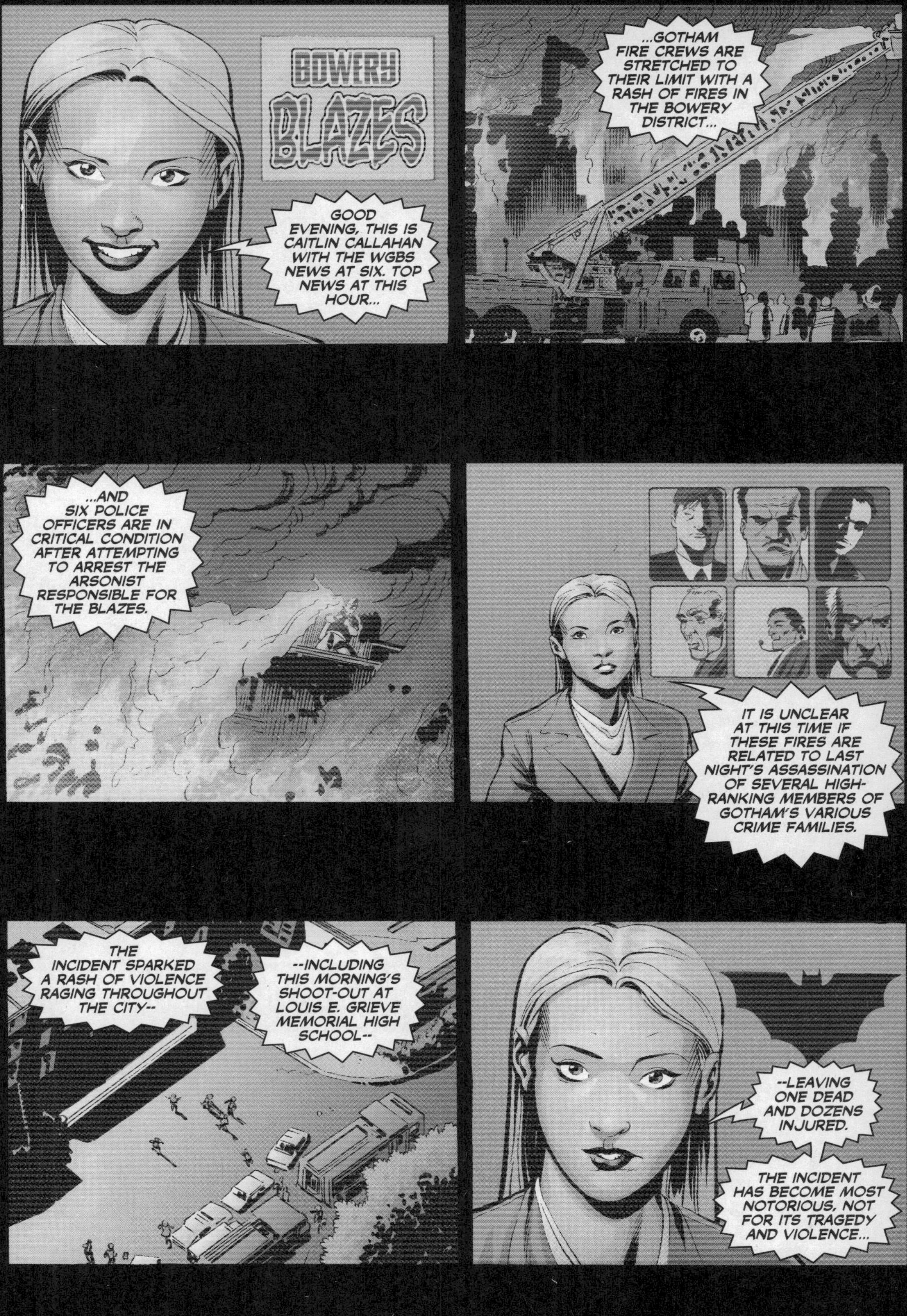
BOWERY BLAZES
GOOD EVENING, THIS IS CAITLIN CALLAHAN WITH THE WGBS NEWS AT SIX. TOP NEWS AT THIS HOUR...
...GOTHAM FIRE CREWS ARE STRETCHED TO THEIR LIMIT WITH A RASH OF FIRES IN THE BOWERY DISTRICT...
...AND SIX POLICE OFFICERS ARE IN CRITICAL CONDITION AFTER ATTEMPTING TO ARREST THE ARSONIST RESPONSIBLE FOR THE BLAZES.
IT IS UNCLEAR AT THIS TIME IF THESE FIRES ARE RELATED TO LAST NIGHT'S ASSASSINATION OF SEVERAL HIGH-RANKING MEMBERS OF GOTHAM'S VARIOUS CRIME FAMILIES.
THE INCIDENT SPARKED A RASH OF VIOLENCE RAGING THROUGHOUT THE CITY--
--INCLUDING THIS MORNING'S SHOOT-OUT AT LOUIS E. GRIEVE MEMORIAL HIGH SCHOOL--
--LEAVING ONE DEAD AND DOZENS INJURED.
THE INCIDENT HAS BECOME MOST NOTORIOUS, NOT FOR ITS TRAGEDY AND VIOLENCE...

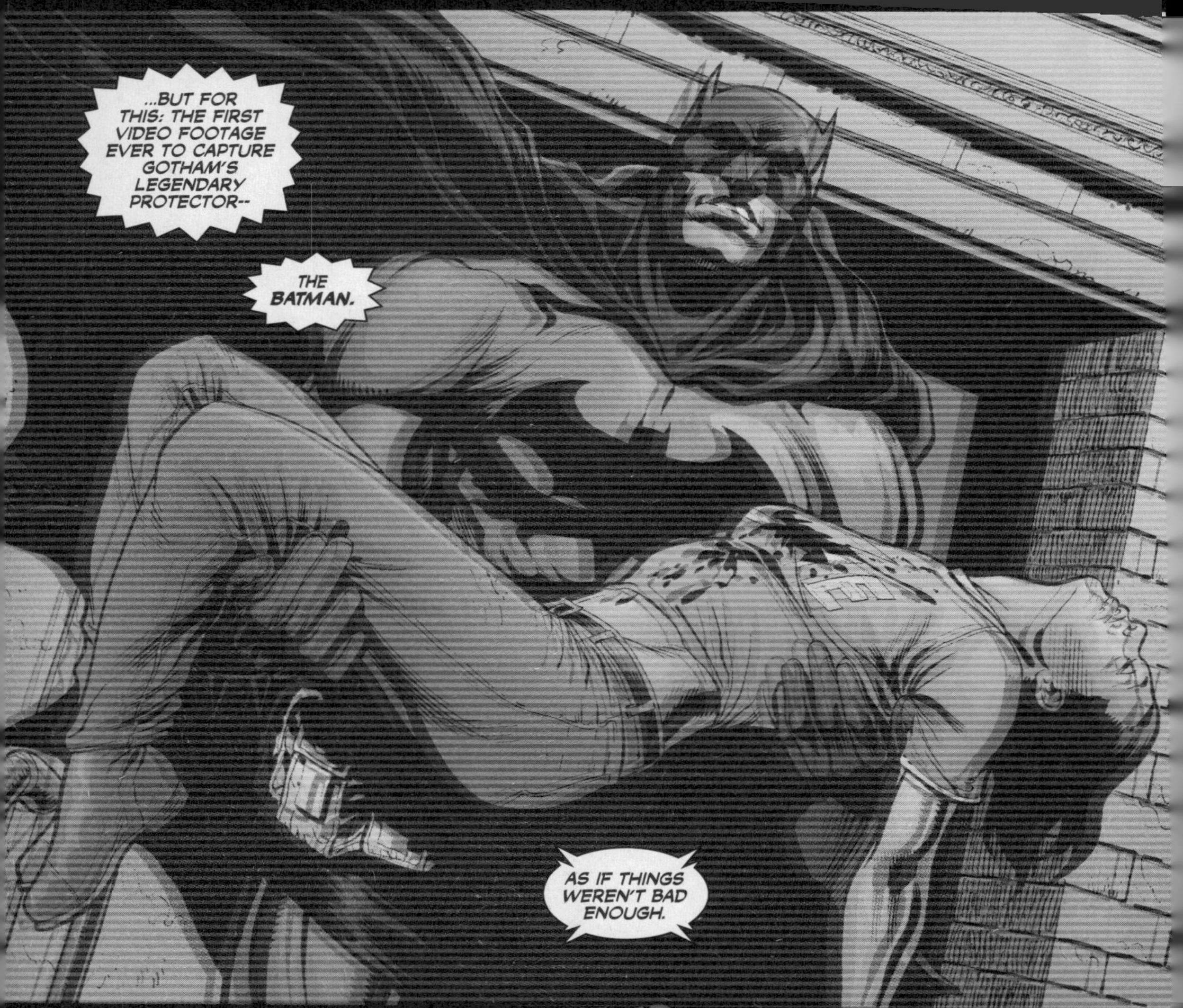
...BUT FOR THIS: THE FIRST VIDEO FOOTAGE EVER TO CAPTURE GOTHAM'S LEGENDARY PROTECTOR--
THE BATMAN.
AS IF THINGS WEREN'T BAD ENOUGH.

WAR GAMES: ACT 2 PART 1
UNDERTOW

ANDERSEN GABRYCH-WRITER PETE WOODS-PENCILLER CAM SMITH-INKER JASON WRIGHT-COLORIST
PAT BROSSEAU-LETTERER BOB SCHRECK-EDITOR MICHAEL WRIGHT-ASSOCIATE EDITOR
BATMAN CREATED BY BOB KANE

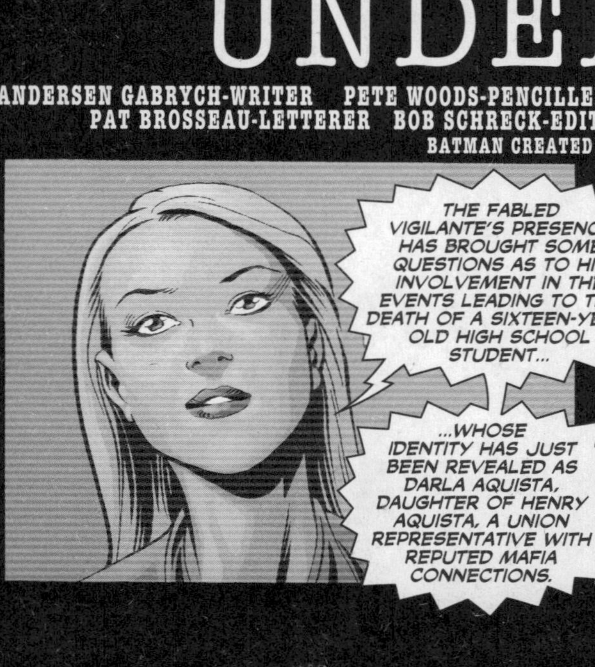
THE FABLED VIGILANTE'S PRESENCE HAS BROUGHT SOME QUESTIONS AS TO HIS INVOLVEMENT IN THE EVENTS LEADING TO THE DEATH OF A SIXTEEN-YEAR-OLD HIGH SCHOOL STUDENT...
...WHOSE IDENTITY HAS JUST BEEN REVEALED AS DARLA AQUISTA, DAUGHTER OF HENRY AQUISTA, A UNION REPRESENTATIVE WITH REPUTED MAFIA CONNECTIONS.

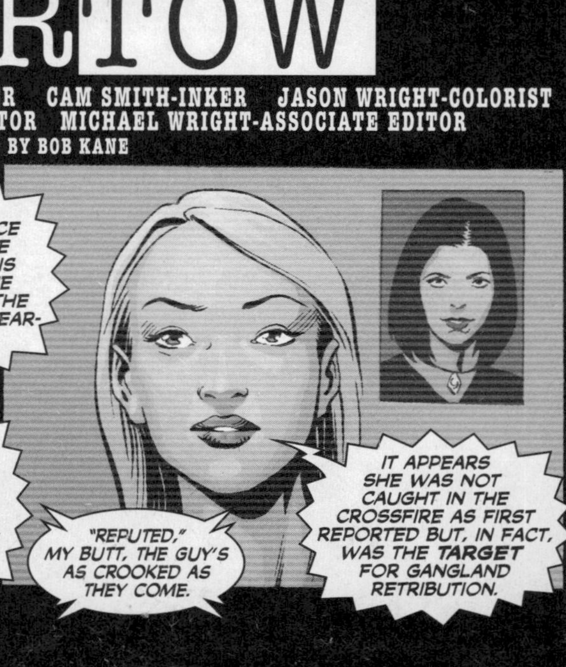
"REPUTED," MY BUTT, THE GUY'S AS CROOKED AS THEY COME.
IT APPEARS SHE WAS NOT CAUGHT IN THE CROSSFIRE AS FIRST REPORTED BUT, IN FACT, WAS THE TARGET FOR GANGLAND RETRIBUTION.

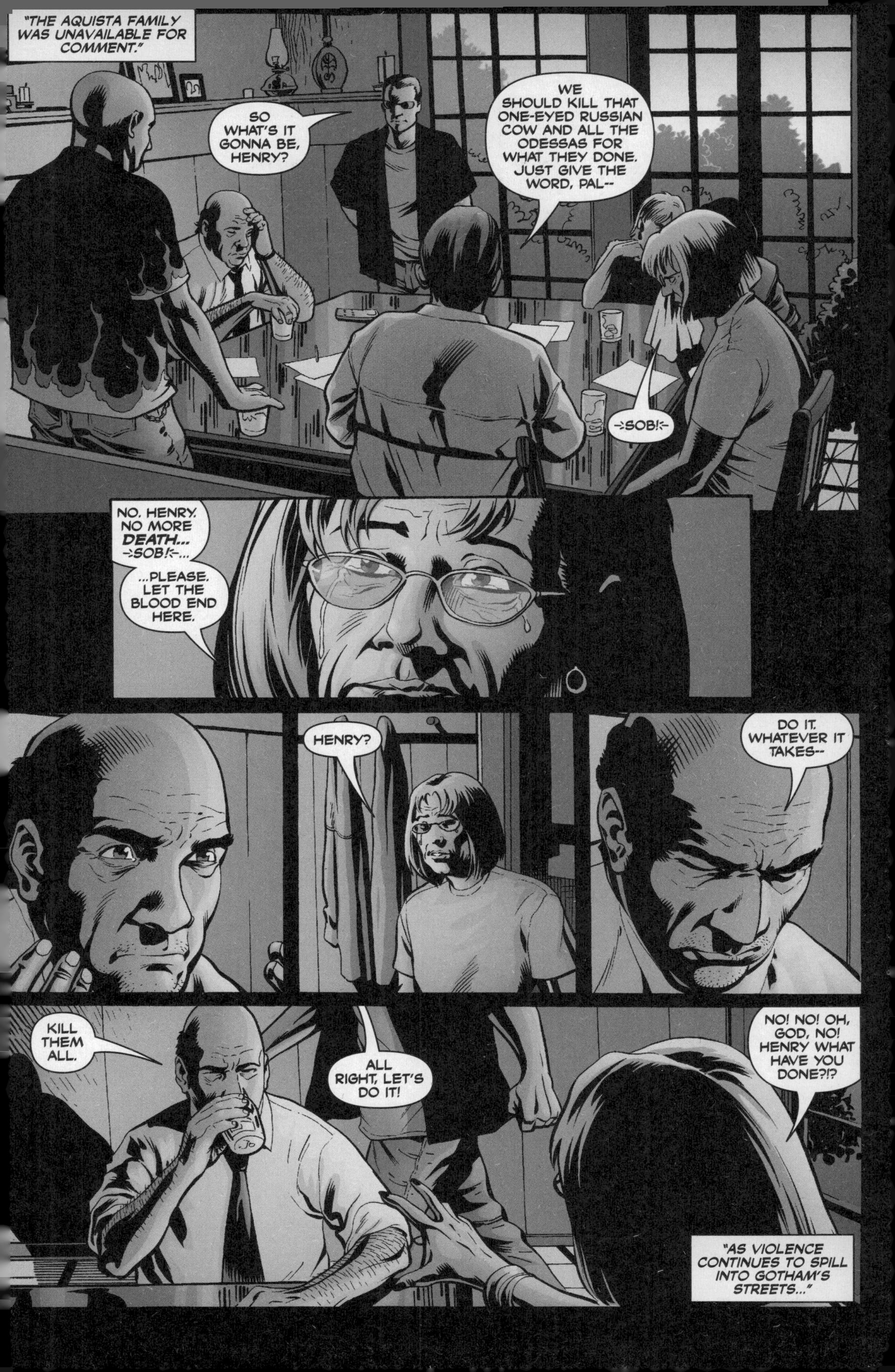
"THE AQUISTA FAMILY WAS UNAVAILABLE FOR COMMENT."
SO WHAT'S IT GONNA BE, HENRY?
WE SHOULD KILL THAT ONE-EYED RUSSIAN COW AND ALL THE ODESSAS FOR WHAT THEY DONE. JUST GIVE THE WORD, PAL--
-SOB!-
NO, HENRY. NO MORE DEATH... -SOB!-...
...PLEASE. LET THE BLOOD END HERE.
HENRY?
DO IT. WHATEVER IT TAKES--
KILL THEM ALL.
ALL RIGHT, LET'S DO IT!
NO! NO! OH, GOD, NO! HENRY WHAT HAVE YOU DONE?!?
"AS VIOLENCE CONTINUES TO SPILL INTO GOTHAM'S STREETS..."

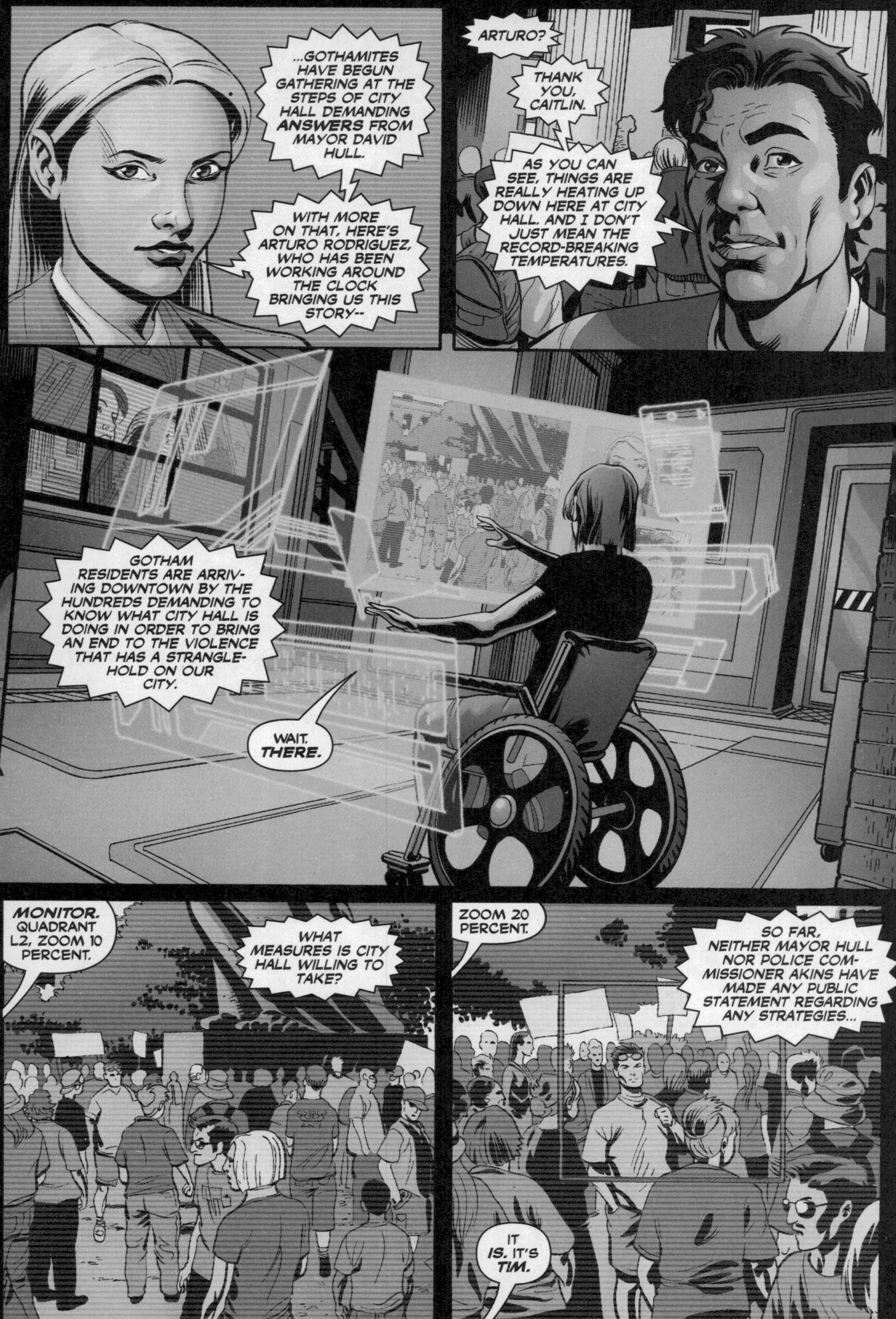
...GOTHAMITES HAVE BEGUN GATHERING AT THE STEPS OF CITY HALL DEMANDING ANSWERS FROM MAYOR DAVID HULL.
WITH MORE ON THAT, HERE'S ARTURO RODRIGUEZ, WHO HAS BEEN WORKING AROUND THE CLOCK BRINGING US THIS STORY--
ARTURO?
THANK YOU, CAITLIN.
AS YOU CAN SEE, THINGS ARE REALLY HEATING UP DOWN HERE AT CITY HALL. AND I DON'T JUST MEAN THE RECORD-BREAKING TEMPERATURES.
GOTHAM RESIDENTS ARE ARRIVING DOWNTOWN BY THE HUNDREDS DEMANDING TO KNOW WHAT CITY HALL IS DOING IN ORDER TO BRING AN END TO THE VIOLENCE THAT HAS A STRANGLEHOLD ON OUR CITY.
WAIT. THERE.
MONITOR. QUADRANT L2, ZOOM 10 PERCENT.
WHAT MEASURES IS CITY HALL WILLING TO TAKE?
ZOOM 20 PERCENT.
SO FAR, NEITHER MAYOR HULL NOR POLICE COMMISSIONER AKINS HAVE MADE ANY PUBLIC STATEMENT REGARDING ANY STRATEGIES...
IT IS. IT'S TIM.

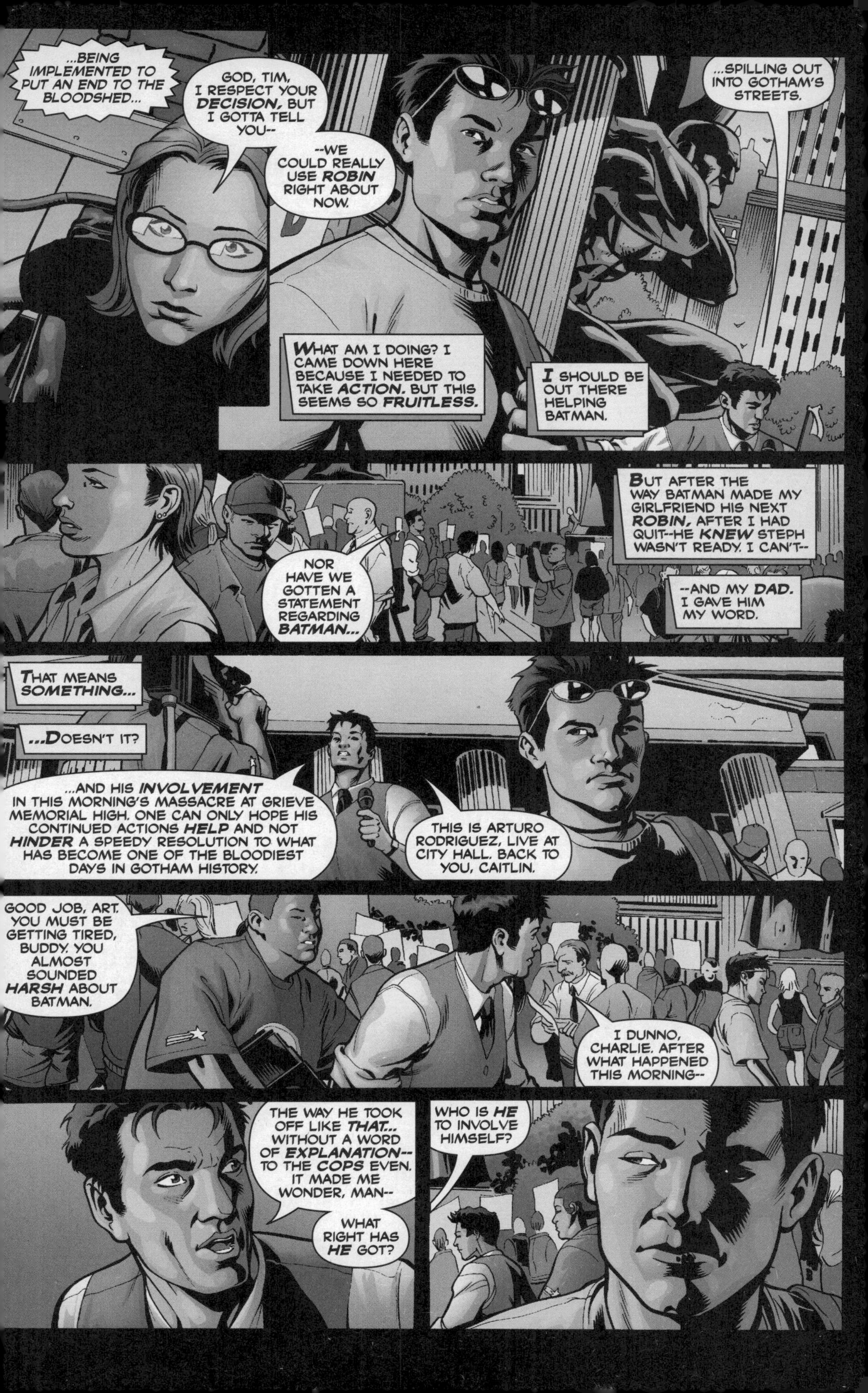
...BEING IMPLEMENTED TO PUT AN END TO THE BLOODSHED...
GOD, TIM, I RESPECT YOUR DECISION, BUT I GOTTA TELL YOU--
--WE COULD REALLY USE ROBIN RIGHT ABOUT NOW.
...SPILLING OUT INTO GOTHAM'S STREETS.
WHAT AM I DOING? I CAME DOWN HERE BECAUSE I NEEDED TO TAKE ACTION. BUT THIS SEEMS SO FRUITLESS.
I SHOULD BE OUT THERE HELPING BATMAN.
NOR HAVE WE GOTTEN A STATEMENT REGARDING BATMAN...
BUT AFTER THE WAY BATMAN MADE MY GIRLFRIEND HIS NEXT ROBIN, AFTER I HAD QUIT--HE KNEW STEPH WASN'T READY. I CAN'T--
--AND MY DAD. I GAVE HIM MY WORD.
THAT MEANS SOMETHING...
...DOESN'T IT?
...AND HIS INVOLVEMENT IN THIS MORNING'S MASSACRE AT GRIEVE MEMORIAL HIGH. ONE CAN ONLY HOPE HIS CONTINUED ACTIONS HELP AND NOT HINDER A SPEEDY RESOLUTION TO WHAT HAS BECOME ONE OF THE BLOODIEST DAYS IN GOTHAM HISTORY.
THIS IS ARTURO RODRIGUEZ, LIVE AT CITY HALL. BACK TO YOU, CAITLIN.
GOOD JOB, ART. YOU MUST BE GETTING TIRED, BUDDY. YOU ALMOST SOUNDED HARSH ABOUT BATMAN.
I DUNNO, CHARLIE. AFTER WHAT HAPPENED THIS MORNING--
THE WAY HE TOOK OFF LIKE THAT... WITHOUT A WORD OF EXPLANATION-- TO THE COPS EVEN. IT MADE ME WONDER, MAN--
WHAT RIGHT HAS HE GOT?
WHO IS HE TO INVOLVE HIMSELF?

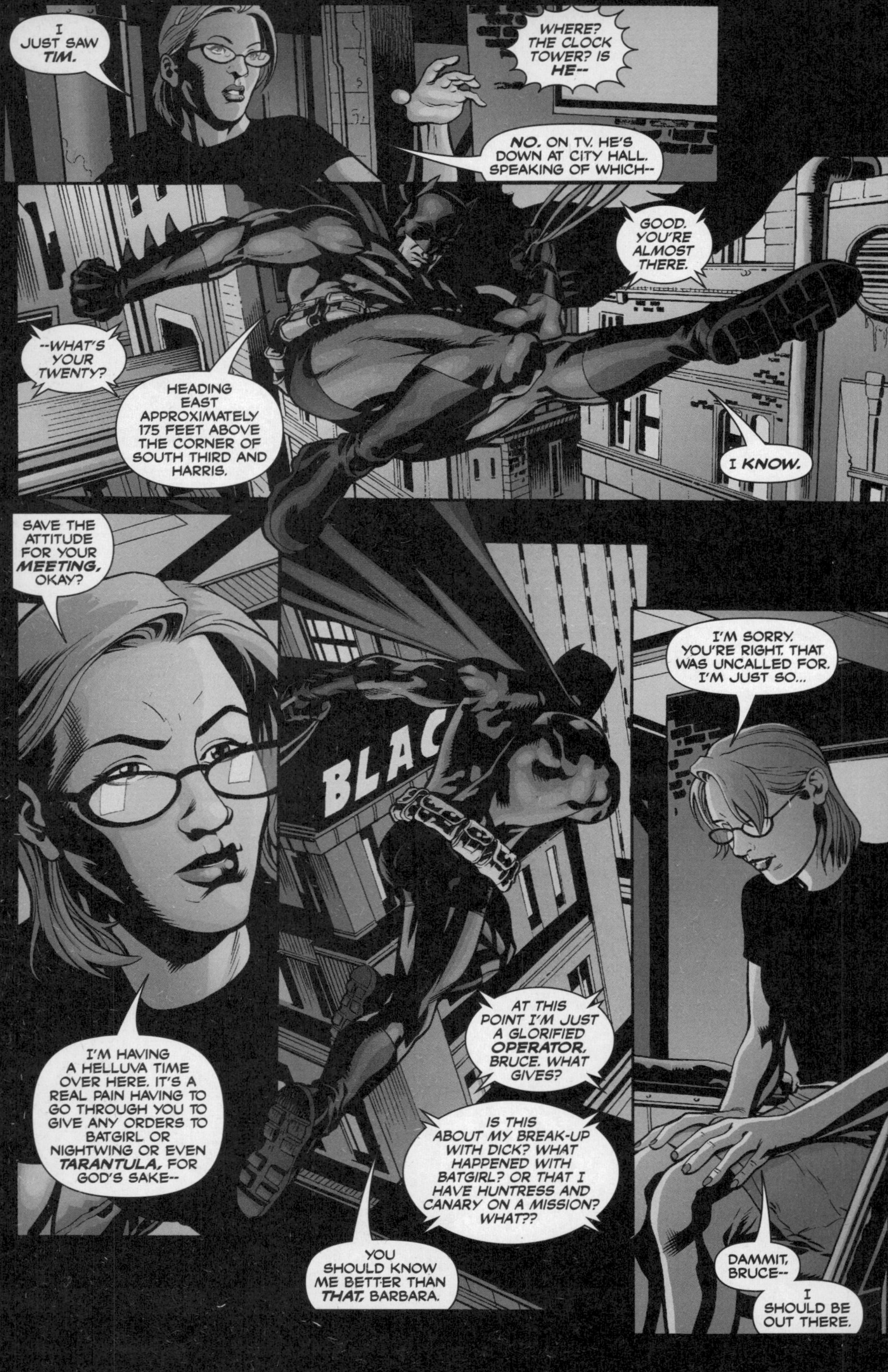
I JUST SAW TIM.
WHERE? THE CLOCK TOWER? IS HE--
NO. ON TV. HE'S DOWN AT CITY HALL. SPEAKING OF WHICH--
--WHAT'S YOUR TWENTY?
HEADING EAST APPROXIMATELY 175 FEET ABOVE THE CORNER OF SOUTH THIRD AND HARRIS.
GOOD. YOU'RE ALMOST THERE.
I KNOW.
SAVE THE ATTITUDE FOR YOUR MEETING, OKAY?
I'M HAVING A HELLUVA TIME OVER HERE. IT'S A REAL PAIN HAVING TO GO THROUGH YOU TO GIVE ANY ORDERS TO BATGIRL OR NIGHTWING OR EVEN TARANTULA, FOR GOD'S SAKE--
BLAC
AT THIS POINT I'M JUST A GLORIFIED OPERATOR, BRUCE. WHAT GIVES?
IS THIS ABOUT MY BREAK-UP WITH DICK? WHAT HAPPENED WITH BATGIRL? OR THAT I HAVE HUNTRESS AND CANARY ON A MISSION? WHAT??
YOU SHOULD KNOW ME BETTER THAN THAT, BARBARA.
I'M SORRY. YOU'RE RIGHT. THAT WAS UNCALLED FOR. I'M JUST SO...
DAMMIT, BRUCE--
I SHOULD BE OUT THERE.

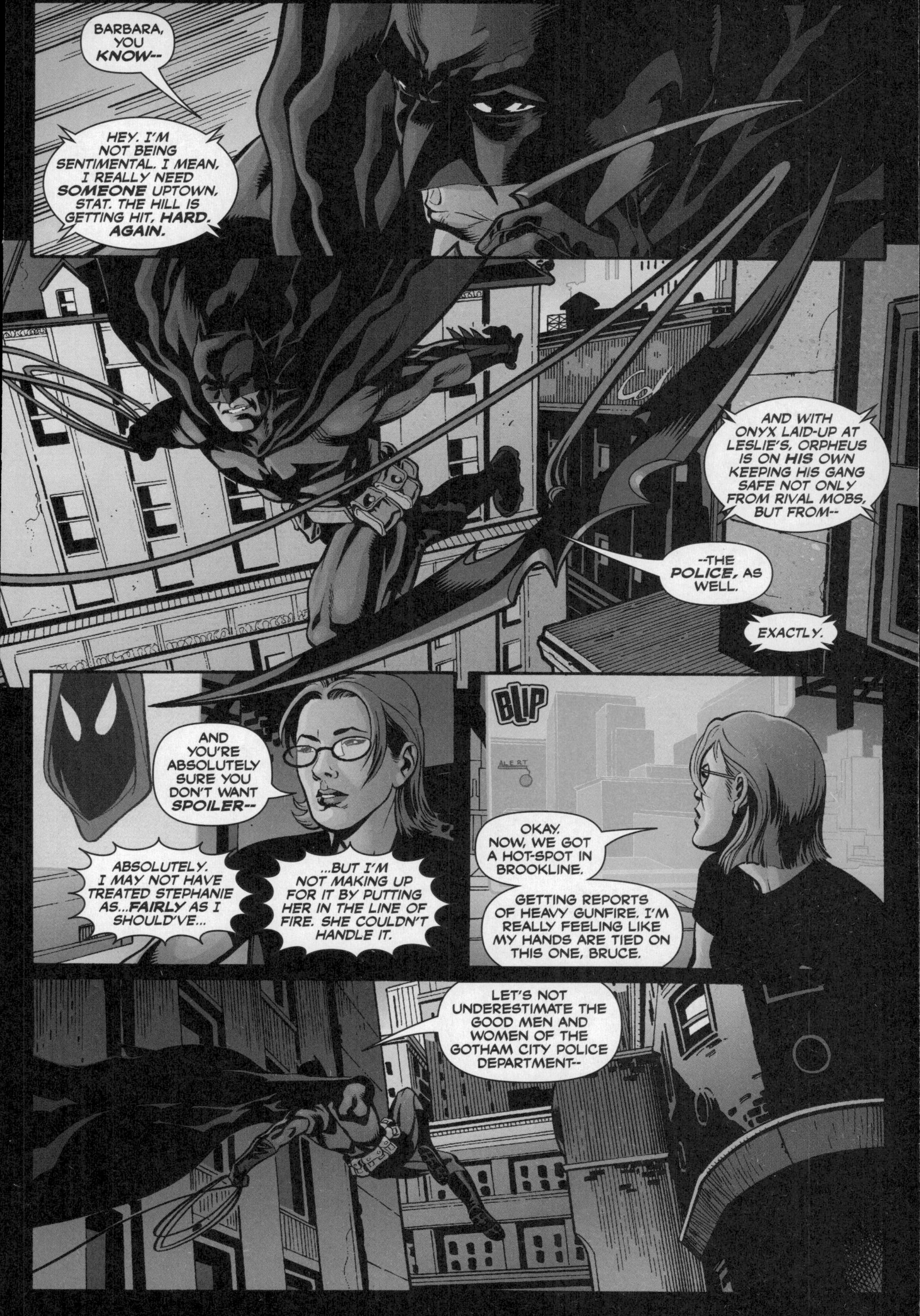

BARBARA, YOU KNOW--
HEY. I'M NOT BEING SENTIMENTAL. I MEAN, I REALLY NEED SOMEONE UPTOWN, STAT. THE HILL IS GETTING HIT, HARD. AGAIN.
AND WITH ONYX LAID-UP AT LESLIE'S, ORPHEUS IS ON HIS OWN KEEPING HIS GANG SAFE NOT ONLY FROM RIVAL MOBS, BUT FROM--
--THE POLICE, AS WELL.
EXACTLY.
AND YOU'RE ABSOLUTELY SURE YOU DON'T WANT SPOILER--
ABSOLUTELY. I MAY NOT HAVE TREATED STEPHANIE AS...FAIRLY AS I SHOULD'VE...
...BUT I'M NOT MAKING UP FOR IT BY PUTTING HER IN THE LINE OF FIRE. SHE COULDN'T HANDLE IT.
BLIP
ALERT
OKAY. NOW, WE GOT A HOT-SPOT IN BROOKLINE.
GETTING REPORTS OF HEAVY GUNFIRE. I'M REALLY FEELING LIKE MY HANDS ARE TIED ON THIS ONE, BRUCE.
LET'S NOT UNDERESTIMATE THE GOOD MEN AND WOMEN OF THE GOTHAM CITY POLICE DEPARTMENT--

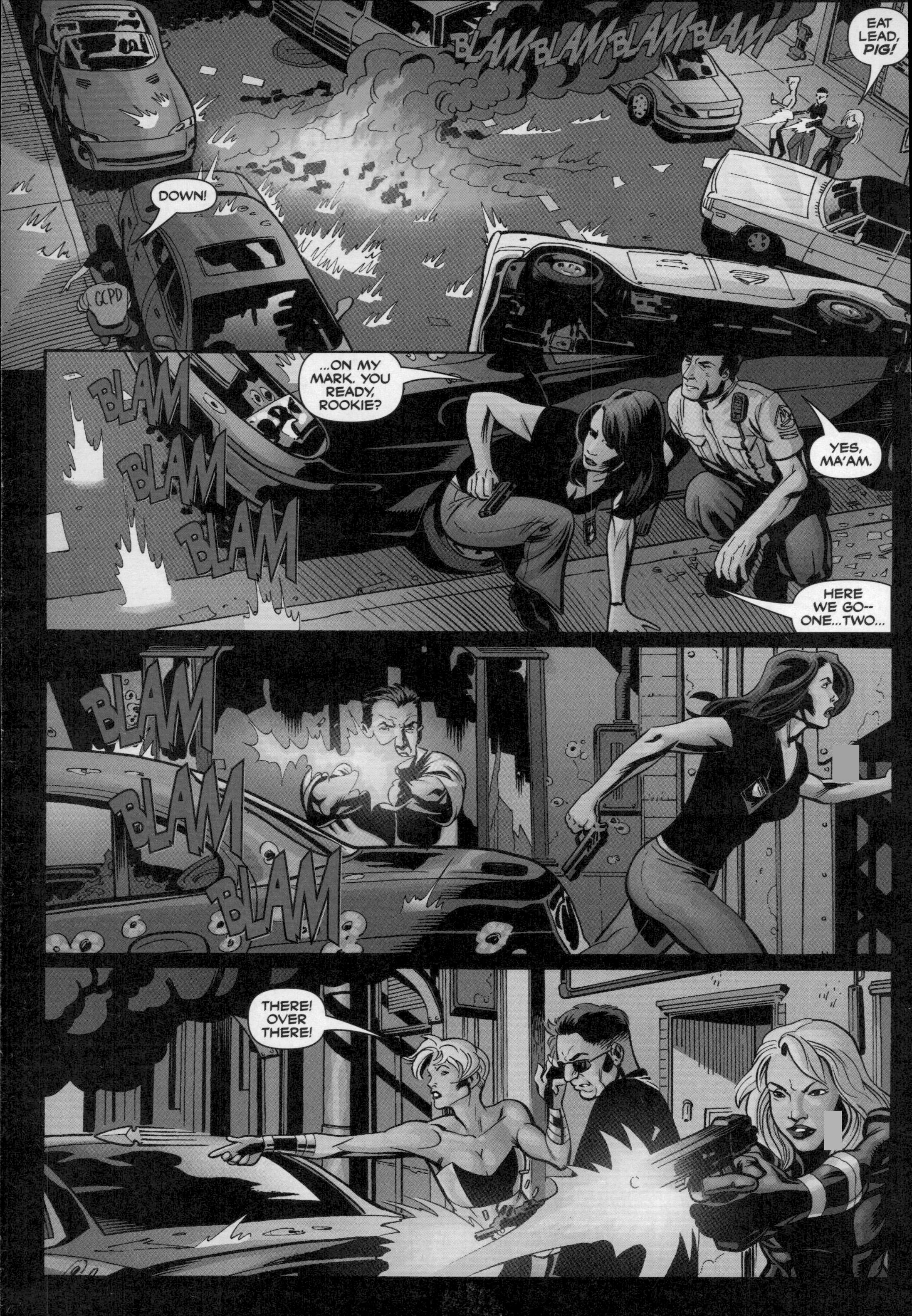
BLAM BLAM BLAM BLAM
EAT LEAD, PIG!
DOWN!
GCPD
BLAM
BLAM
BLAM
...ON MY MARK. YOU READY, ROOKIE?
YES, MA'AM.
HERE WE GO-- ONE...TWO...
BLAM
BLAM
BLAM
THERE! OVER THERE!

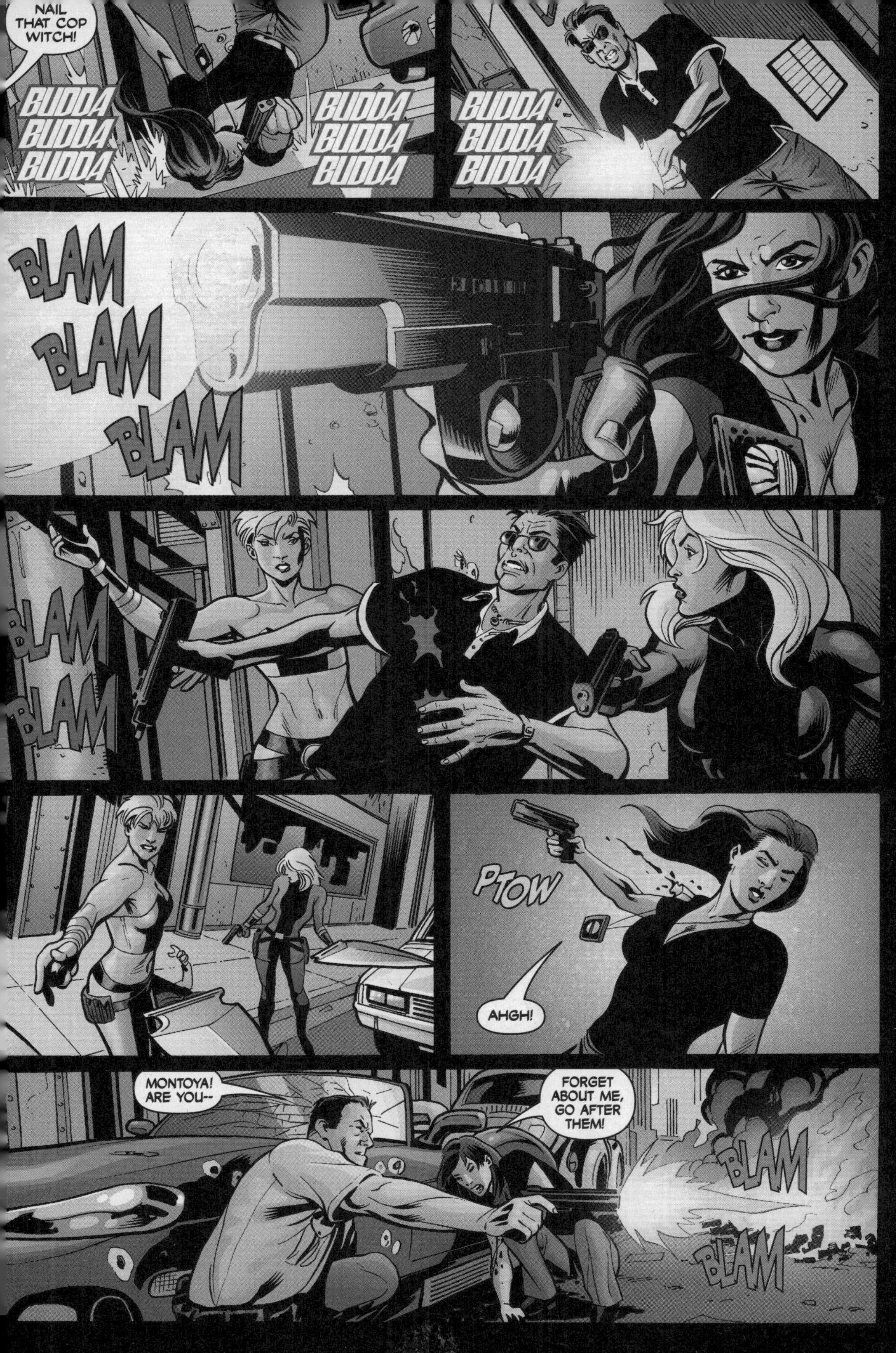
NAIL THAT COP WITCH!
BUDDA BUDDA BUDDA
BUDDA BUDDA BUDDA
BUDDA BUDDA BUDDA
BLAM BLAM BLAM
BLAM BLAM
PTOW
AHGH!
MONTOYA! ARE YOU--
FORGET ABOUT ME, GO AFTER THEM!
BLAM
BLAM

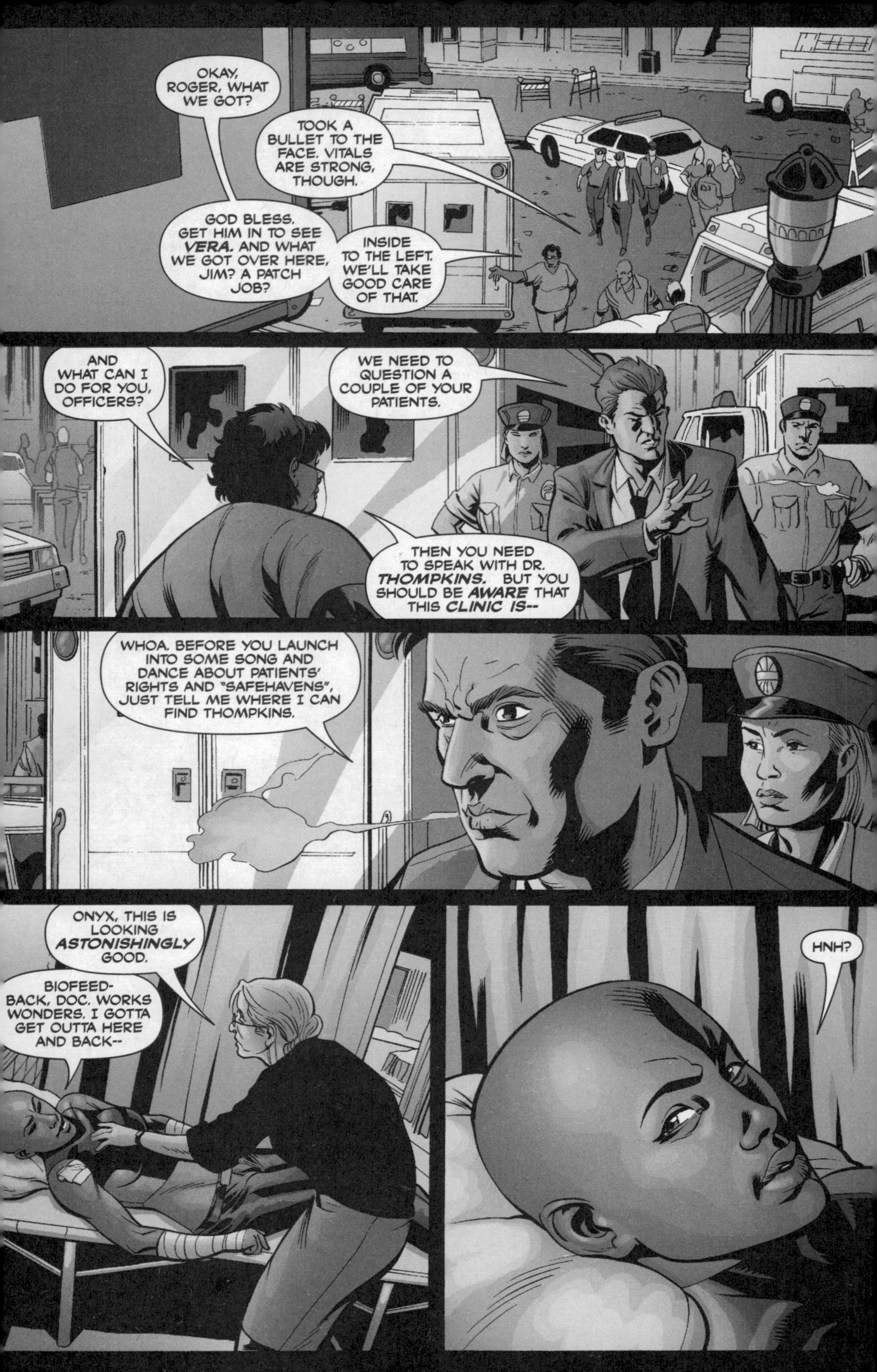
OKAY, ROGER, WHAT WE GOT?
TOOK A BULLET TO THE FACE. VITALS ARE STRONG, THOUGH.
GOD BLESS. GET HIM IN TO SEE VERA. AND WHAT WE GOT OVER HERE, JIM? A PATCH JOB?
INSIDE TO THE LEFT. WE'LL TAKE GOOD CARE OF THAT.
AND WHAT CAN I DO FOR YOU, OFFICERS?
WE NEED TO QUESTION A COUPLE OF YOUR PATIENTS.
THEN YOU NEED TO SPEAK WITH DR. THOMPKINS. BUT YOU SHOULD BE AWARE THAT THIS CLINIC IS--
WHOA. BEFORE YOU LAUNCH INTO SOME SONG AND DANCE ABOUT PATIENTS' RIGHTS AND "SAFEHAVENS", JUST TELL ME WHERE I CAN FIND THOMPKINS.
ONYX, THIS IS LOOKING ASTONISHINGLY GOOD.
BIOFEED-BACK, DOC. WORKS WONDERS. I GOTTA GET OUTTA HERE AND BACK--
HNH?

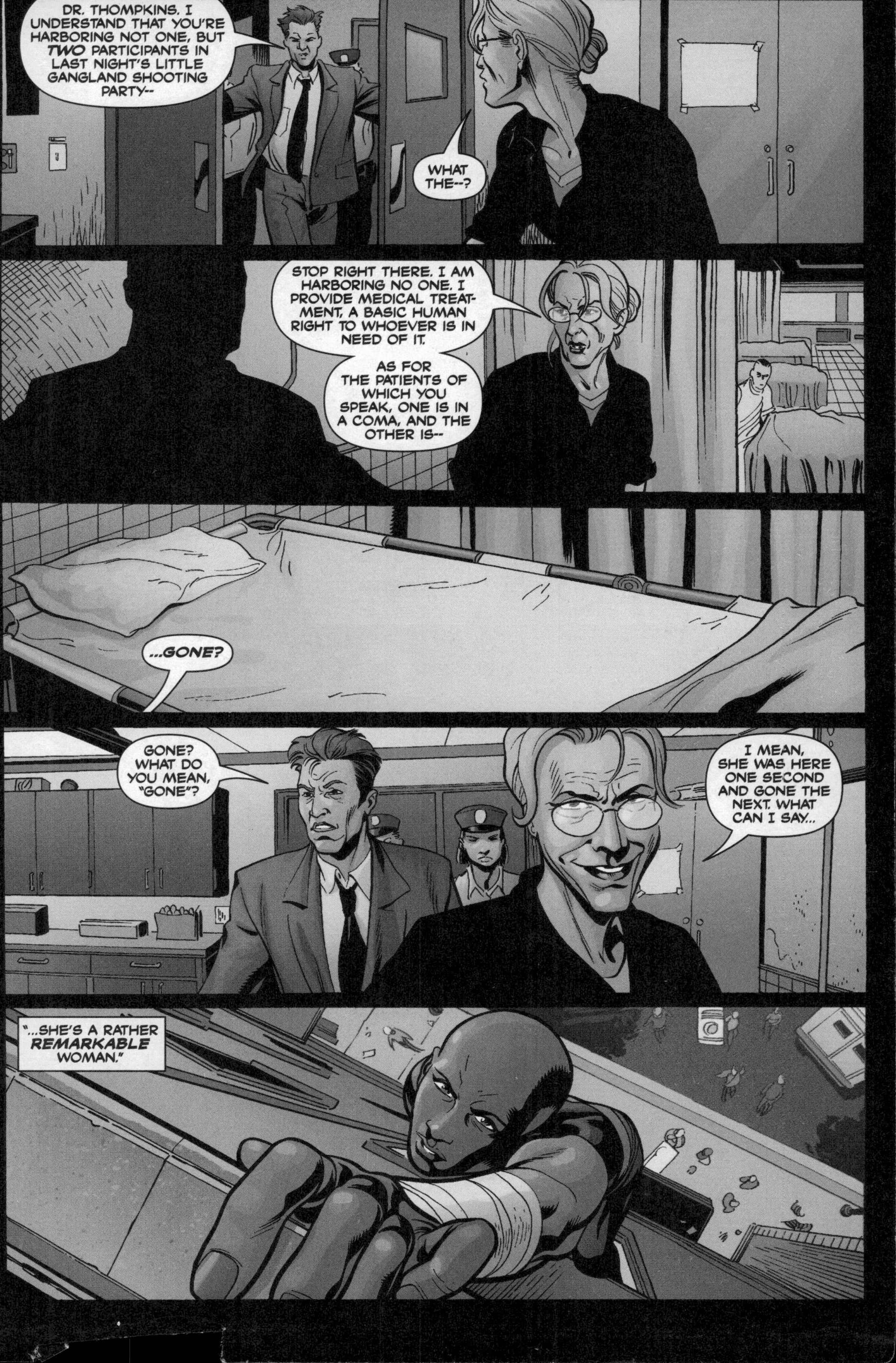
DR. THOMPKINS. I UNDERSTAND THAT YOU'RE HARBORING NOT ONE, BUT *TWO* PARTICIPANTS IN LAST NIGHT'S LITTLE GANGLAND SHOOTING PARTY--
WHAT THE--?
STOP RIGHT THERE. I AM HARBORING NO ONE. I PROVIDE MEDICAL TREATMENT, A BASIC HUMAN RIGHT TO WHOEVER IS IN NEED OF IT.
AS FOR THE PATIENTS OF WHICH YOU SPEAK, ONE IS IN A COMA, AND THE OTHER IS--
...GONE?
GONE? WHAT DO YOU MEAN, "GONE"?
I MEAN, SHE WAS HERE ONE SECOND AND GONE THE NEXT. WHAT CAN I SAY...
"...SHE'S A RATHER *REMARKABLE* WOMAN."

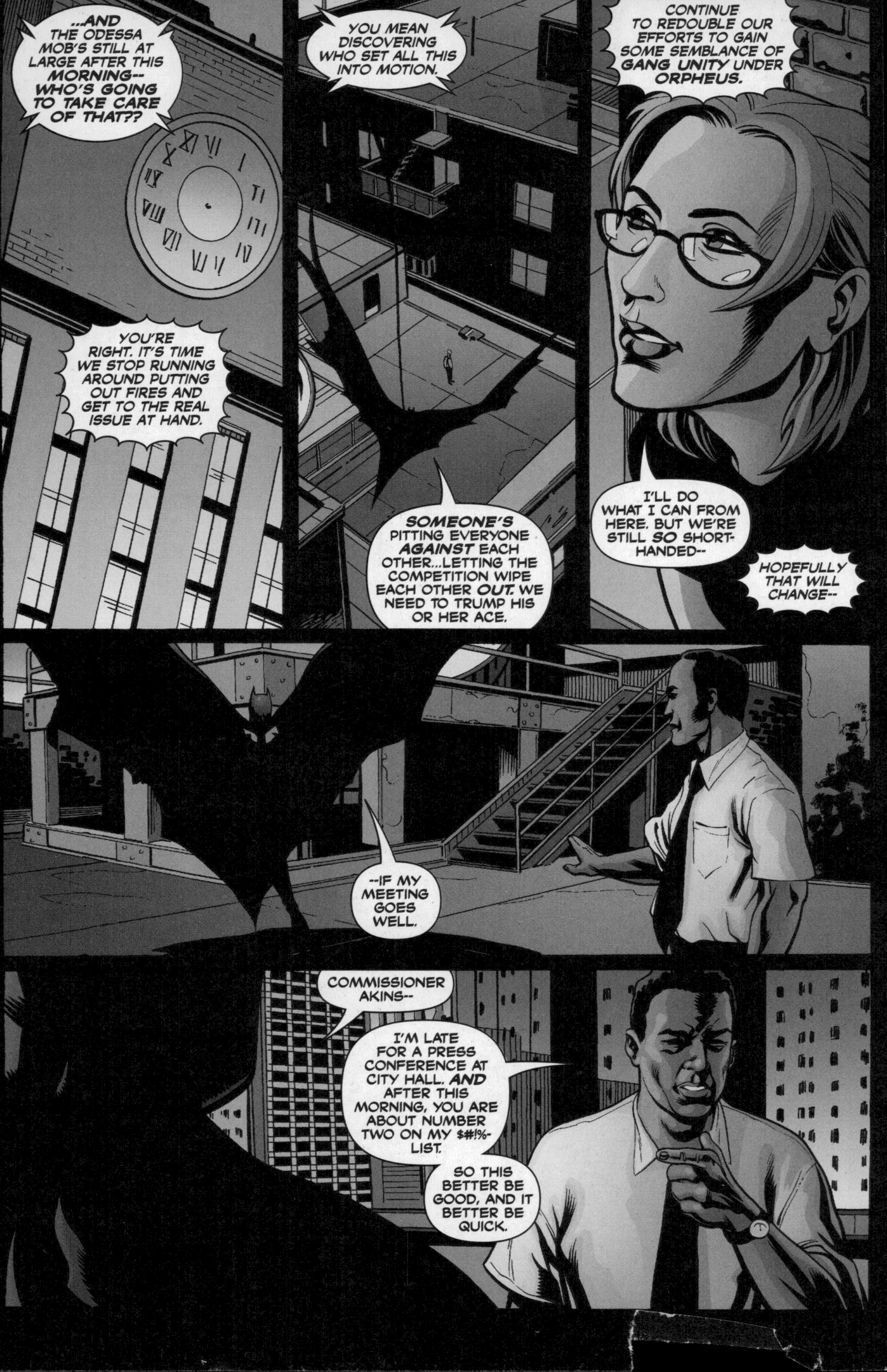
...AND THE ODESSA MOB'S STILL AT LARGE AFTER THIS MORNING-- WHO'S GOING TO TAKE CARE OF THAT??
YOU'RE RIGHT. IT'S TIME WE STOP RUNNING AROUND PUTTING OUT FIRES AND GET TO THE REAL ISSUE AT HAND.
YOU MEAN DISCOVERING WHO SET ALL THIS INTO MOTION.
SOMEONE'S PITTING EVERYONE AGAINST EACH OTHER...LETTING THE COMPETITION WIPE EACH OTHER OUT. WE NEED TO TRUMP HIS OR HER ACE.
CONTINUE TO REDOUBLE OUR EFFORTS TO GAIN SOME SEMBLANCE OF GANG UNITY UNDER ORPHEUS.
I'LL DO WHAT I CAN FROM HERE. BUT WE'RE STILL SO SHORT-HANDED--
HOPEFULLY THAT WILL CHANGE--
--IF MY MEETING GOES WELL.
COMMISSIONER AKINS--
I'M LATE FOR A PRESS CONFERENCE AT CITY HALL. AND AFTER THIS MORNING, YOU ARE ABOUT NUMBER TWO ON MY $#!%- LIST.
SO THIS BETTER BE GOOD, AND IT BETTER BE QUICK.

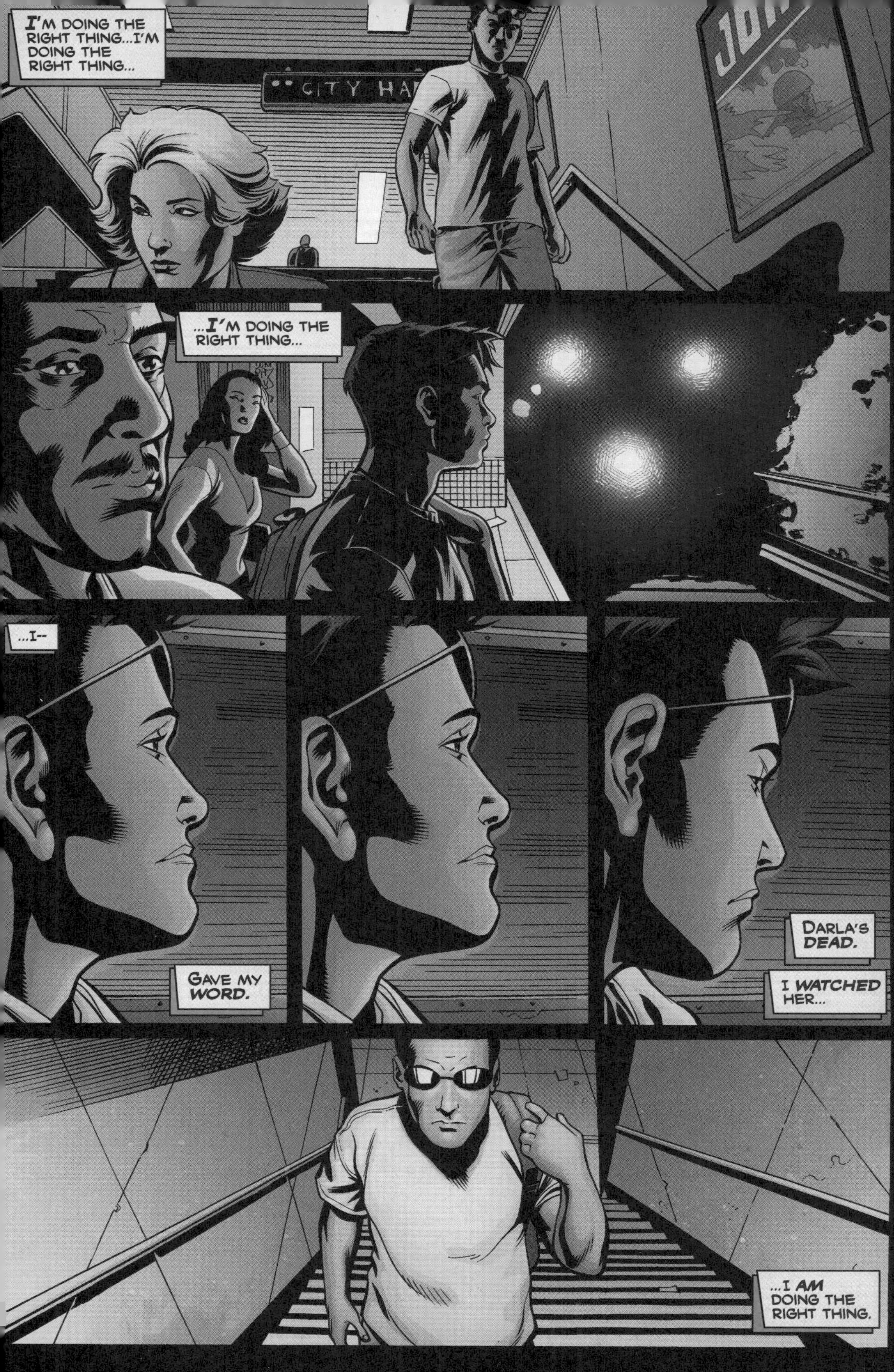
I'M DOING THE RIGHT THING...I'M DOING THE RIGHT THING...
CITY HA
...I'M DOING THE RIGHT THING...
...I--
GAVE MY WORD.
DARLA'S DEAD.
I WATCHED HER...
...I AM DOING THE RIGHT THING.

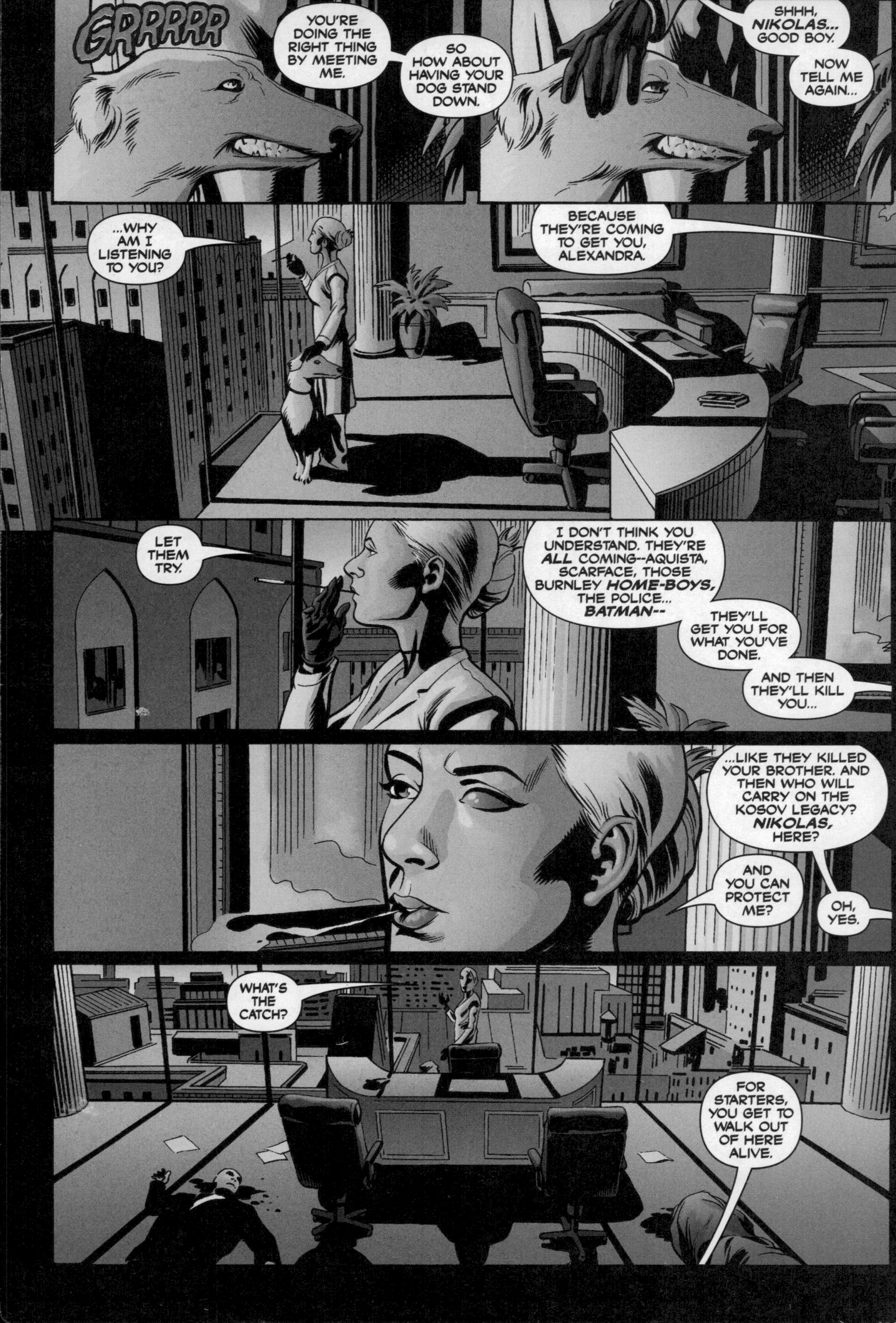
GRRRRR
YOU'RE DOING THE RIGHT THING BY MEETING ME.
SO HOW ABOUT HAVING YOUR DOG STAND DOWN.
SHHH, NIKOLAS... GOOD BOY.
NOW TELL ME AGAIN...
...WHY AM I LISTENING TO YOU?
BECAUSE THEY'RE COMING TO GET YOU, ALEXANDRA.
LET THEM TRY.
I DON'T THINK YOU UNDERSTAND. THEY'RE ALL COMING--AQUISTA, SCARFACE, THOSE BURNLEY HOME-BOYS, THE POLICE... BATMAN--
THEY'LL GET YOU FOR WHAT YOU'VE DONE.
AND THEN THEY'LL KILL YOU...
...LIKE THEY KILLED YOUR BROTHER. AND THEN WHO WILL CARRY ON THE KOSOV LEGACY? NIKOLAS, HERE?
AND YOU CAN PROTECT ME?
OH, YES.
WHAT'S THE CATCH?
FOR STARTERS, YOU GET TO WALK OUT OF HERE ALIVE.

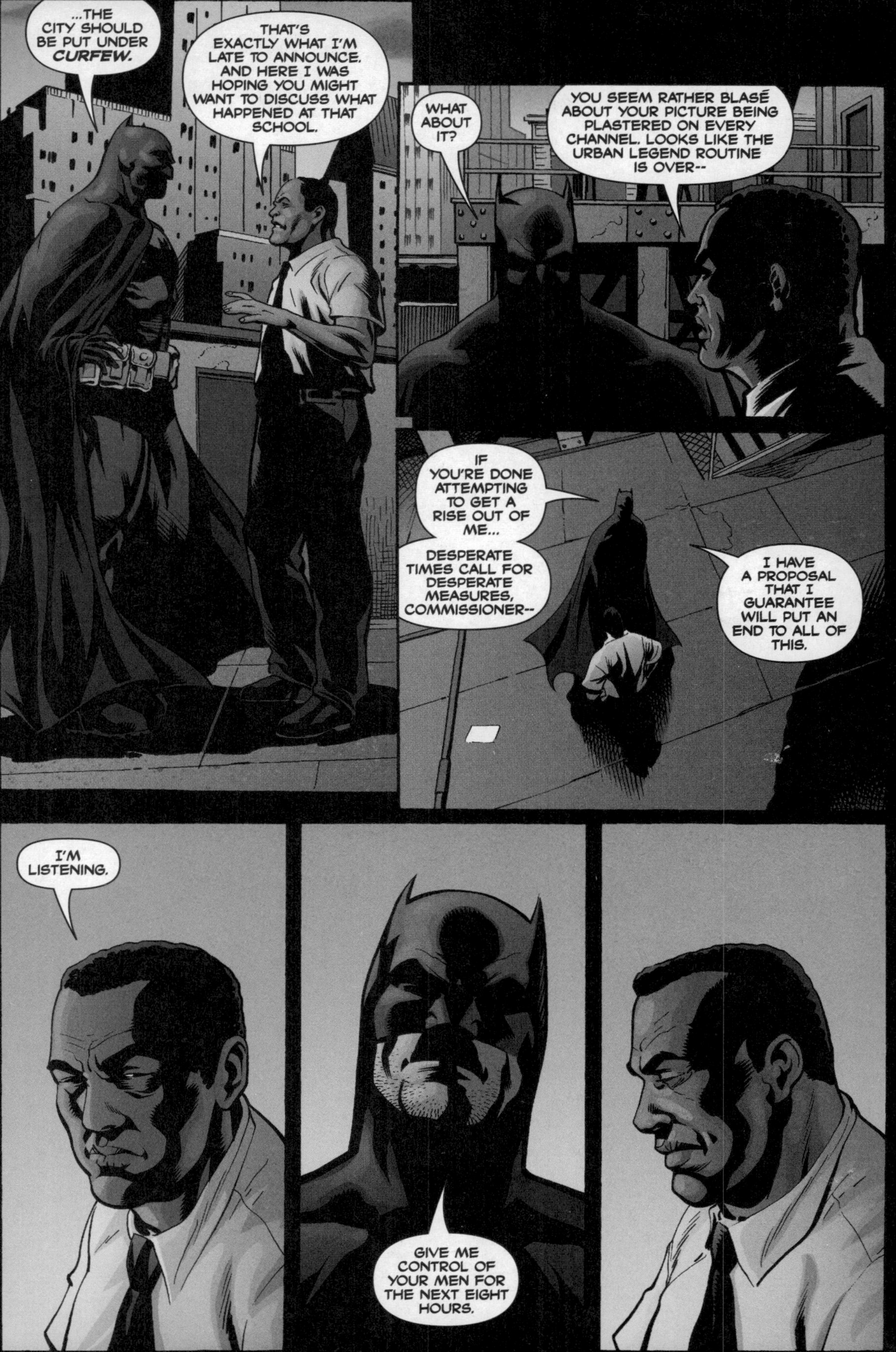
...THE CITY SHOULD BE PUT UNDER *CURFEW.*
THAT'S EXACTLY WHAT I'M LATE TO ANNOUNCE. AND HERE I WAS HOPING YOU MIGHT WANT TO DISCUSS WHAT HAPPENED AT THAT SCHOOL.
WHAT ABOUT IT?
YOU SEEM RATHER BLASÉ ABOUT YOUR PICTURE BEING PLASTERED ON EVERY CHANNEL. LOOKS LIKE THE URBAN LEGEND ROUTINE IS OVER--
IF YOU'RE DONE ATTEMPTING TO GET A RISE OUT OF ME...
DESPERATE TIMES CALL FOR DESPERATE MEASURES, COMMISSIONER--
I HAVE A PROPOSAL THAT I GUARANTEE WILL PUT AN END TO ALL OF THIS.
I'M LISTENING.
GIVE ME CONTROL OF YOUR MEN FOR THE NEXT EIGHT HOURS.

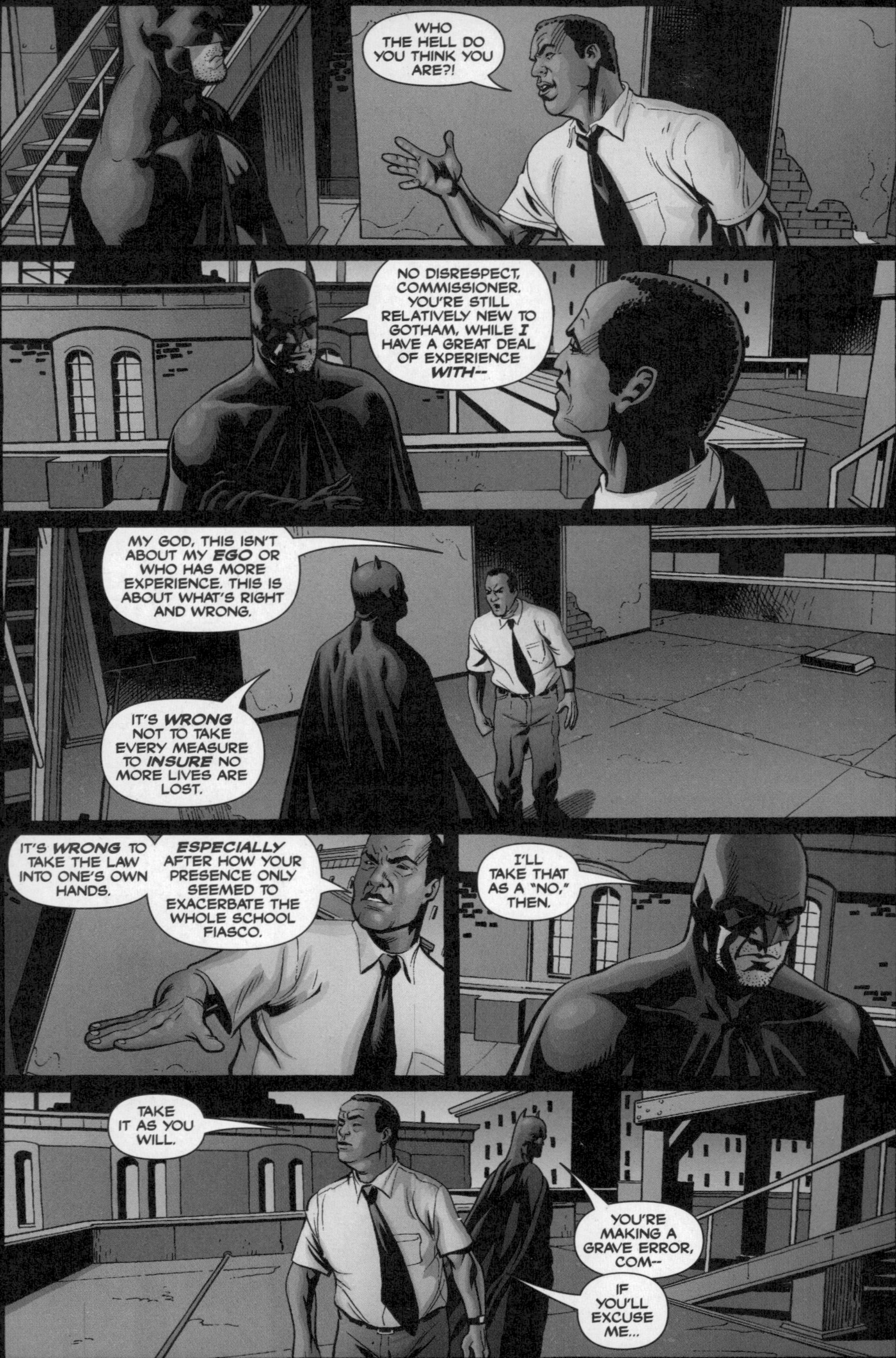
WHO THE HELL DO YOU THINK YOU ARE?!
NO DISRESPECT, COMMISSIONER. YOU'RE STILL RELATIVELY NEW TO GOTHAM, WHILE *I* HAVE A GREAT DEAL OF EXPERIENCE *WITH*--
MY GOD, THIS ISN'T ABOUT MY *EGO* OR WHO HAS MORE EXPERIENCE. THIS IS ABOUT WHAT'S RIGHT AND WRONG.
IT'S *WRONG* NOT TO TAKE EVERY MEASURE TO *INSURE* NO MORE LIVES ARE LOST.
IT'S *WRONG* TO TAKE THE LAW INTO ONE'S OWN HANDS.
ESPECIALLY AFTER HOW YOUR PRESENCE ONLY SEEMED TO EXACERBATE THE WHOLE SCHOOL FIASCO.
I'LL TAKE THAT AS A "NO," THEN.
TAKE IT AS YOU WILL.
YOU'RE MAKING A GRAVE ERROR, COM--
IF YOU'LL EXCUSE ME...

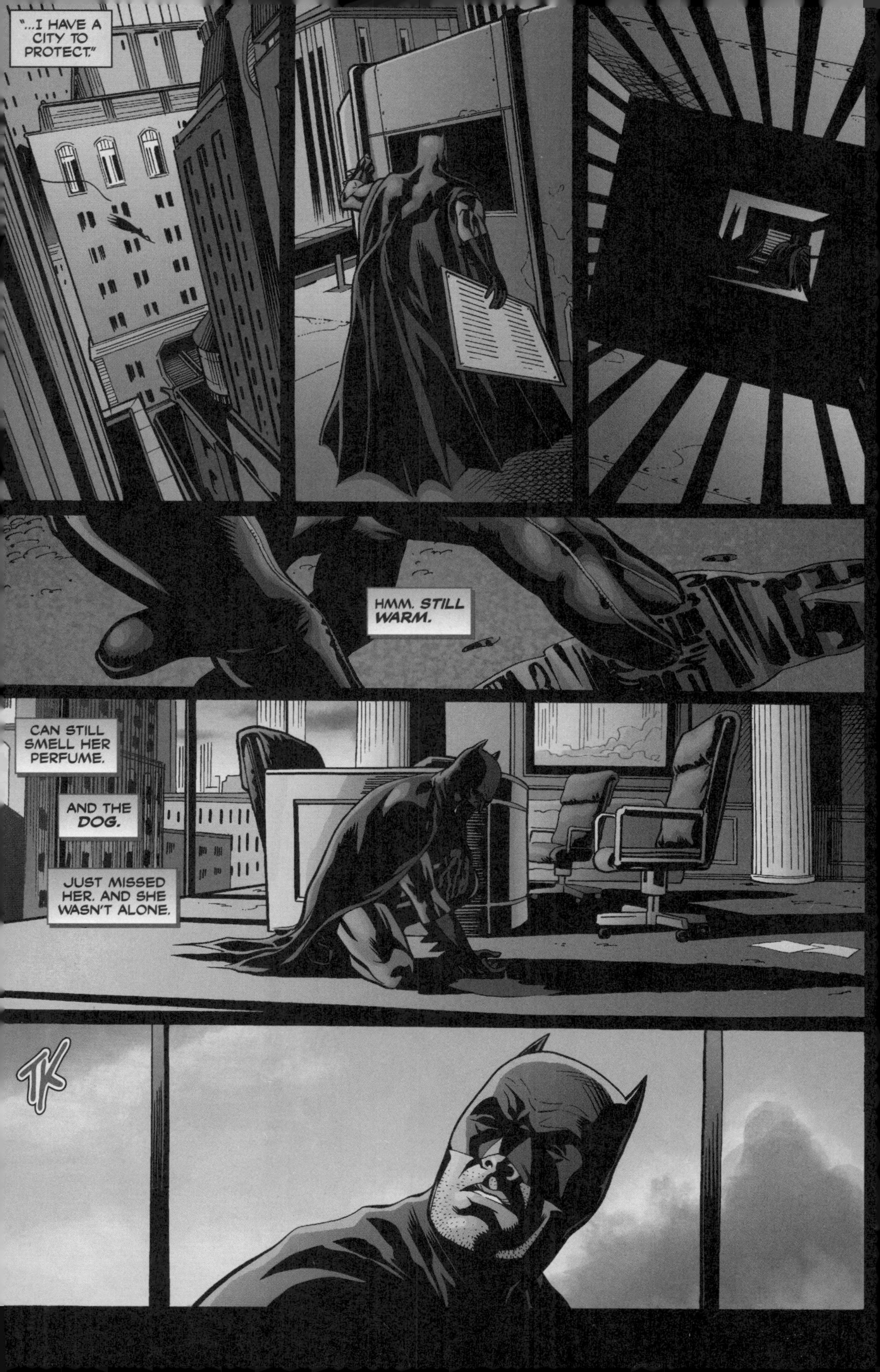
"...I HAVE A CITY TO PROTECT."
HMM. STILL WARM.
CAN STILL SMELL HER PERFUME.
AND THE DOG.
JUST MISSED HER. AND SHE WASN'T ALONE.
TK

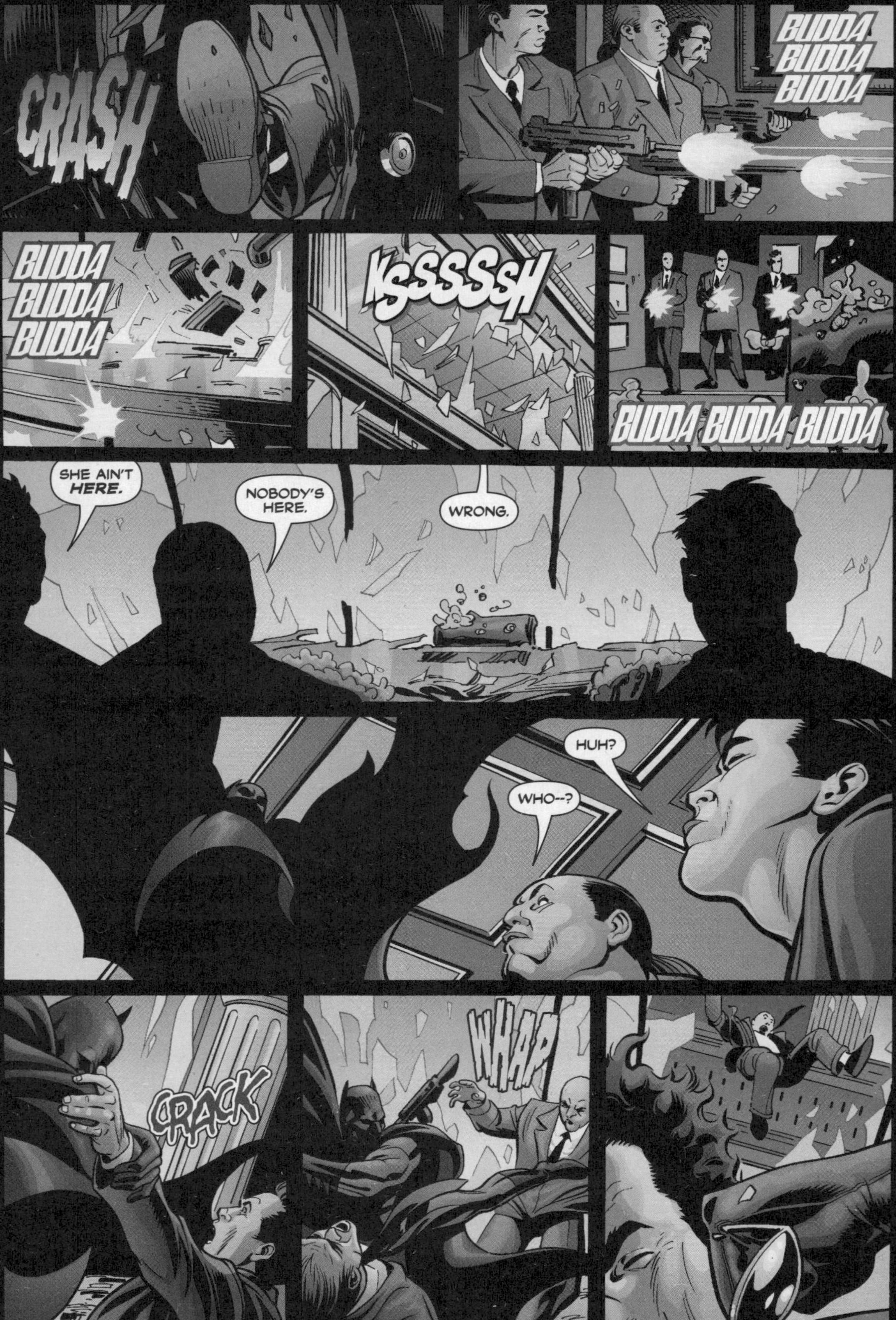
CRASH
BUDDA BUDDA BUDDA
BUDDA BUDDA BUDDA
KSSSSSH
BUDDA BUDDA BUDDA
SHE AIN'T *HERE.*
NOBODY'S HERE.
WRONG.
HUH?
WHO--?
CRACK
WHAP

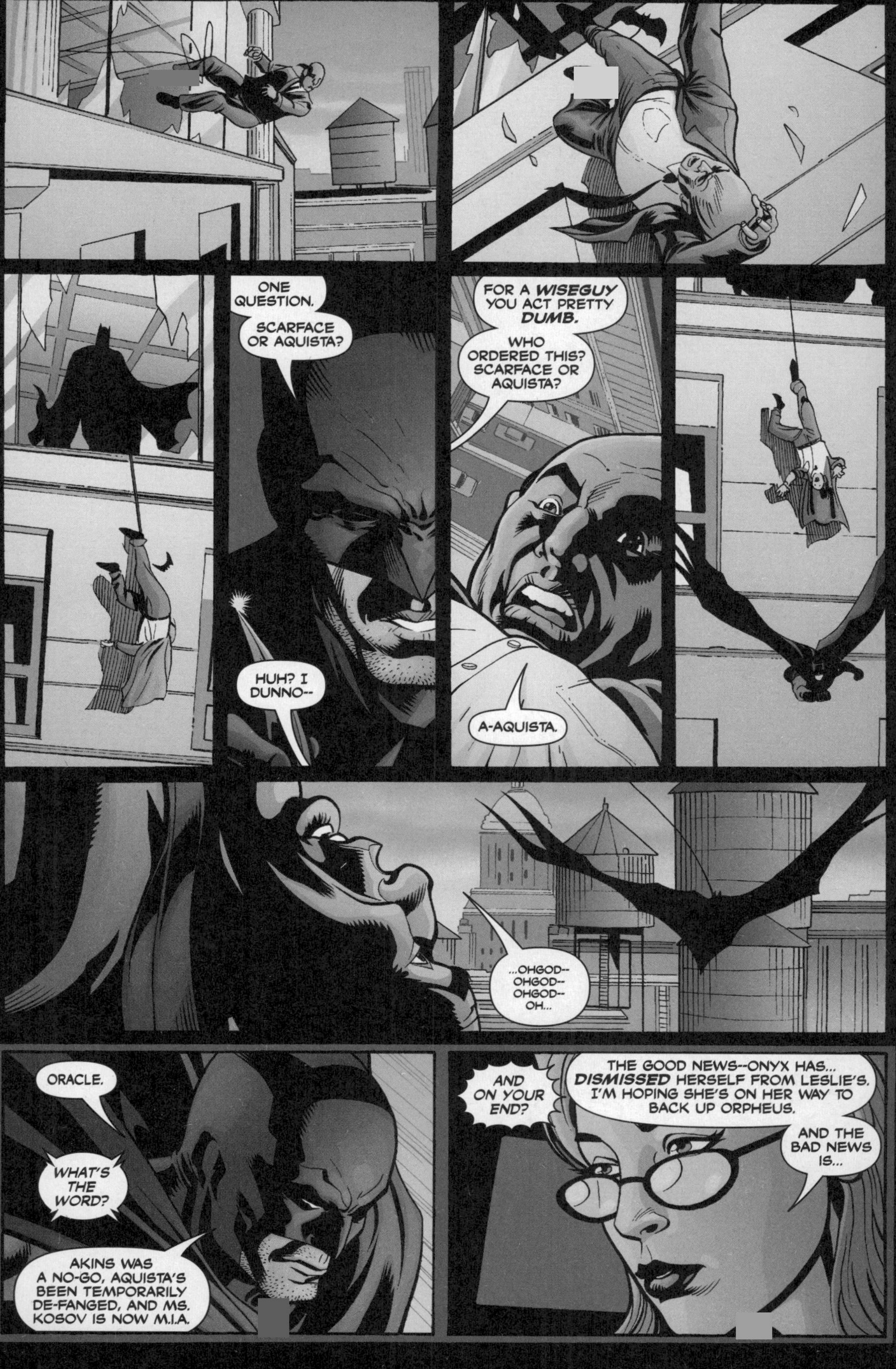
ONE QUESTION.
SCARFACE OR AQUISTA?
HUH? I DUNNO--
FOR A *WISEGUY* YOU ACT PRETTY *DUMB.*
WHO ORDERED THIS? SCARFACE OR AQUISTA?
A-AQUISTA.
...OHGOD-- OHGOD-- OHGOD-- OH...
ORACLE.
WHAT'S THE WORD?
AKINS WAS A NO-GO, AQUISTA'S BEEN TEMPORARILY DE-FANGED, AND MS. KOSOV IS NOW M.I.A.
AND ON YOUR END?
THE GOOD NEWS--ONYX HAS... *DISMISSED* HERSELF FROM LESLIE'S. I'M HOPING SHE'S ON HER WAY TO BACK UP ORPHEUS.
AND THE BAD NEWS IS...

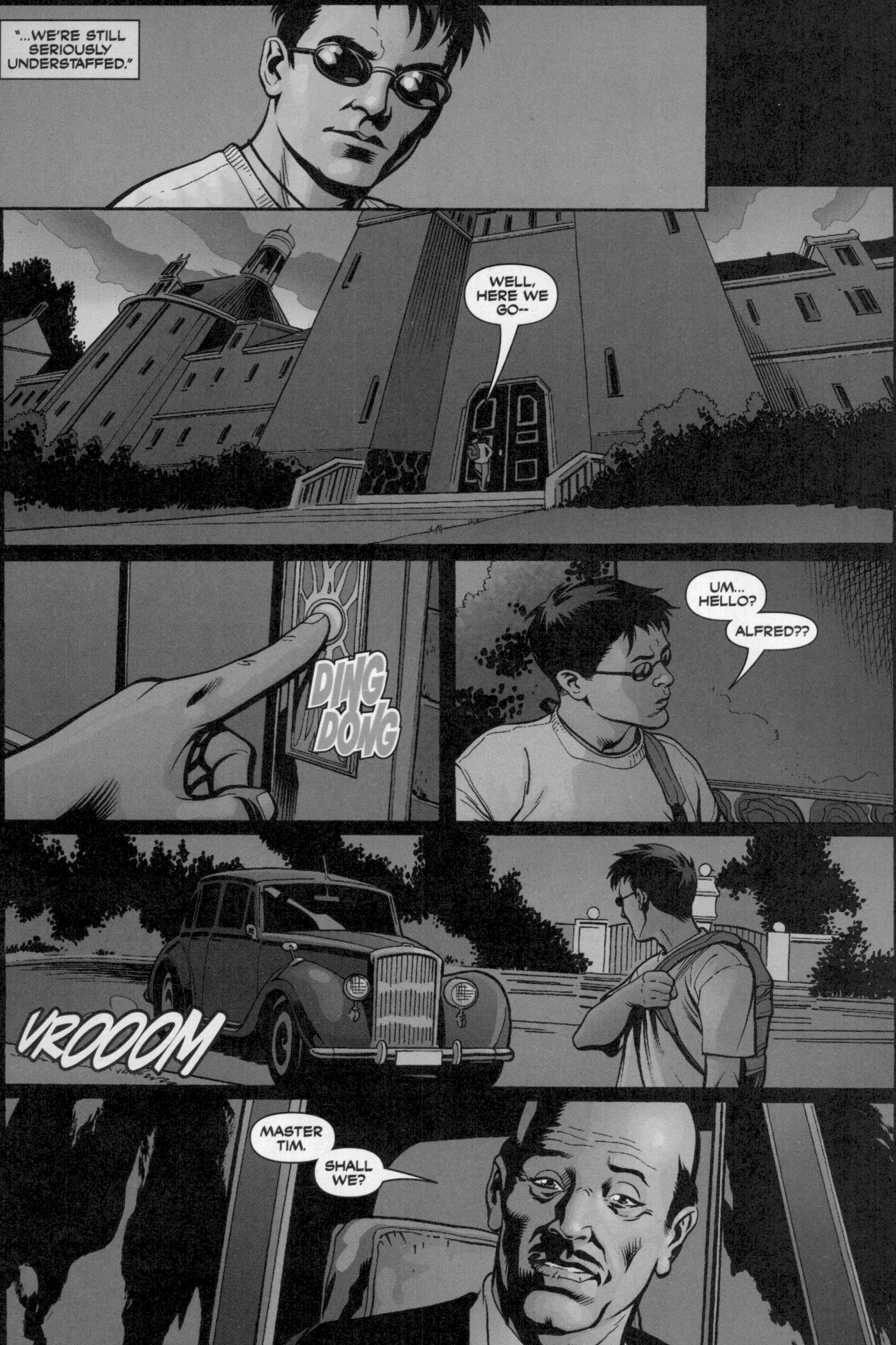
"...WE'RE STILL SERIOUSLY UNDERSTAFFED."
WELL, HERE WE GO--
DING DONG
UM... HELLO?
ALFRED??
VROOOM
MASTER TIM.
SHALL WE?

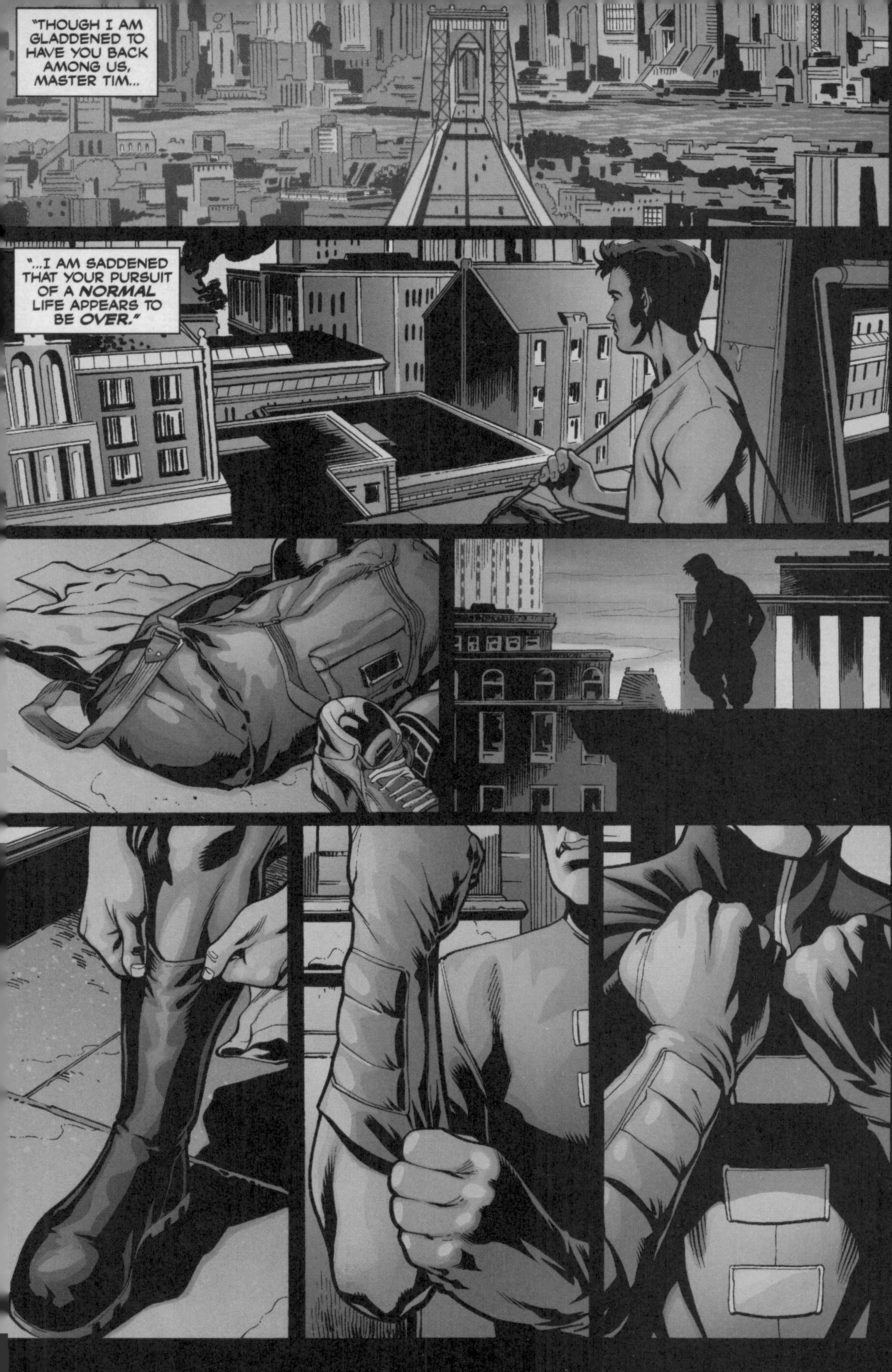
"THOUGH I AM GLADDENED TO HAVE YOU BACK AMONG US, MASTER TIM...
"...I AM SADDENED THAT YOUR PURSUIT OF A NORMAL LIFE APPEARS TO BE OVER."

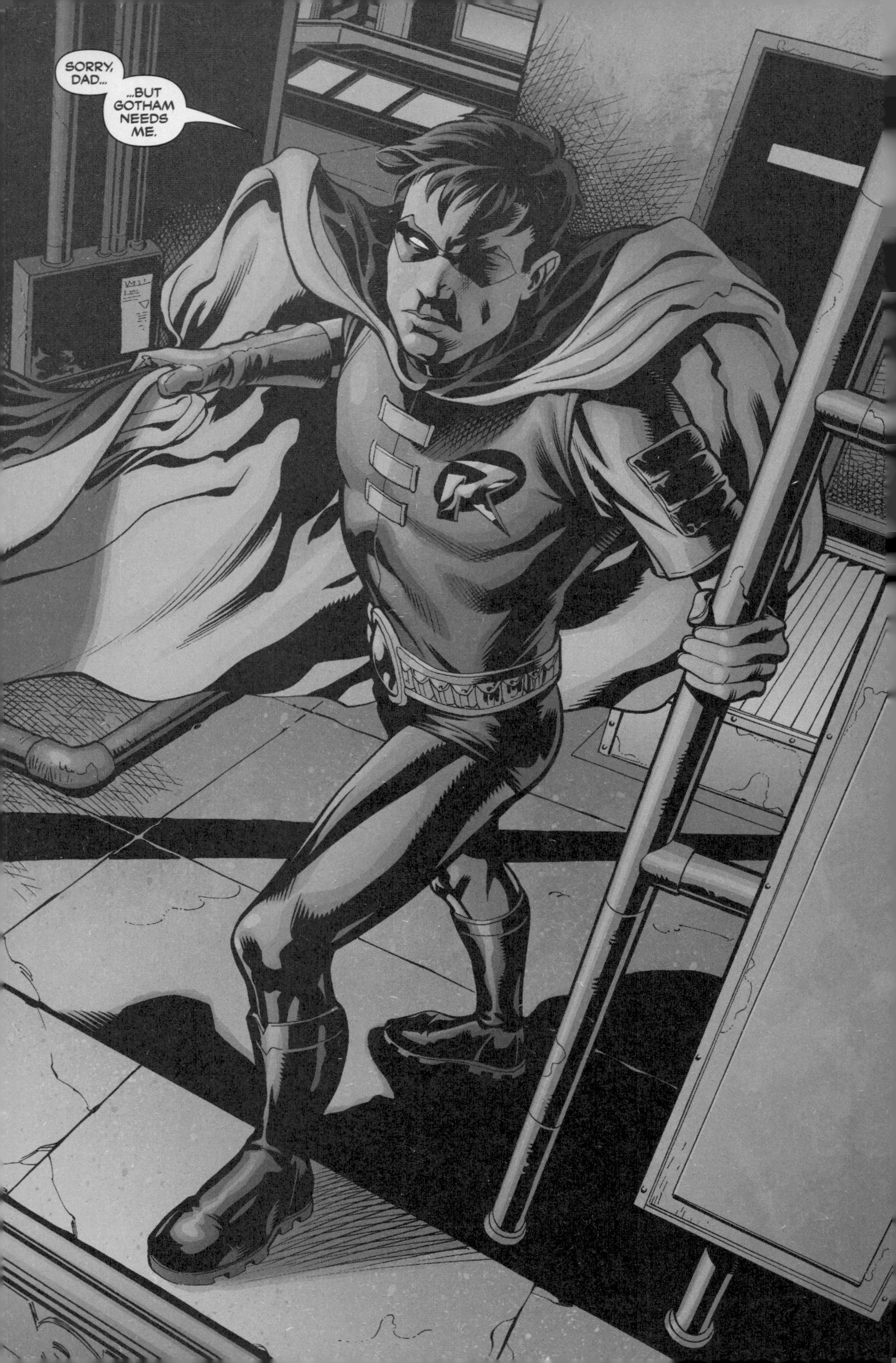
SORRY, DAD...
...BUT GOTHAM NEEDS ME.

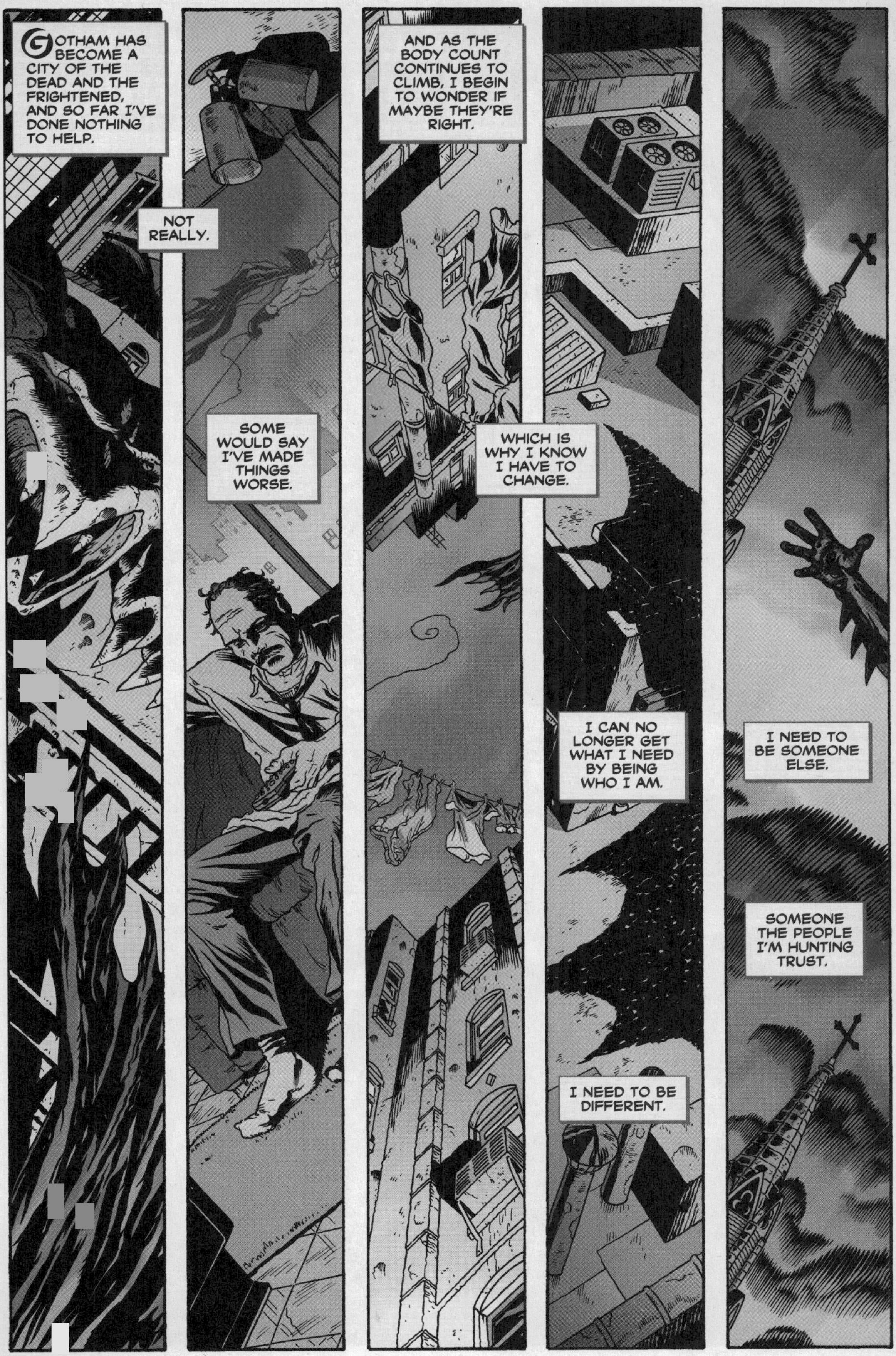
GOTHAM HAS BECOME A CITY OF THE DEAD AND THE FRIGHTENED, AND SO FAR I'VE DONE NOTHING TO HELP.
NOT REALLY.
SOME WOULD SAY I'VE MADE THINGS WORSE.
AND AS THE BODY COUNT CONTINUES TO CLIMB, I BEGIN TO WONDER IF MAYBE THEY'RE RIGHT.
WHICH IS WHY I KNOW I HAVE TO CHANGE.
I CAN NO LONGER GET WHAT I NEED BY BEING WHO I AM.
I NEED TO BE DIFFERENT.
I NEED TO BE SOMEONE ELSE.
SOMEONE THE PEOPLE I'M HUNTING TRUST.

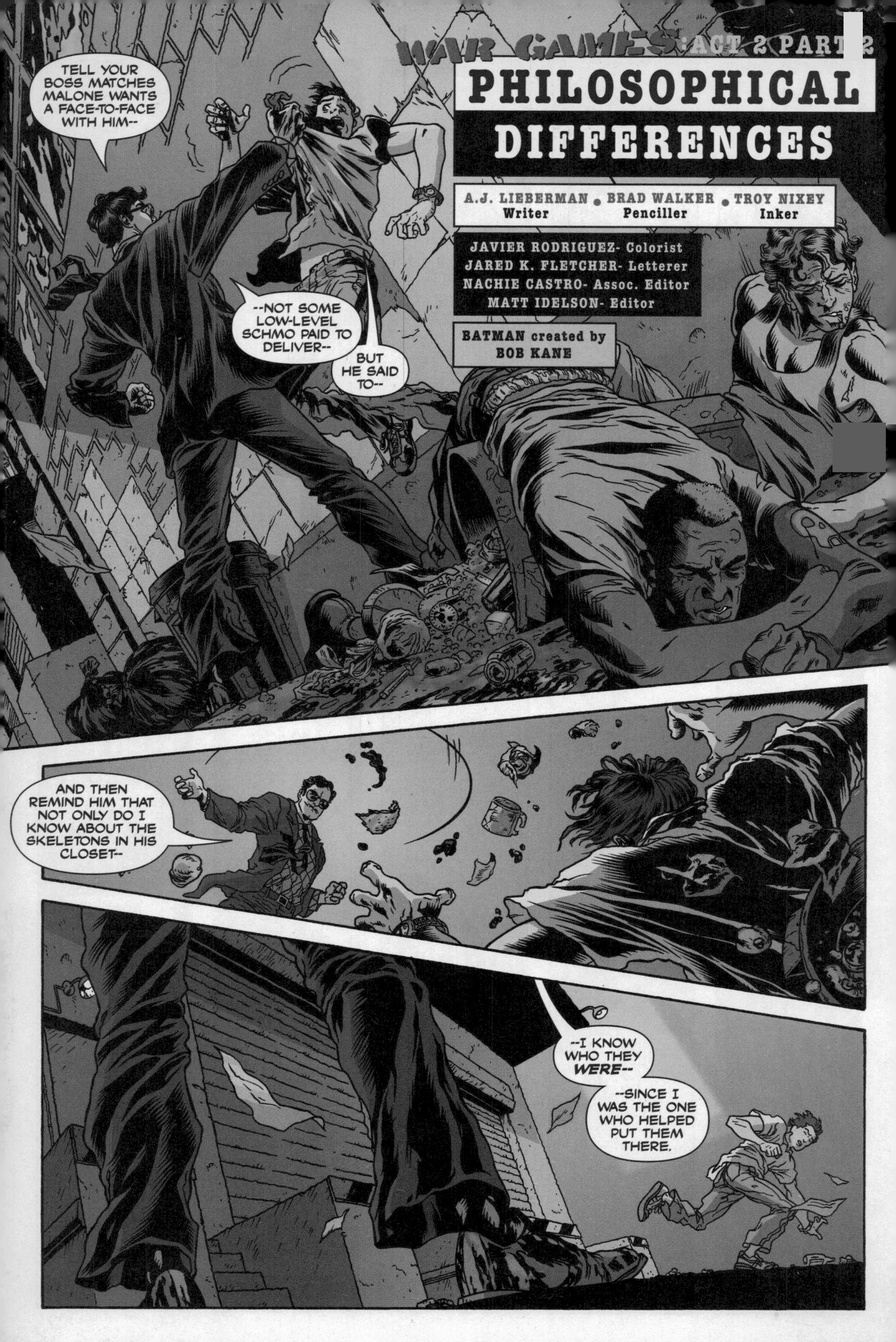
WAR GAMES: ACT 2 PART 2
PHILOSOPHICAL DIFFERENCES
A.J. LIEBERMAN Writer • BRAD WALKER Penciller • TROY NIXEY Inker
JAVIER RODRIGUEZ- Colorist
JARED K. FLETCHER- Letterer
NACHIE CASTRO- Assoc. Editor
MATT IDELSON- Editor
BATMAN created by BOB KANE
TELL YOUR BOSS MATCHES MALONE WANTS A FACE-TO-FACE WITH HIM--
--NOT SOME LOW-LEVEL SCHMO PAID TO DELIVER--
BUT HE SAID TO--
AND THEN REMIND HIM THAT NOT ONLY DO I KNOW ABOUT THE SKELETONS IN HIS CLOSET--
--I KNOW WHO THEY WERE--
--SINCE I WAS THE ONE WHO HELPED PUT THEM THERE.

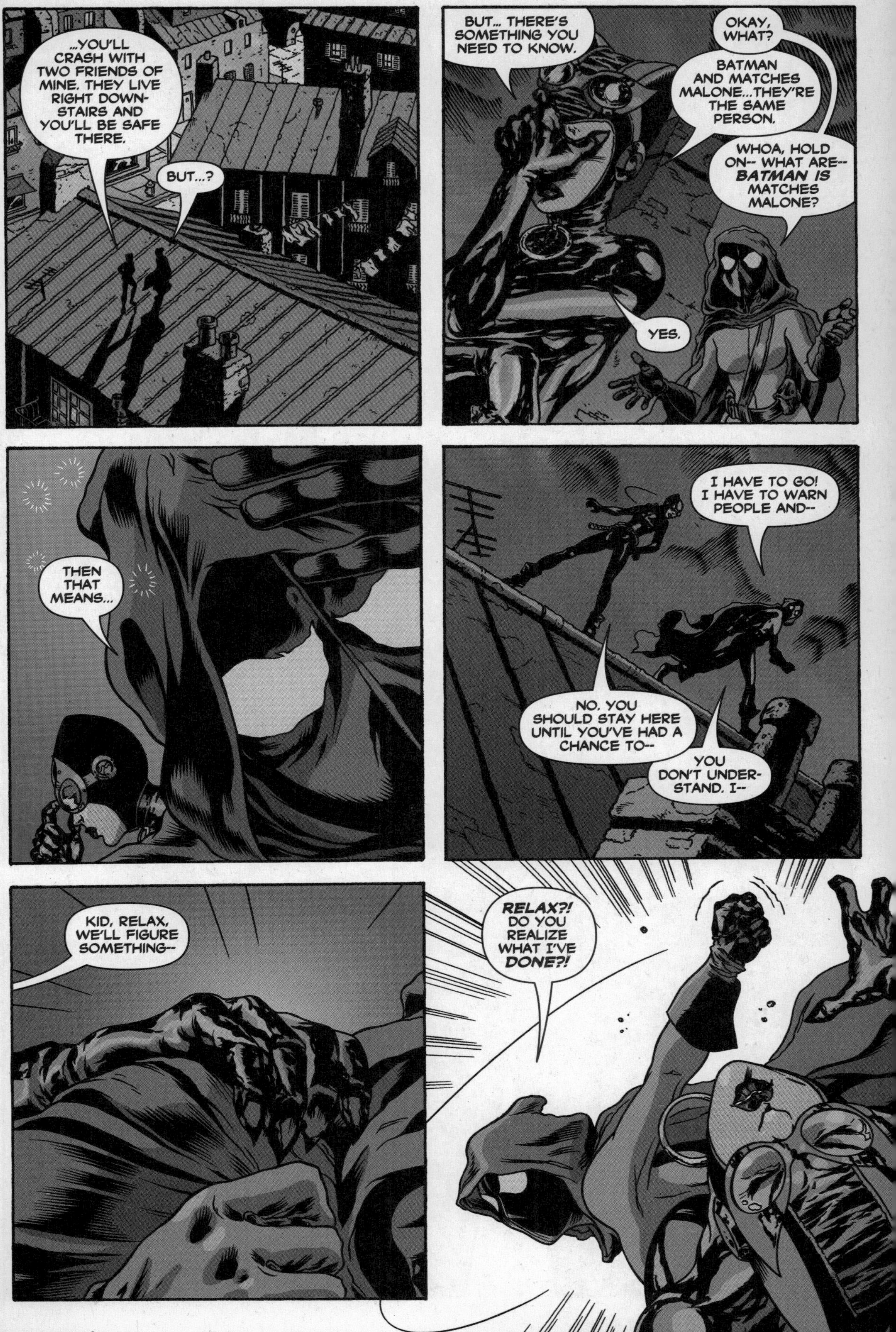
...YOU'LL CRASH WITH TWO FRIENDS OF MINE. THEY LIVE RIGHT DOWN-STAIRS AND YOU'LL BE SAFE THERE.
BUT...?
BUT... THERE'S SOMETHING YOU NEED TO KNOW.
OKAY, WHAT?
BATMAN AND MATCHES MALONE...THEY'RE THE SAME PERSON.
WHOA, HOLD ON-- WHAT ARE-- BATMAN IS MATCHES MALONE?
YES.
THEN THAT MEANS...
I HAVE TO GO! I HAVE TO WARN PEOPLE AND--
NO. YOU SHOULD STAY HERE UNTIL YOU'VE HAD A CHANCE TO--
YOU DON'T UNDER-STAND. I--
KID, RELAX, WE'LL FIGURE SOMETHING--
RELAX?! DO YOU REALIZE WHAT I'VE DONE?!

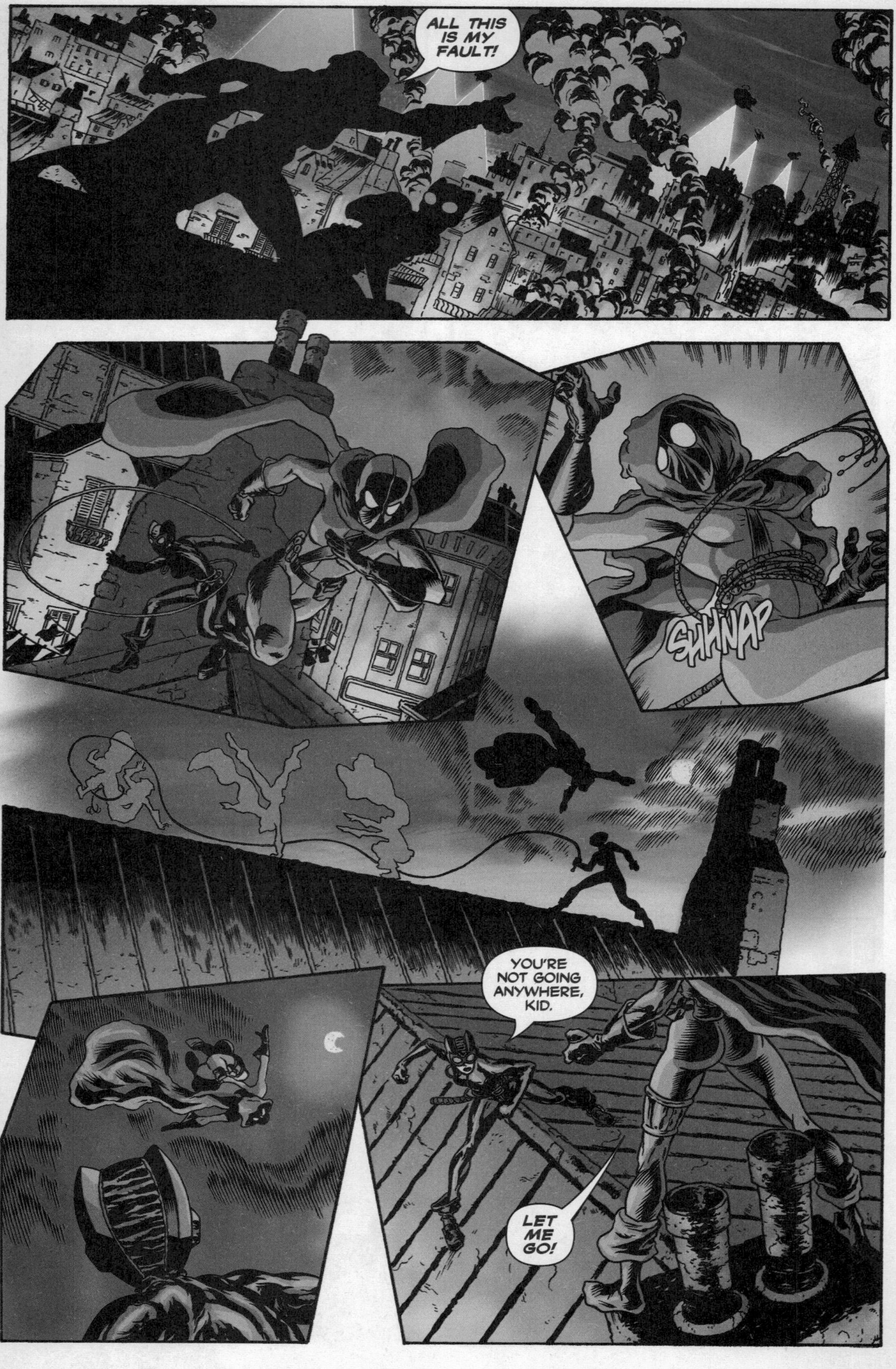
ALL THIS IS MY FAULT!
SHNAP
YOU'RE NOT GOING ANYWHERE, KID.
LET ME GO!

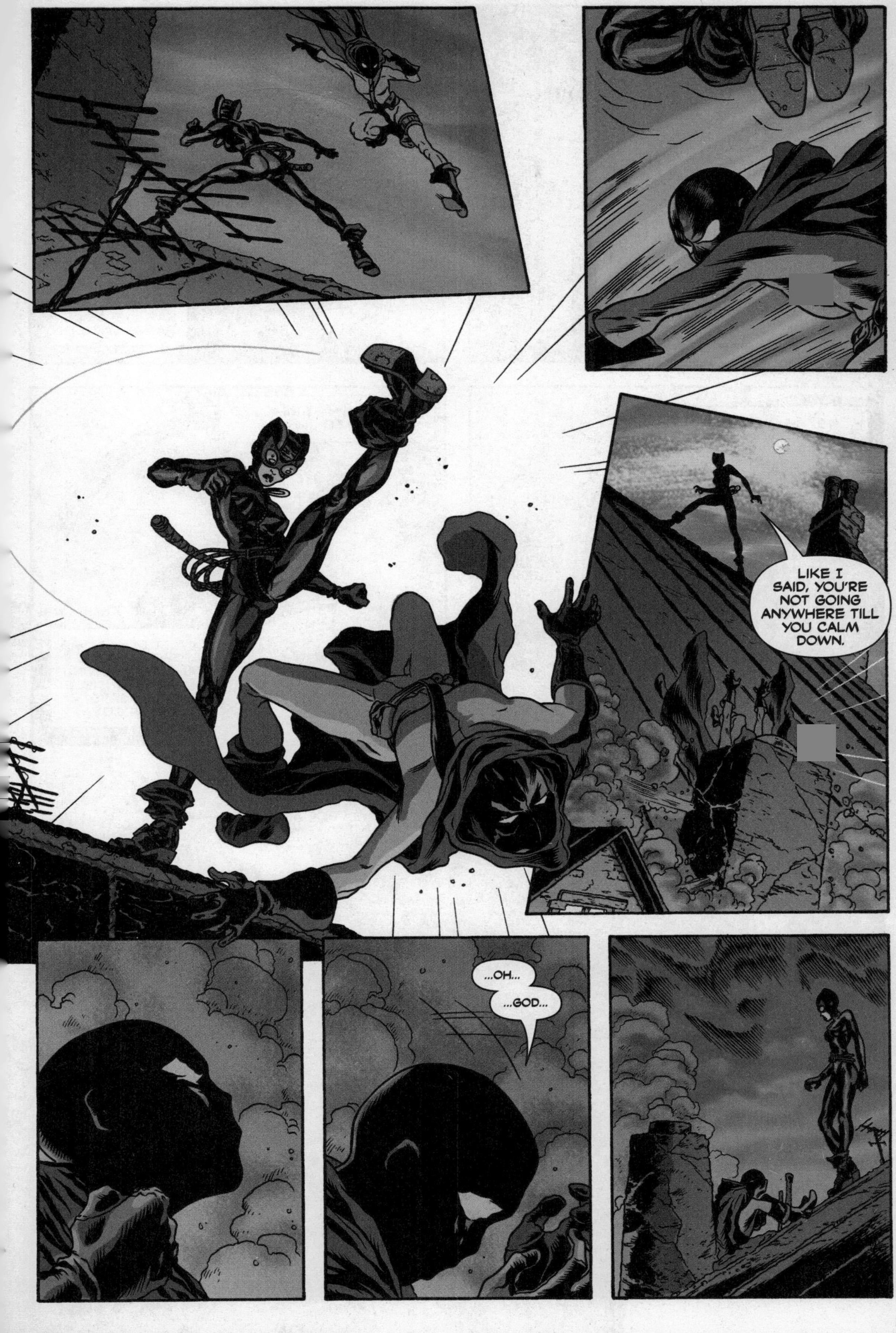
LIKE I SAID, YOU'RE NOT GOING ANYWHERE TILL YOU CALM DOWN.
...OH...
...GOD...

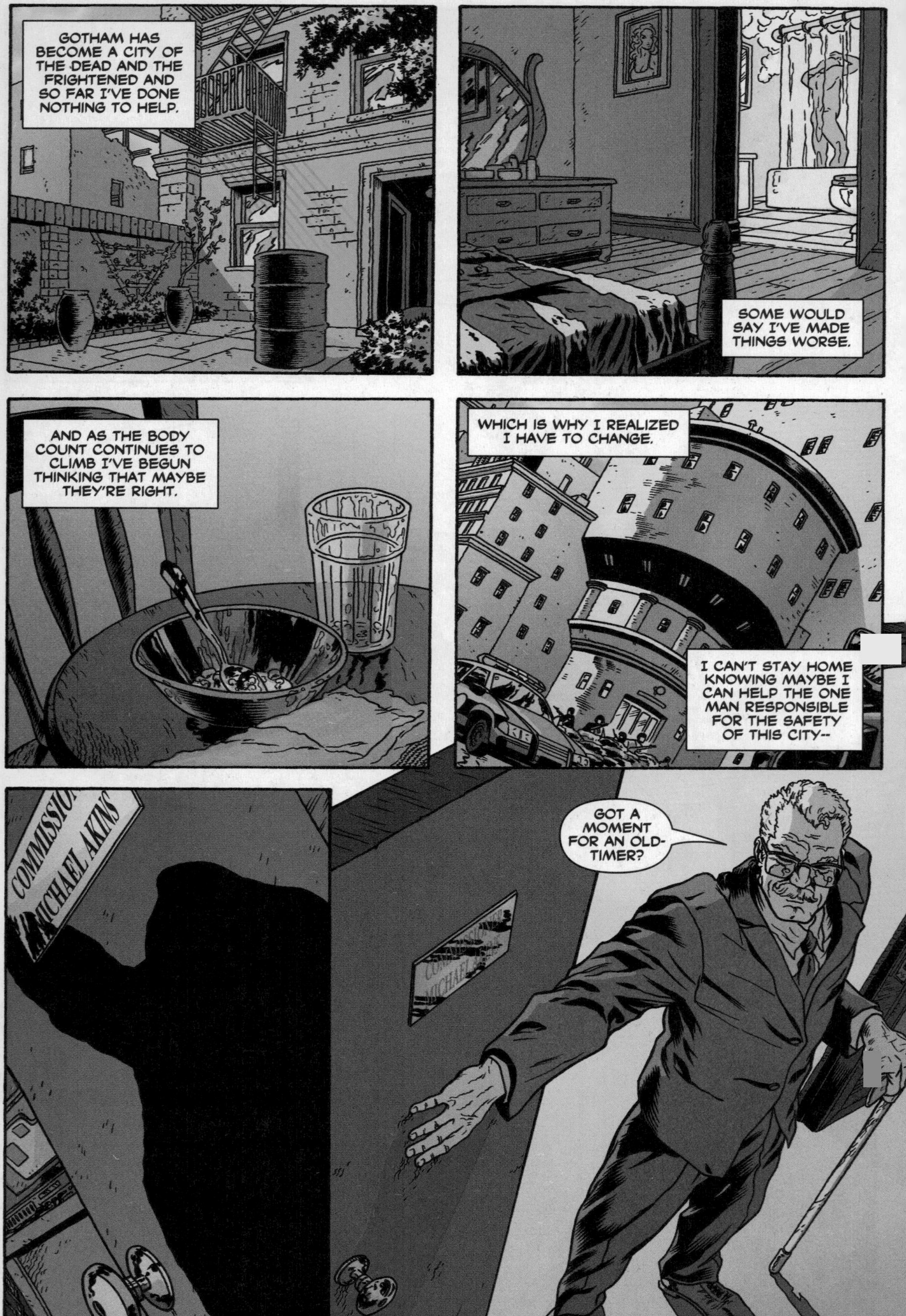
GOTHAM HAS BECOME A CITY OF THE DEAD AND THE FRIGHTENED AND SO FAR I'VE DONE NOTHING TO HELP.
SOME WOULD SAY I'VE MADE THINGS WORSE.
AND AS THE BODY COUNT CONTINUES TO CLIMB I'VE BEGUN THINKING THAT MAYBE THEY'RE RIGHT.
WHICH IS WHY I REALIZED I HAVE TO CHANGE.
I CAN'T STAY HOME KNOWING MAYBE I CAN HELP THE ONE MAN RESPONSIBLE FOR THE SAFETY OF THIS CITY--
COMMISSIONER
MICHAEL AKINS
GOT A MOMENT FOR AN OLD-TIMER?

FOR YOU, ABSOLUTELY.

I THOUGHT YOU MIGHT WANT SOME--

HELP? THAT WAS HOURS AGO. NOW I'M SHOPPING FOR MIRACLES.

HOW ARE YOU DOING?

I... DON'T KNOW ANYMORE.

I CAN COME BACK. IF YOU'RE BUSY, I MEAN. I SHOULD'VE CALLED.

IN THE LAST FORTY-EIGHT HOURS YOU'RE THE ONLY PERSON I'VE ACTUALLY BEEN GLAD TO SEE.

I THOUGHT MAYBE SINCE I'VE BEEN THROUGH THIS BEFORE I COULD HELP. OR AT LEAST LISTEN.

OR BOTH.

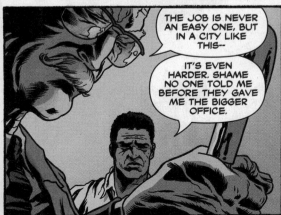

THE JOB IS NEVER AN EASY ONE, BUT IN A CITY LIKE THIS--

IT'S EVEN HARDER. SHAME NO ONE TOLD ME BEFORE THEY GAVE ME THE BIGGER OFFICE.

HAS HE BEEN HERE?

YEAH.

AND?

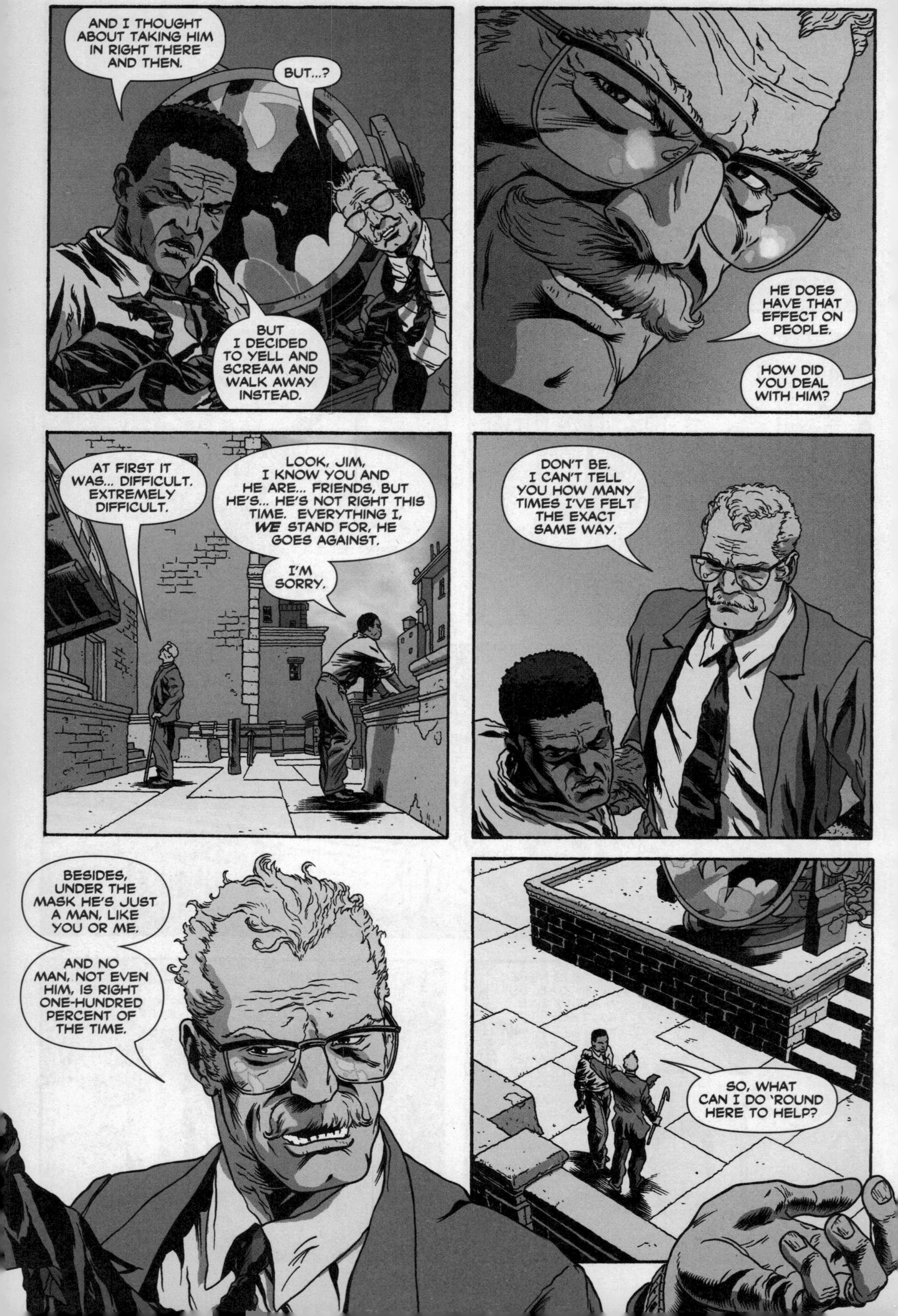
AND I THOUGHT ABOUT TAKING HIM IN RIGHT THERE AND THEN.
BUT...?
BUT I DECIDED TO YELL AND SCREAM AND WALK AWAY INSTEAD.
HE DOES HAVE THAT EFFECT ON PEOPLE.
HOW DID YOU DEAL WITH HIM?
AT FIRST IT WAS... DIFFICULT. EXTREMELY DIFFICULT.
LOOK, JIM, I KNOW YOU AND HE ARE... FRIENDS, BUT HE'S... HE'S NOT RIGHT THIS TIME. EVERYTHING I, *WE* STAND FOR, HE GOES AGAINST.
I'M SORRY.
DON'T BE. I CAN'T TELL YOU HOW MANY TIMES I'VE FELT THE EXACT SAME WAY.
BESIDES, UNDER THE MASK HE'S JUST A MAN, LIKE YOU OR ME.
AND NO MAN, NOT EVEN HIM, IS RIGHT ONE-HUNDRED PERCENT OF THE TIME.
SO, WHAT CAN I DO 'ROUND HERE TO HELP?

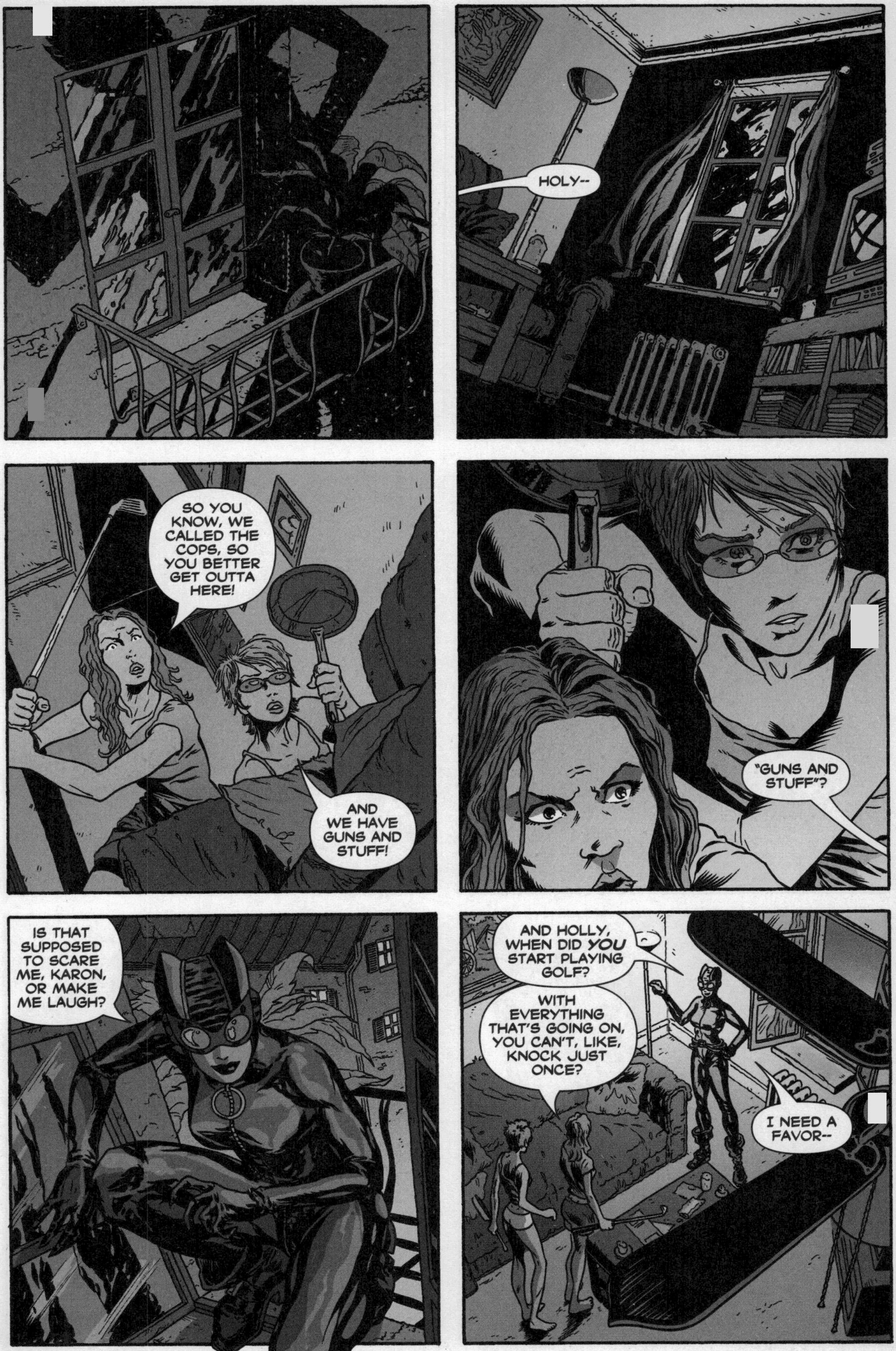
HOLY--
SO YOU KNOW, WE CALLED THE COPS, SO YOU BETTER GET OUTTA HERE!
AND WE HAVE GUNS AND STUFF!
"GUNS AND STUFF"?
IS THAT SUPPOSED TO SCARE ME, KARON, OR MAKE ME LAUGH?
AND HOLLY, WHEN DID *YOU* START PLAYING GOLF?
WITH EVERYTHING THAT'S GOING ON, YOU CAN'T, LIKE, KNOCK JUST ONCE?
I NEED A FAVOR--

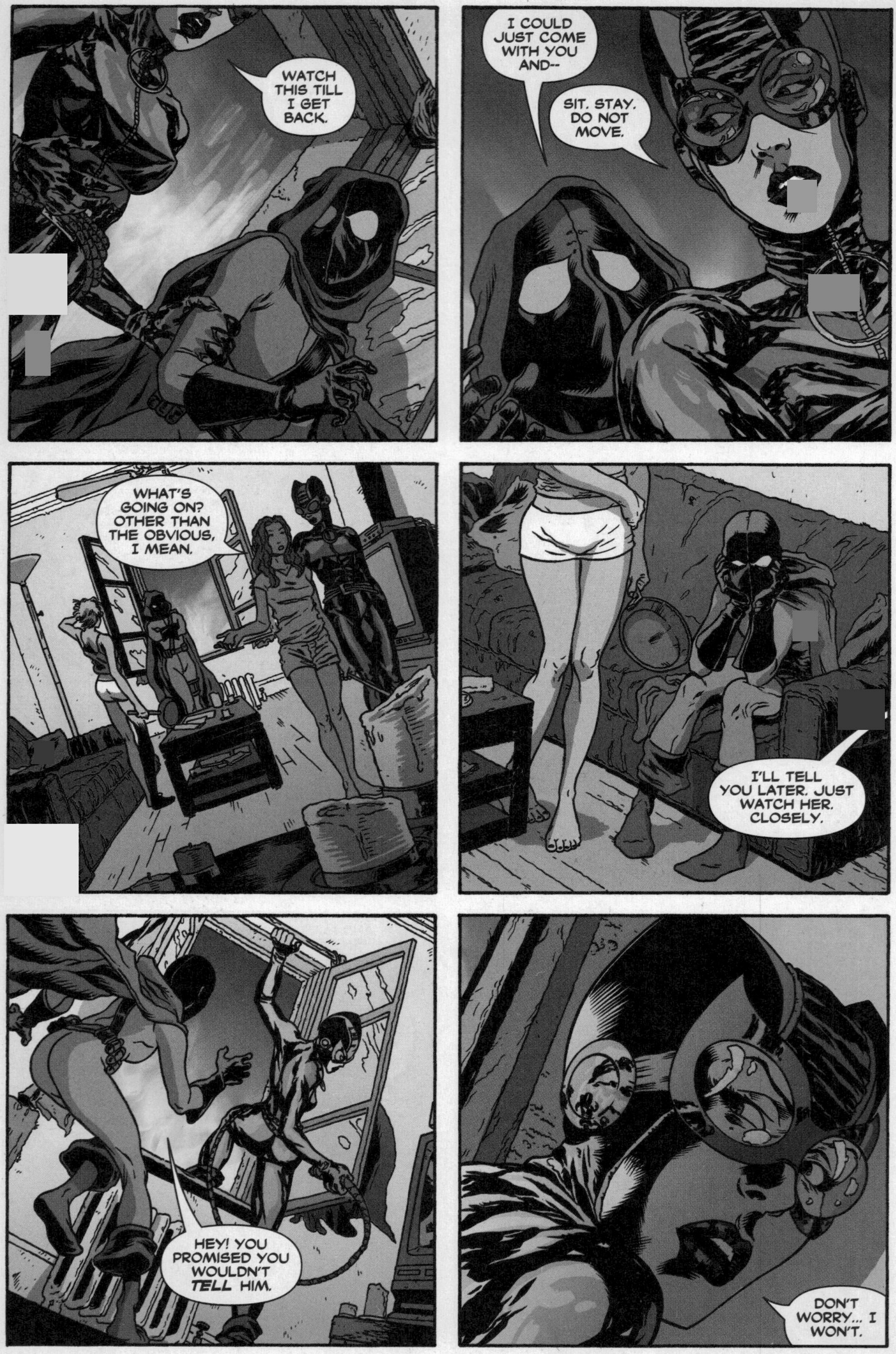
WATCH THIS TILL I GET BACK.
I COULD JUST COME WITH YOU AND--
SIT. STAY. DO NOT MOVE.
WHAT'S GOING ON? OTHER THAN THE OBVIOUS, I MEAN.
I'LL TELL YOU LATER. JUST WATCH HER. CLOSELY.
HEY! YOU PROMISED YOU WOULDN'T *TELL* HIM.
DON'T WORRY... I WON'T.

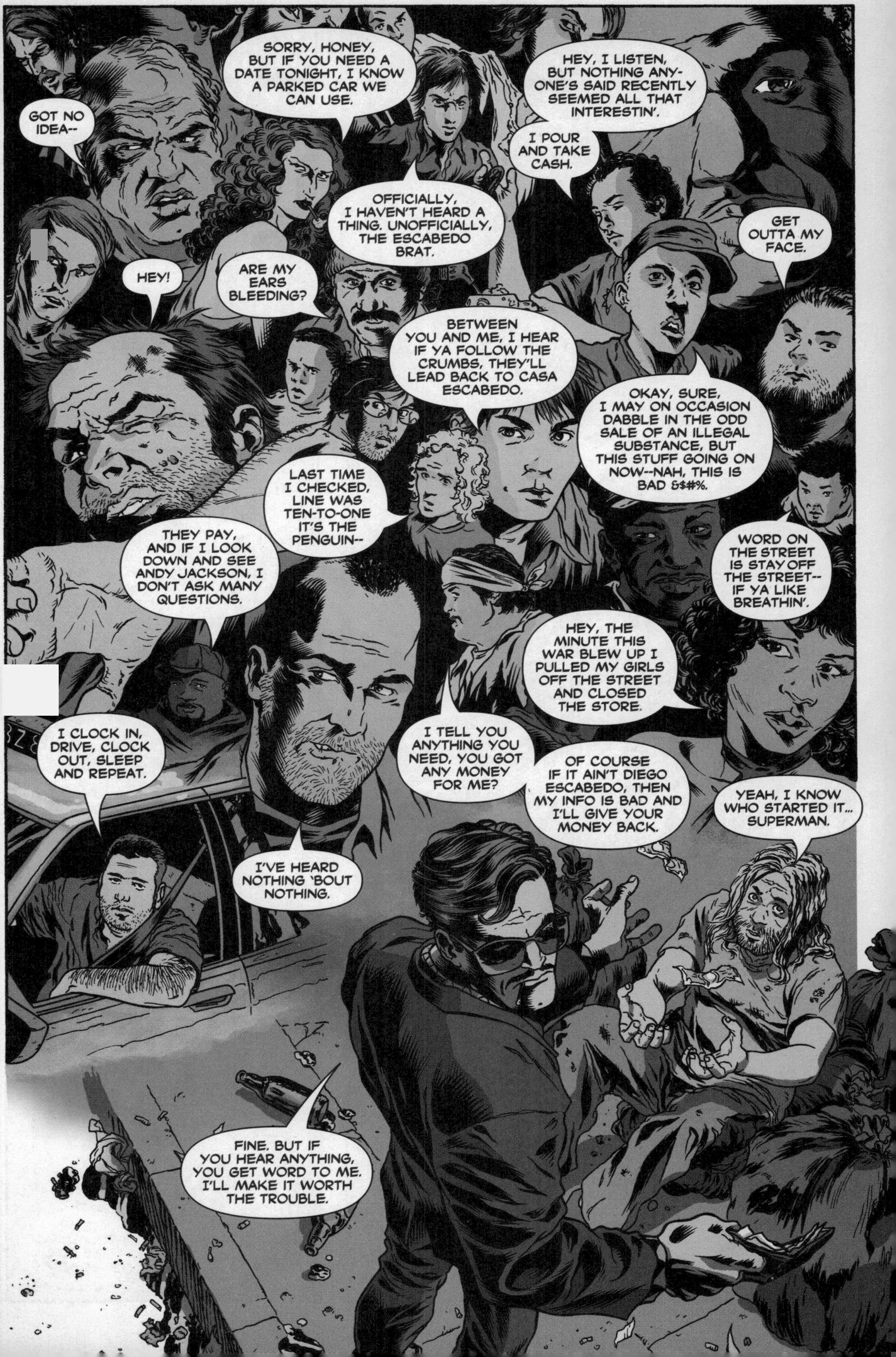
GOT NO IDEA--
SORRY, HONEY, BUT IF YOU NEED A DATE TONIGHT, I KNOW A PARKED CAR WE CAN USE.
HEY, I LISTEN, BUT NOTHING ANY-ONE'S SAID RECENTLY SEEMED ALL THAT INTERESTIN'.
I POUR AND TAKE CASH.
OFFICIALLY, I HAVEN'T HEARD A THING. UNOFFICIALLY, THE ESCABEDO BRAT.
GET OUTTA MY FACE.
HEY!
ARE MY EARS BLEEDING?
BETWEEN YOU AND ME, I HEAR IF YA FOLLOW THE CRUMBS, THEY'LL LEAD BACK TO CASA ESCABEDO.
OKAY, SURE, I MAY ON OCCASION DABBLE IN THE ODD SALE OF AN ILLEGAL SUBSTANCE, BUT THIS STUFF GOING ON NOW--NAH, THIS IS BAD &$#%.
LAST TIME I CHECKED, LINE WAS TEN-TO-ONE IT'S THE PENGUIN--
THEY PAY, AND IF I LOOK DOWN AND SEE ANDY JACKSON, I DON'T ASK MANY QUESTIONS.
WORD ON THE STREET IS STAY OFF THE STREET-- IF YA LIKE BREATHIN'.
HEY, THE MINUTE THIS WAR BLEW UP I PULLED MY GIRLS OFF THE STREET AND CLOSED THE STORE.
I CLOCK IN, DRIVE, CLOCK OUT, SLEEP AND REPEAT.
I TELL YOU ANYTHING YOU NEED, YOU GOT ANY MONEY FOR ME?
OF COURSE IF IT AIN'T DIEGO ESCABEDO, THEN MY INFO IS BAD AND I'LL GIVE YOUR MONEY BACK.
YEAH, I KNOW WHO STARTED IT... SUPERMAN.
I'VE HEARD NOTHING 'BOUT NOTHING.
FINE. BUT IF YOU HEAR ANYTHING, YOU GET WORD TO ME. I'LL MAKE IT WORTH THE TROUBLE.

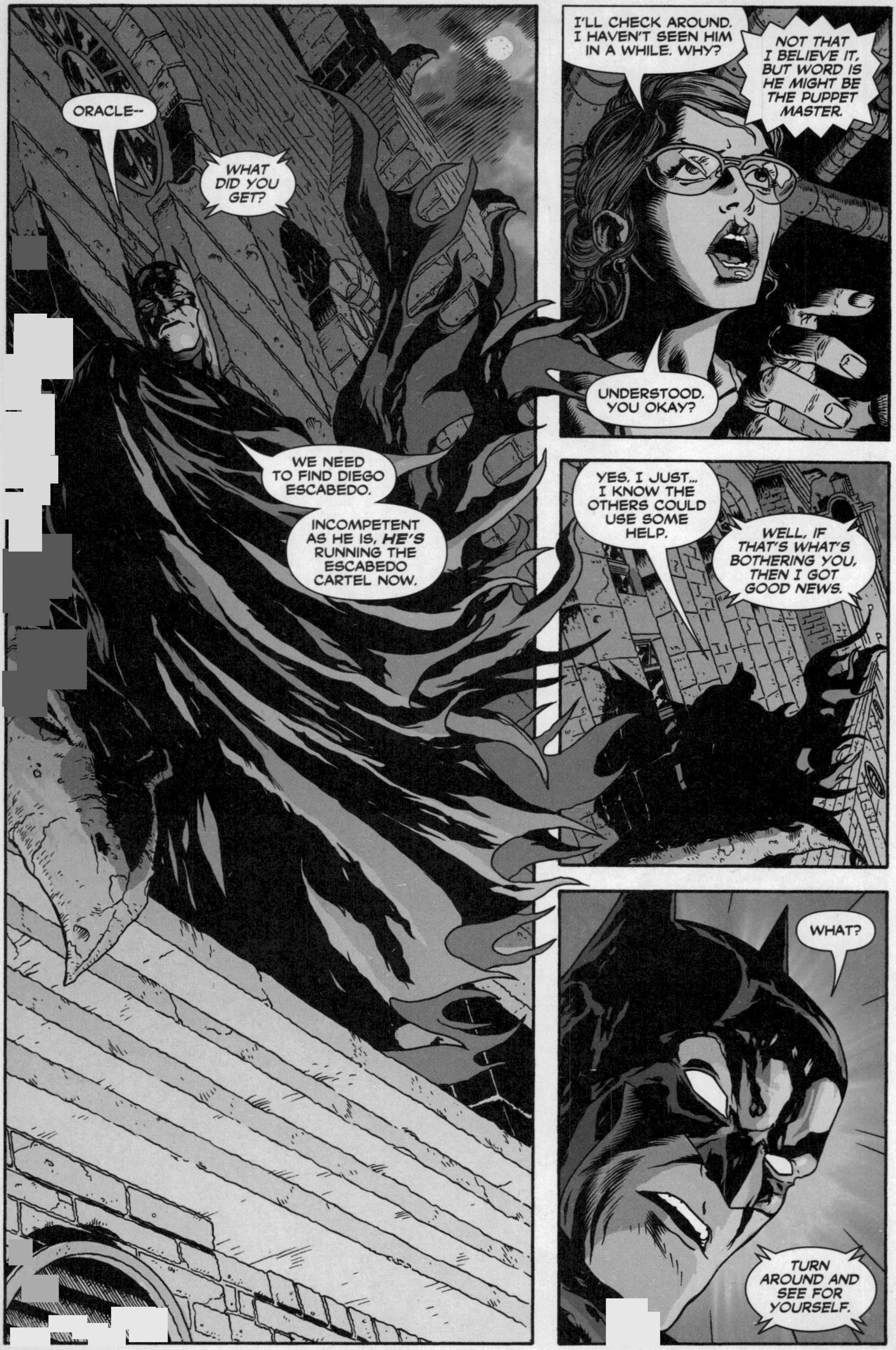
ORACLE--
WHAT DID YOU GET?
WE NEED TO FIND DIEGO ESCABEDO.
INCOMPETENT AS HE IS, **HE'S** RUNNING THE ESCABEDO CARTEL NOW.
I'LL CHECK AROUND. I HAVEN'T SEEN HIM IN A WHILE. WHY?
NOT THAT I BELIEVE IT, BUT WORD IS HE MIGHT BE THE PUPPET MASTER.
UNDERSTOOD. YOU OKAY?
YES. I JUST... I KNOW THE OTHERS COULD USE SOME HELP.
WELL, IF THAT'S WHAT'S BOTHERING YOU, THEN I GOT GOOD NEWS.
WHAT?
TURN AROUND AND SEE FOR YOURSELF.

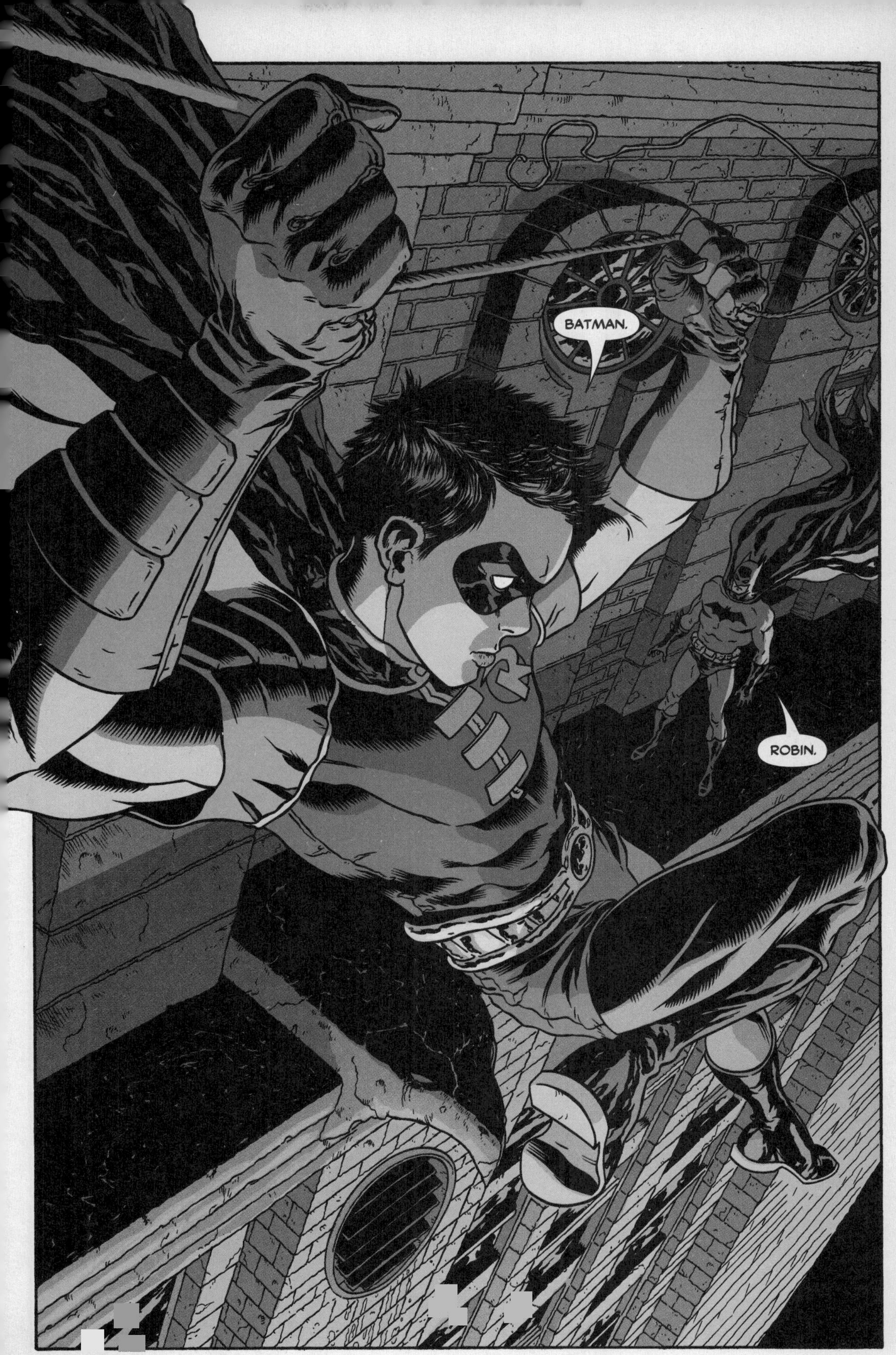
BATMAN.
ROBIN.

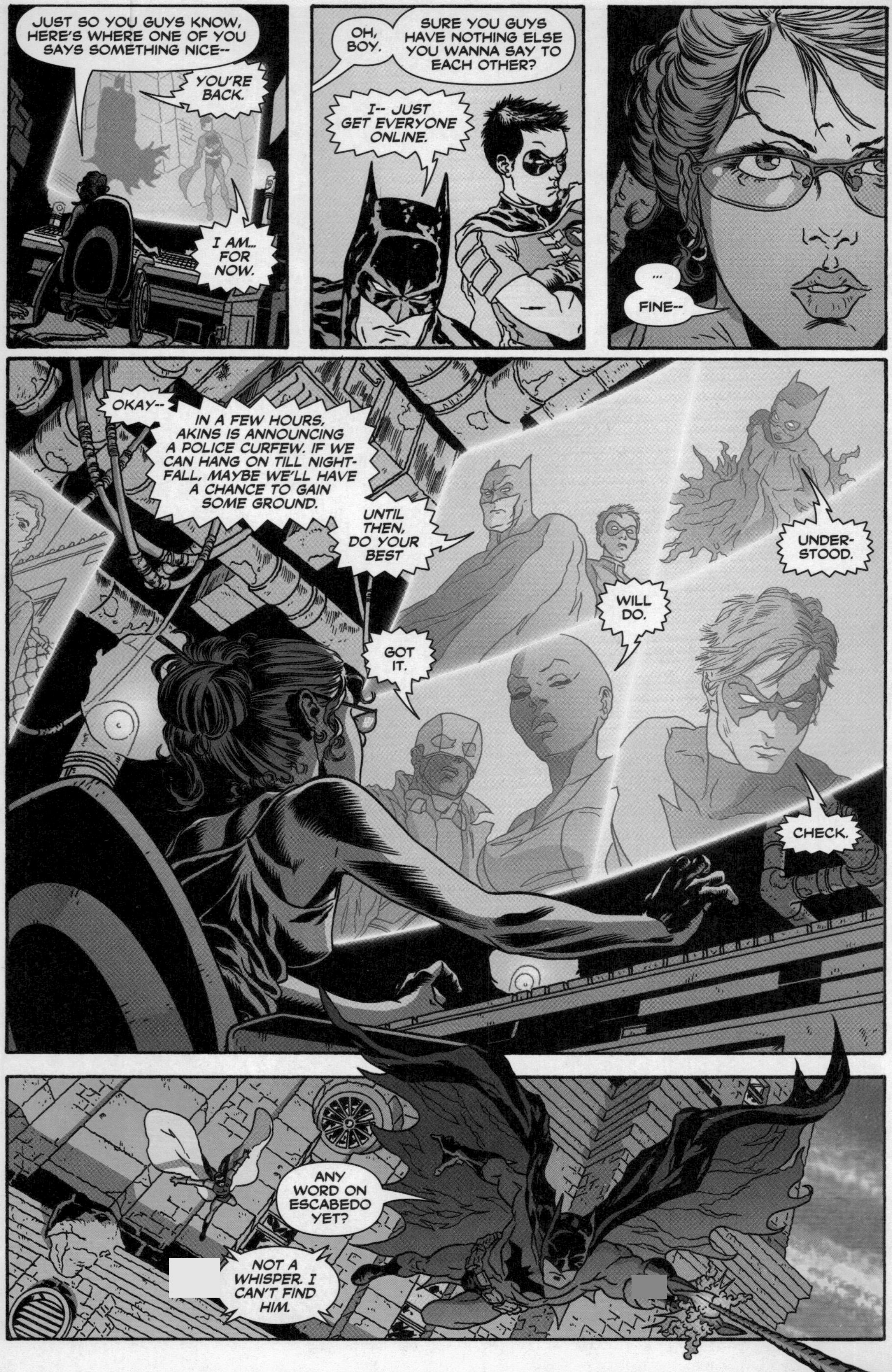
JUST SO YOU GUYS KNOW, HERE'S WHERE ONE OF YOU SAYS SOMETHING NICE--
YOU'RE BACK.
I AM... FOR NOW.
OH, BOY.
SURE YOU GUYS HAVE NOTHING ELSE YOU WANNA SAY TO EACH OTHER?
I-- JUST GET EVERYONE ONLINE.
...
FINE--
OKAY--
IN A FEW HOURS, AKINS IS ANNOUNCING A POLICE CURFEW. IF WE CAN HANG ON TILL NIGHT-FALL, MAYBE WE'LL HAVE A CHANCE TO GAIN SOME GROUND.
UNTIL THEN, DO YOUR BEST
UNDER-STOOD.
GOT IT.
WILL DO.
CHECK.
ANY WORD ON ESCABEDO YET?
NOT A WHISPER. I CAN'T FIND HIM.

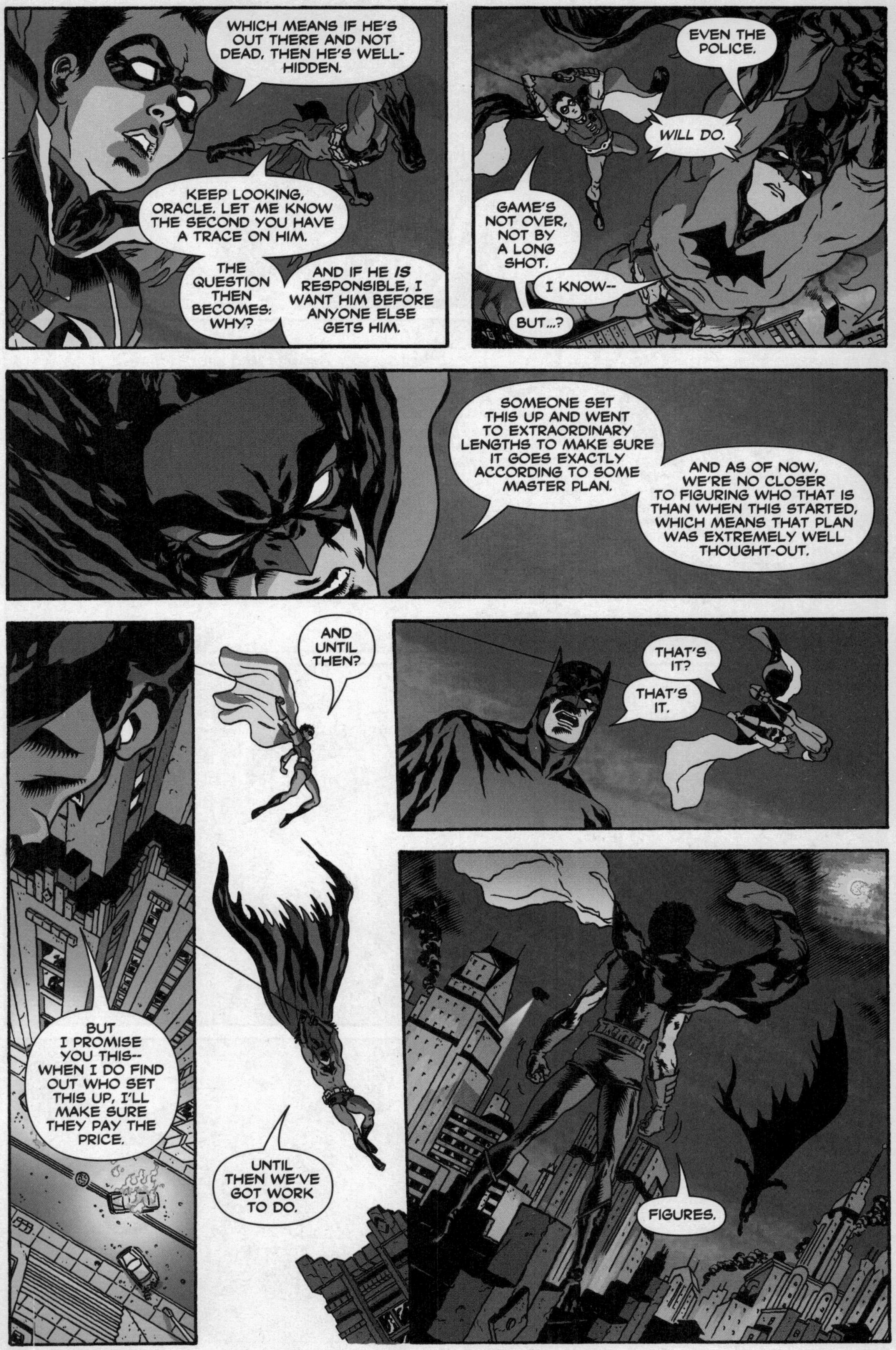
WHICH MEANS IF HE'S OUT THERE AND NOT DEAD, THEN HE'S WELL-HIDDEN.
KEEP LOOKING, ORACLE. LET ME KNOW THE SECOND YOU HAVE A TRACE ON HIM.
THE QUESTION THEN BECOMES: WHY?
AND IF HE *IS* RESPONSIBLE, I WANT HIM BEFORE ANYONE ELSE GETS HIM.
EVEN THE POLICE.
WILL DO.
GAME'S NOT OVER, NOT BY A LONG SHOT.
I KNOW--
BUT...?
SOMEONE SET THIS UP AND WENT TO EXTRAORDINARY LENGTHS TO MAKE SURE IT GOES EXACTLY ACCORDING TO SOME MASTER PLAN.
AND AS OF NOW, WE'RE NO CLOSER TO FIGURING WHO THAT IS THAN WHEN THIS STARTED, WHICH MEANS THAT PLAN WAS EXTREMELY WELL THOUGHT-OUT.
AND UNTIL THEN?
BUT I PROMISE YOU THIS-- WHEN I DO FIND OUT WHO SET THIS UP, I'LL MAKE SURE THEY PAY THE PRICE.
UNTIL THEN WE'VE GOT WORK TO DO.
THAT'S IT?
THAT'S IT.
FIGURES.

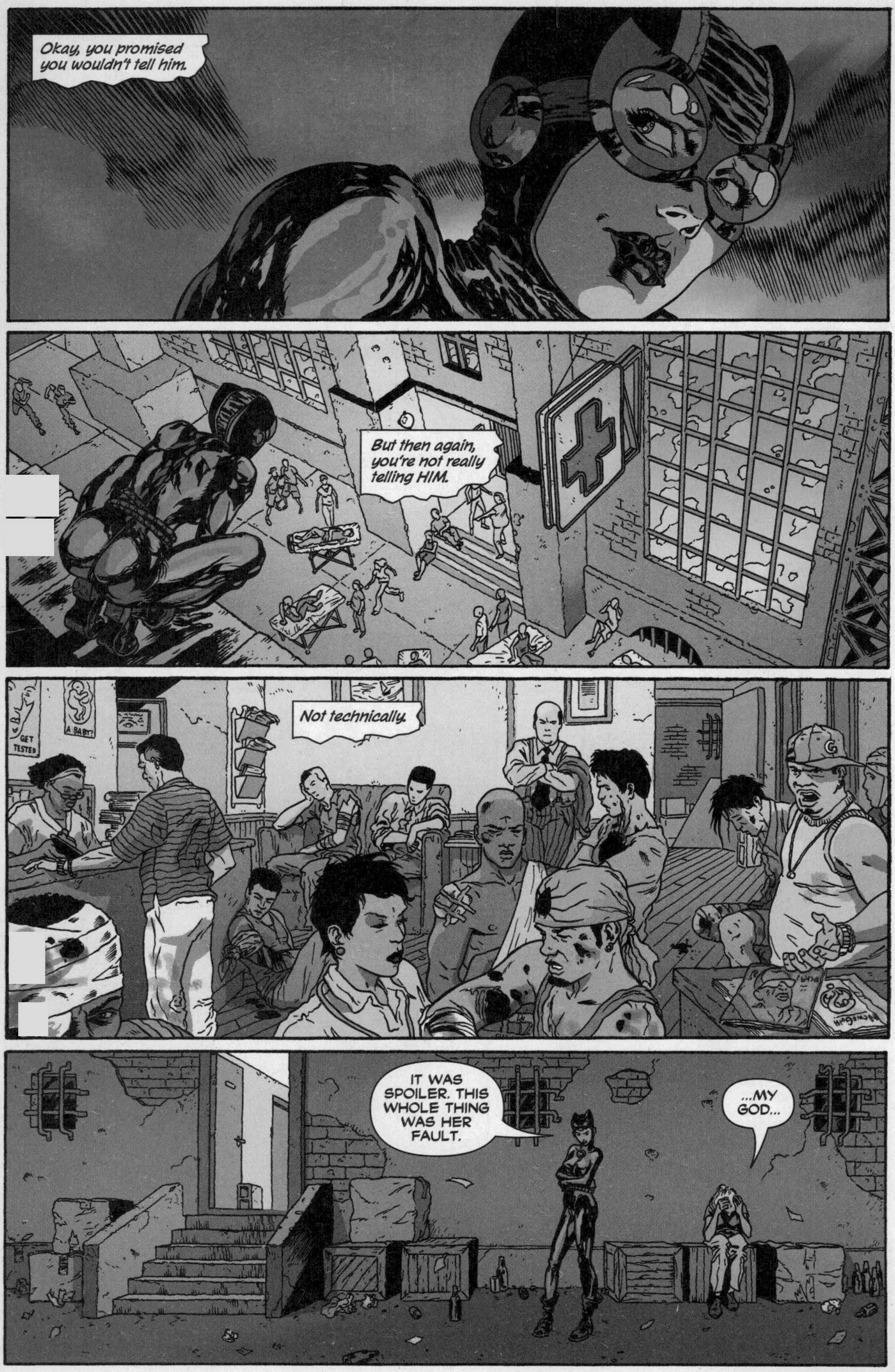
Okay, you promised you wouldn't tell him.
But then again, you're not really telling HIM.
Not technically.
GET TESTED
IT WAS SPOILER. THIS WHOLE THING WAS HER FAULT.
...MY GOD...

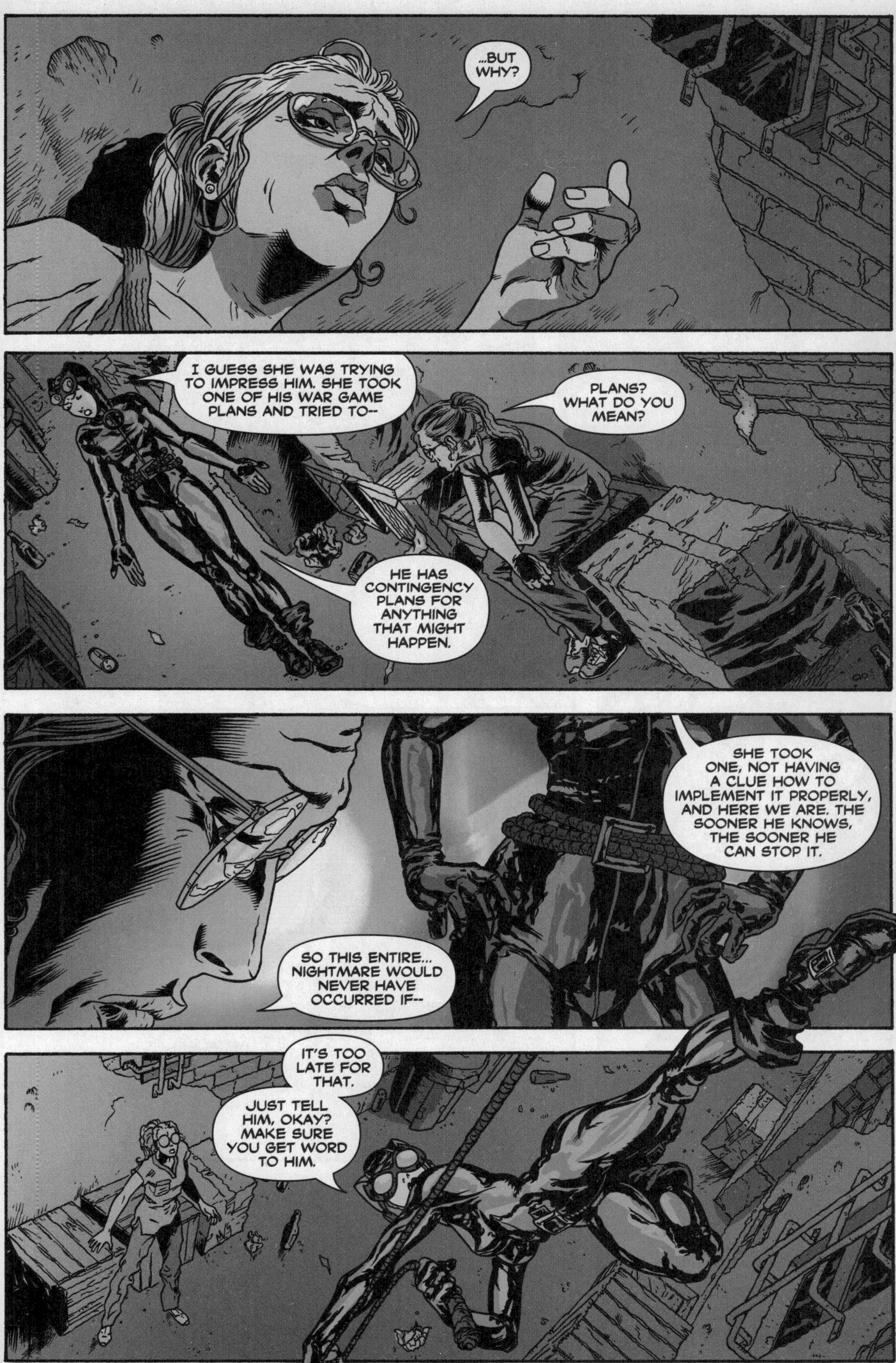
...BUT WHY?
I GUESS SHE WAS TRYING TO IMPRESS HIM. SHE TOOK ONE OF HIS WAR GAME PLANS AND TRIED TO--
PLANS? WHAT DO YOU MEAN?
HE HAS CONTINGENCY PLANS FOR ANYTHING THAT MIGHT HAPPEN.
SHE TOOK ONE, NOT HAVING A CLUE HOW TO IMPLEMENT IT PROPERLY, AND HERE WE ARE. THE SOONER HE KNOWS, THE SOONER HE CAN STOP IT.
SO THIS ENTIRE... NIGHTMARE WOULD NEVER HAVE OCCURRED IF--
IT'S TOO LATE FOR THAT.
JUST TELL HIM, OKAY? MAKE SURE YOU GET WORD TO HIM.

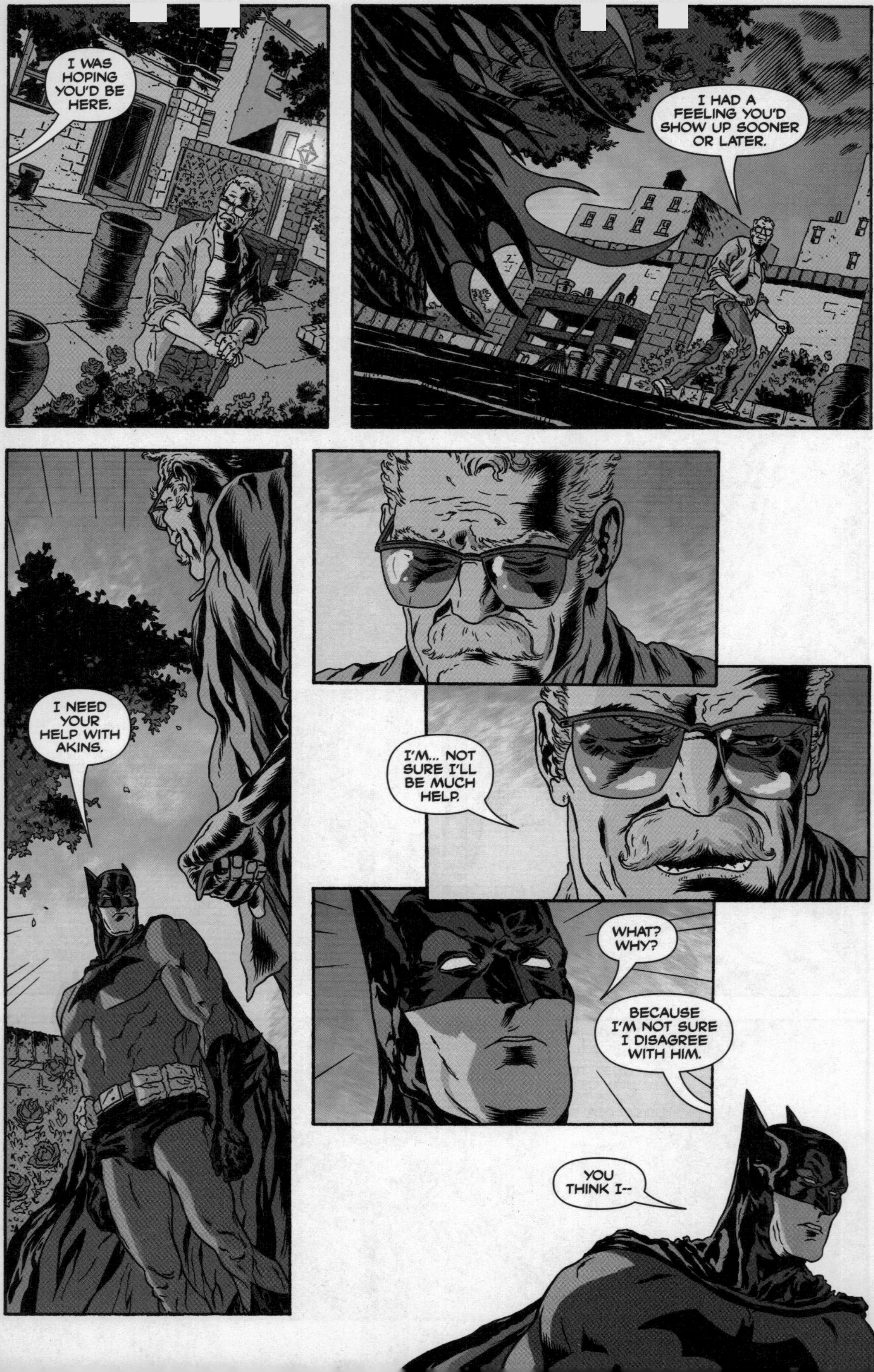
I WAS HOPING YOU'D BE HERE.
I HAD A FEELING YOU'D SHOW UP SOONER OR LATER.
I NEED YOUR HELP WITH AKINS.
I'M... NOT SURE I'LL BE MUCH HELP.
WHAT? WHY?
BECAUSE I'M NOT SURE I DISAGREE WITH HIM.
YOU THINK I--

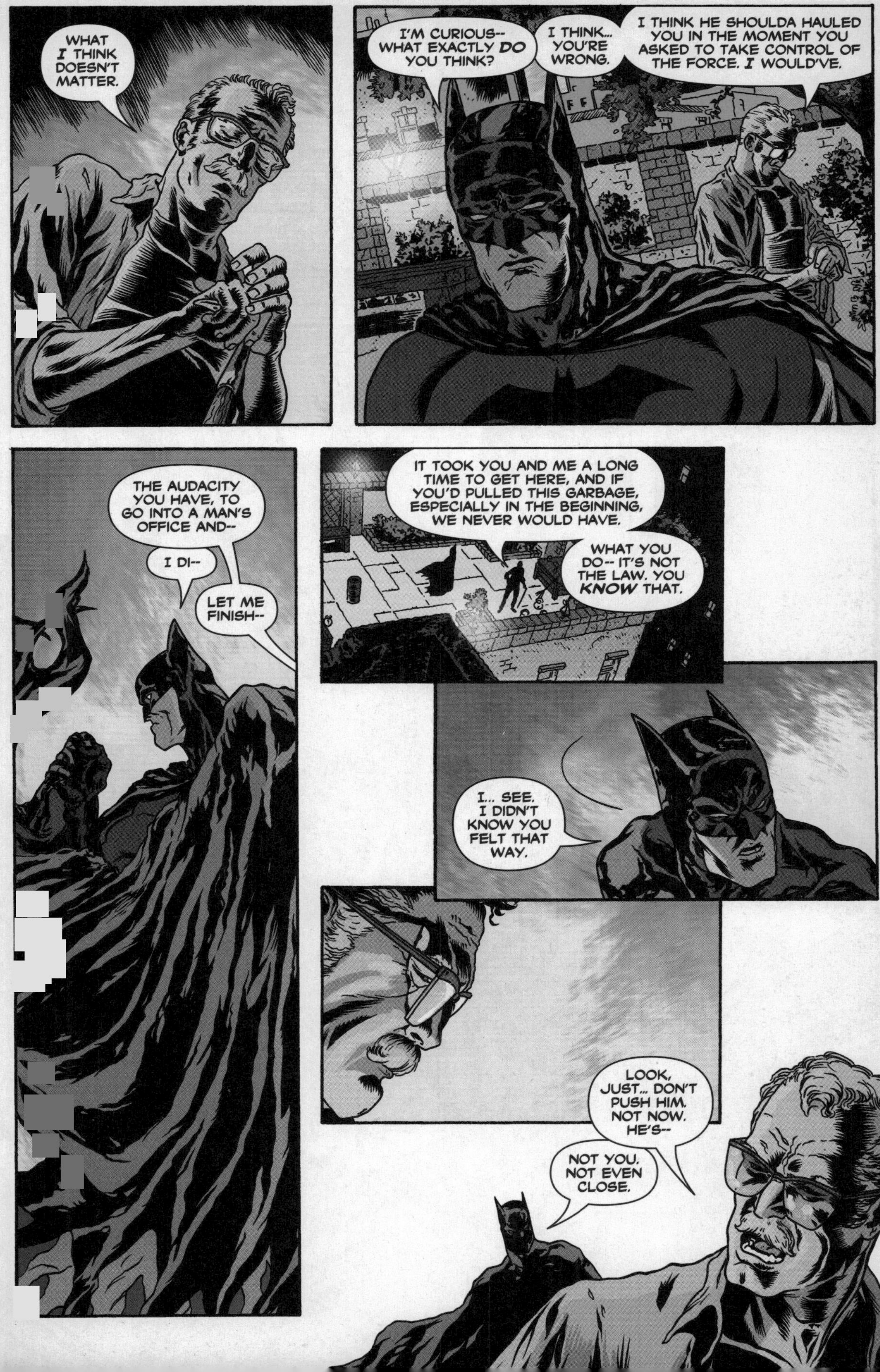
WHAT I THINK DOESN'T MATTER.
I'M CURIOUS-- WHAT EXACTLY DO YOU THINK?
I THINK... YOU'RE WRONG.
I THINK HE SHOULDA HAULED YOU IN THE MOMENT YOU ASKED TO TAKE CONTROL OF THE FORCE. I WOULD'VE.
THE AUDACITY YOU HAVE, TO GO INTO A MAN'S OFFICE AND--
I DI--
LET ME FINISH--
IT TOOK YOU AND ME A LONG TIME TO GET HERE, AND IF YOU'D PULLED THIS GARBAGE, ESPECIALLY IN THE BEGINNING, WE NEVER WOULD HAVE.
WHAT YOU DO-- IT'S NOT THE LAW. YOU KNOW THAT.
I... SEE. I DIDN'T KNOW YOU FELT THAT WAY.
LOOK, JUST... DON'T PUSH HIM. NOT NOW. HE'S--
NOT YOU. NOT EVEN CLOSE.

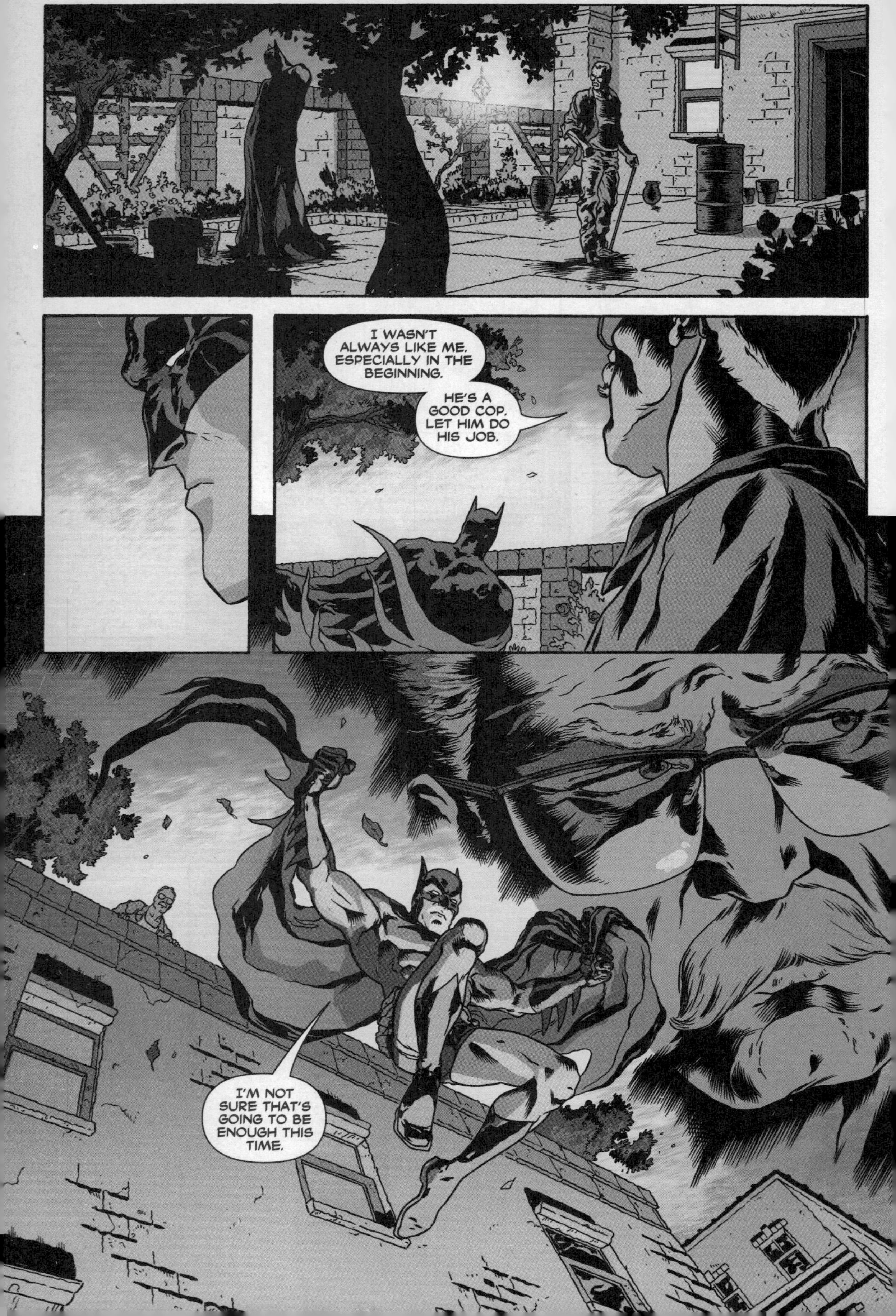
I WASN'T ALWAYS LIKE ME. ESPECIALLY IN THE BEGINNING.
HE'S A GOOD COP. LET HIM DO HIS JOB.
I'M NOT SURE THAT'S GOING TO BE ENOUGH THIS TIME.

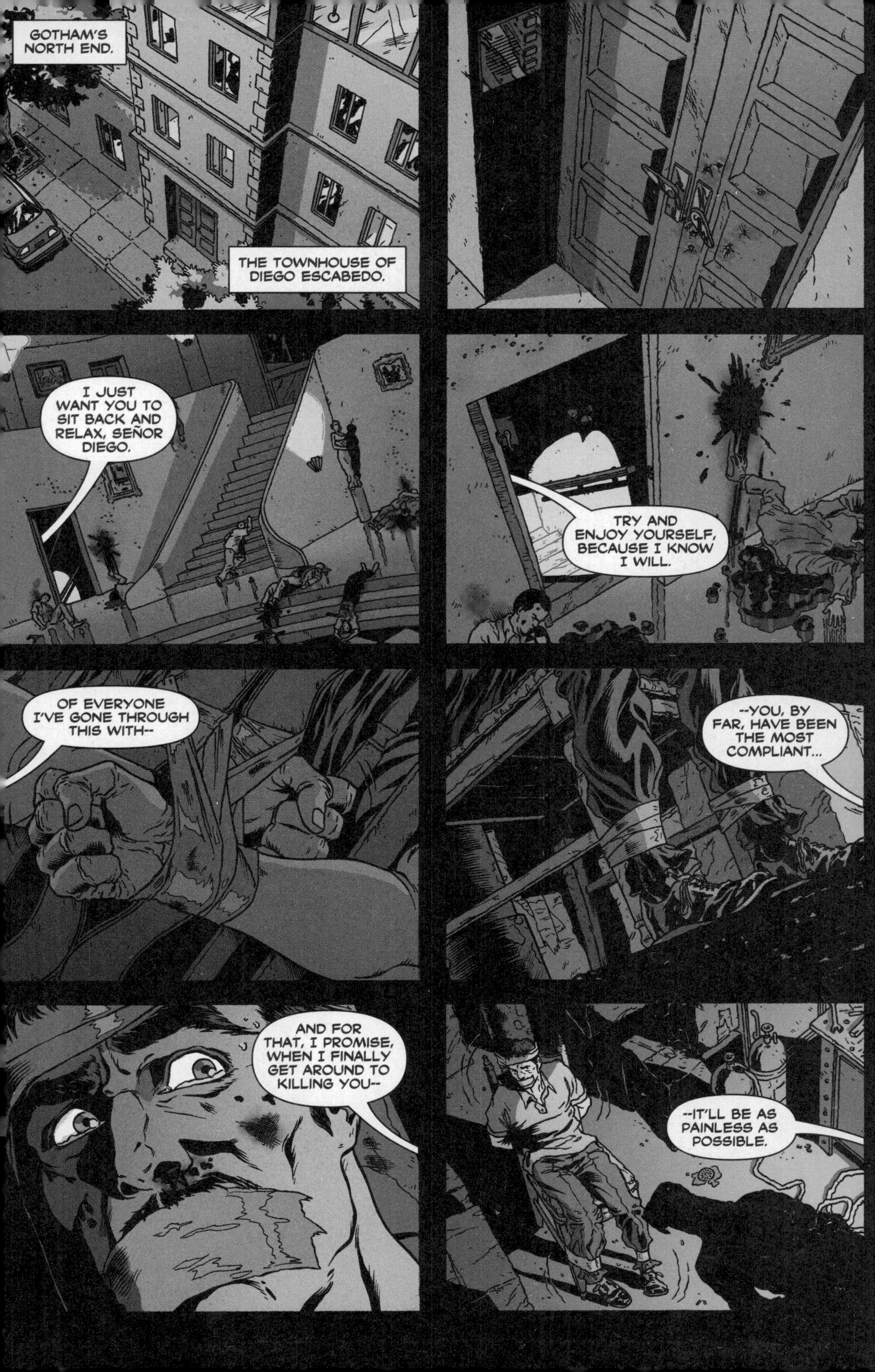
GOTHAM'S NORTH END.
THE TOWNHOUSE OF DIEGO ESCABEDO.
I JUST WANT YOU TO SIT BACK AND RELAX, SEÑOR DIEGO.
TRY AND ENJOY YOURSELF, BECAUSE I KNOW I WILL.
OF EVERYONE I'VE GONE THROUGH THIS WITH--
--YOU, BY FAR, HAVE BEEN THE MOST COMPLIANT...
AND FOR THAT, I PROMISE, WHEN I FINALLY GET AROUND TO KILLING YOU--
--IT'LL BE AS PAINLESS AS POSSIBLE.

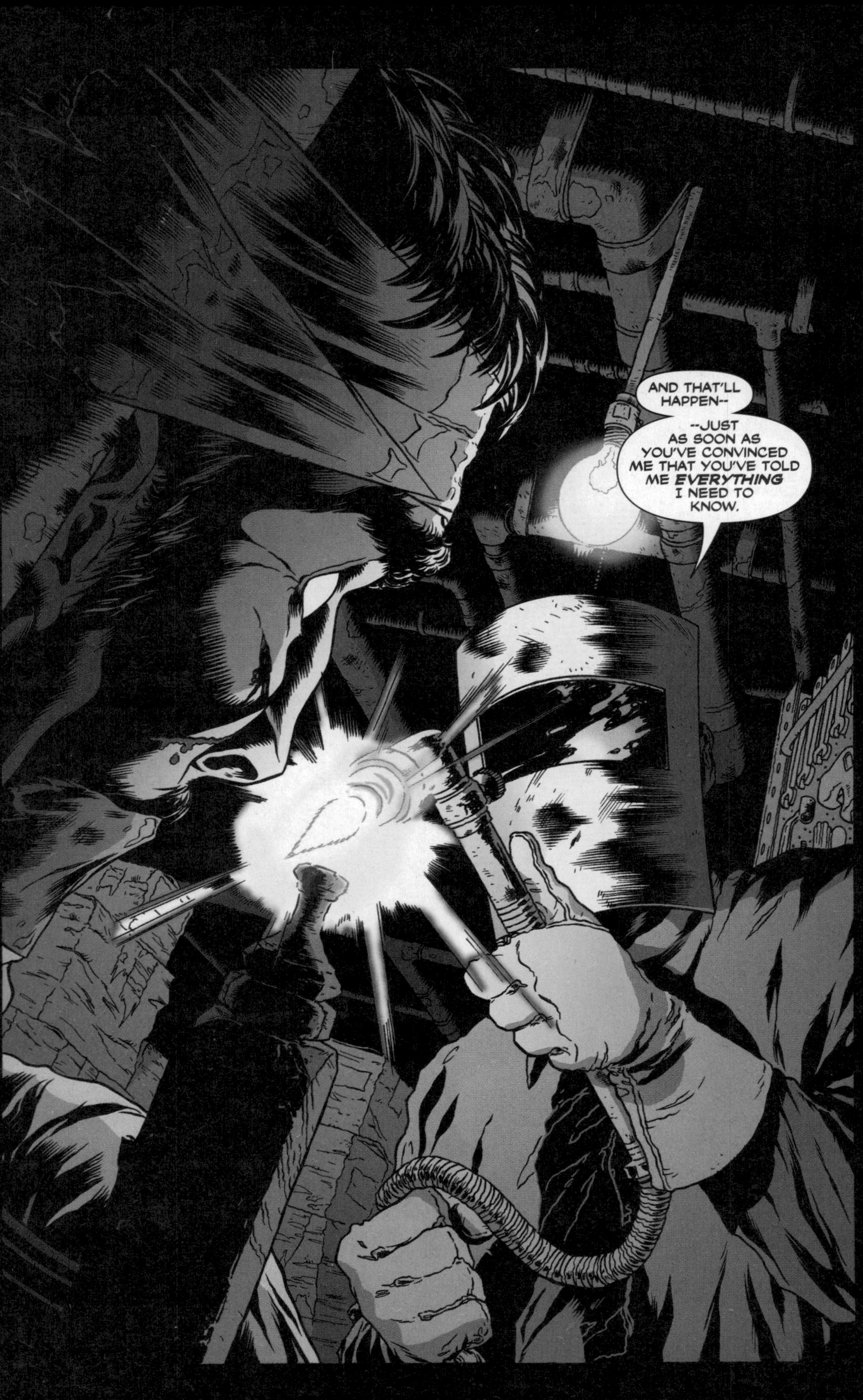
AND THAT'LL HAPPEN--
--JUST AS SOON AS YOU'VE CONVINCED ME THAT YOU'VE TOLD ME EVERYTHING I NEED TO KNOW.

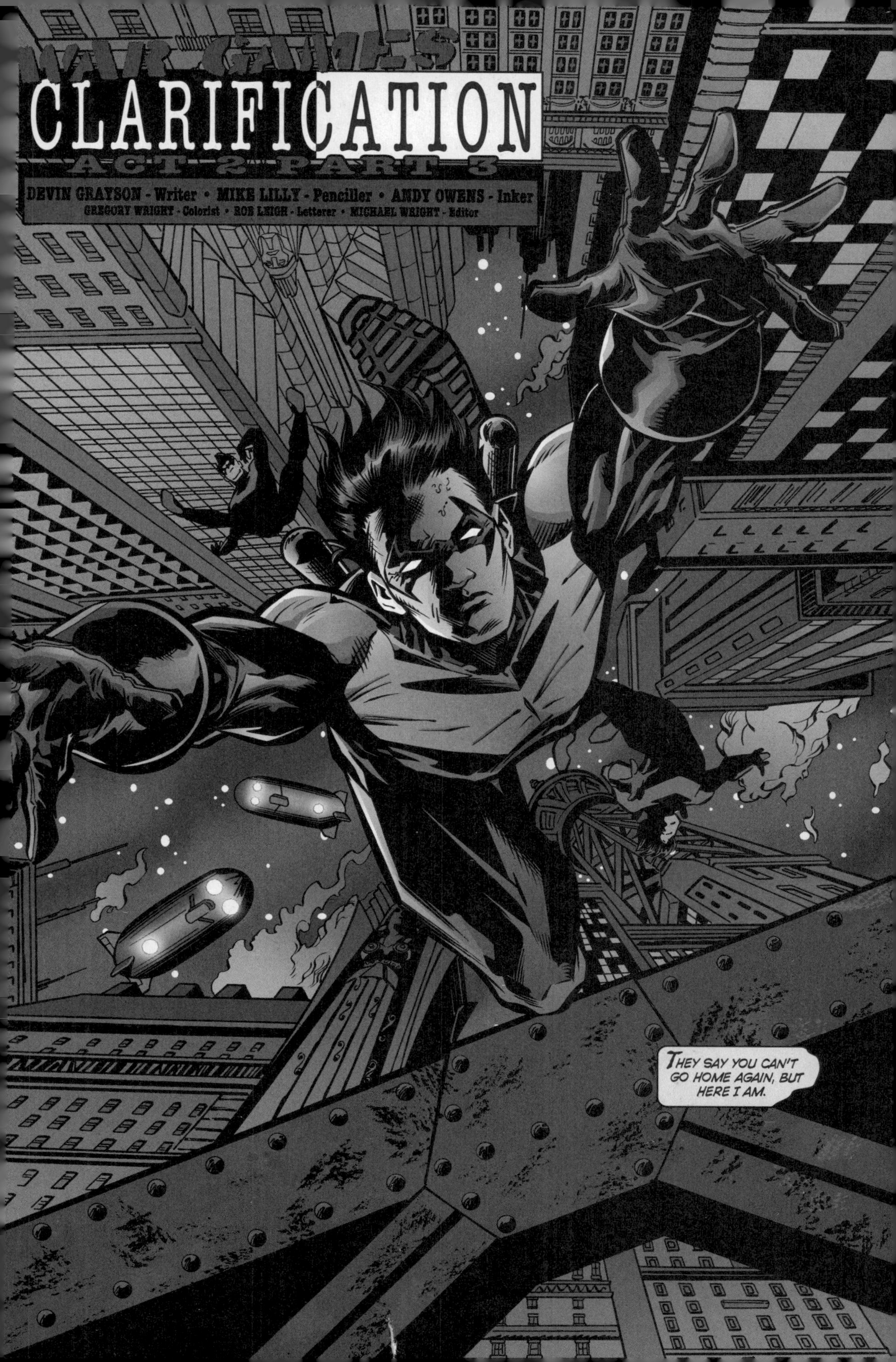
WAR GAMES
CLARIFICATION
ACT 2 PART 3
DEVIN GRAYSON - Writer • MIKE LILLY - Penciller • ANDY OWENS - Inker
GREGORY WRIGHT - Colorist • ROB LEIGH - Letterer • MICHAEL WRIGHT - Editor
THEY SAY YOU CAN'T GO HOME AGAIN, BUT HERE I AM.

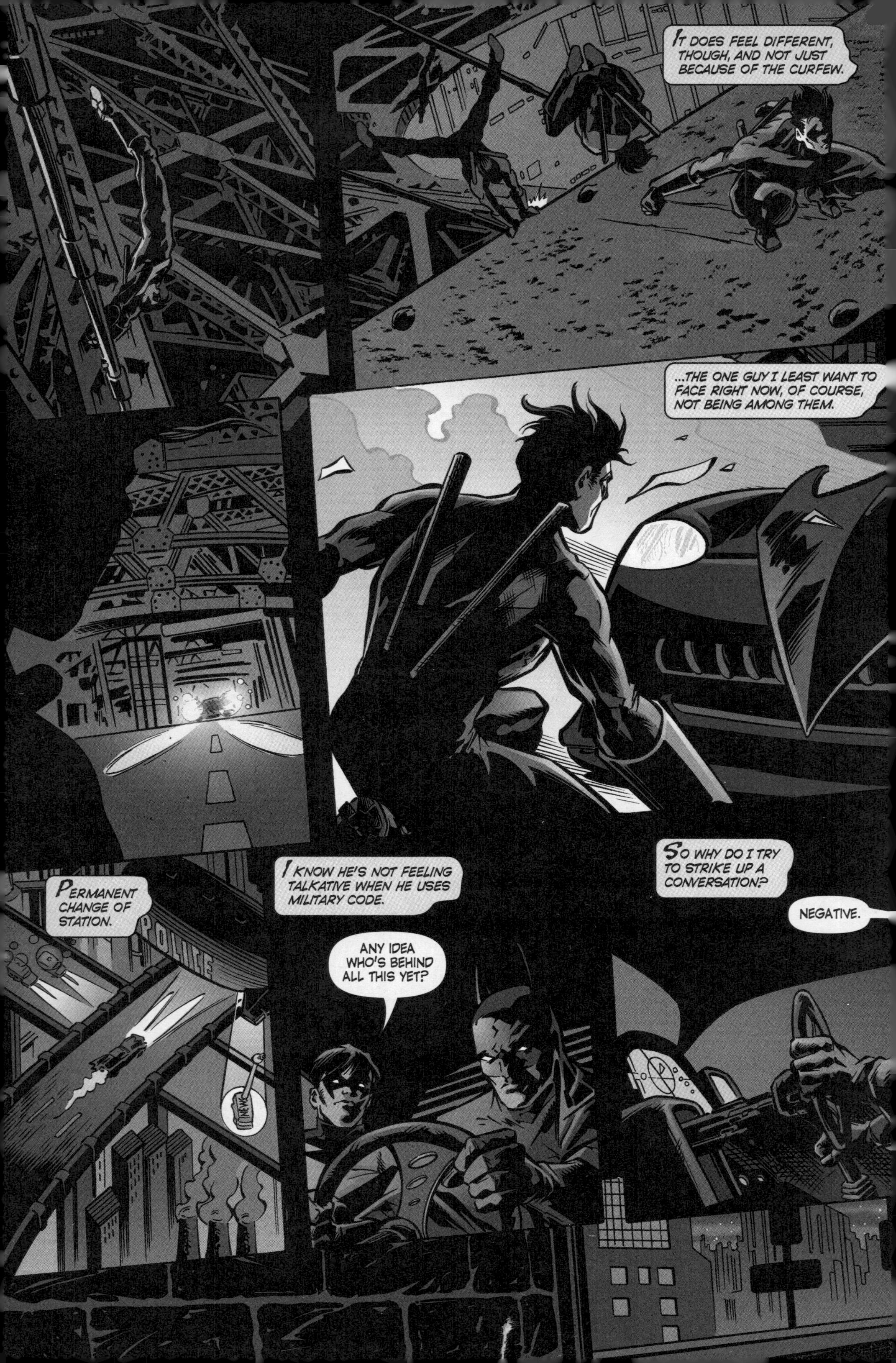

IT DOES FEEL DIFFERENT, THOUGH, AND NOT JUST BECAUSE OF THE CURFEW.
...THE ONE GUY I LEAST WANT TO FACE RIGHT NOW, OF COURSE, NOT BEING AMONG THEM.
PERMANENT CHANGE OF STATION.
POLICE
NEWS
I KNOW HE'S NOT FEELING TALKATIVE WHEN HE USES MILITARY CODE.
ANY IDEA WHO'S BEHIND ALL THIS YET?
SO WHY DO I TRY TO STRIKE UP A CONVERSATION?
NEGATIVE.

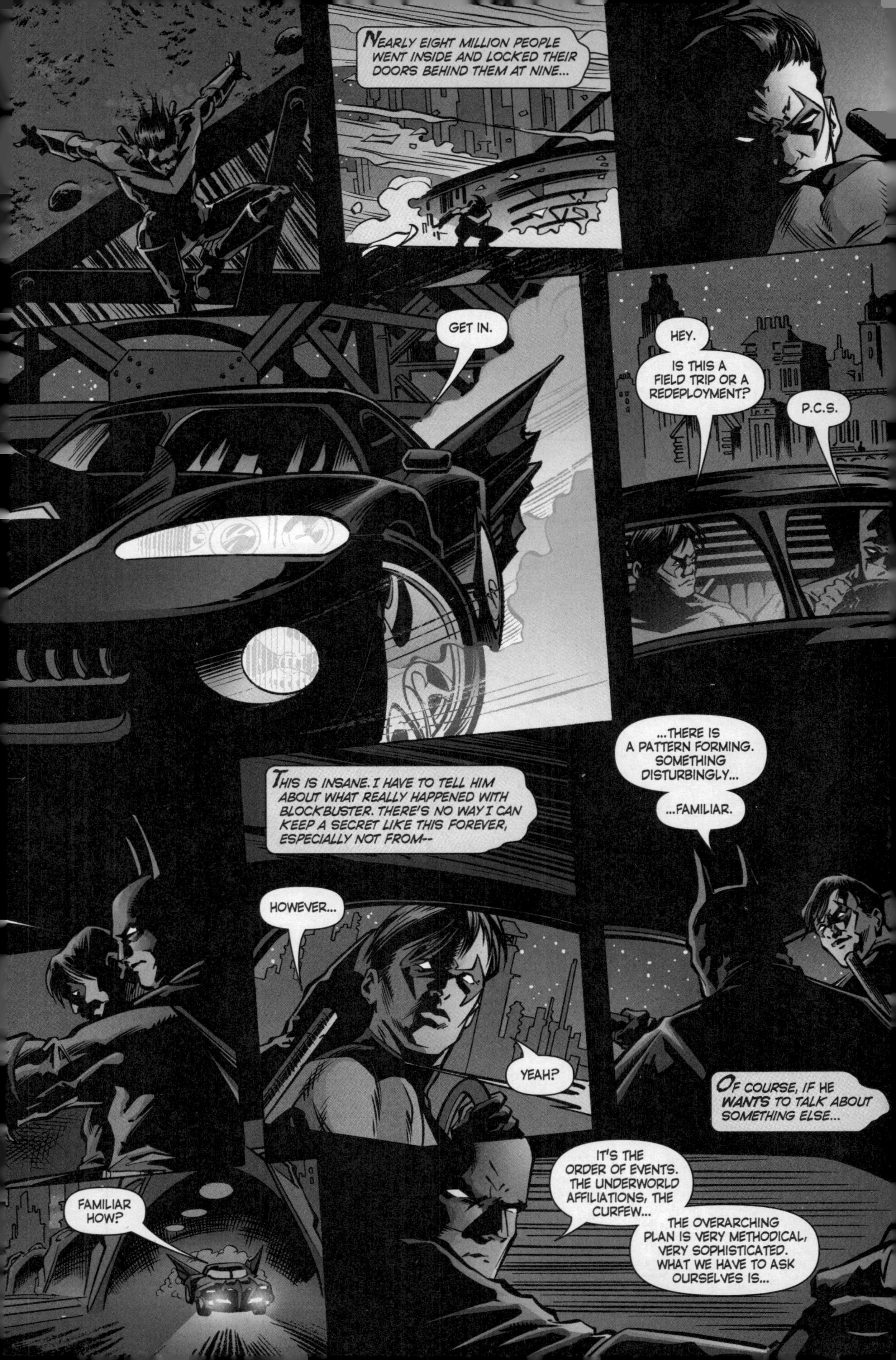
NEARLY EIGHT MILLION PEOPLE WENT INSIDE AND LOCKED THEIR DOORS BEHIND THEM AT NINE...
GET IN.
HEY.
IS THIS A FIELD TRIP OR A REDEPLOYMENT?
P.C.S.
THIS IS INSANE. I HAVE TO TELL HIM ABOUT WHAT REALLY HAPPENED WITH BLOCKBUSTER. THERE'S NO WAY I CAN KEEP A SECRET LIKE THIS FOREVER, ESPECIALLY NOT FROM--
HOWEVER...
YEAH?
...THERE IS A PATTERN FORMING. SOMETHING DISTURBINGLY...
...FAMILIAR.
OF COURSE, IF HE WANTS TO TALK ABOUT SOMETHING ELSE...
FAMILIAR HOW?
IT'S THE ORDER OF EVENTS. THE UNDERWORLD AFFILIATIONS, THE CURFEW...
THE OVERARCHING PLAN IS VERY METHODICAL, VERY SOPHISTICATED. WHAT WE HAVE TO ASK OURSELVES IS...

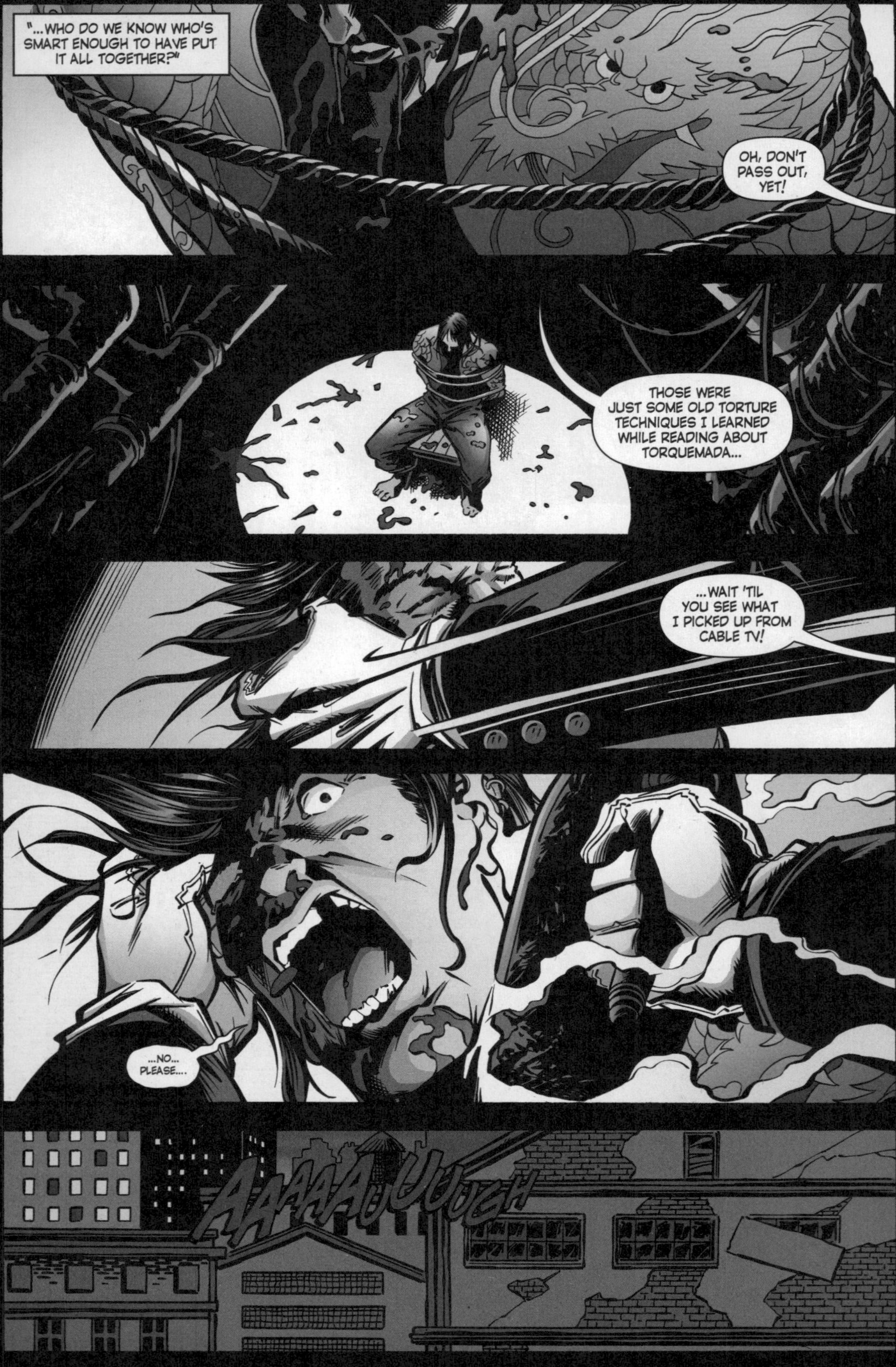
"...WHO DO WE KNOW WHO'S SMART ENOUGH TO HAVE PUT IT ALL TOGETHER?"
OH, DON'T PASS OUT, YET!
THOSE WERE JUST SOME OLD TORTURE TECHNIQUES I LEARNED WHILE READING ABOUT TORQUEMADA...
...WAIT 'TIL YOU SEE WHAT I PICKED UP FROM CABLE TV!
...NO... PLEASE...
AAAAAUUUGH

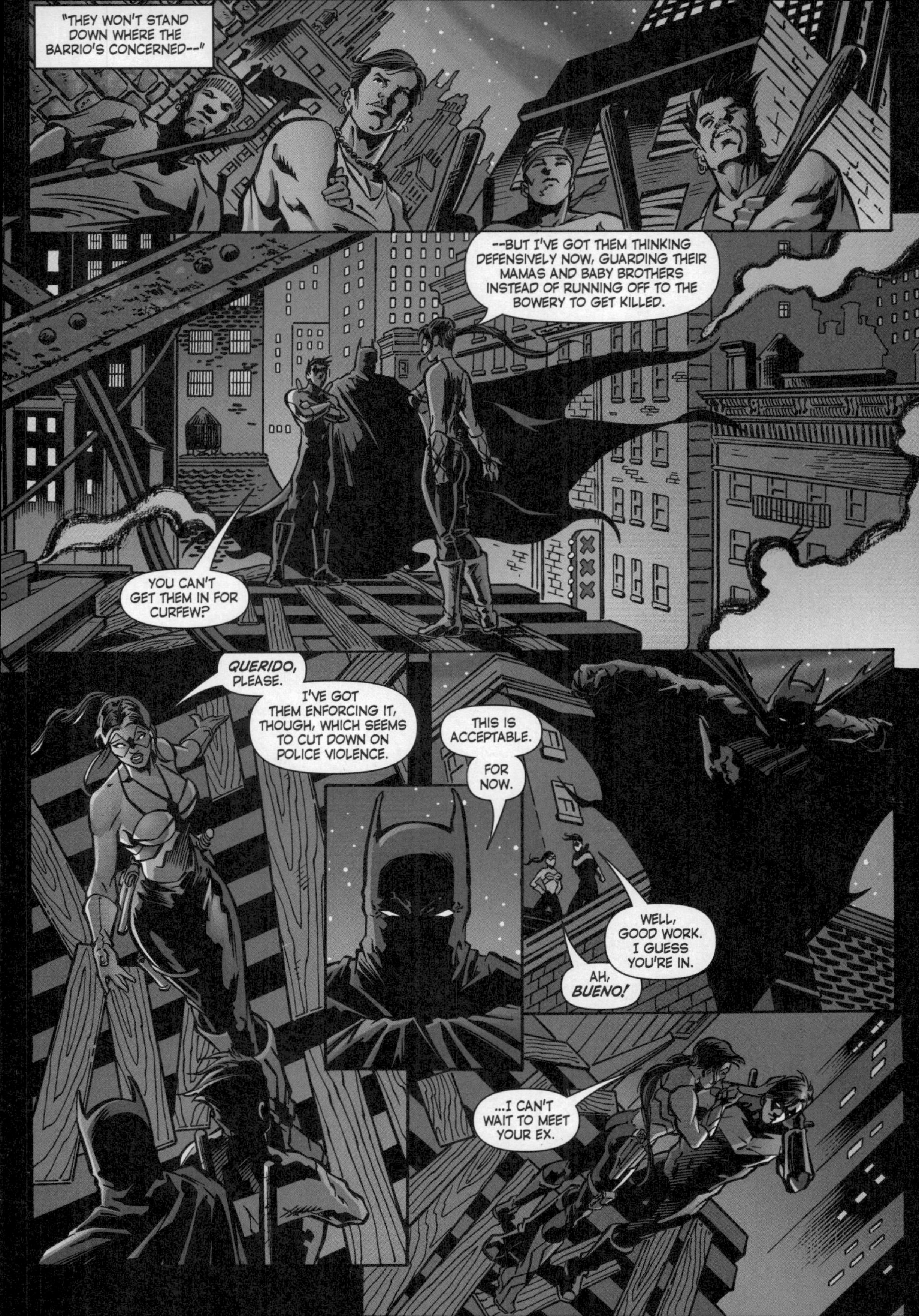
"THEY WON'T STAND DOWN WHERE THE BARRIO'S CONCERNED--"
--BUT I'VE GOT THEM THINKING DEFENSIVELY NOW, GUARDING THEIR MAMAS AND BABY BROTHERS INSTEAD OF RUNNING OFF TO THE BOWERY TO GET KILLED.
YOU CAN'T GET THEM IN FOR CURFEW?
QUERIDO, PLEASE.
I'VE GOT THEM ENFORCING IT, THOUGH, WHICH SEEMS TO CUT DOWN ON POLICE VIOLENCE.
THIS IS ACCEPTABLE.
FOR NOW.
WELL, GOOD WORK. I GUESS YOU'RE IN.
AH, *BUENO!*
...I CAN'T WAIT TO MEET YOUR EX.

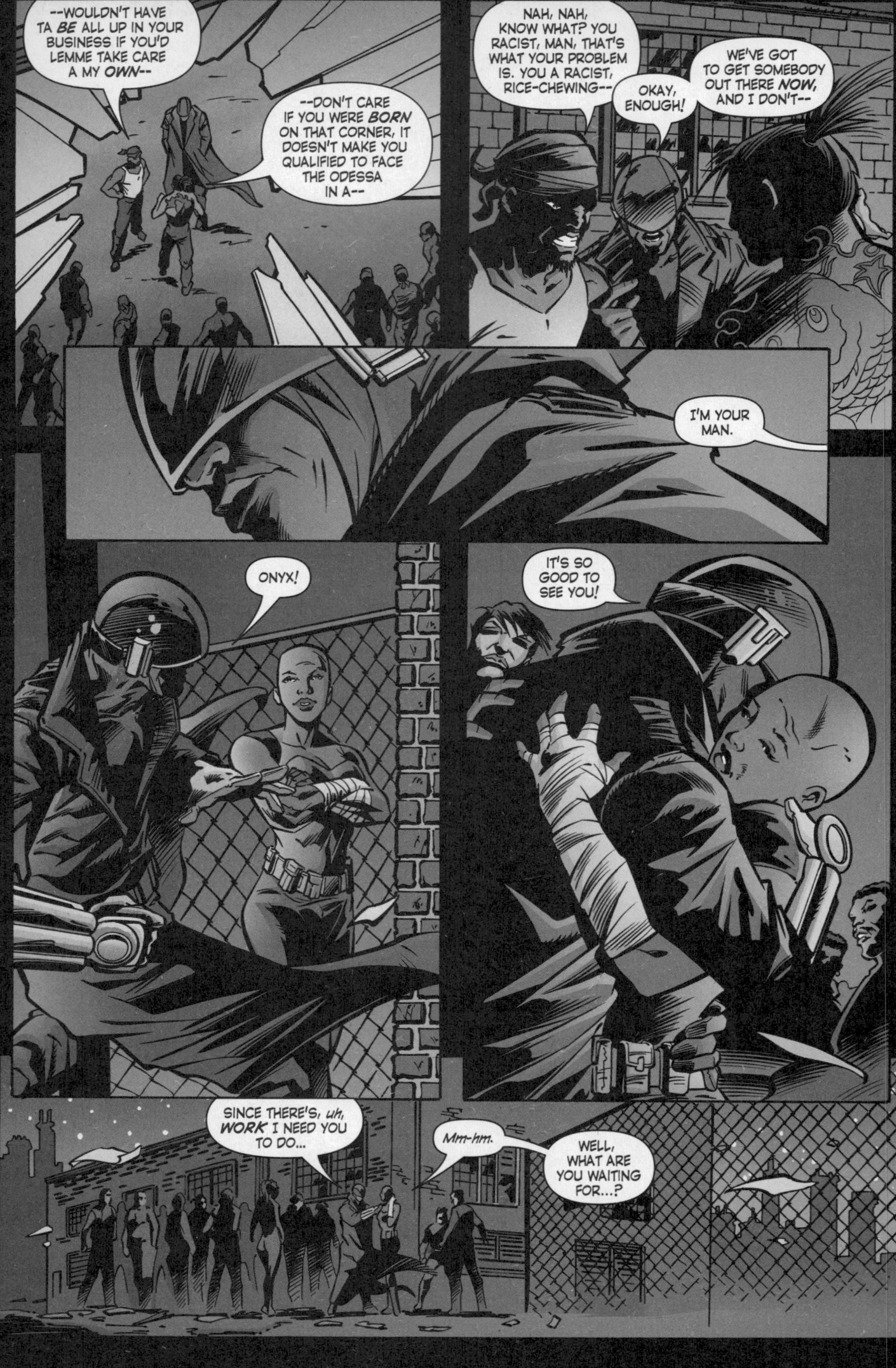
--WOULDN'T HAVE TA *BE* ALL UP IN YOUR BUSINESS IF YOU'D LEMME TAKE CARE A MY *OWN*--
--DON'T CARE IF YOU WERE *BORN* ON THAT CORNER, IT DOESN'T MAKE YOU QUALIFIED TO FACE THE ODESSA IN A--
NAH, NAH, KNOW WHAT? YOU RACIST, MAN, THAT'S WHAT YOUR PROBLEM IS. YOU A RACIST, RICE-CHEWING--
OKAY, ENOUGH!
WE'VE GOT TO GET SOMEBODY OUT THERE *NOW*, AND I DON'T--
I'M YOUR MAN.
ONYX!
IT'S SO GOOD TO SEE YOU!
SINCE THERE'S, *uh*, *WORK* I NEED YOU TO DO...
Mm-hm.
WELL, WHAT ARE YOU WAITING FOR...?

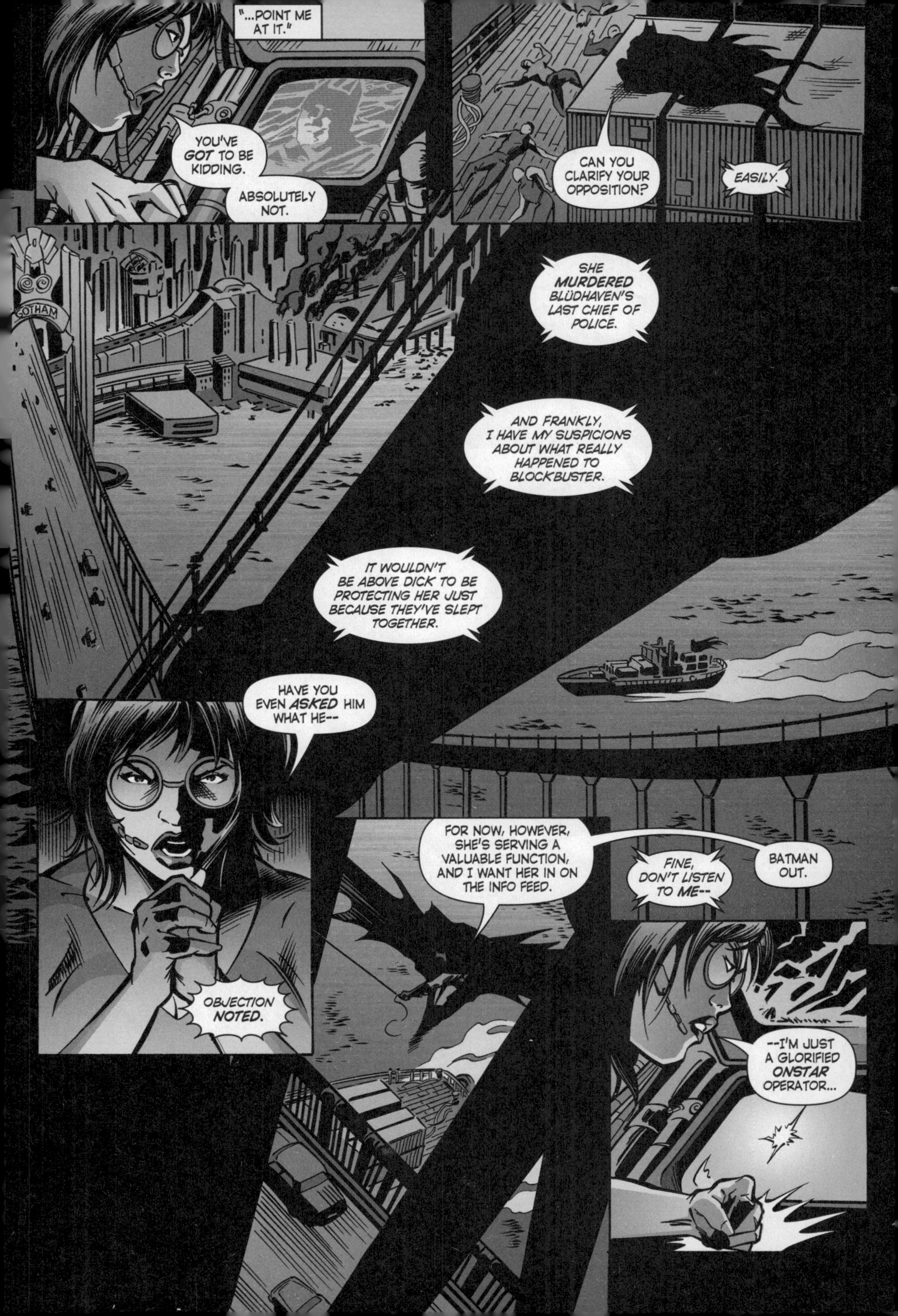
"...POINT ME AT IT."
YOU'VE GOT TO BE KIDDING.
ABSOLUTELY NOT.
CAN YOU CLARIFY YOUR OPPOSITION?
EASILY.
GOTHAM
SHE MURDERED BLÜDHAVEN'S LAST CHIEF OF POLICE.
AND FRANKLY, I HAVE MY SUSPICIONS ABOUT WHAT REALLY HAPPENED TO BLOCKBUSTER.
IT WOULDN'T BE ABOVE DICK TO BE PROTECTING HER JUST BECAUSE THEY'VE SLEPT TOGETHER.
HAVE YOU EVEN ASKED HIM WHAT HE--
OBJECTION NOTED.
FOR NOW, HOWEVER, SHE'S SERVING A VALUABLE FUNCTION, AND I WANT HER IN ON THE INFO FEED.
FINE, DON'T LISTEN TO ME--
BATMAN OUT.
--I'M JUST A GLORIFIED ONSTAR OPERATOR...

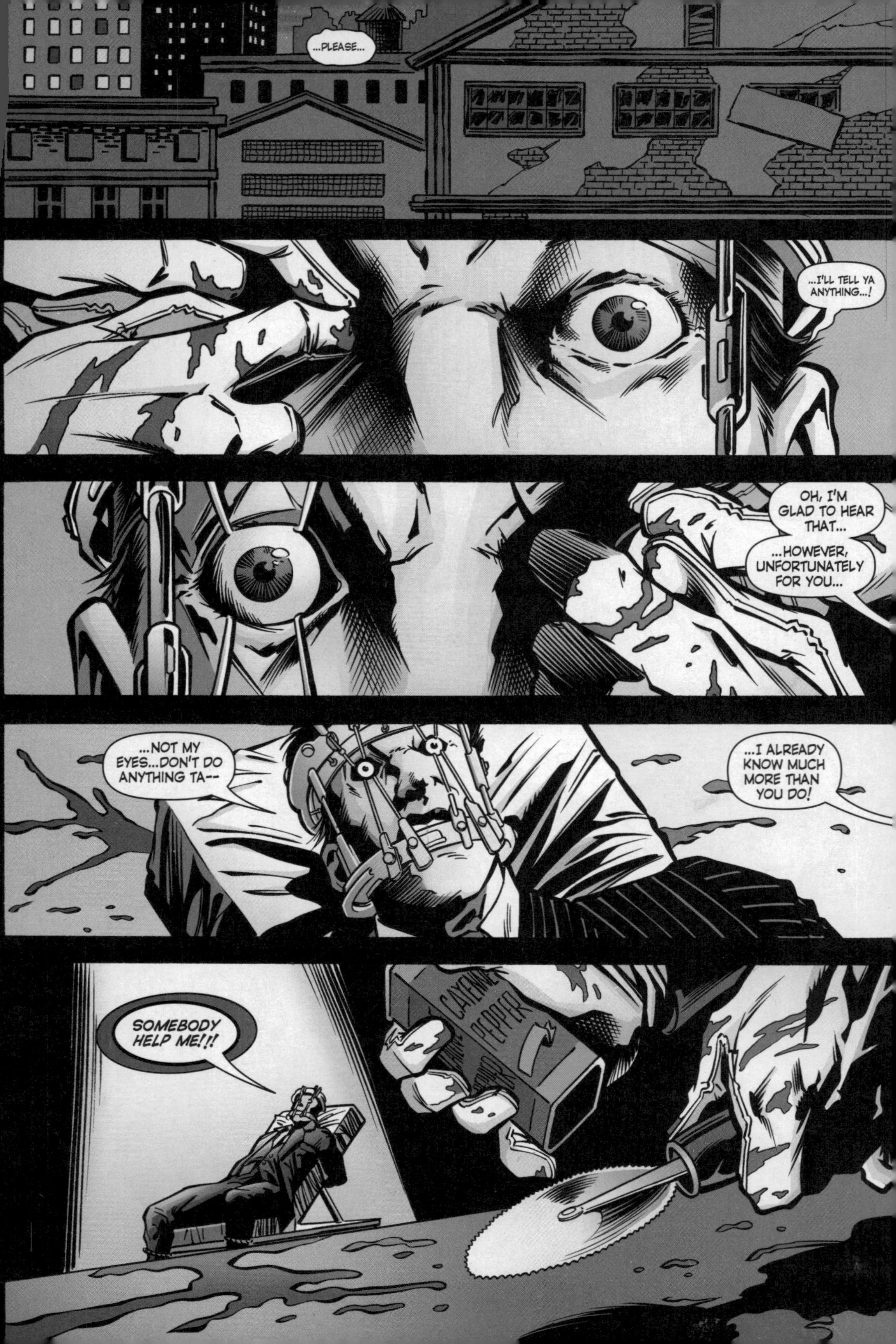
...PLEASE...
...I'LL TELL YA ANYTHING...!
OH, I'M GLAD TO HEAR THAT...
...HOWEVER, UNFORTUNATELY FOR YOU...
...NOT MY EYES...DON'T DO ANYTHING TA--
...I ALREADY KNOW MUCH MORE THAN YOU DO!
SOMEBODY HELP ME!!!
CAYENNE PEPPER

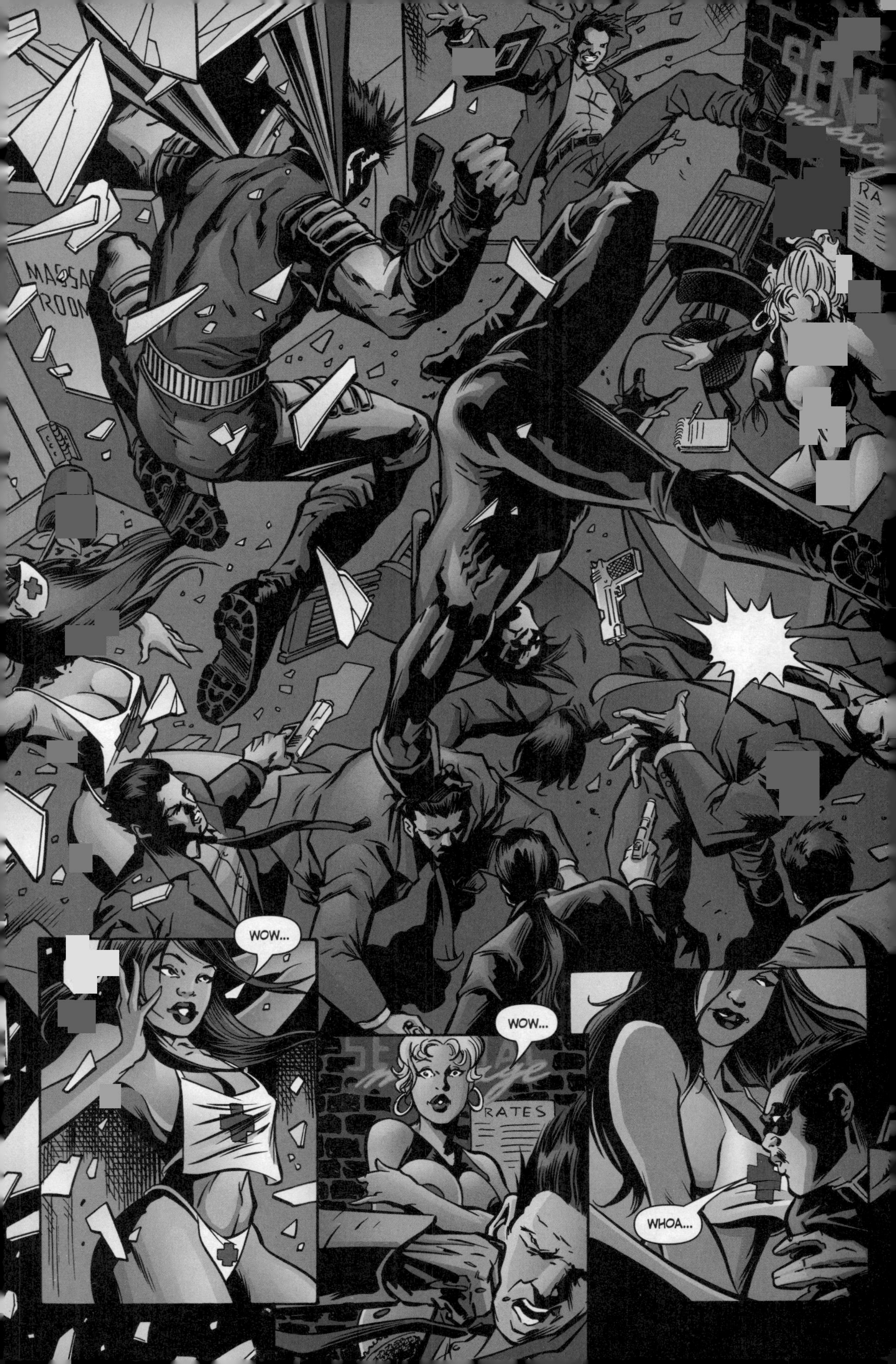
WOW...
WOW...
RATES
WHOA...

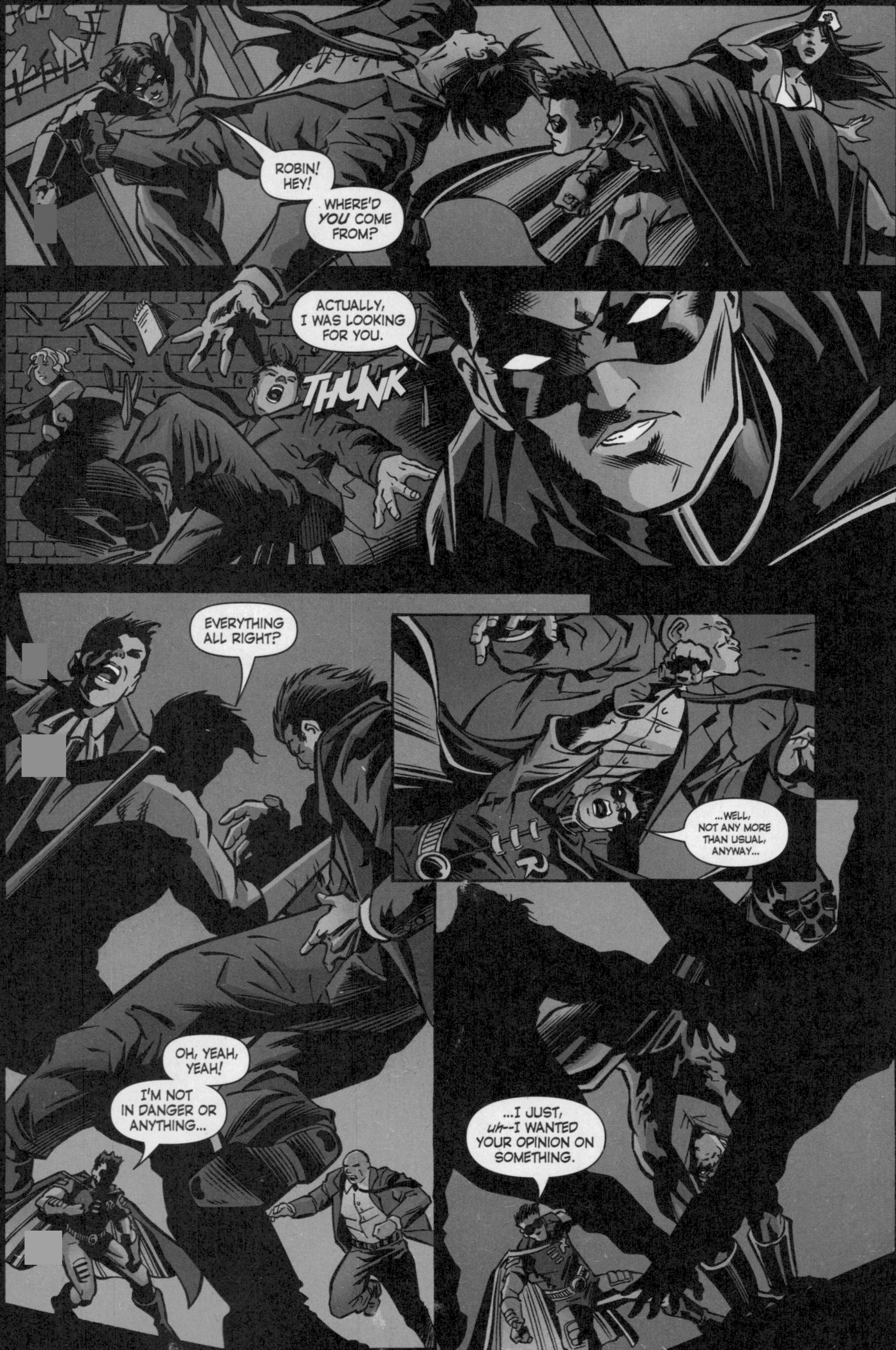
ROBIN! HEY!
WHERE'D YOU COME FROM?
ACTUALLY, I WAS LOOKING FOR YOU.
THUNK
EVERYTHING ALL RIGHT?
...WELL, NOT ANY MORE THAN USUAL, ANYWAY...
OH, YEAH, YEAH!
I'M NOT IN DANGER OR ANYTHING...
...I JUST, uh--I WANTED YOUR OPINION ON SOMETHING.

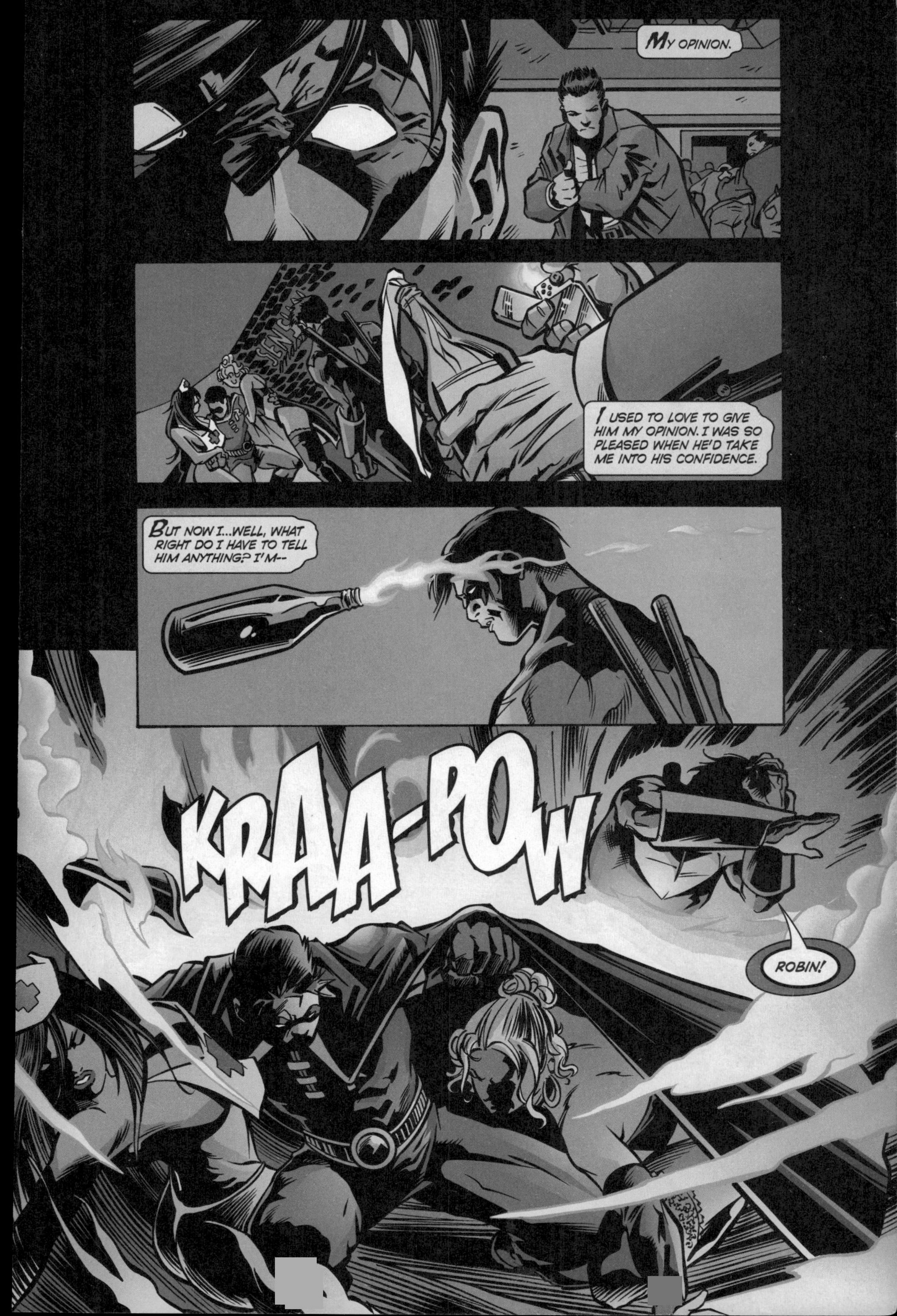
MY OPINION.
I USED TO LOVE TO GIVE HIM MY OPINION. I WAS SO PLEASED WHEN HE'D TAKE ME INTO HIS CONFIDENCE.
BUT NOW I...WELL, WHAT RIGHT DO I HAVE TO TELL HIM ANYTHING? I'M--
KRAA-POW
ROBIN!

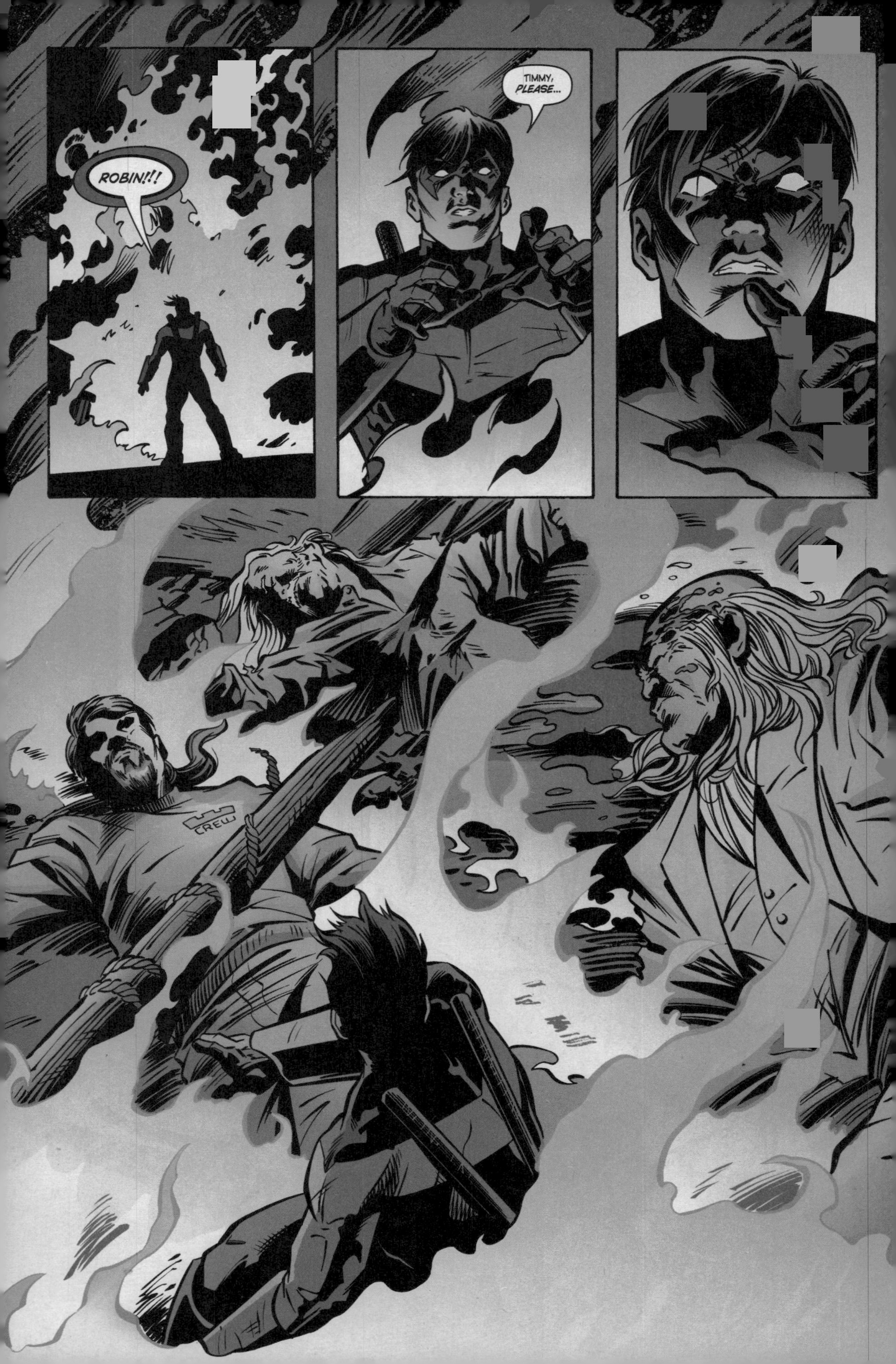
ROBIN!!!
TIMMY, PLEASE...
CREW

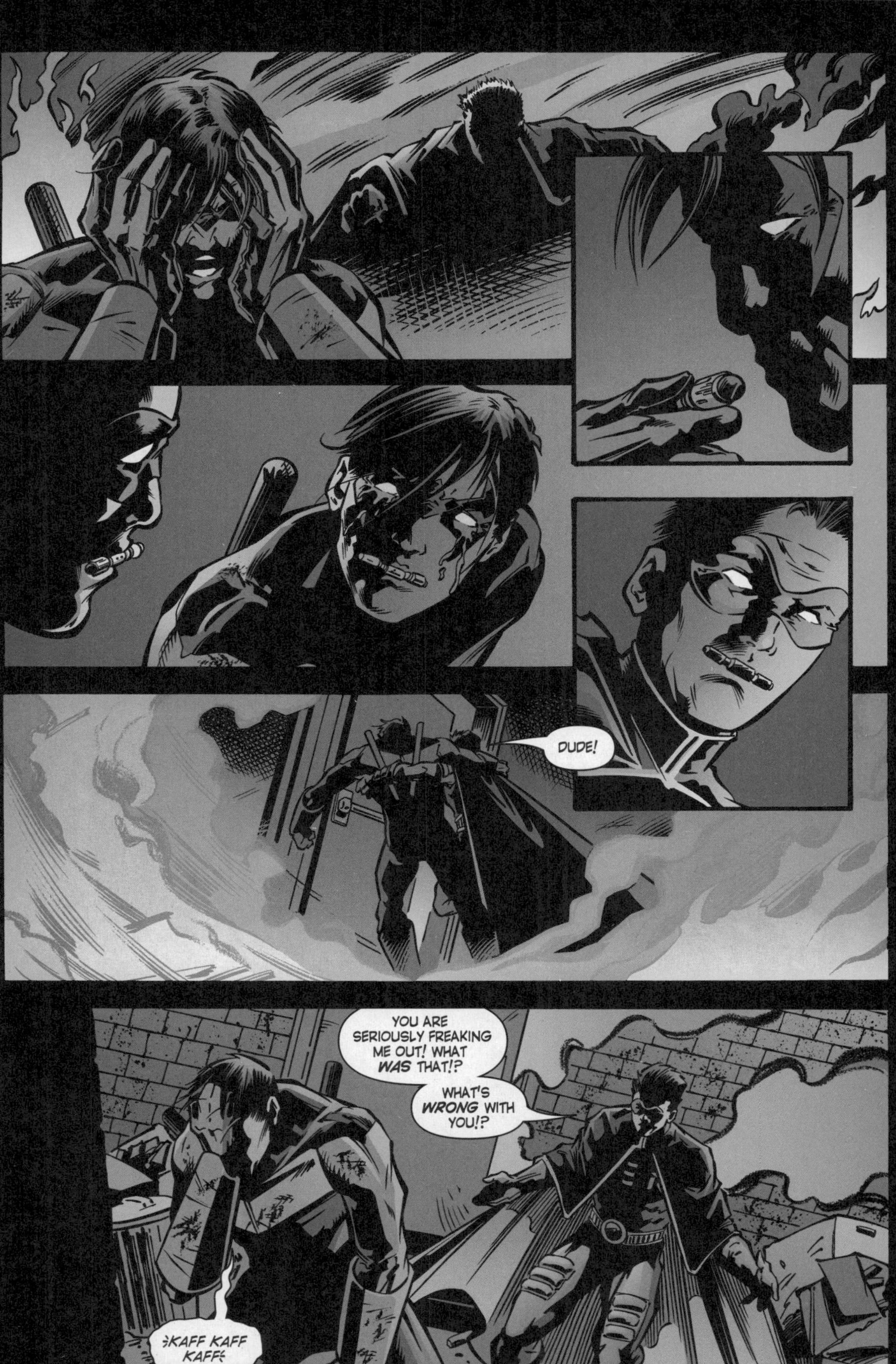
DUDE!
YOU ARE SERIOUSLY FREAKING ME OUT! WHAT WAS THAT!?
WHAT'S WRONG WITH YOU!?
KAFF KAFF KAFF

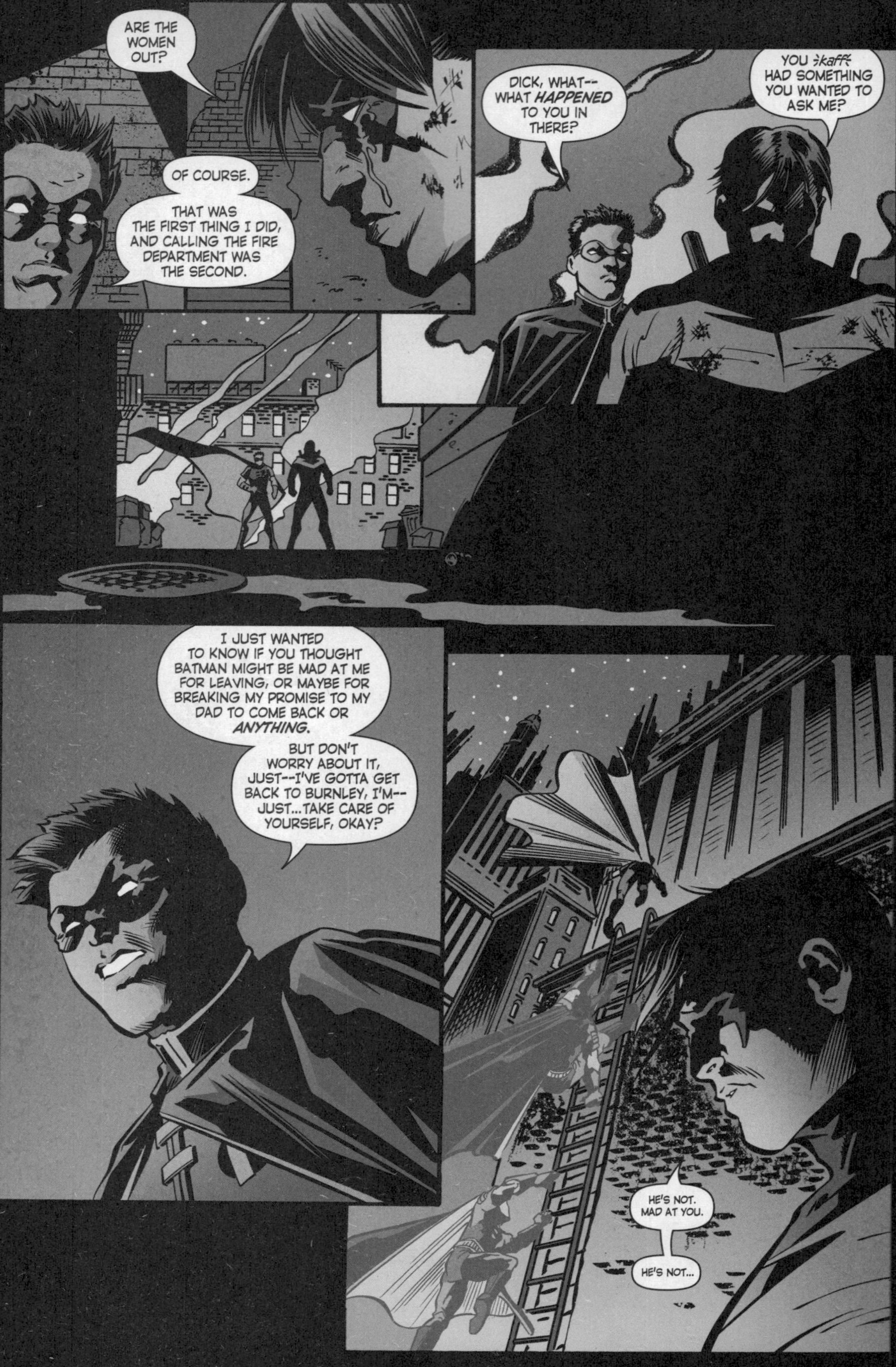

ARE THE WOMEN OUT?
OF COURSE.
THAT WAS THE FIRST THING I DID, AND CALLING THE FIRE DEPARTMENT WAS THE SECOND.
DICK, WHAT-- WHAT *HAPPENED* TO YOU IN THERE?
YOU *kaff* HAD SOMETHING YOU WANTED TO ASK ME?
I JUST WANTED TO KNOW IF YOU THOUGHT BATMAN MIGHT BE MAD AT ME FOR LEAVING, OR MAYBE FOR BREAKING MY PROMISE TO MY DAD TO COME BACK OR *ANYTHING*.
BUT DON'T WORRY ABOUT IT, JUST--I'VE GOTTA GET BACK TO BURNLEY, I'M-- JUST...TAKE CARE OF YOURSELF, OKAY?
HE'S NOT. MAD AT YOU.
HE'S NOT...

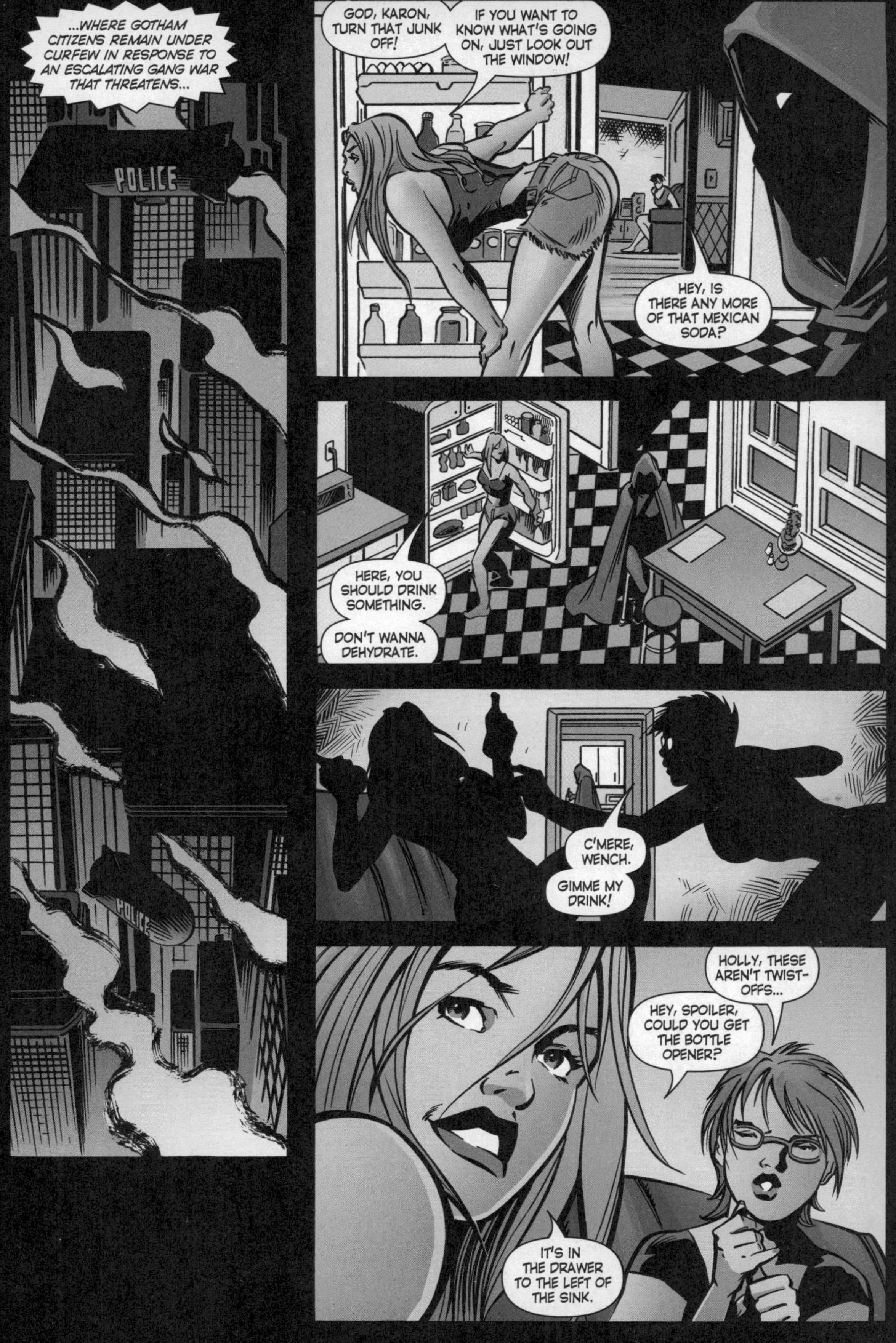
...WHERE GOTHAM CITIZENS REMAIN UNDER CURFEW IN RESPONSE TO AN ESCALATING GANG WAR THAT THREATENS...
POLICE
GOD, KARON, TURN THAT JUNK OFF!
IF YOU WANT TO KNOW WHAT'S GOING ON, JUST LOOK OUT THE WINDOW!
HEY, IS THERE ANY MORE OF THAT MEXICAN SODA?
HERE, YOU SHOULD DRINK SOMETHING.
DON'T WANNA DEHYDRATE.
C'MERE, WENCH.
GIMME MY DRINK!
POLICE
HOLLY, THESE AREN'T TWIST-OFFS...
HEY, SPOILER, COULD YOU GET THE BOTTLE OPENER?
IT'S IN THE DRAWER TO THE LEFT OF THE SINK.

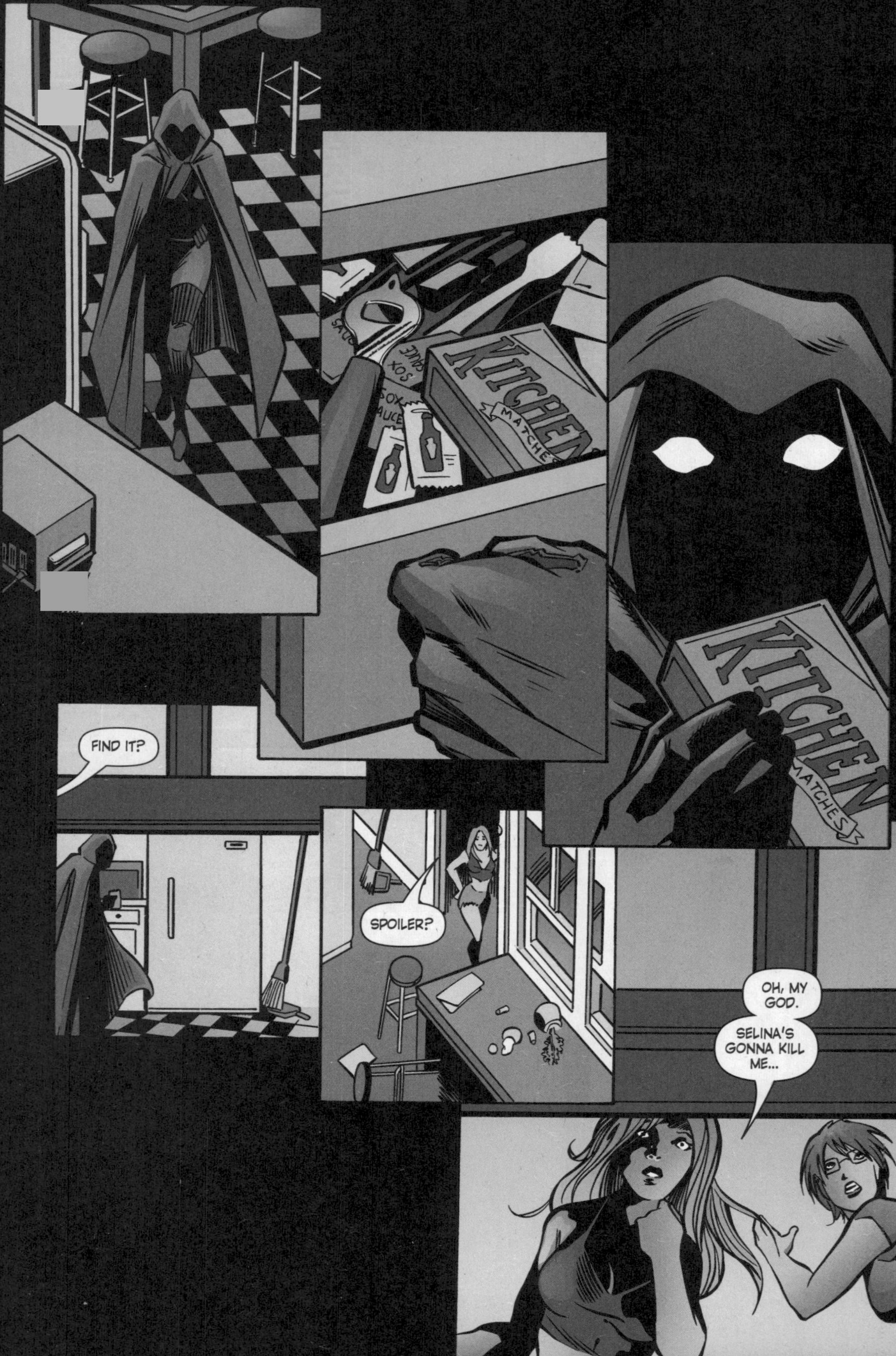
KITCHEN MATCHES
FIND IT?
SPOILER?
OH, MY GOD.
SELINA'S GONNA KILL ME...

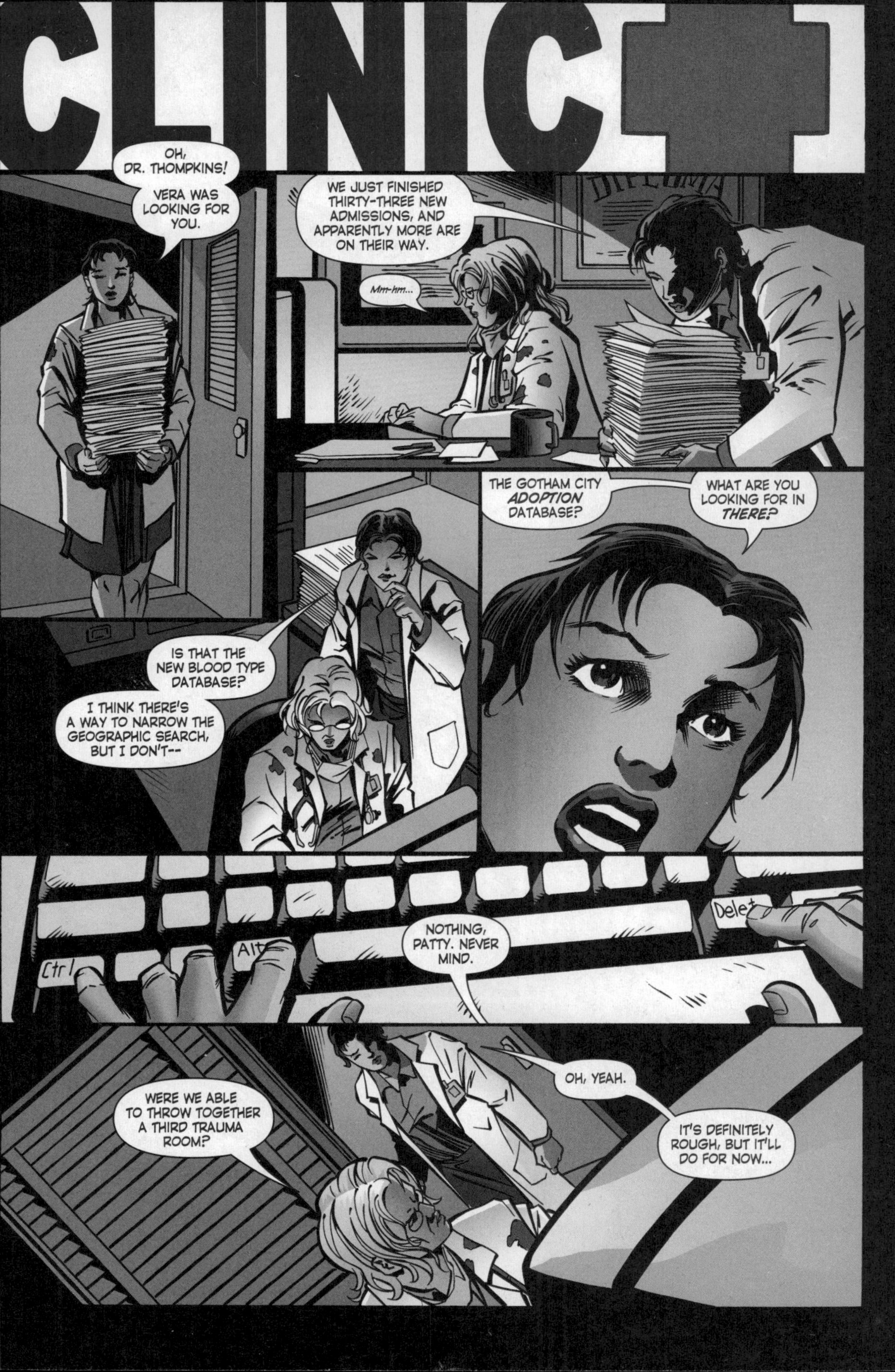
CLINIC
OH, DR. THOMPKINS!
VERA WAS LOOKING FOR YOU.
WE JUST FINISHED THIRTY-THREE NEW ADMISSIONS, AND APPARENTLY MORE ARE ON THEIR WAY.
Mm-hm...
DIPLOMA
IS THAT THE NEW BLOOD TYPE DATABASE?
I THINK THERE'S A WAY TO NARROW THE GEOGRAPHIC SEARCH, BUT I DON'T--
THE GOTHAM CITY *ADOPTION* DATABASE?
WHAT ARE YOU LOOKING FOR IN *THERE?*
Ctrl
Alt
Delet
NOTHING, PATTY. NEVER MIND.
WERE WE ABLE TO THROW TOGETHER A THIRD TRAUMA ROOM?
OH, YEAH.
IT'S DEFINITELY ROUGH, BUT IT'LL DO FOR NOW...

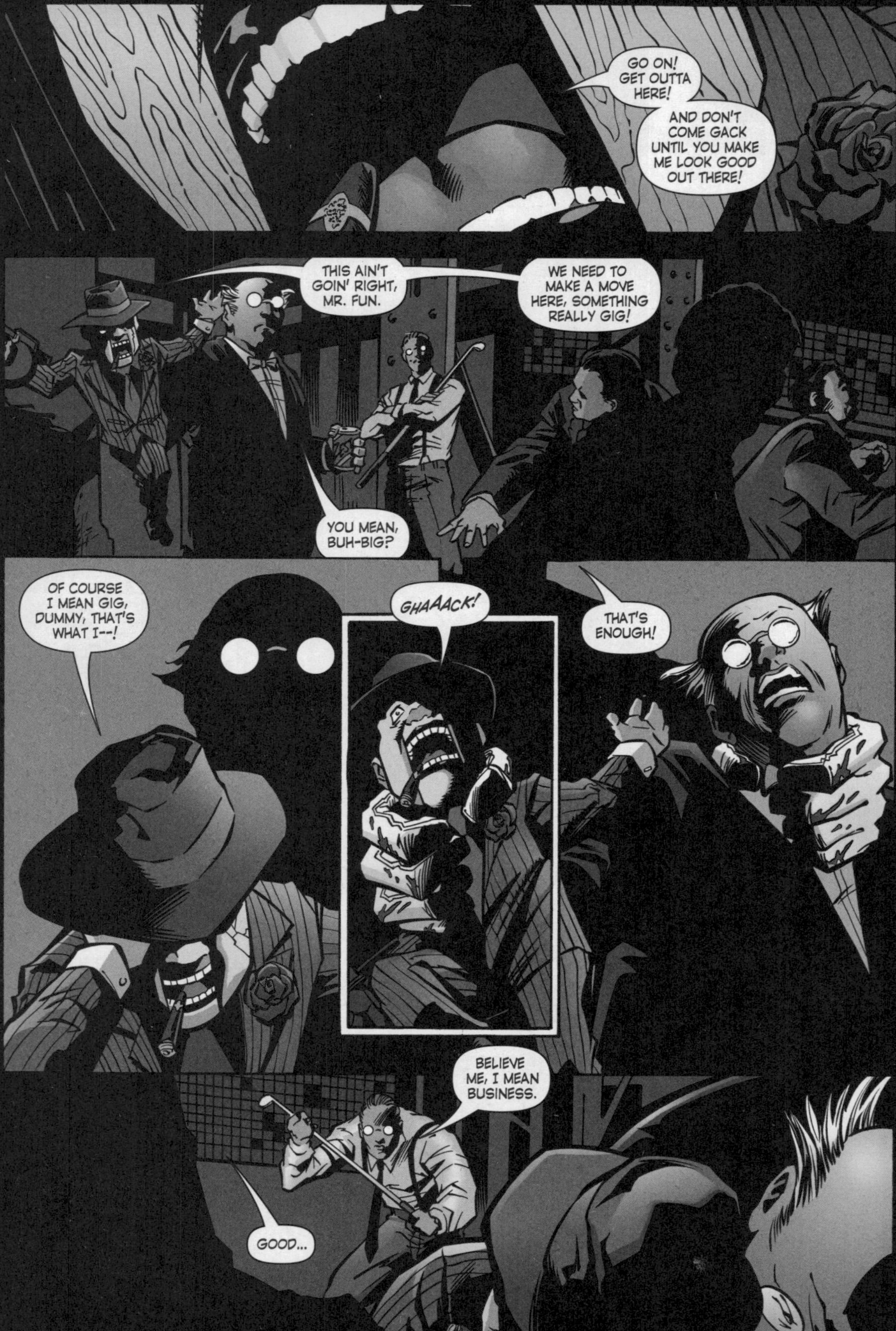
GO ON! GET OUTTA HERE!
AND DON'T COME GACK UNTIL YOU MAKE ME LOOK GOOD OUT THERE!
THIS AIN'T GOIN' RIGHT, MR. FUN.
WE NEED TO MAKE A MOVE HERE, SOMETHING REALLY GIG!
YOU MEAN, BUH-BIG?
OF COURSE I MEAN GIG, DUMMY, THAT'S WHAT I--!
GHAAACK!
THAT'S ENOUGH!
BELIEVE ME, I MEAN BUSINESS.
GOOD...

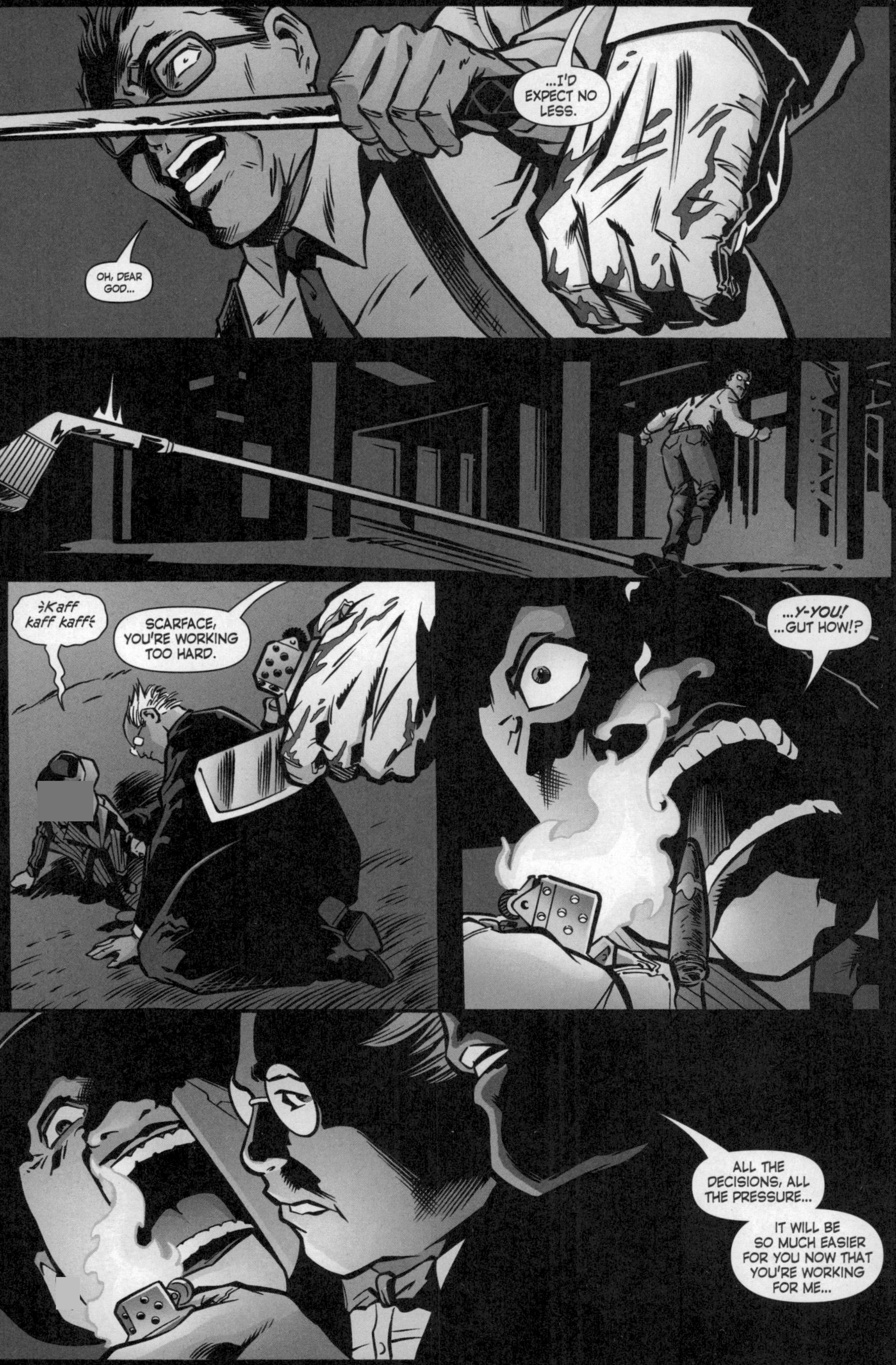
...I'D EXPECT NO LESS.
OH, DEAR GOD...
Kaff kaff kaff
SCARFACE, YOU'RE WORKING TOO HARD.
...Y-YOU! ...GUT HOW!?
ALL THE DECISIONS, ALL THE PRESSURE...
IT WILL BE SO MUCH EASIER FOR YOU NOW THAT YOU'RE WORKING FOR ME...

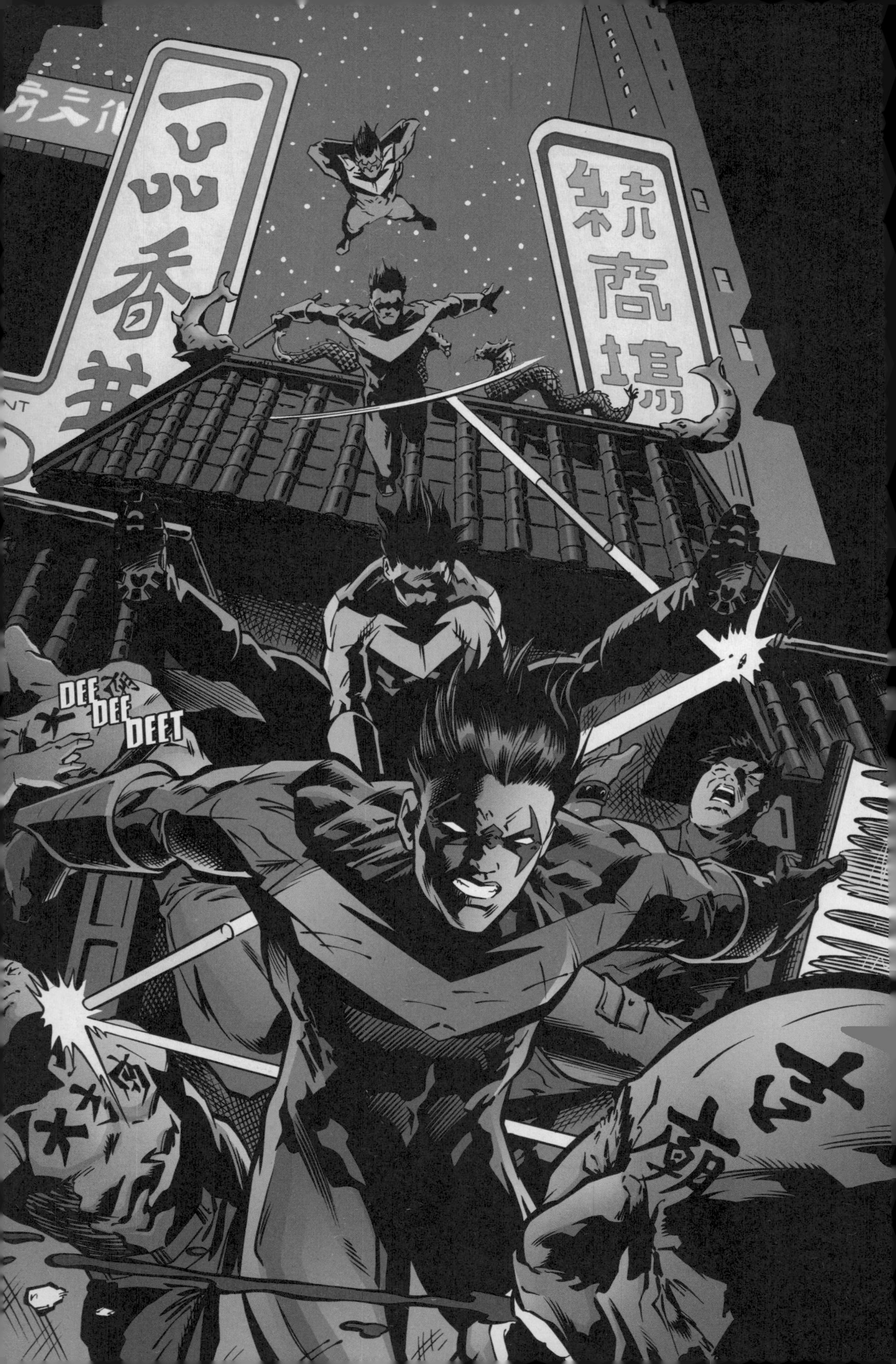
DEE DEE DEET

WHAT?
HELLO TO YOU TOO, QUERIDO.
SORRY IF I'M INTERRUPTING SOMETHING, I'M JUST CHECKING OUT THE BATTERIES ON MY BRAND-NEW COMMUNICATOR!
YOUR NEW TEMPORARY COMMUNICATOR, TARANTULA.
BUT DON'T WORRY ABOUT THAT-- WHAT YOU NEED TO BE CHECKING IS YOUR FLASHLIGHT.
MY FLASHLIGHT? WHY?
BECAUSE BATMAN SAID HE THINKS HE KNOWS WHAT'S GOING ON NOW, AND WE SHOULD BE PREPARED FOR THE LIGHTS TO--
DAMN. I GUESS YOU CAN SEE FOR YOURSELF.
NIGHTWING OUT.

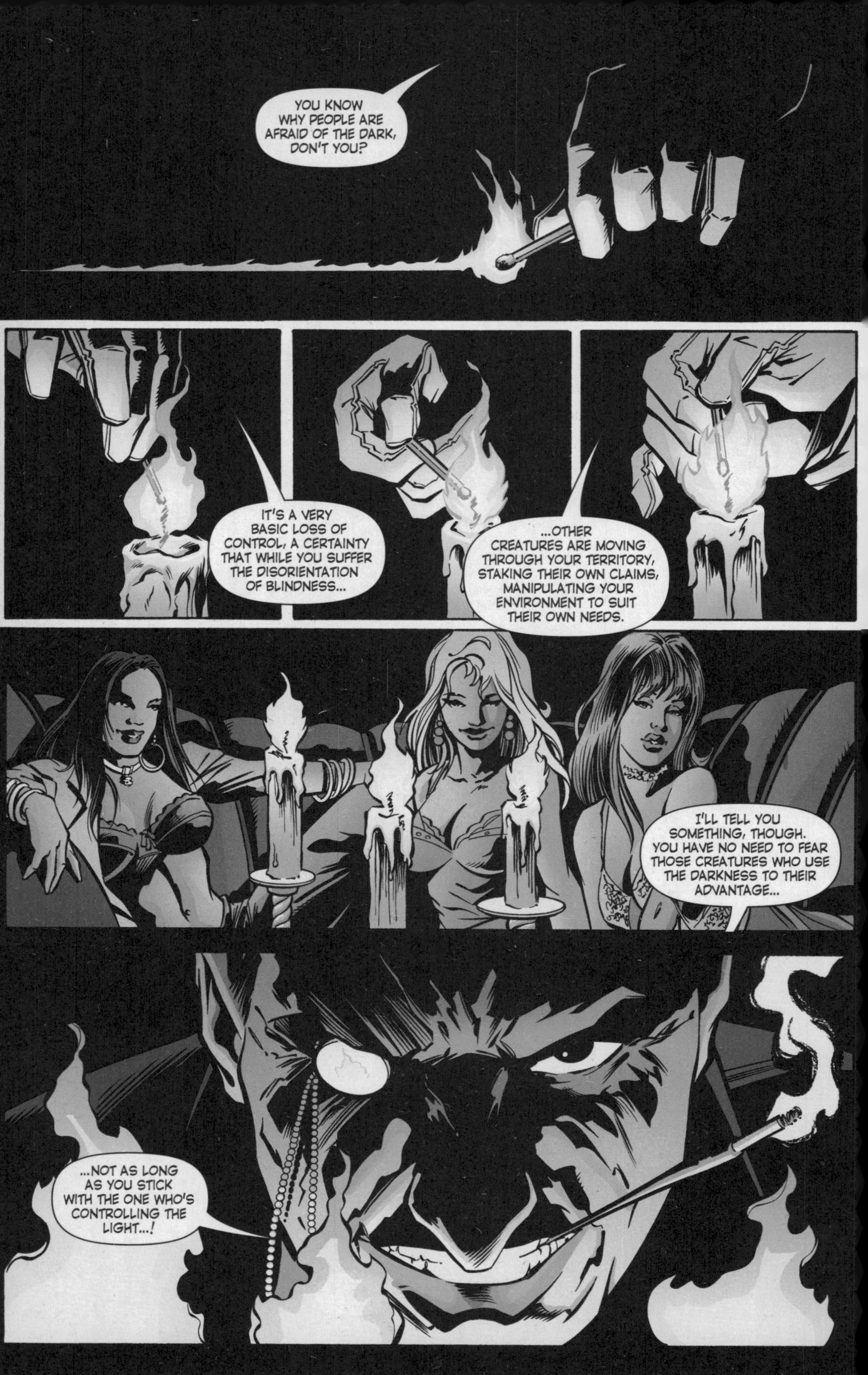
YOU KNOW WHY PEOPLE ARE AFRAID OF THE DARK, DON'T YOU?
IT'S A VERY BASIC LOSS OF CONTROL, A CERTAINTY THAT WHILE YOU SUFFER THE DISORIENTATION OF BLINDNESS...
...OTHER CREATURES ARE MOVING THROUGH YOUR TERRITORY, STAKING THEIR OWN CLAIMS, MANIPULATING YOUR ENVIRONMENT TO SUIT THEIR OWN NEEDS.
I'LL TELL YOU SOMETHING, THOUGH. YOU HAVE NO NEED TO FEAR THOSE CREATURES WHO USE THE DARKNESS TO THEIR ADVANTAGE...
...NOT AS LONG AS YOU STICK WITH THE ONE WHO'S CONTROLLING THE LIGHT...!

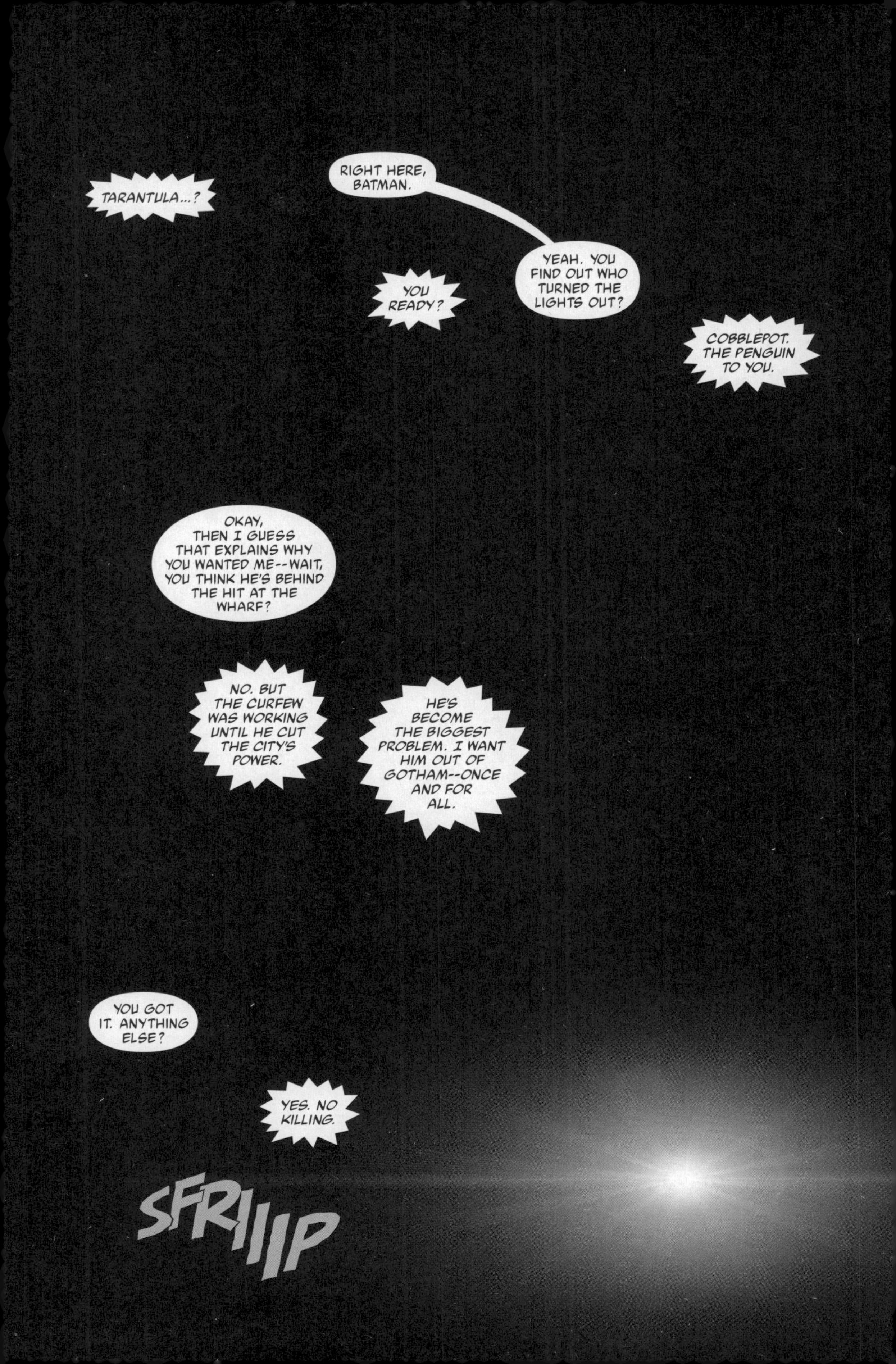
TARANTULA...?
RIGHT HERE, BATMAN.
YOU READY?
YEAH. YOU FIND OUT WHO TURNED THE LIGHTS OUT?
COBBLEPOT. THE PENGUIN TO YOU.
OKAY, THEN I GUESS THAT EXPLAINS WHY YOU WANTED ME--WAIT, YOU THINK HE'S BEHIND THE HIT AT THE WHARF?
NO. BUT THE CURFEW WAS WORKING UNTIL HE CUT THE CITY'S POWER.
HE'S BECOME THE BIGGEST PROBLEM. I WANT HIM OUT OF GOTHAM--ONCE AND FOR ALL.
YOU GOT IT. ANYTHING ELSE?
YES. NO KILLING.
SFRIIIP

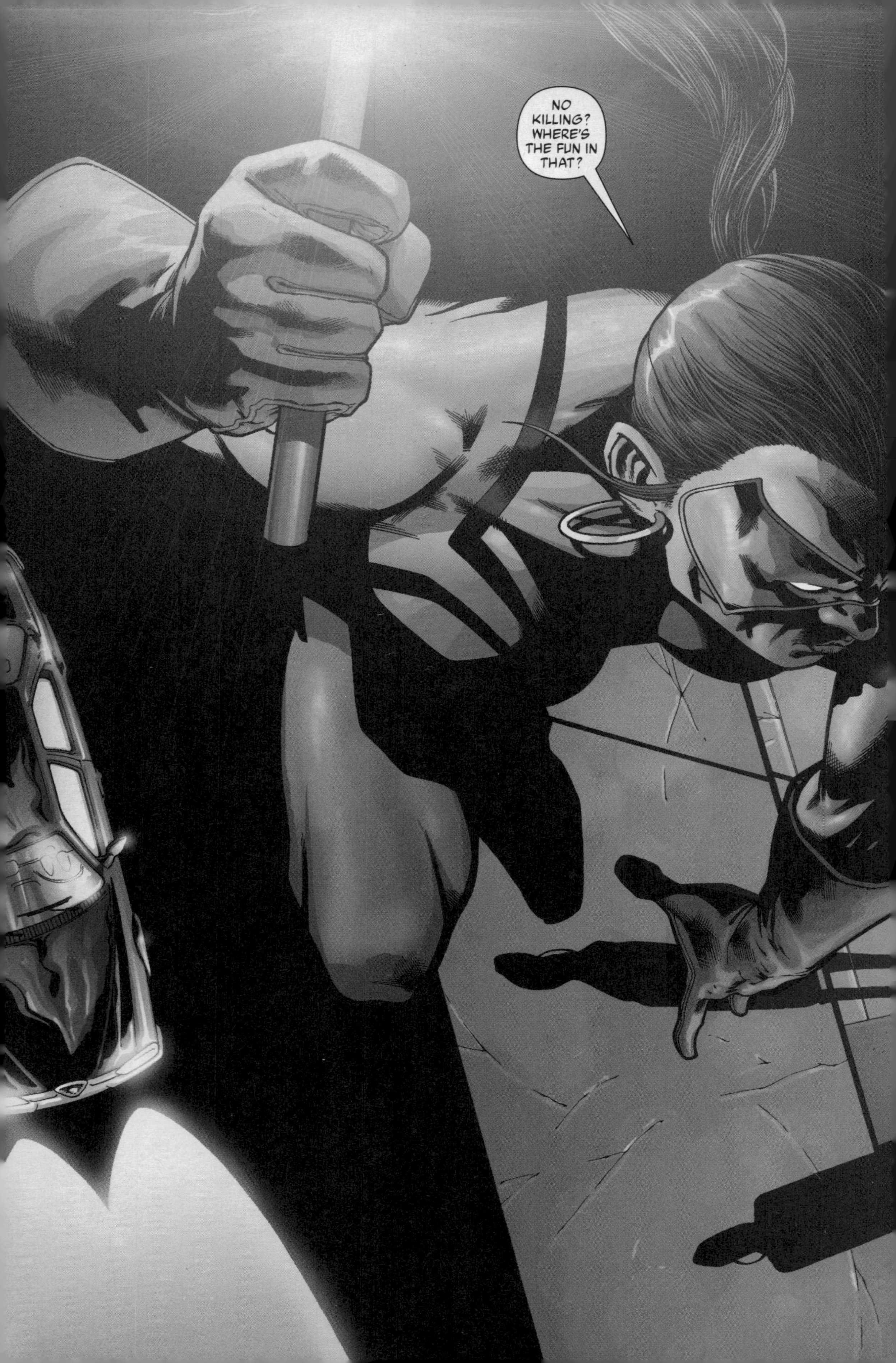
NO KILLING? WHERE'S THE FUN IN THAT?

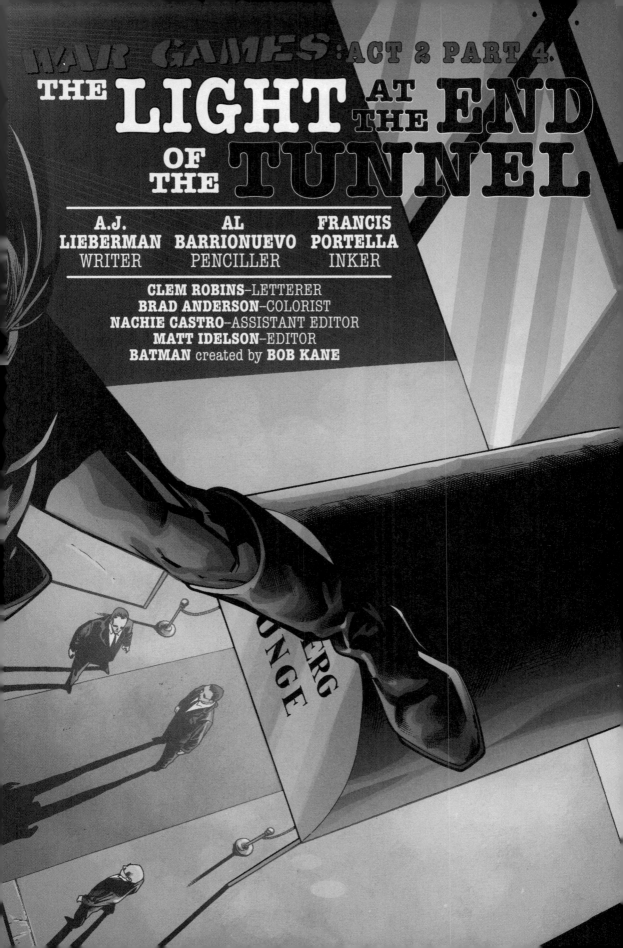

WAR GAMES: ACT 2 PART 4:

THE LIGHT AT THE END OF THE TUNNEL

A.J. LIEBERMAN — WRITER

AL BARRIONUEVO — PENCILLER

FRANCIS PORTELLA — INKER

CLEM ROBINS—LETTERER

BRAD ANDERSON—COLORIST

NACHIE CASTRO—ASSISTANT EDITOR

MATT IDELSON—EDITOR

BATMAN created by BOB KANE

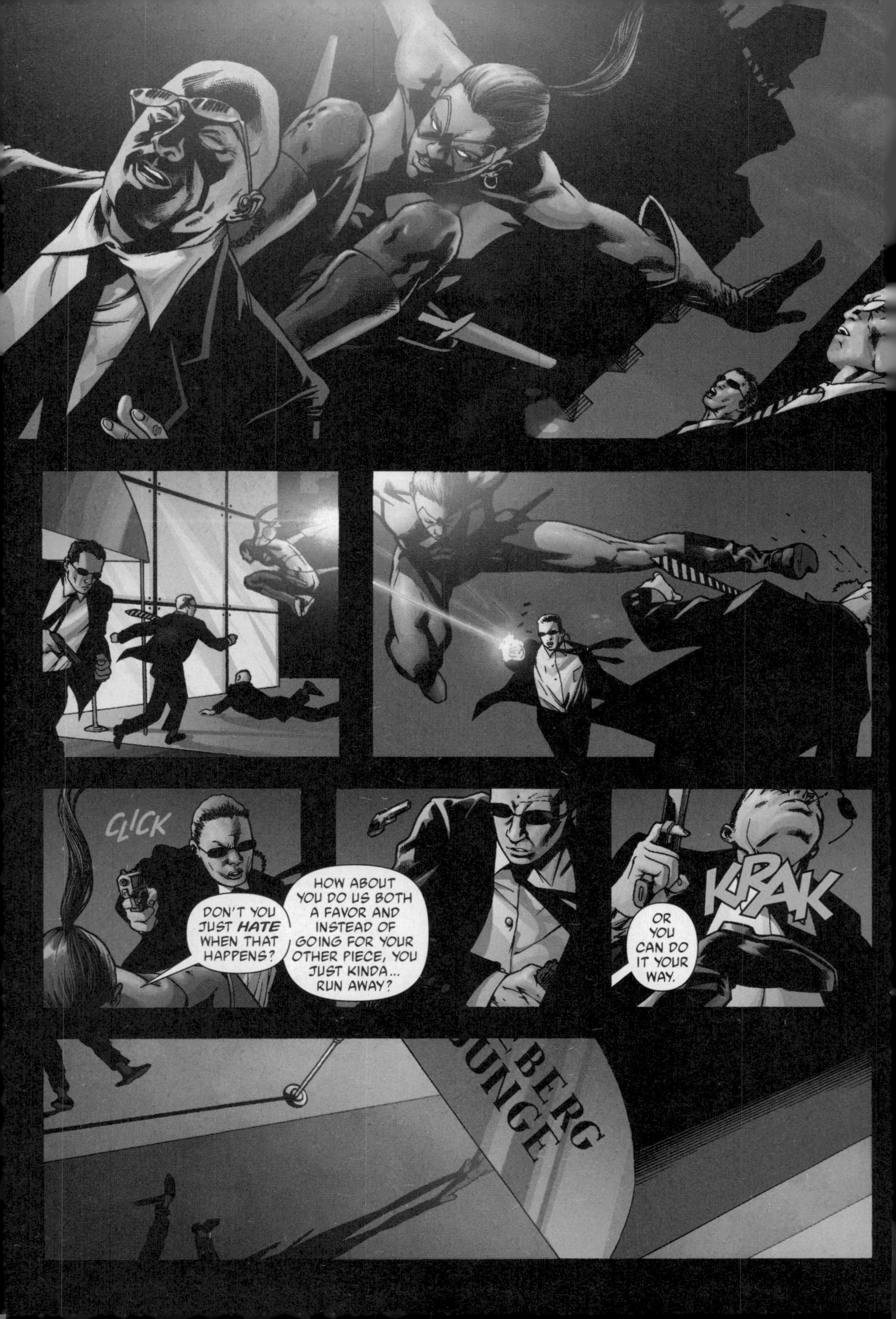
CLICK
DON'T YOU JUST *HATE* WHEN THAT HAPPENS?
HOW ABOUT YOU DO US BOTH A FAVOR AND INSTEAD OF GOING FOR YOUR OTHER PIECE, YOU JUST KINDA... RUN AWAY?
KRAK
OR YOU CAN DO IT YOUR WAY.

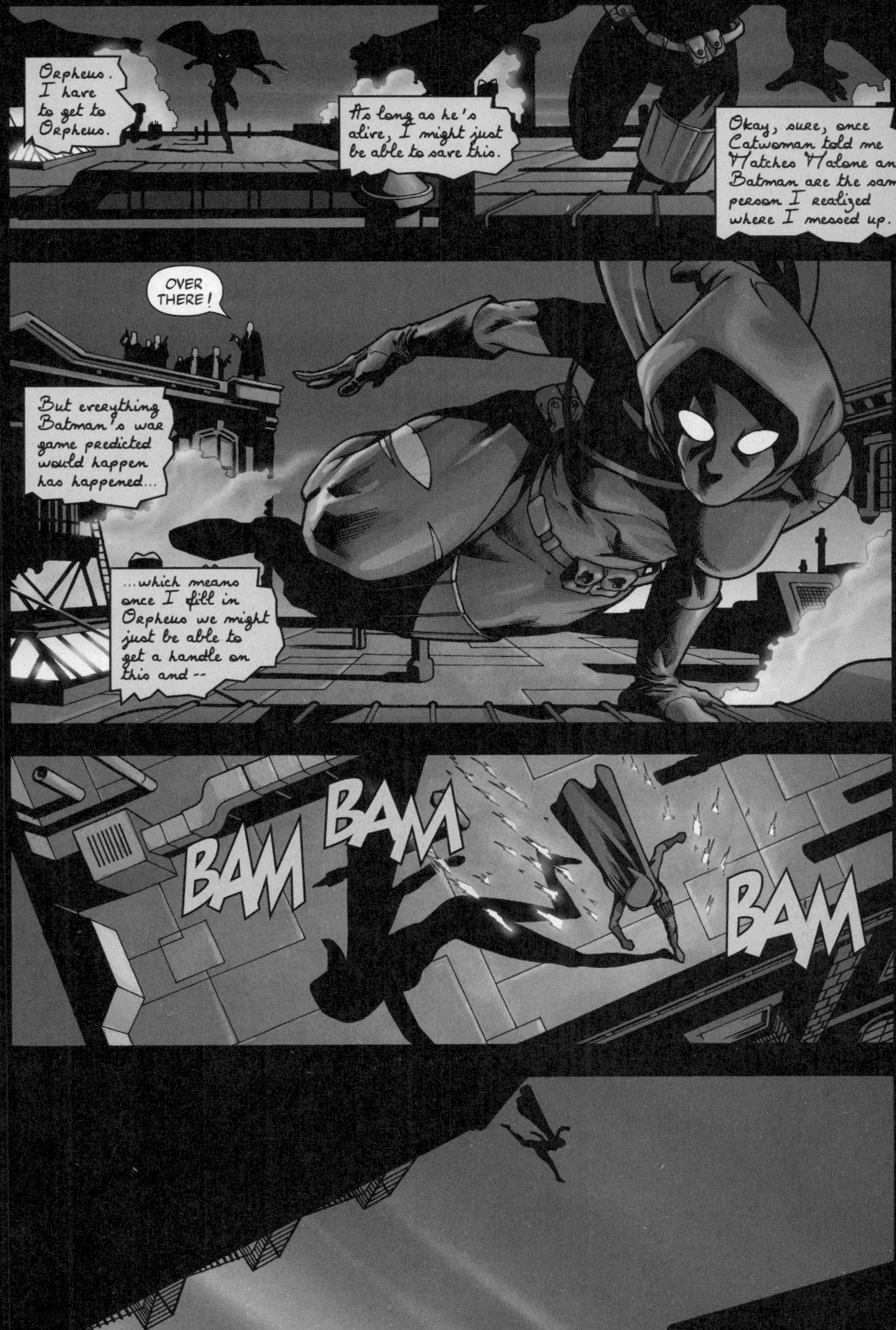
Orpheus. I have to get to Orpheus.
As long as he's alive, I might just be able to save this.
Okay, sure, once Catwoman told me Matches Malone and Batman are the same person I realized where I messed up.
OVER THERE!
But everything Batman's war game predicted would happen has happened...
...which means once I fill in Orpheus we might just be able to get a handle on this and --
BAM
BAM
BAM

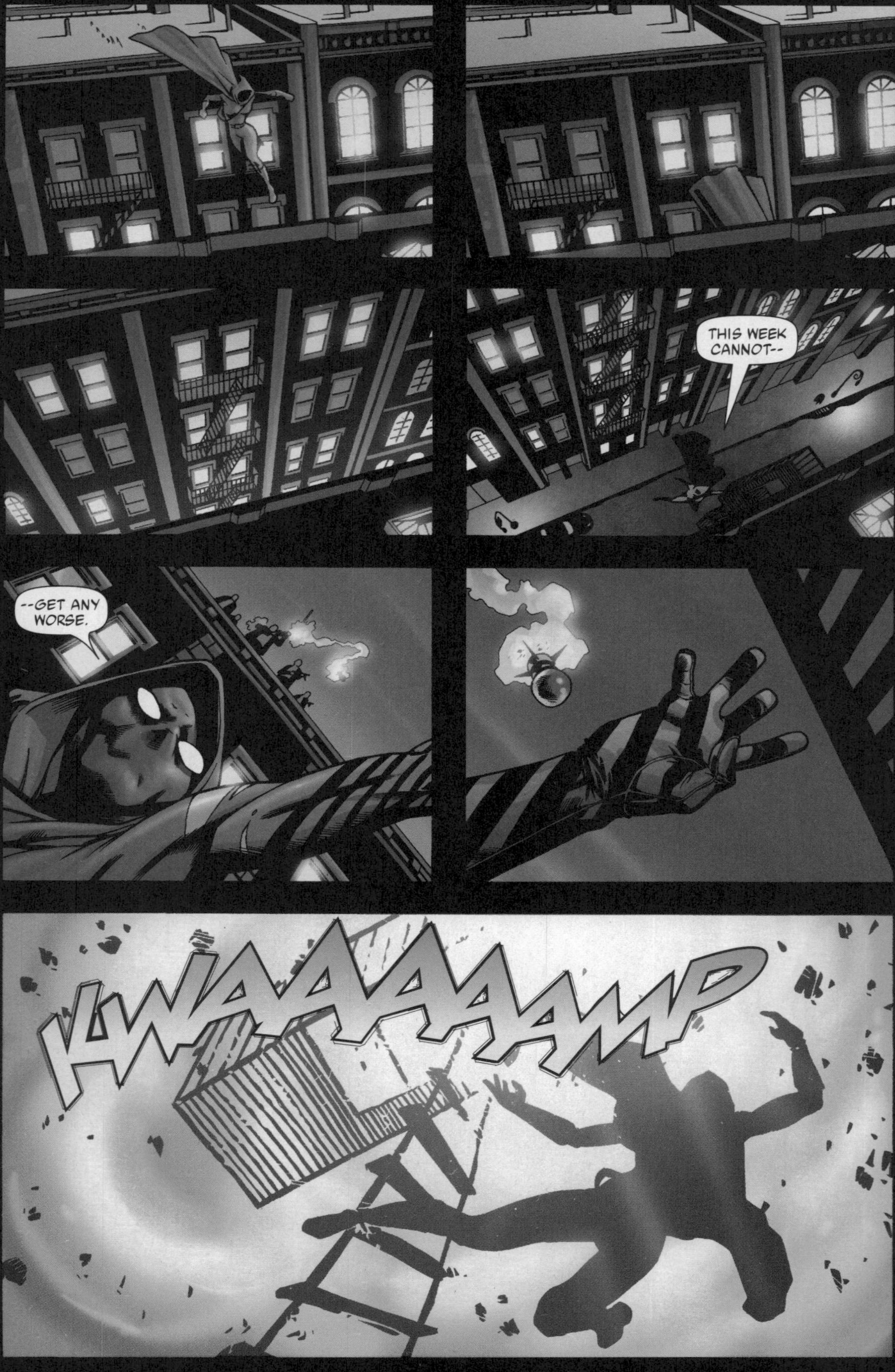
THIS WEEK CANNOT--
--GET ANY WORSE.
KWAAAAAMP

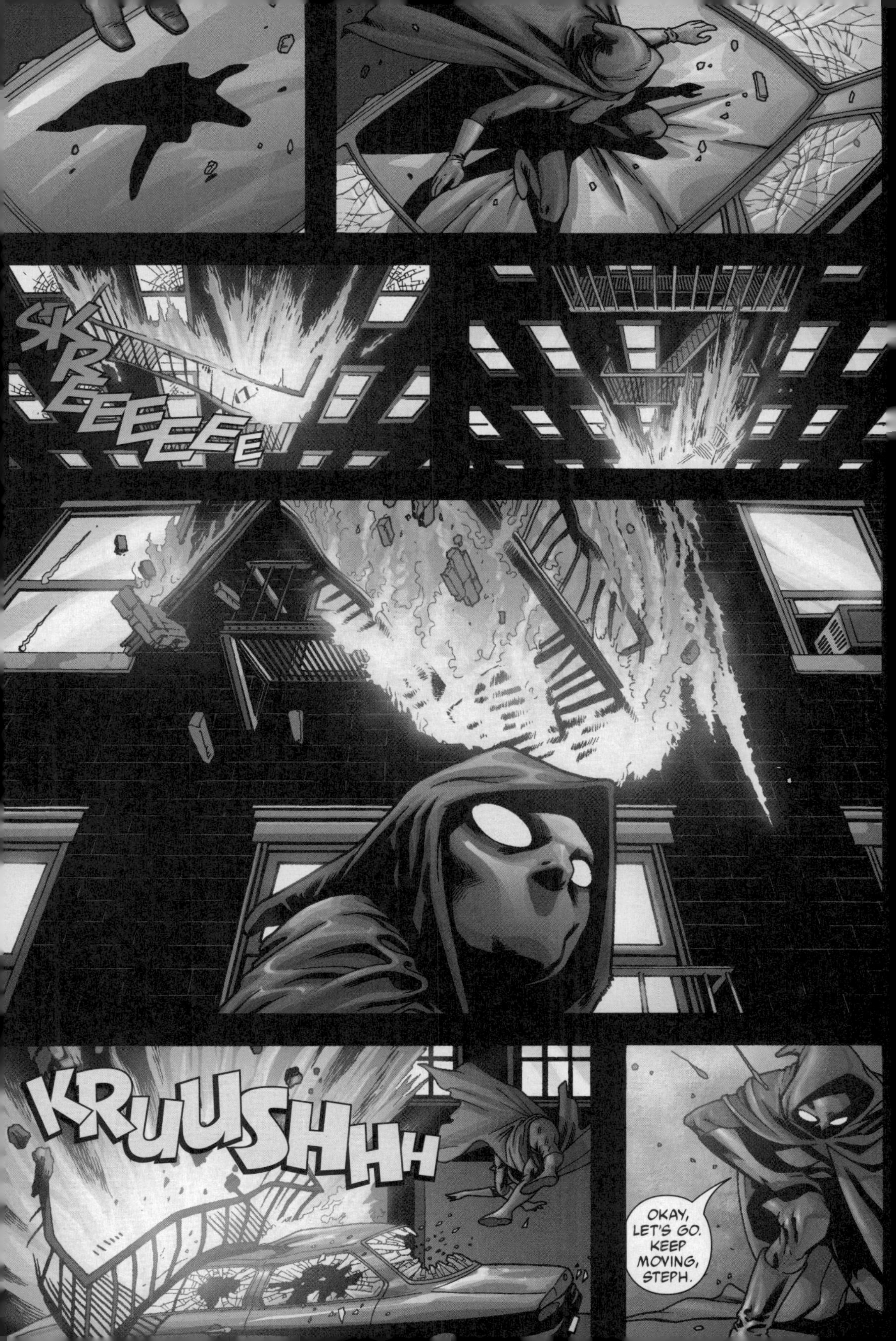
SKREEEEEEE
KRUUSHHH
OKAY, LET'S GO. KEEP MOVING, STEPH.

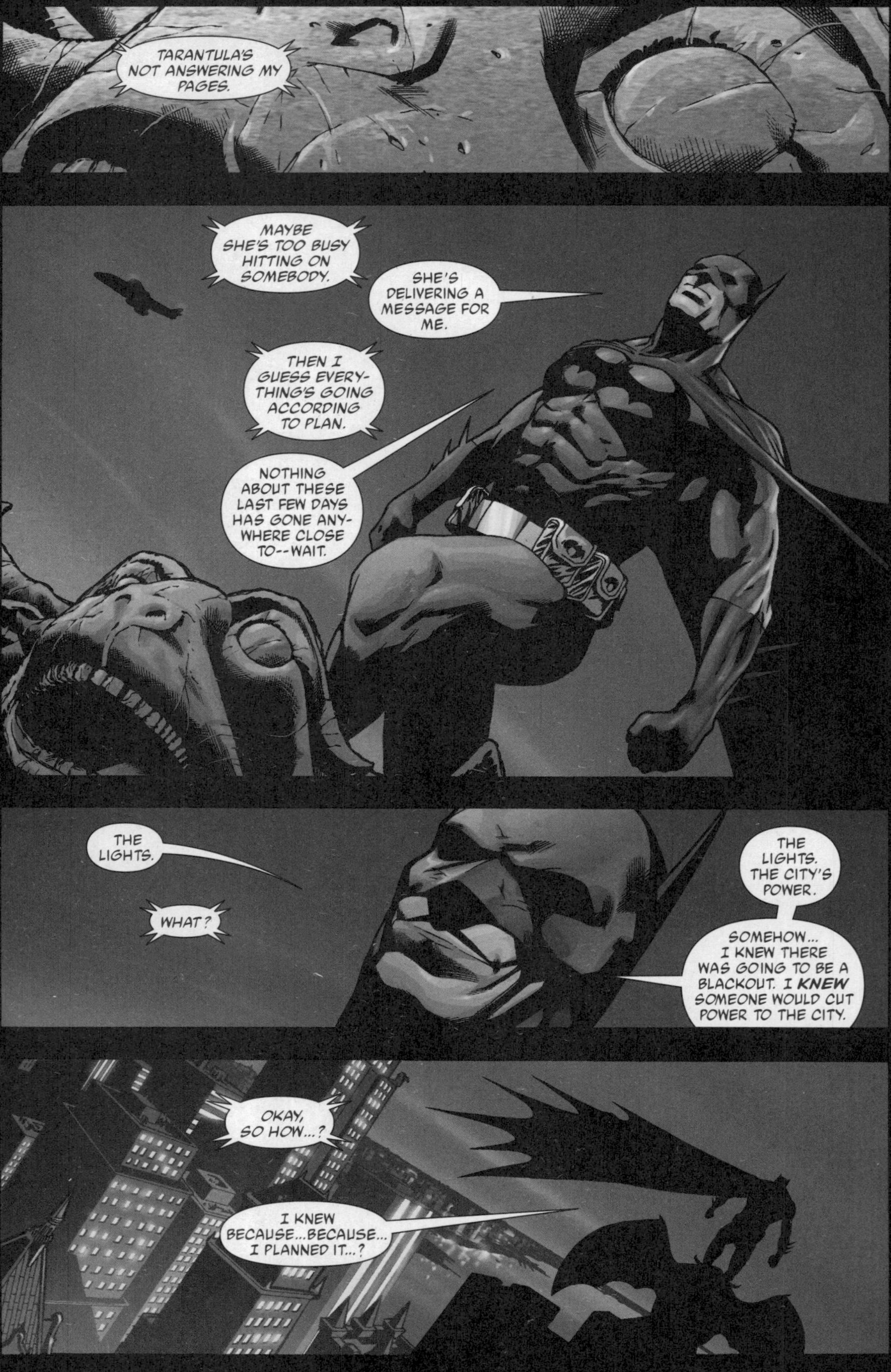
TARANTULA'S NOT ANSWERING MY PAGES.
MAYBE SHE'S TOO BUSY HITTING ON SOMEBODY.
SHE'S DELIVERING A MESSAGE FOR ME.
THEN I GUESS EVERY-THING'S GOING ACCORDING TO PLAN.
NOTHING ABOUT THESE LAST FEW DAYS HAS GONE ANY-WHERE CLOSE TO--WAIT.
THE LIGHTS.
WHAT?
THE LIGHTS. THE CITY'S POWER.
SOMEHOW... I KNEW THERE WAS GOING TO BE A BLACKOUT. I KNEW SOMEONE WOULD CUT POWER TO THE CITY.
OKAY, SO HOW...?
I KNEW BECAUSE...BECAUSE... I PLANNED IT...?

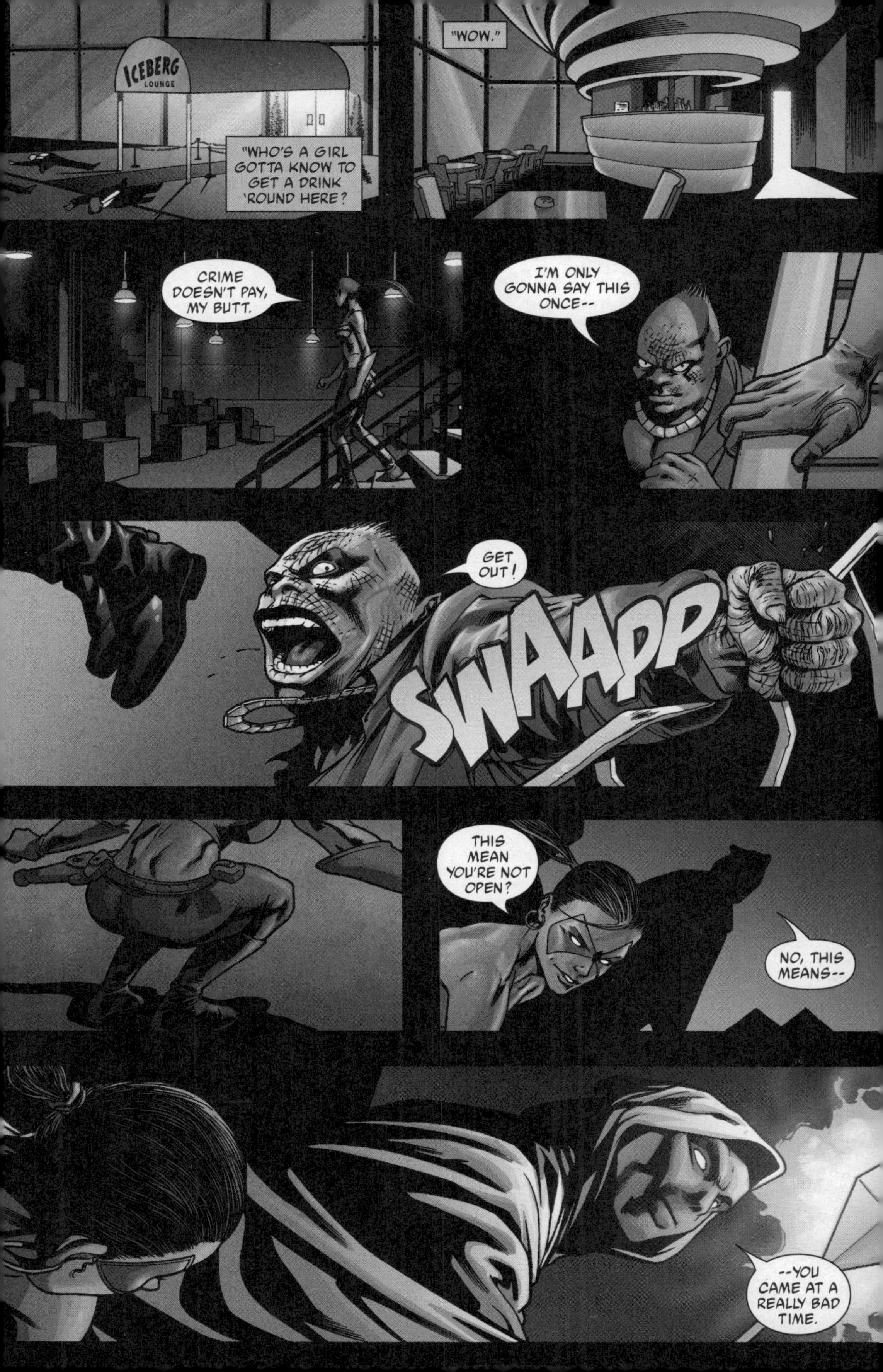
ICEBERG
LOUNGE
"WHO'S A GIRL GOTTA KNOW TO GET A DRINK 'ROUND HERE?
"WOW."
CRIME DOESN'T PAY, MY BUTT.
I'M ONLY GONNA SAY THIS ONCE--
GET OUT!
SWAAPP
THIS MEAN YOU'RE NOT OPEN?
NO, THIS MEANS--
--YOU CAME AT A REALLY BAD TIME.

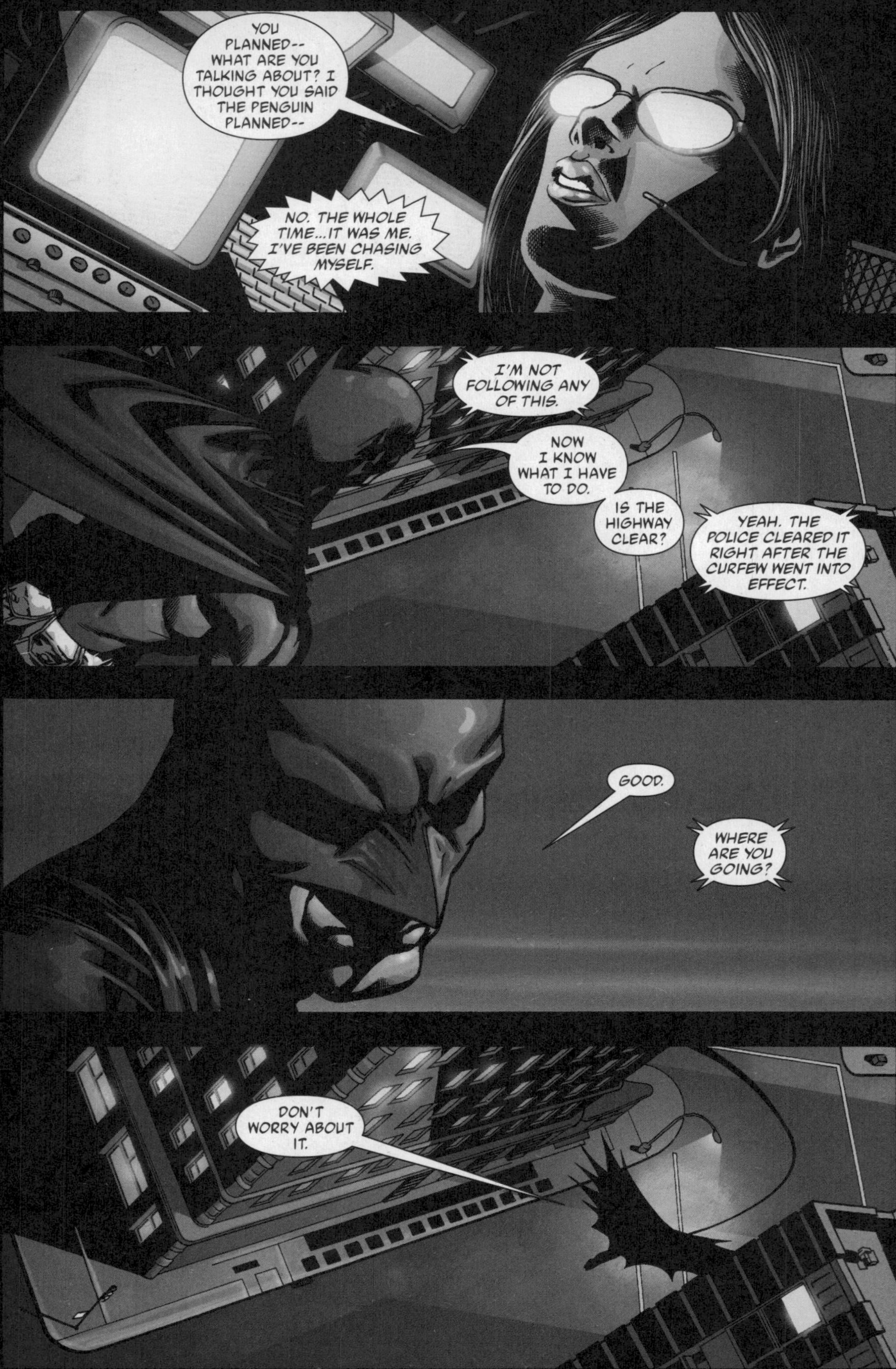
YOU PLANNED-- WHAT ARE YOU TALKING ABOUT? I THOUGHT YOU SAID THE PENGUIN PLANNED--
NO. THE WHOLE TIME...IT WAS ME. I'VE BEEN CHASING MYSELF.
I'M NOT FOLLOWING ANY OF THIS.
NOW I KNOW WHAT I HAVE TO DO.
IS THE HIGHWAY CLEAR?
YEAH. THE POLICE CLEARED IT RIGHT AFTER THE CURFEW WENT INTO EFFECT.
GOOD.
WHERE ARE YOU GOING?
DON'T WORRY ABOUT IT.

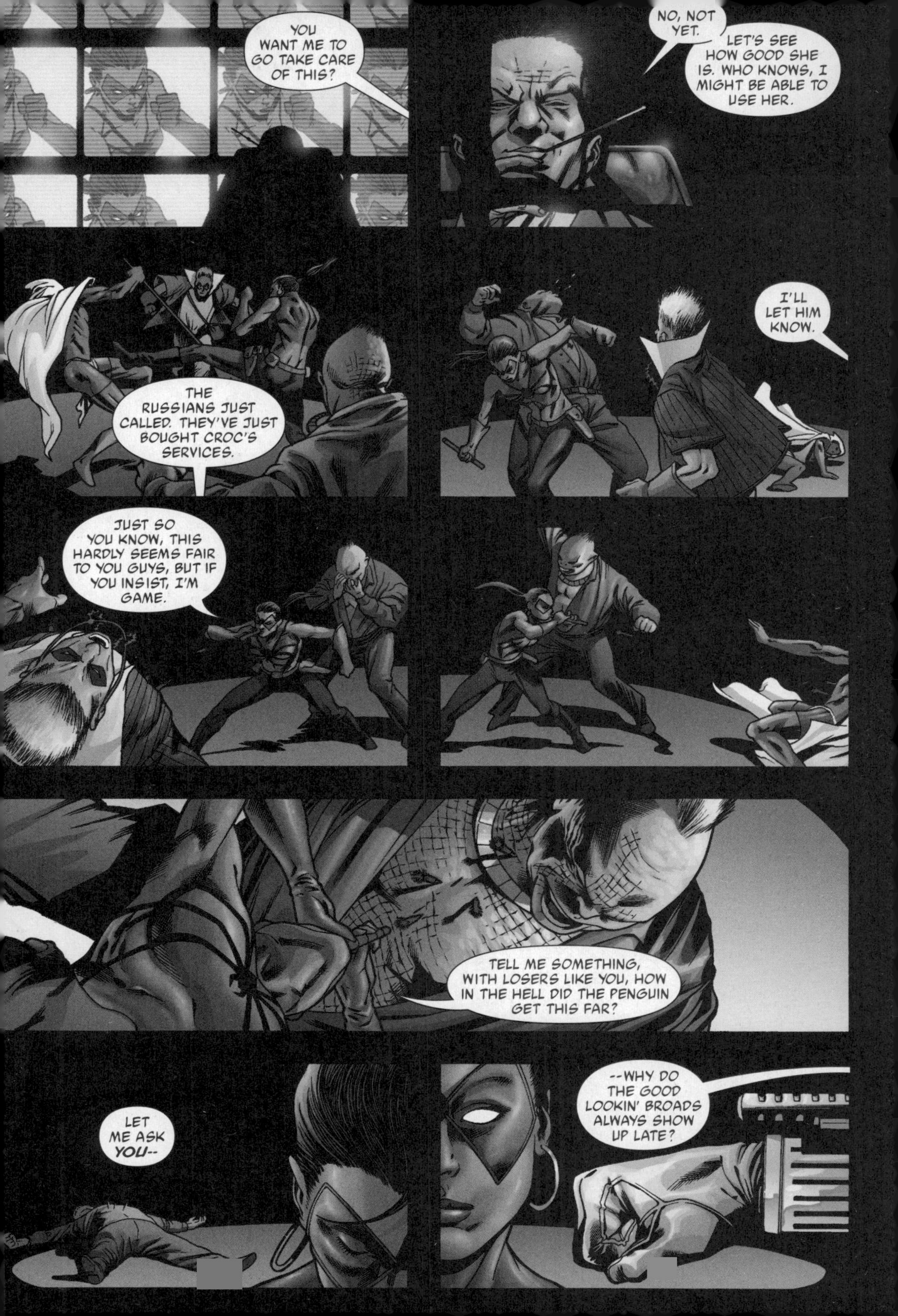
YOU WANT ME TO GO TAKE CARE OF THIS?
NO, NOT YET.
LET'S SEE HOW GOOD SHE IS. WHO KNOWS, I MIGHT BE ABLE TO USE HER.
THE RUSSIANS JUST CALLED. THEY'VE JUST BOUGHT CROC'S SERVICES.
I'LL LET HIM KNOW.
JUST SO YOU KNOW, THIS HARDLY SEEMS FAIR TO YOU GUYS, BUT IF YOU INSIST, I'M GAME.
TELL ME SOMETHING, WITH LOSERS LIKE YOU, HOW IN THE HELL DID THE PENGUIN GET THIS FAR?
LET ME ASK *YOU*--
--WHY DO THE GOOD LOOKIN' BROADS ALWAYS SHOW UP LATE?

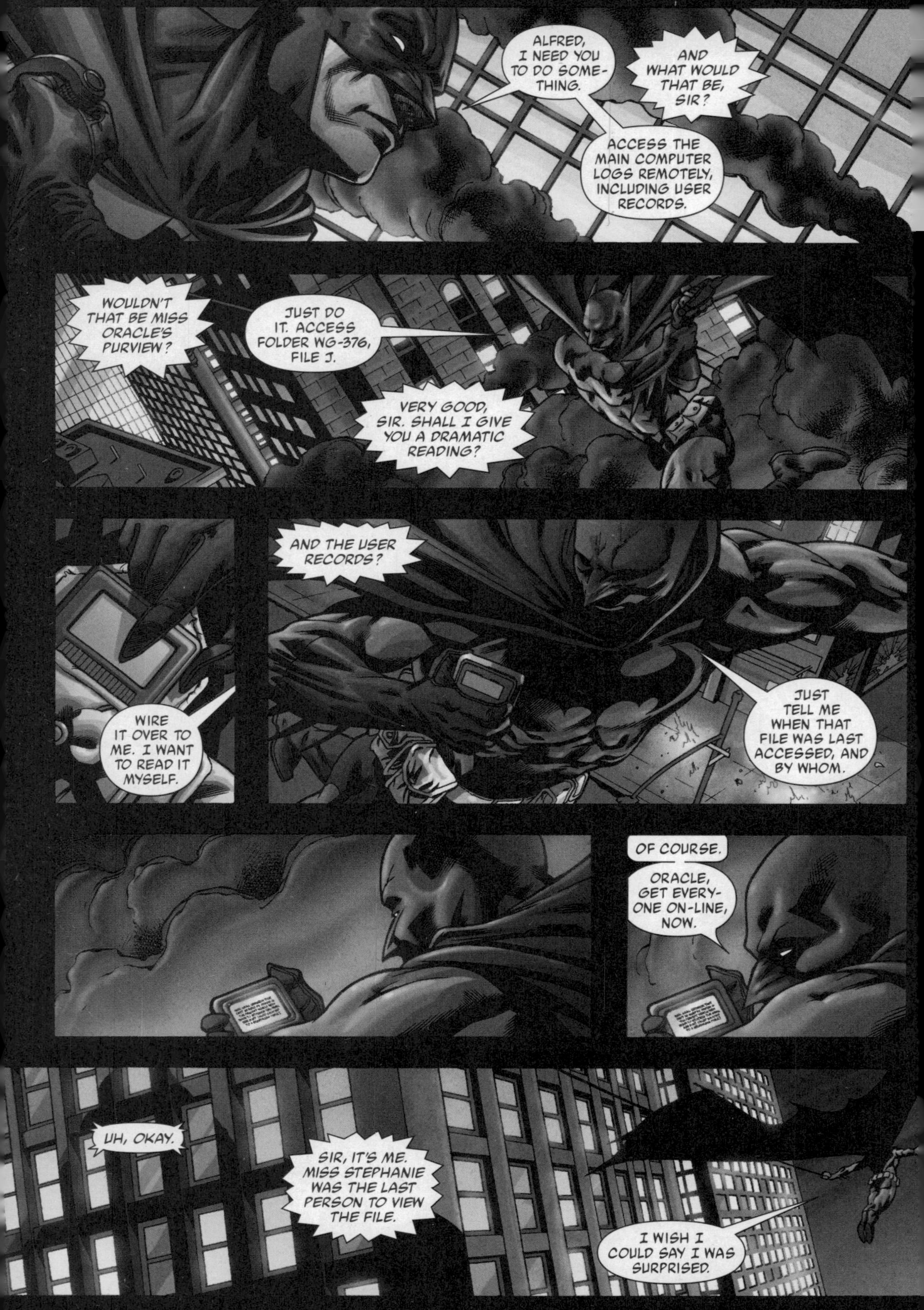
ALFRED, I NEED YOU TO DO SOME-THING.
AND WHAT WOULD THAT BE, SIR?
ACCESS THE MAIN COMPUTER LOGS REMOTELY, INCLUDING USER RECORDS.
WOULDN'T THAT BE MISS ORACLE'S PURVIEW?
JUST DO IT. ACCESS FOLDER WG-376, FILE J.
VERY GOOD, SIR. SHALL I GIVE YOU A DRAMATIC READING?
WIRE IT OVER TO ME. I WANT TO READ IT MYSELF.
AND THE USER RECORDS?
JUST TELL ME WHEN THAT FILE WAS LAST ACCESSED, AND BY WHOM.
OF COURSE.
ORACLE, GET EVERY-ONE ON-LINE, NOW.
UH, OKAY.
SIR, IT'S ME. MISS STEPHANIE WAS THE LAST PERSON TO VIEW THE FILE.
I WISH I COULD SAY I WAS SURPRISED.

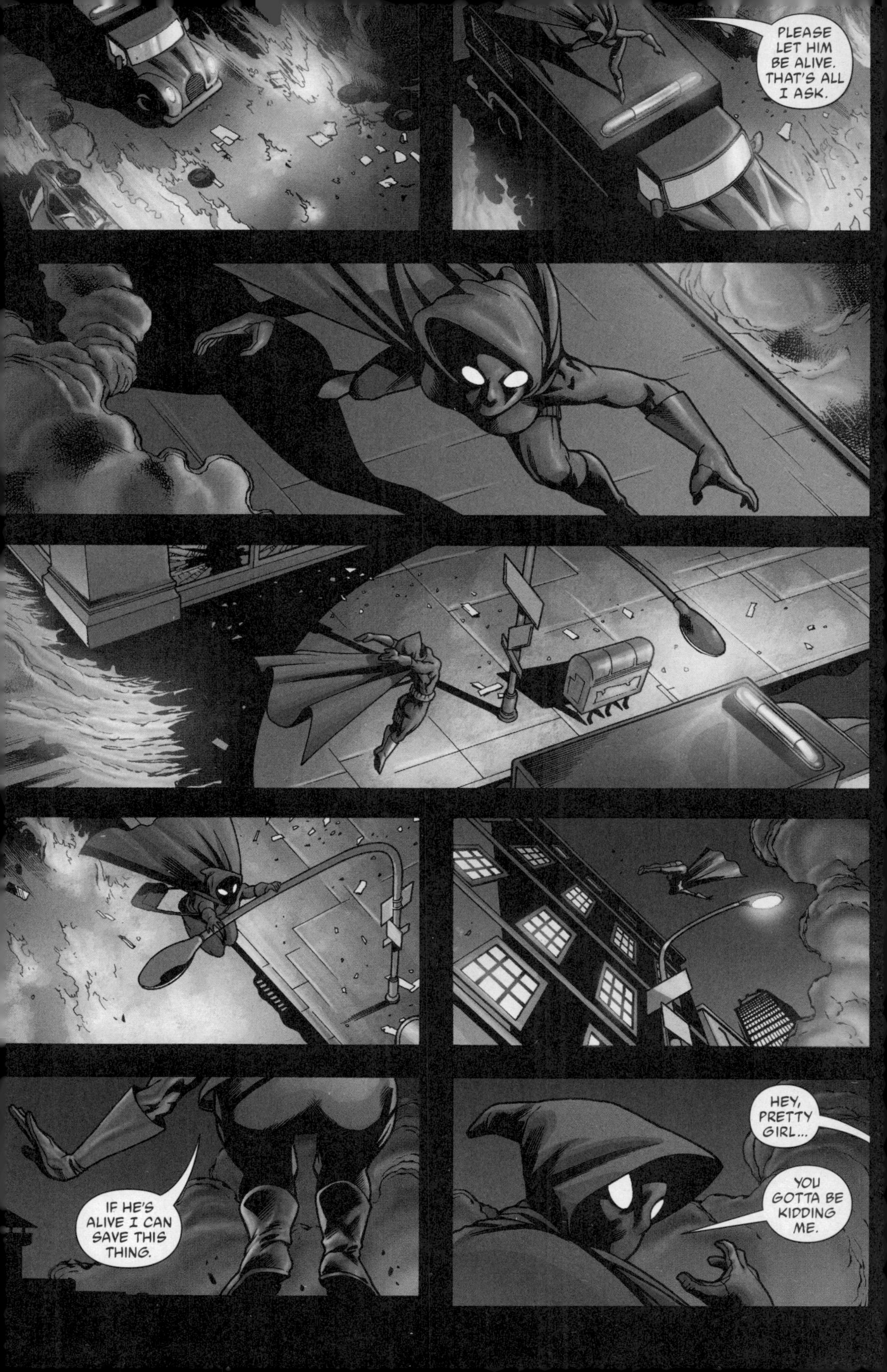
PLEASE LET HIM BE ALIVE. THAT'S ALL I ASK.
IF HE'S ALIVE I CAN SAVE THIS THING.
HEY, PRETTY GIRL...
YOU GOTTA BE KIDDING ME.

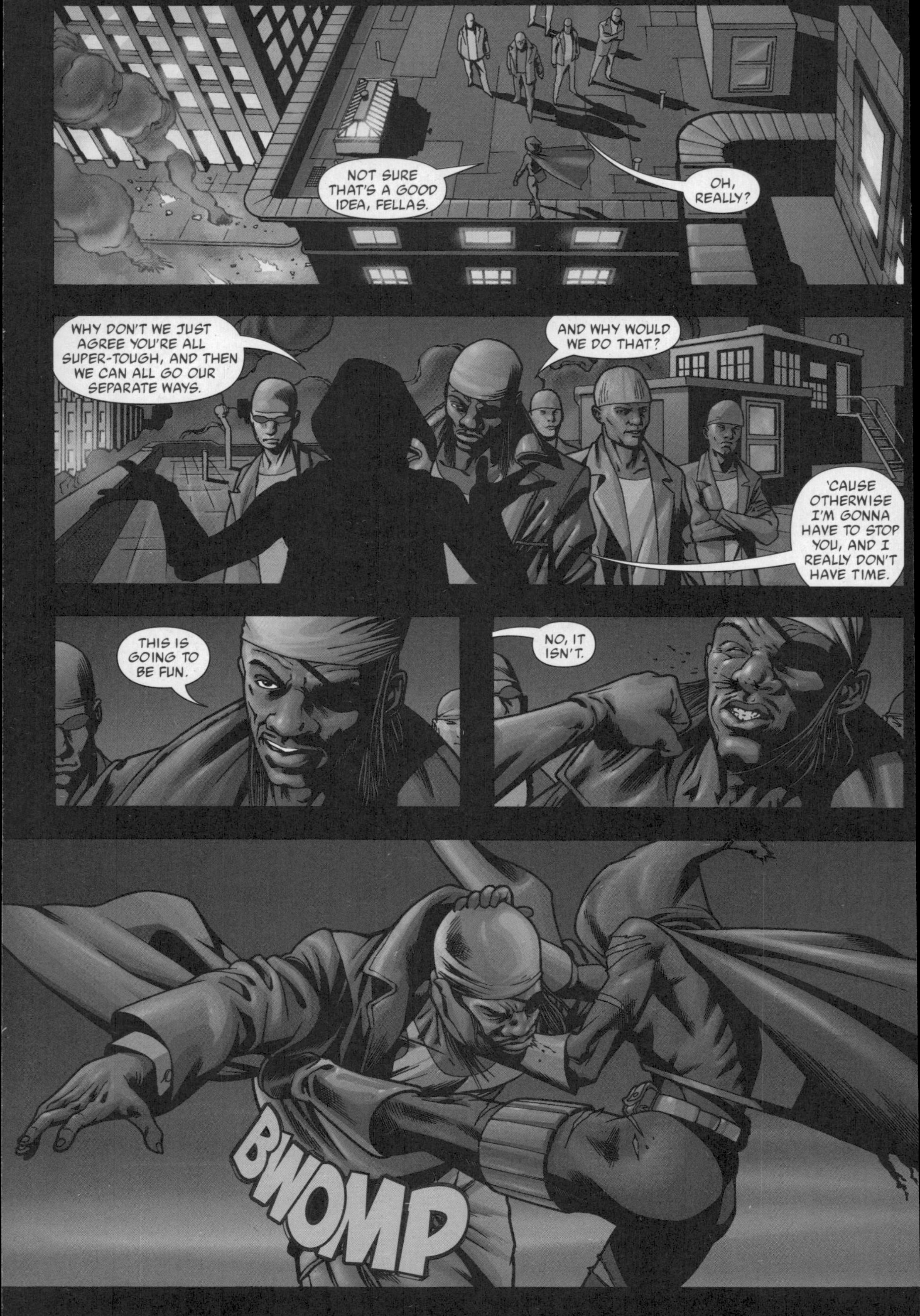
NOT SURE THAT'S A GOOD IDEA, FELLAS.
OH, REALLY?
WHY DON'T WE JUST AGREE YOU'RE ALL SUPER-TOUGH, AND THEN WE CAN ALL GO OUR SEPARATE WAYS.
AND WHY WOULD WE DO THAT?
'CAUSE OTHERWISE I'M GONNA HAVE TO STOP YOU, AND I REALLY DON'T HAVE TIME.
THIS IS GOING TO BE FUN.
NO, IT ISN'T.
BWOMP

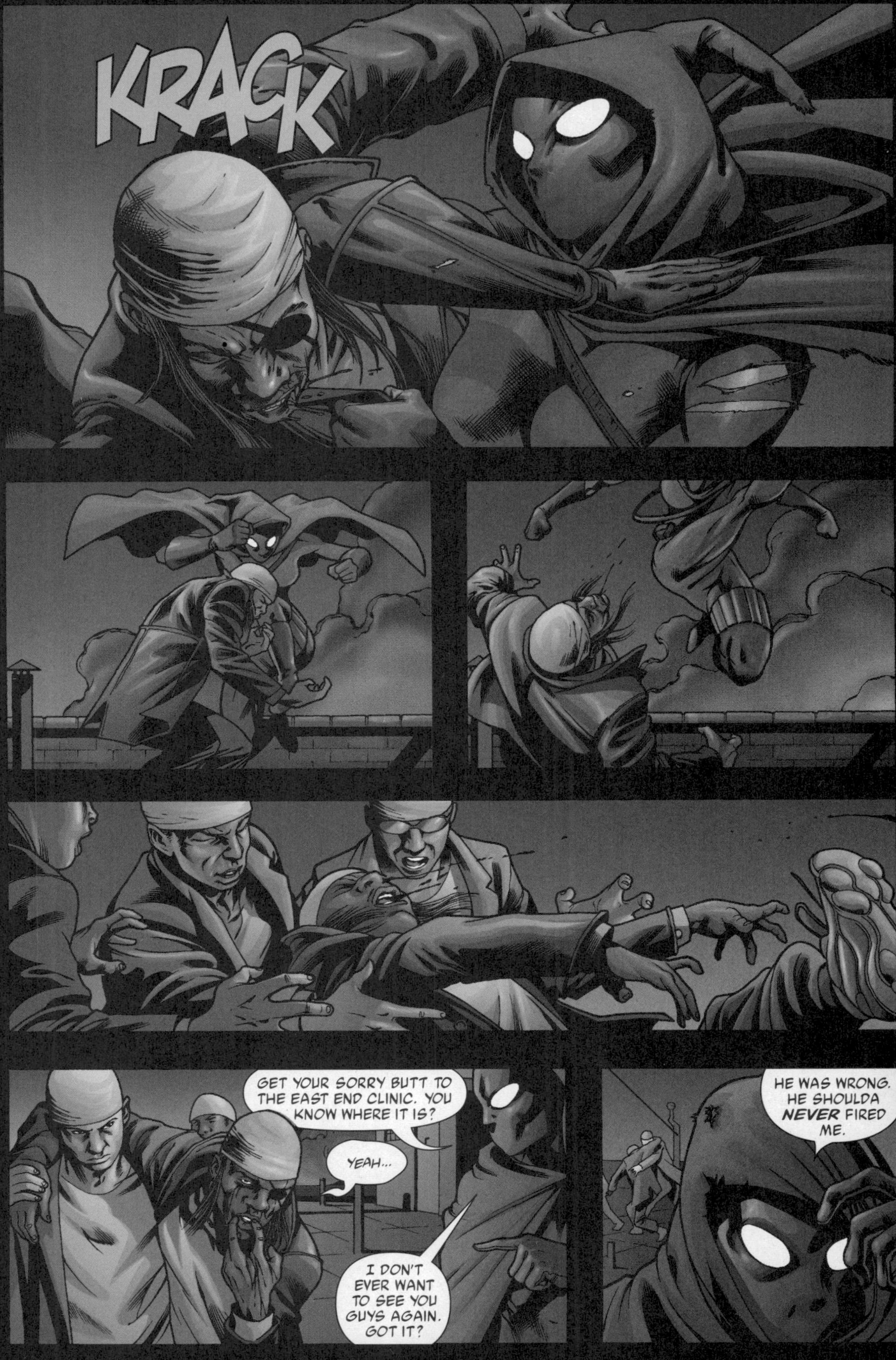
KRACK
GET YOUR SORRY BUTT TO THE EAST END CLINIC. YOU KNOW WHERE IT IS?
YEAH...
I DON'T EVER WANT TO SEE YOU GUYS AGAIN. GOT IT?
HE WAS WRONG. HE SHOULDA NEVER FIRED ME.

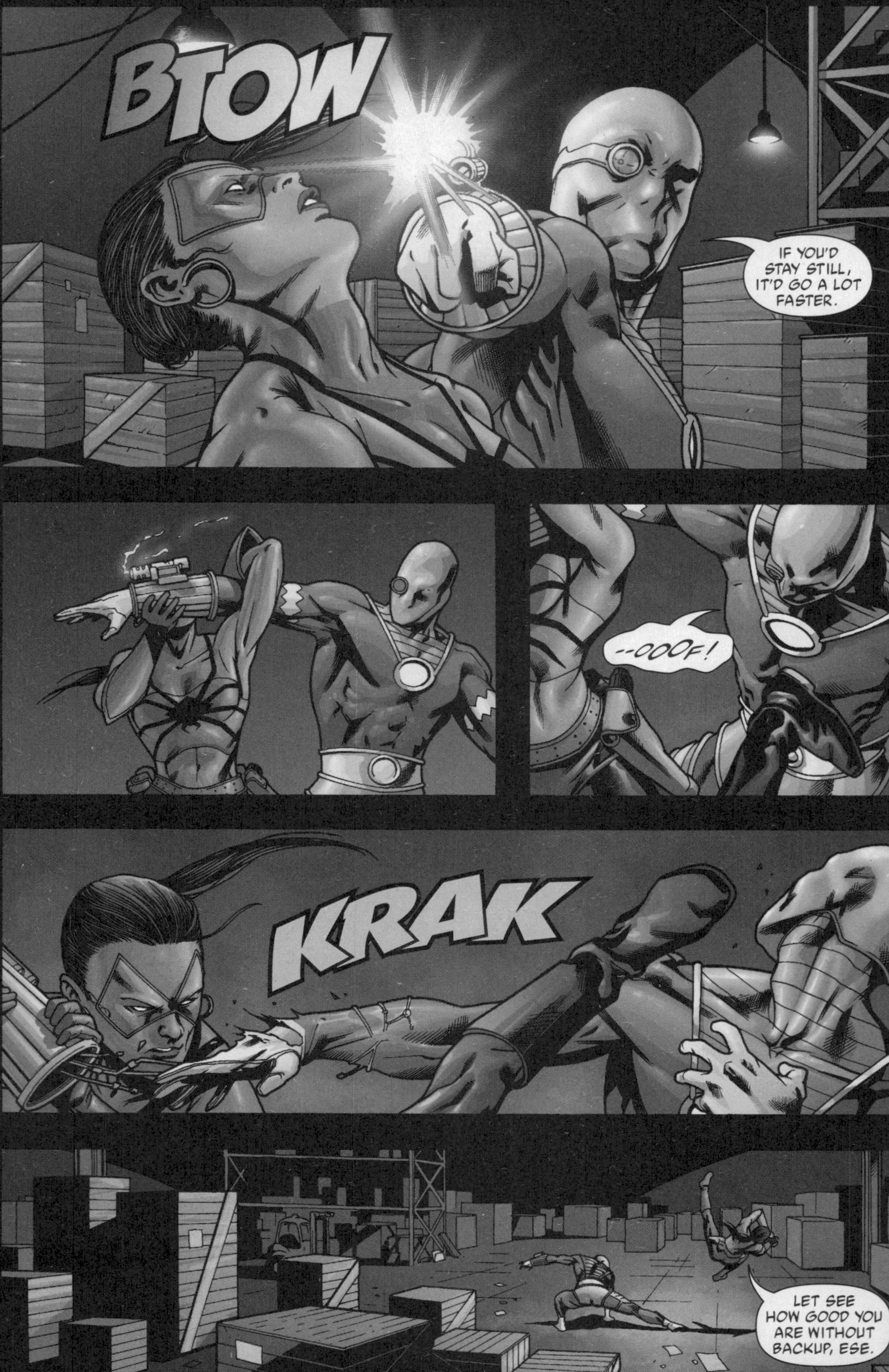
BTOW
IF YOU'D STAY STILL, IT'D GO A LOT FASTER.
--OOOF!
KRAK
LET SEE HOW GOOD YOU ARE WITHOUT BACKUP, ESE.

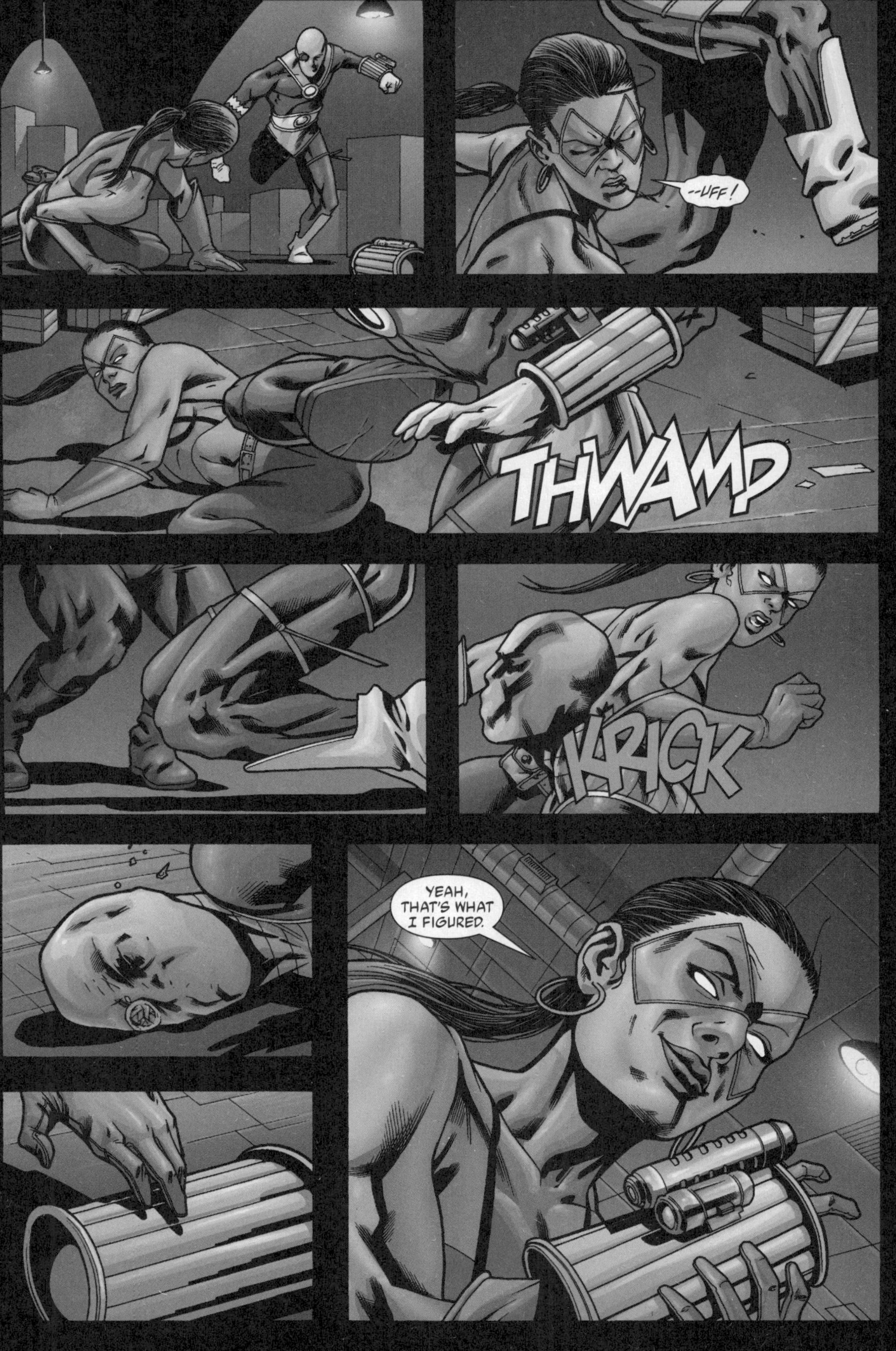
--UFF!
THWAMP
KRICK
YEAH, THAT'S WHAT I FIGURED.

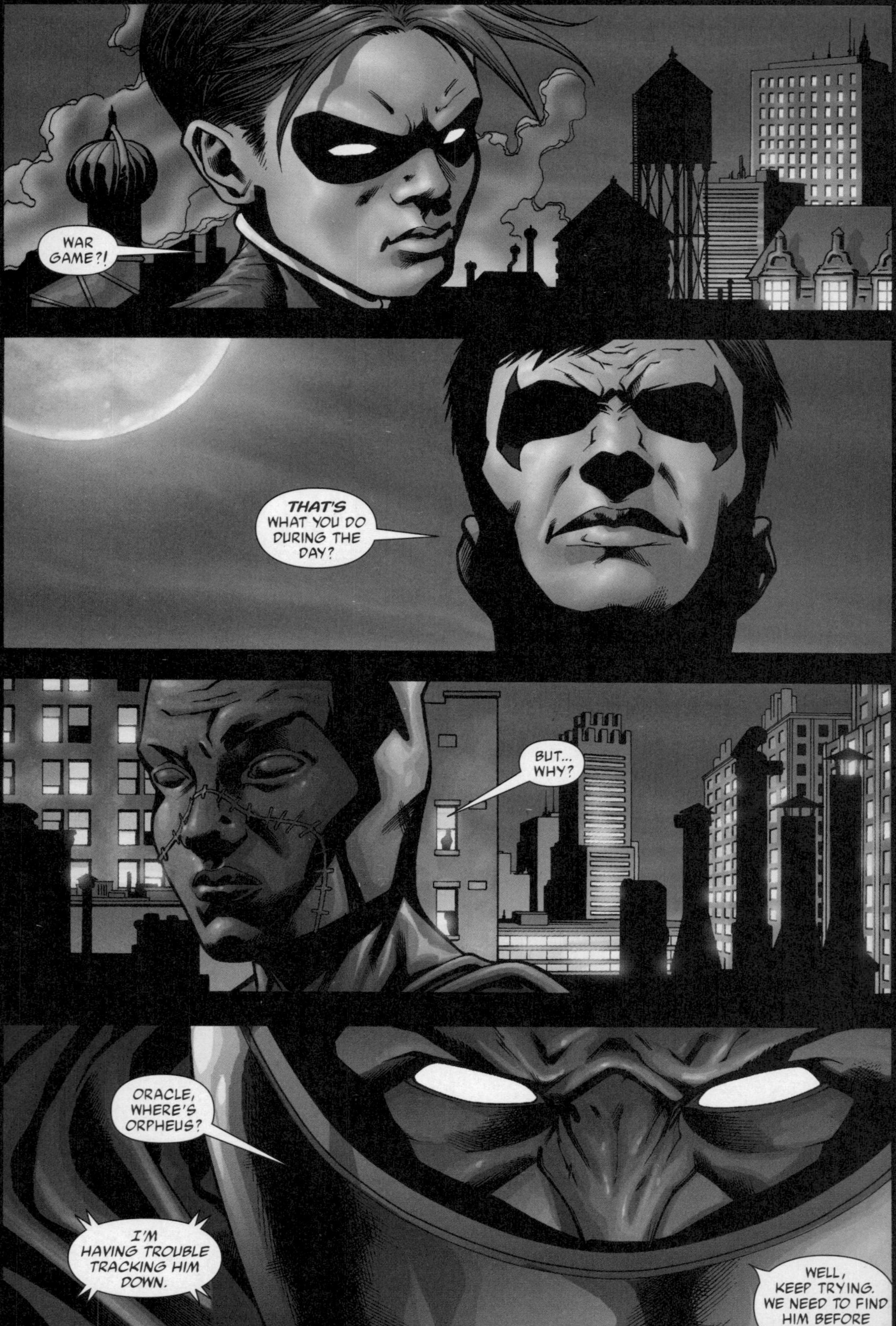
WAR GAME?!
THAT'S WHAT YOU DO DURING THE DAY?
BUT... WHY?
ORACLE, WHERE'S ORPHEUS?
I'M HAVING TROUBLE TRACKING HIM DOWN.
WELL, KEEP TRYING. WE NEED TO FIND HIM BEFORE ANYTHING--

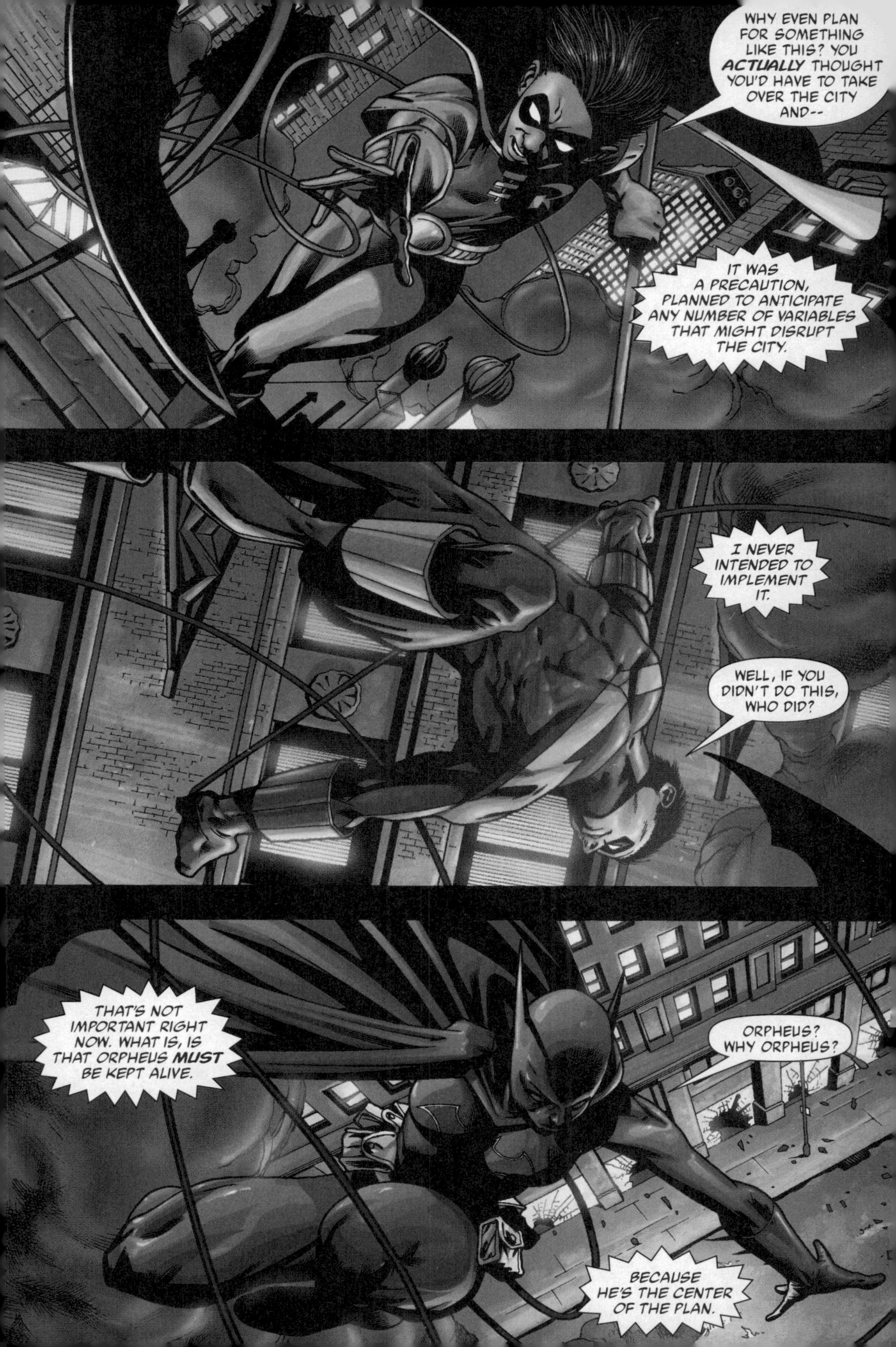
WHY EVEN PLAN FOR SOMETHING LIKE THIS? YOU ACTUALLY THOUGHT YOU'D HAVE TO TAKE OVER THE CITY AND--
IT WAS A PRECAUTION, PLANNED TO ANTICIPATE ANY NUMBER OF VARIABLES THAT MIGHT DISRUPT THE CITY.
I NEVER INTENDED TO IMPLEMENT IT.
WELL, IF YOU DIDN'T DO THIS, WHO DID?
THAT'S NOT IMPORTANT RIGHT NOW. WHAT IS, IS THAT ORPHEUS MUST BE KEPT ALIVE.
ORPHEUS? WHY ORPHEUS?
BECAUSE HE'S THE CENTER OF THE PLAN.

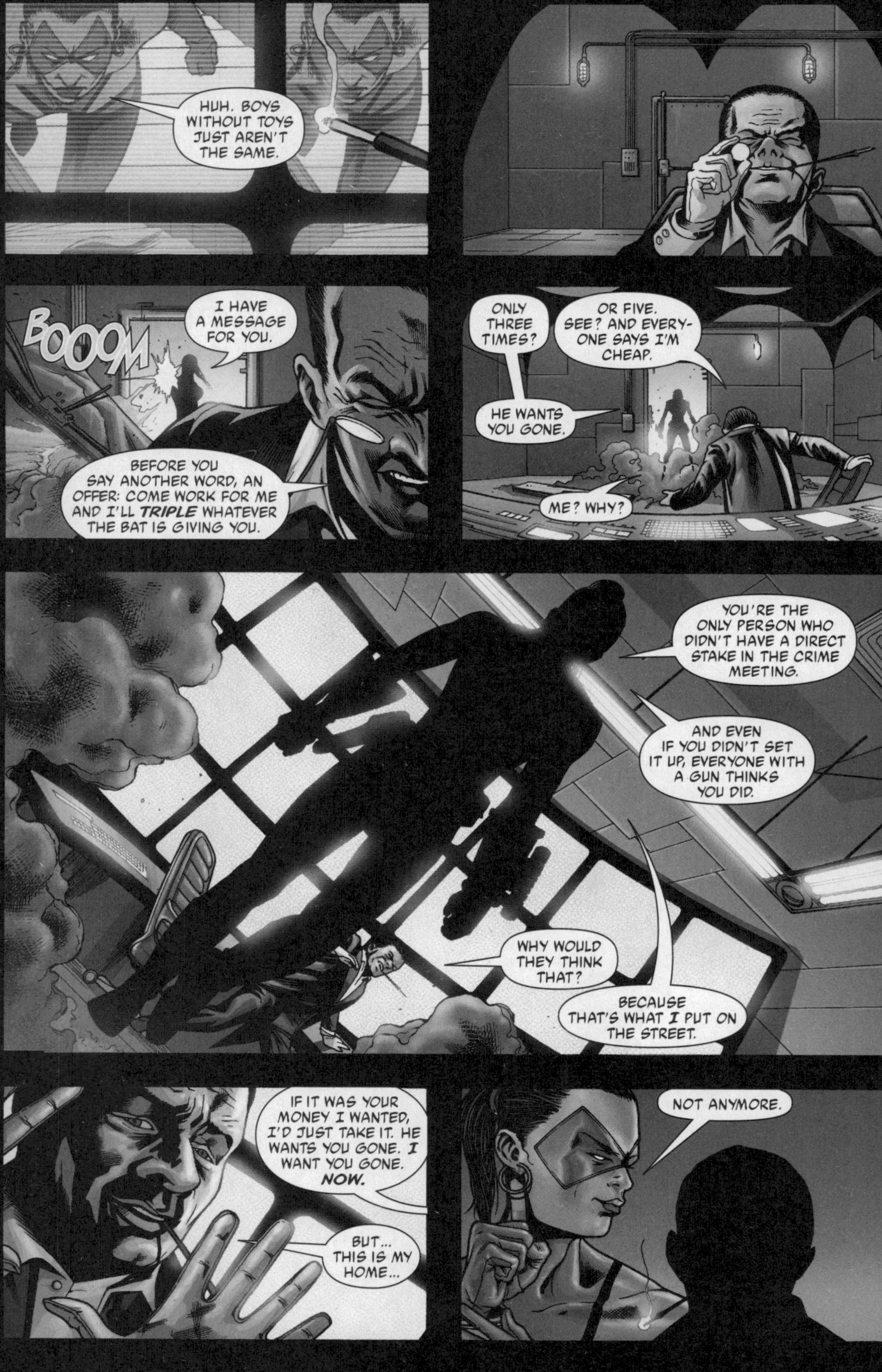
HUH. BOYS WITHOUT TOYS JUST AREN'T THE SAME.
BOOOM
I HAVE A MESSAGE FOR YOU.
BEFORE YOU SAY ANOTHER WORD, AN OFFER: COME WORK FOR ME AND I'LL TRIPLE WHATEVER THE BAT IS GIVING YOU.
ONLY THREE TIMES?
OR FIVE. SEE? AND EVERY-ONE SAYS I'M CHEAP.
HE WANTS YOU GONE.
ME? WHY?
YOU'RE THE ONLY PERSON WHO DIDN'T HAVE A DIRECT STAKE IN THE CRIME MEETING.
AND EVEN IF YOU DIDN'T SET IT UP, EVERYONE WITH A GUN THINKS YOU DID.
WHY WOULD THEY THINK THAT?
BECAUSE THAT'S WHAT I PUT ON THE STREET.
IF IT WAS YOUR MONEY I WANTED, I'D JUST TAKE IT. HE WANTS YOU GONE. I WANT YOU GONE. NOW.
BUT... THIS IS MY HOME...
NOT ANYMORE.

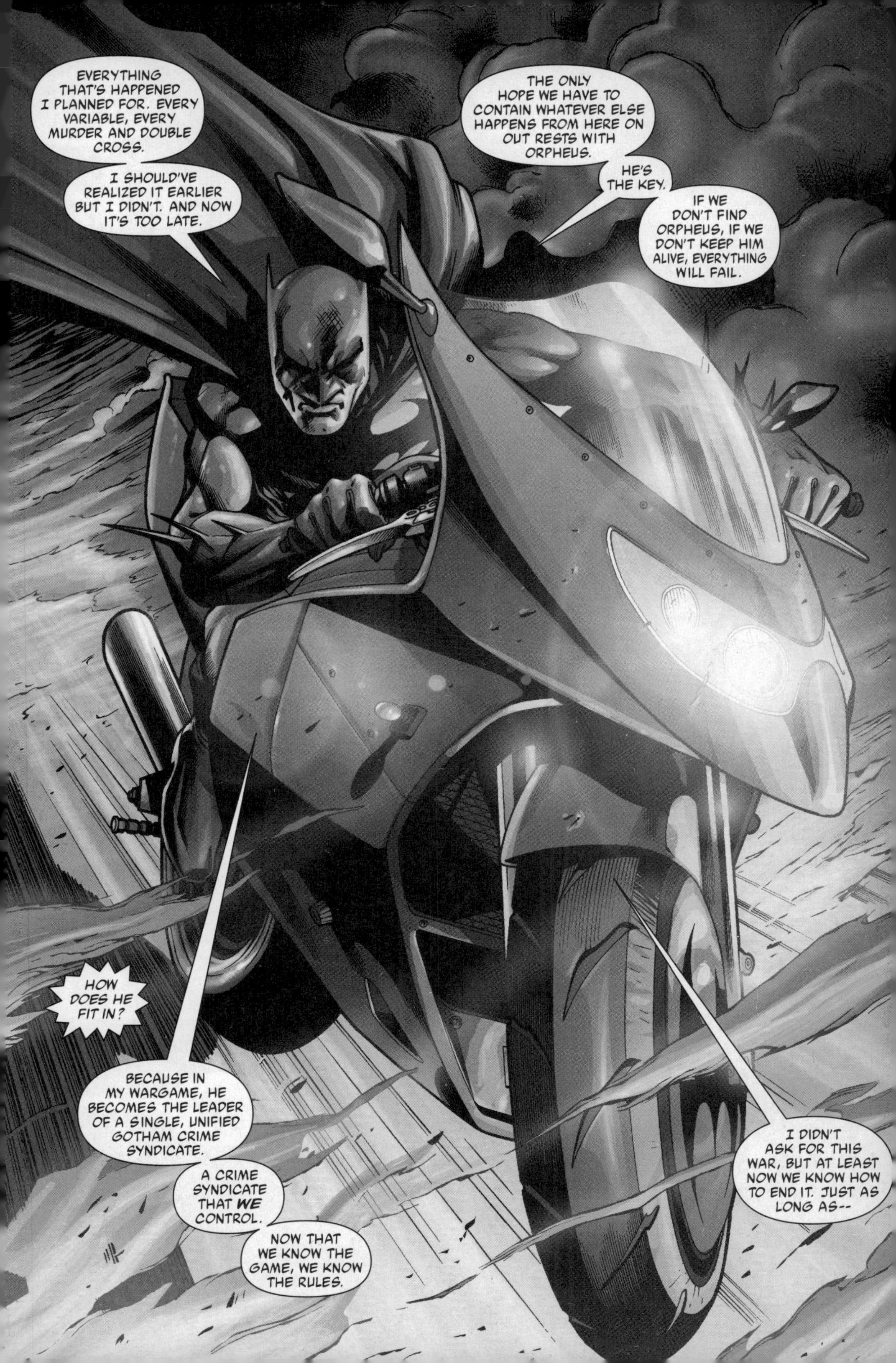
EVERYTHING THAT'S HAPPENED I PLANNED FOR. EVERY VARIABLE, EVERY MURDER AND DOUBLE CROSS.
I SHOULD'VE REALIZED IT EARLIER BUT I DIDN'T. AND NOW IT'S TOO LATE.
THE ONLY HOPE WE HAVE TO CONTAIN WHATEVER ELSE HAPPENS FROM HERE ON OUT RESTS WITH ORPHEUS.
HE'S THE KEY.
IF WE DON'T FIND ORPHEUS, IF WE DON'T KEEP HIM ALIVE, EVERYTHING WILL FAIL.
HOW DOES HE FIT IN?
BECAUSE IN MY WARGAME, HE BECOMES THE LEADER OF A SINGLE, UNIFIED GOTHAM CRIME SYNDICATE.
A CRIME SYNDICATE THAT ***WE*** CONTROL.
NOW THAT WE KNOW THE GAME, WE KNOW THE RULES.
I DIDN'T ASK FOR THIS WAR, BUT AT LEAST NOW WE KNOW HOW TO END IT. JUST AS LONG AS--

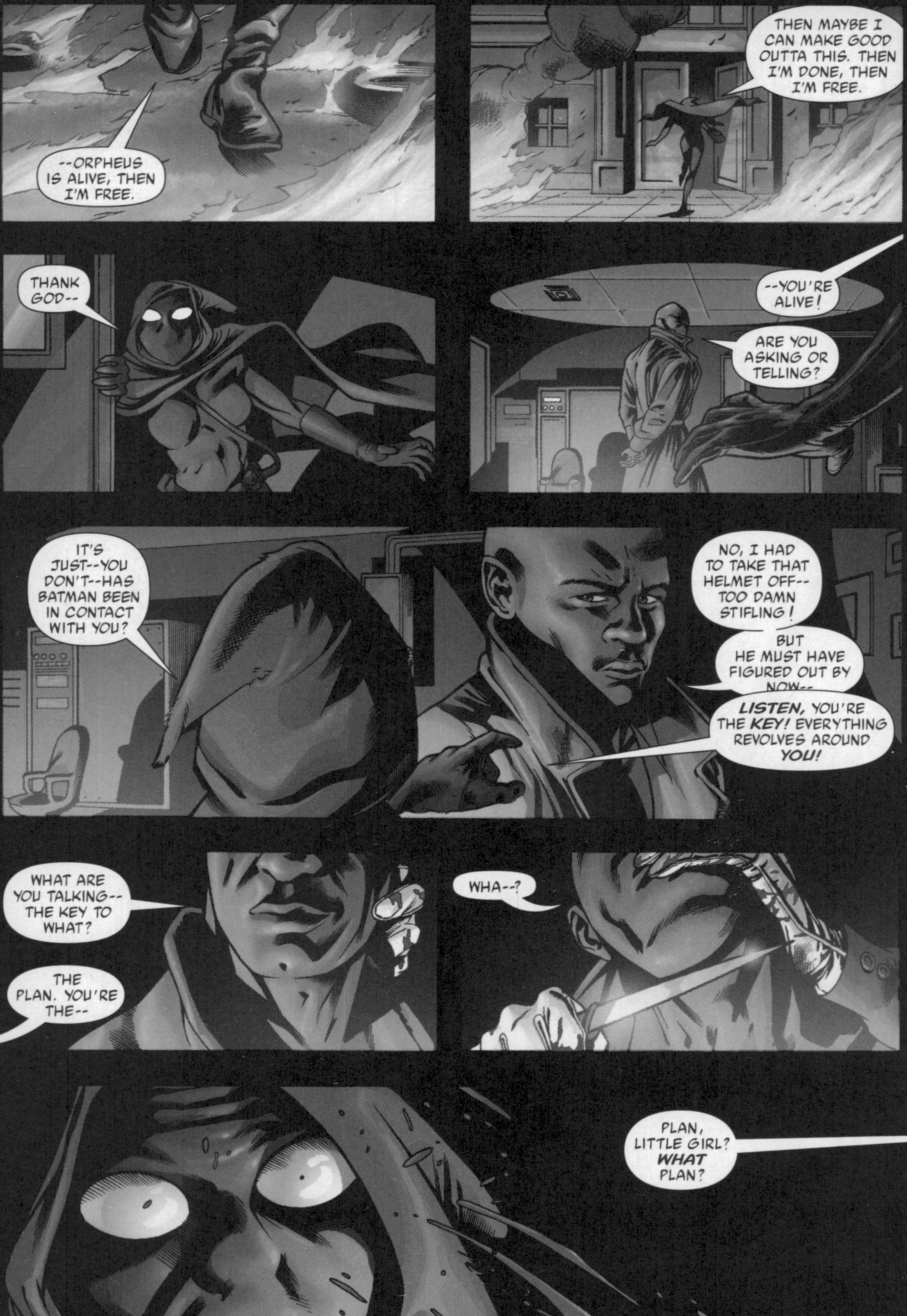
--ORPHEUS IS ALIVE, THEN I'M FREE.
THEN MAYBE I CAN MAKE GOOD OUTTA THIS. THEN I'M DONE, THEN I'M FREE.
THANK GOD--
--YOU'RE ALIVE!
ARE YOU ASKING OR TELLING?
IT'S JUST--YOU DON'T--HAS BATMAN BEEN IN CONTACT WITH YOU?
NO, I HAD TO TAKE THAT HELMET OFF--TOO DAMN STIFLING!
BUT HE MUST HAVE FIGURED OUT BY NOW--
LISTEN, YOU'RE THE KEY! EVERYTHING REVOLVES AROUND YOU!
WHAT ARE YOU TALKING--THE KEY TO WHAT?
THE PLAN. YOU'RE THE--
WHA--?
PLAN, LITTLE GIRL? WHAT PLAN?

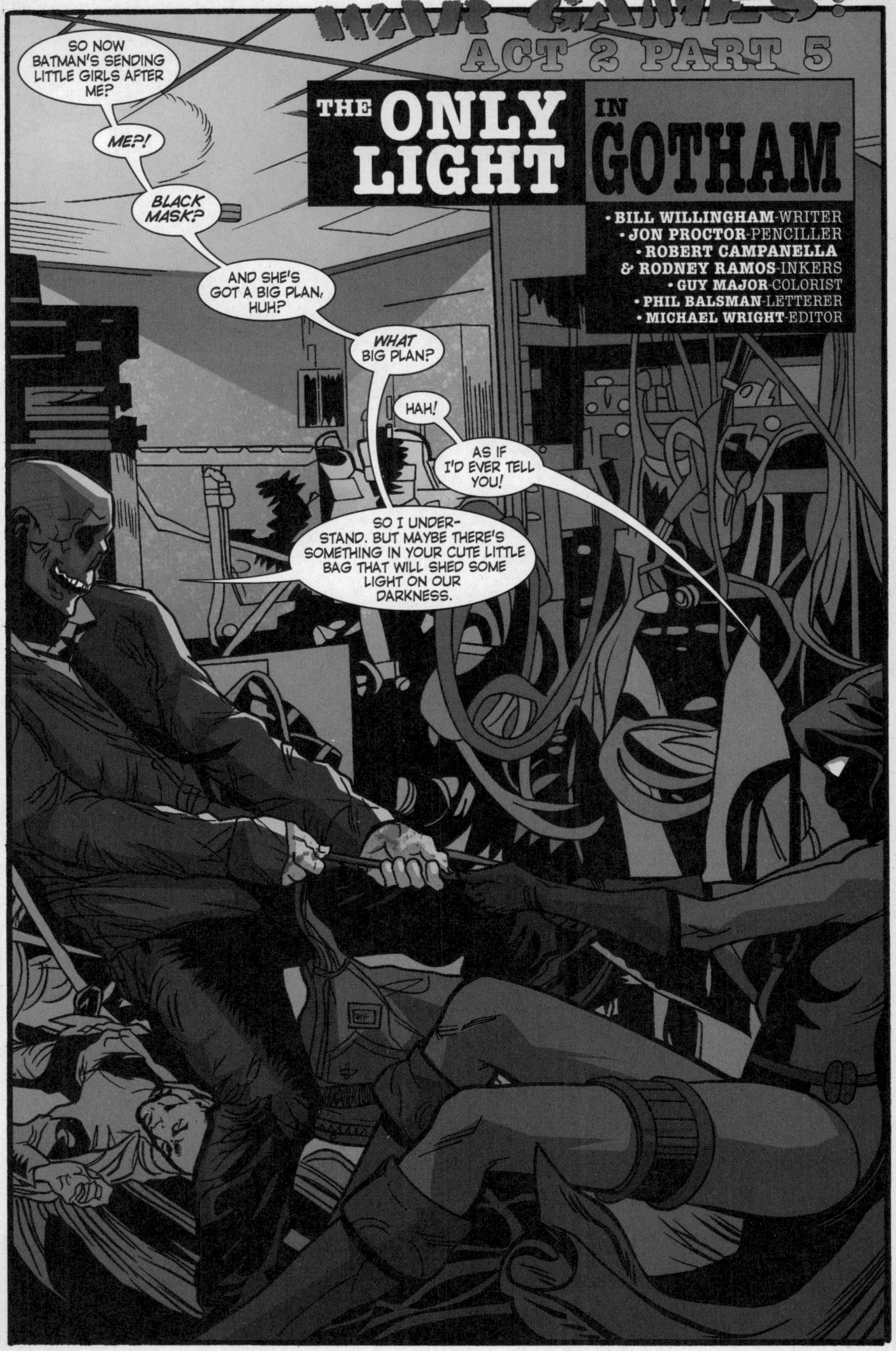
WAR GAMES:
ACT 2 PART 5
THE ONLY LIGHT IN GOTHAM
• BILL WILLINGHAM-WRITER
• JON PROCTOR-PENCILLER
• ROBERT CAMPANELLA & RODNEY RAMOS-INKERS
• GUY MAJOR-COLORIST
• PHIL BALSMAN-LETTERER
• MICHAEL WRIGHT-EDITOR
SO NOW BATMAN'S SENDING LITTLE GIRLS AFTER ME?
ME?!
BLACK MASK?
AND SHE'S GOT A BIG PLAN, HUH?
WHAT BIG PLAN?
HAH!
AS IF I'D EVER TELL YOU!
SO I UNDER-STAND. BUT MAYBE THERE'S SOMETHING IN YOUR CUTE LITTLE BAG THAT WILL SHED SOME LIGHT ON OUR DARKNESS.

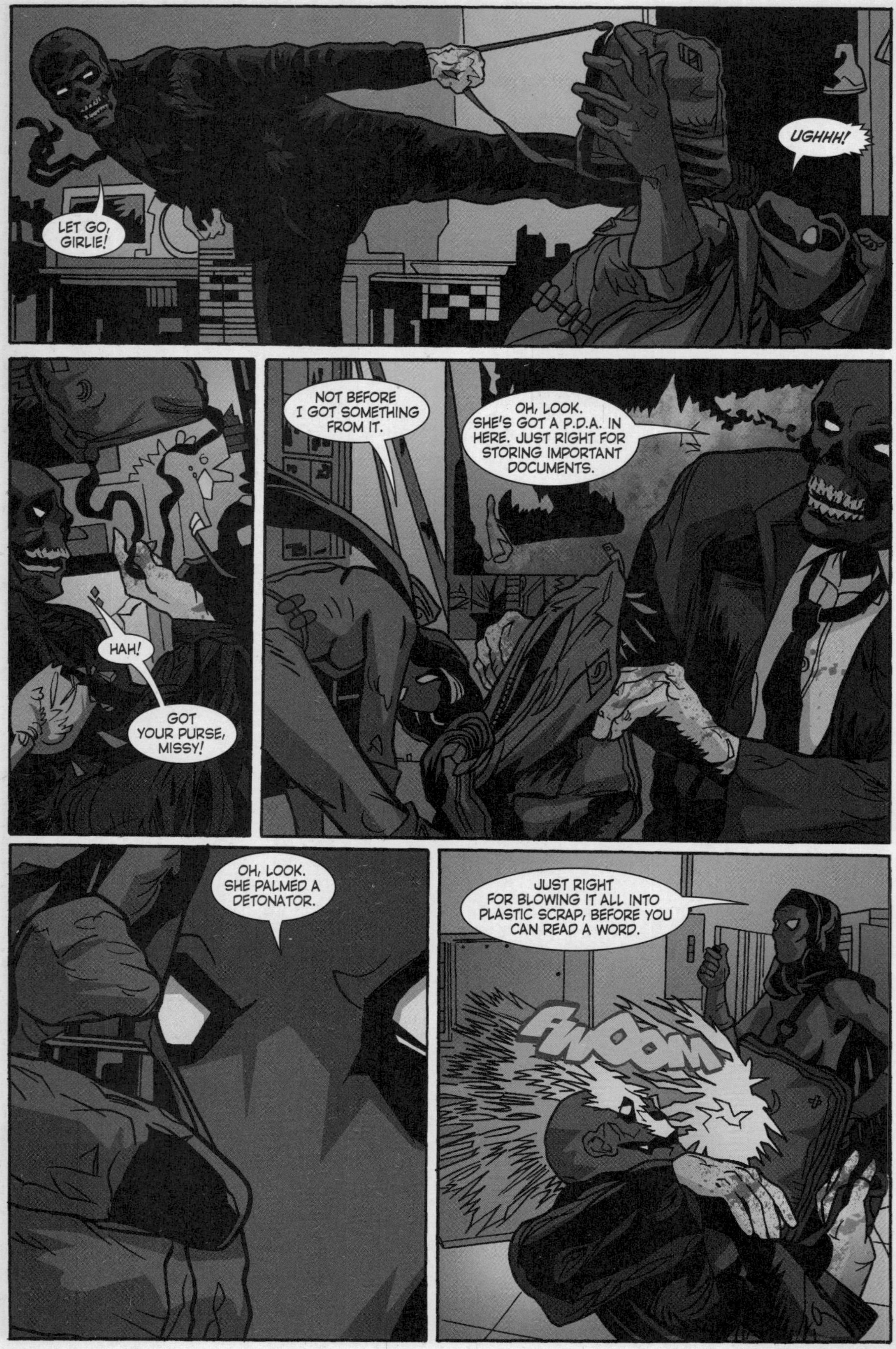
UGHHH!
LET GO, GIRLIE!
HAH!
GOT YOUR PURSE, MISSY!
NOT BEFORE I GOT SOMETHING FROM IT.
OH, LOOK. SHE'S GOT A P.D.A. IN HERE. JUST RIGHT FOR STORING IMPORTANT DOCUMENTS.
OH, LOOK. SHE PALMED A DETONATOR.
JUST RIGHT FOR BLOWING IT ALL INTO PLASTIC SCRAP, BEFORE YOU CAN READ A WORD.
FWOOM

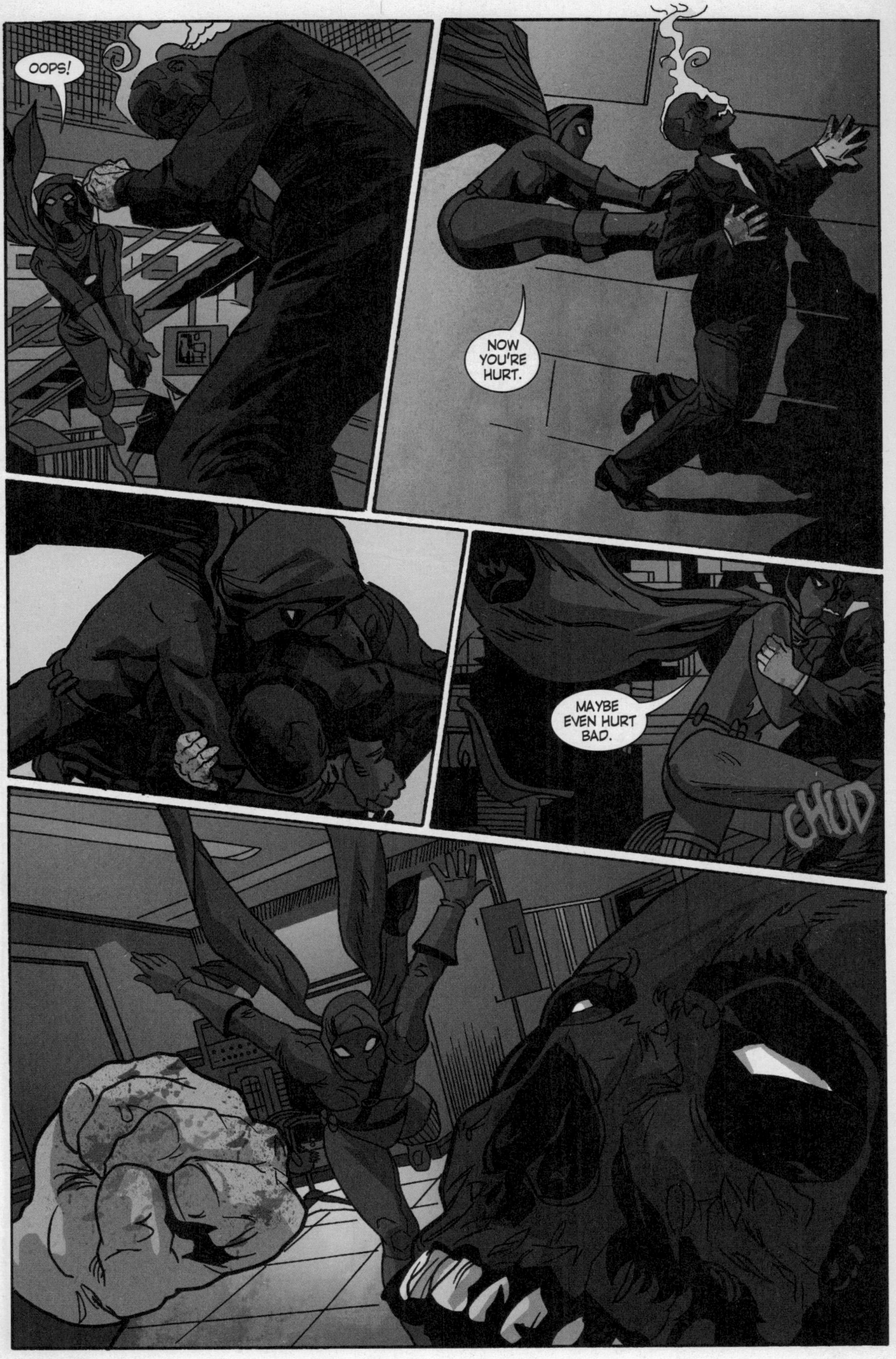
OOPS!
NOW YOU'RE HURT.
MAYBE EVEN HURT BAD.
CHUD

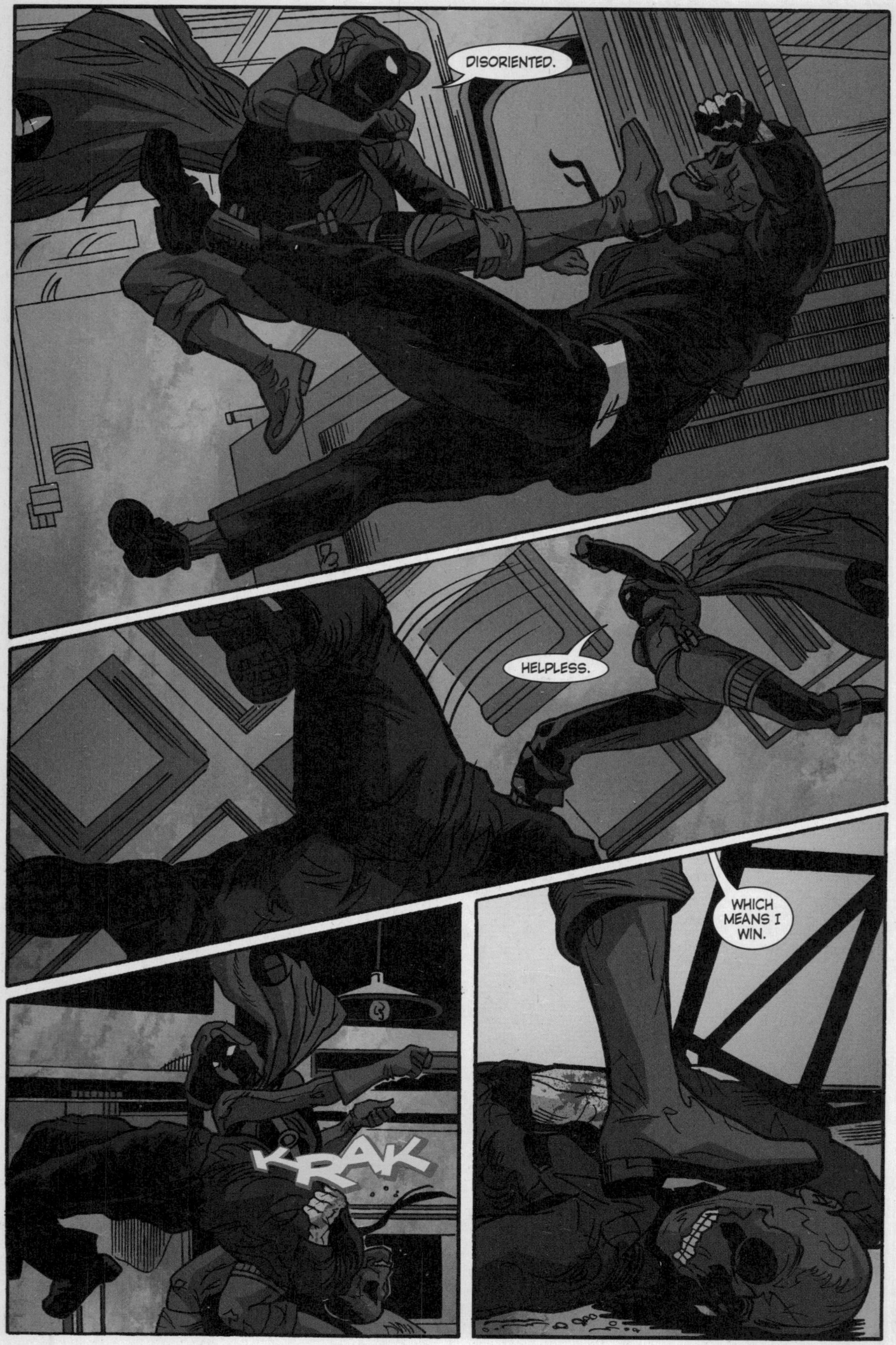
DISORIENTED.
HELPLESS.
KRAK
WHICH MEANS I WIN.

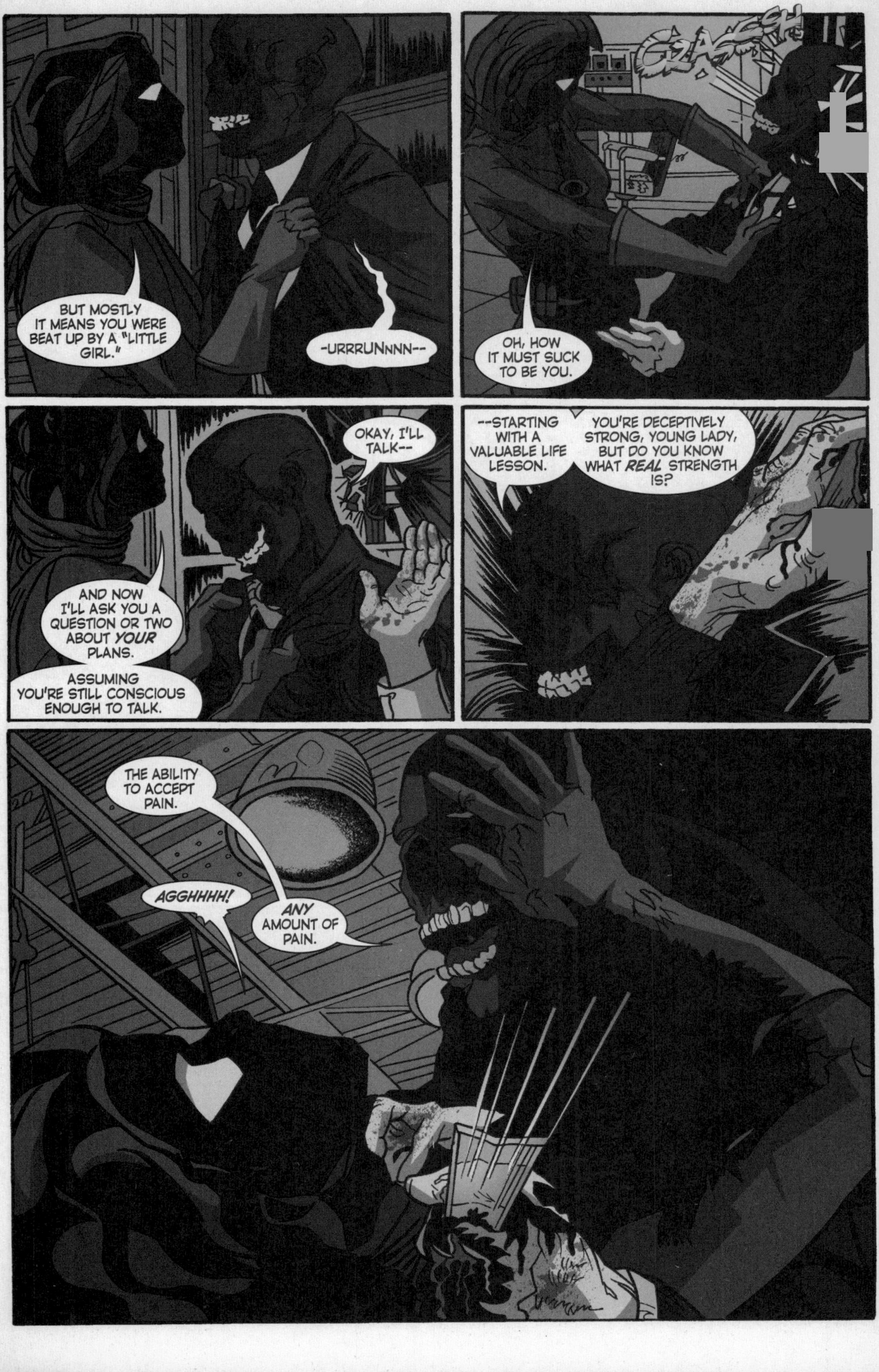
BUT MOSTLY IT MEANS YOU WERE BEAT UP BY A "LITTLE GIRL."
-URRRUNNNN--
OH, HOW IT MUST SUCK TO BE YOU.
OKAY, I'LL TALK--
AND NOW I'LL ASK YOU A QUESTION OR TWO ABOUT *YOUR* PLANS.
ASSUMING YOU'RE STILL CONSCIOUS ENOUGH TO TALK.
YOU'RE DECEPTIVELY STRONG, YOUNG LADY, BUT DO YOU KNOW WHAT *REAL* STRENGTH IS?
--STARTING WITH A VALUABLE LIFE LESSON.
THE ABILITY TO ACCEPT PAIN.
AGGHHHH!
ANY AMOUNT OF PAIN.

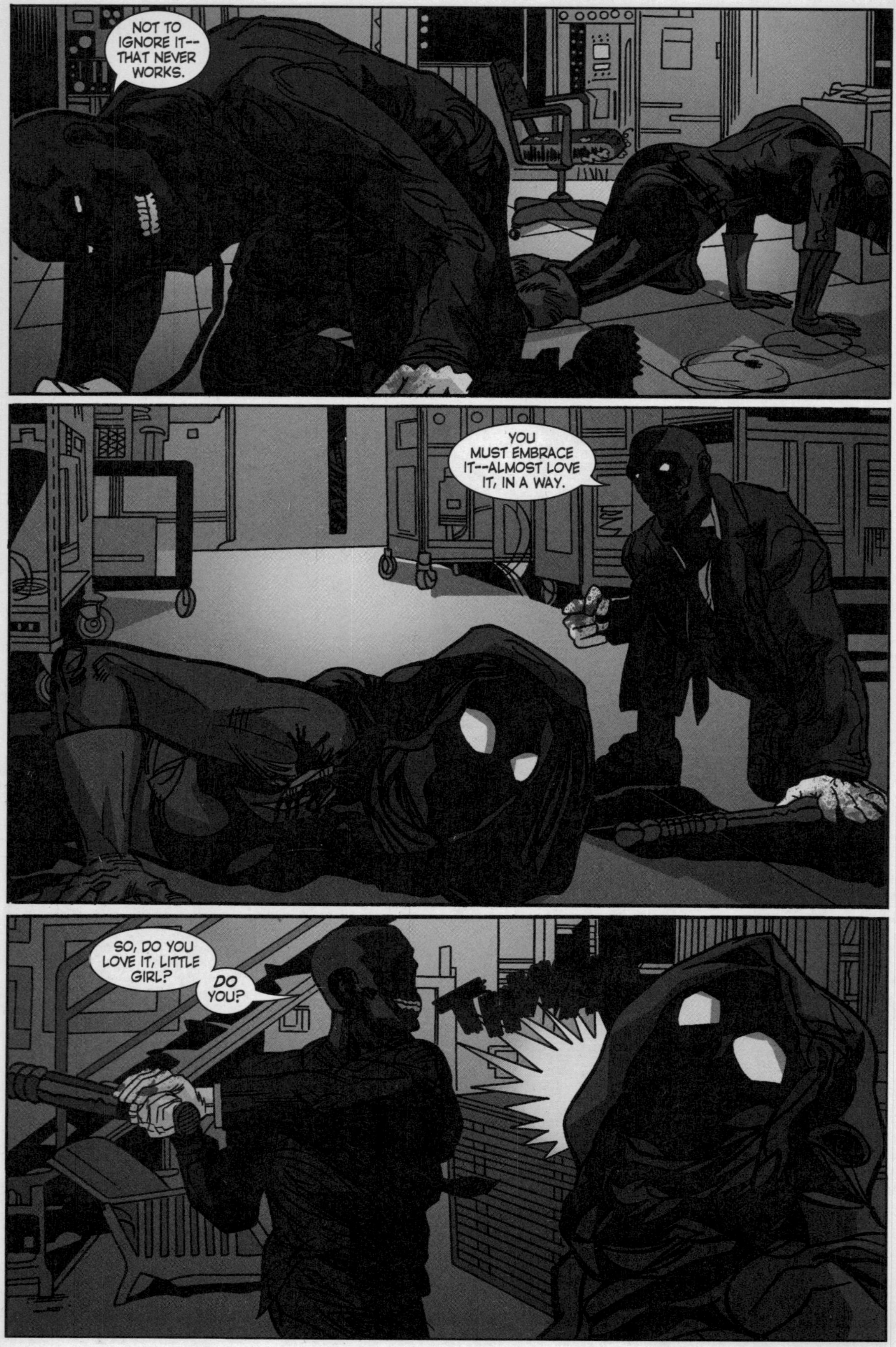
NOT TO IGNORE IT--THAT NEVER WORKS.
YOU MUST EMBRACE IT--ALMOST LOVE IT, IN A WAY.
SO, DO YOU LOVE IT, LITTLE GIRL?
DO YOU?

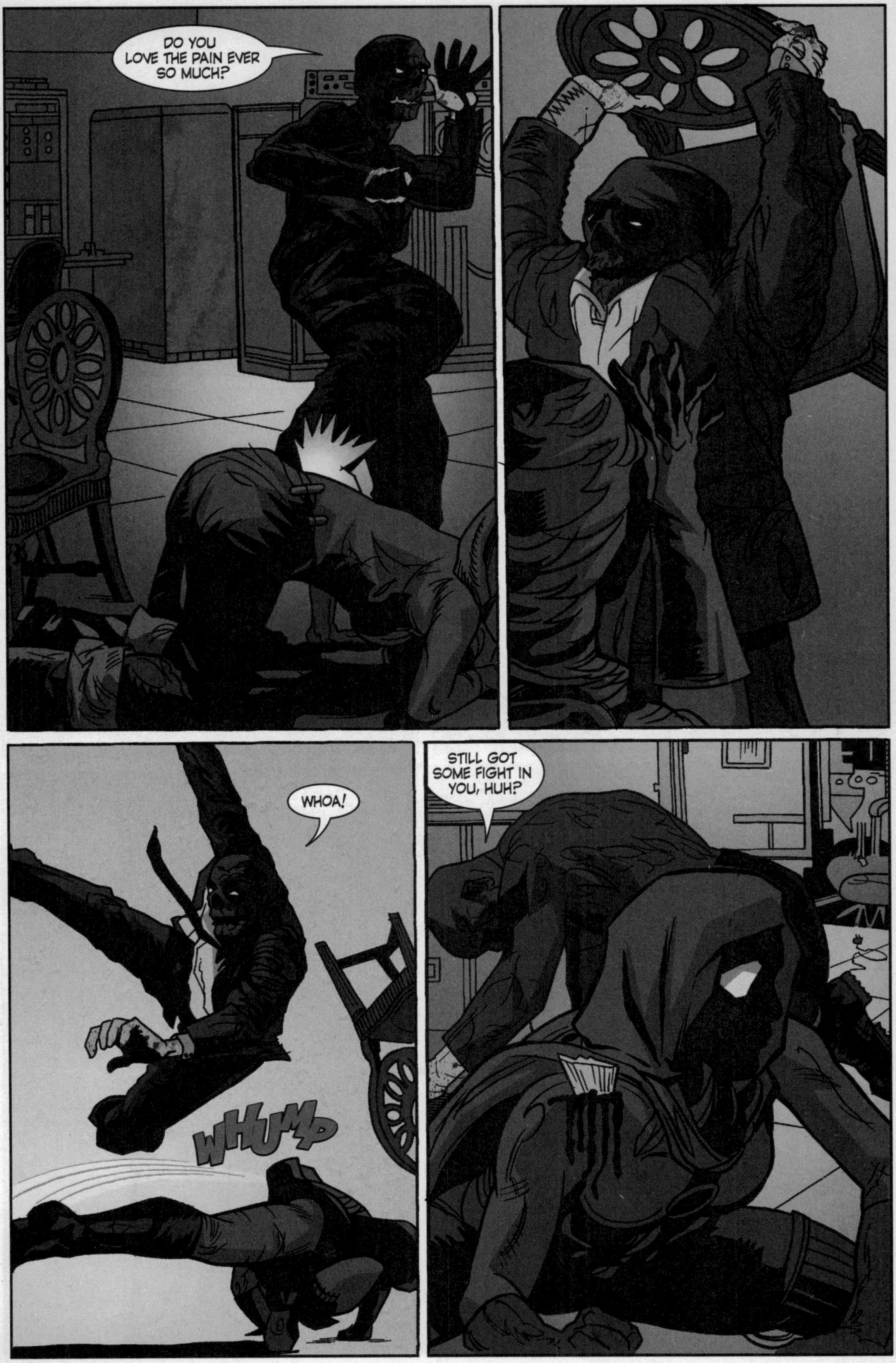
DO YOU LOVE THE PAIN EVER SO MUCH?
WHOA!
WHUMP
STILL GOT SOME FIGHT IN YOU, HUH?

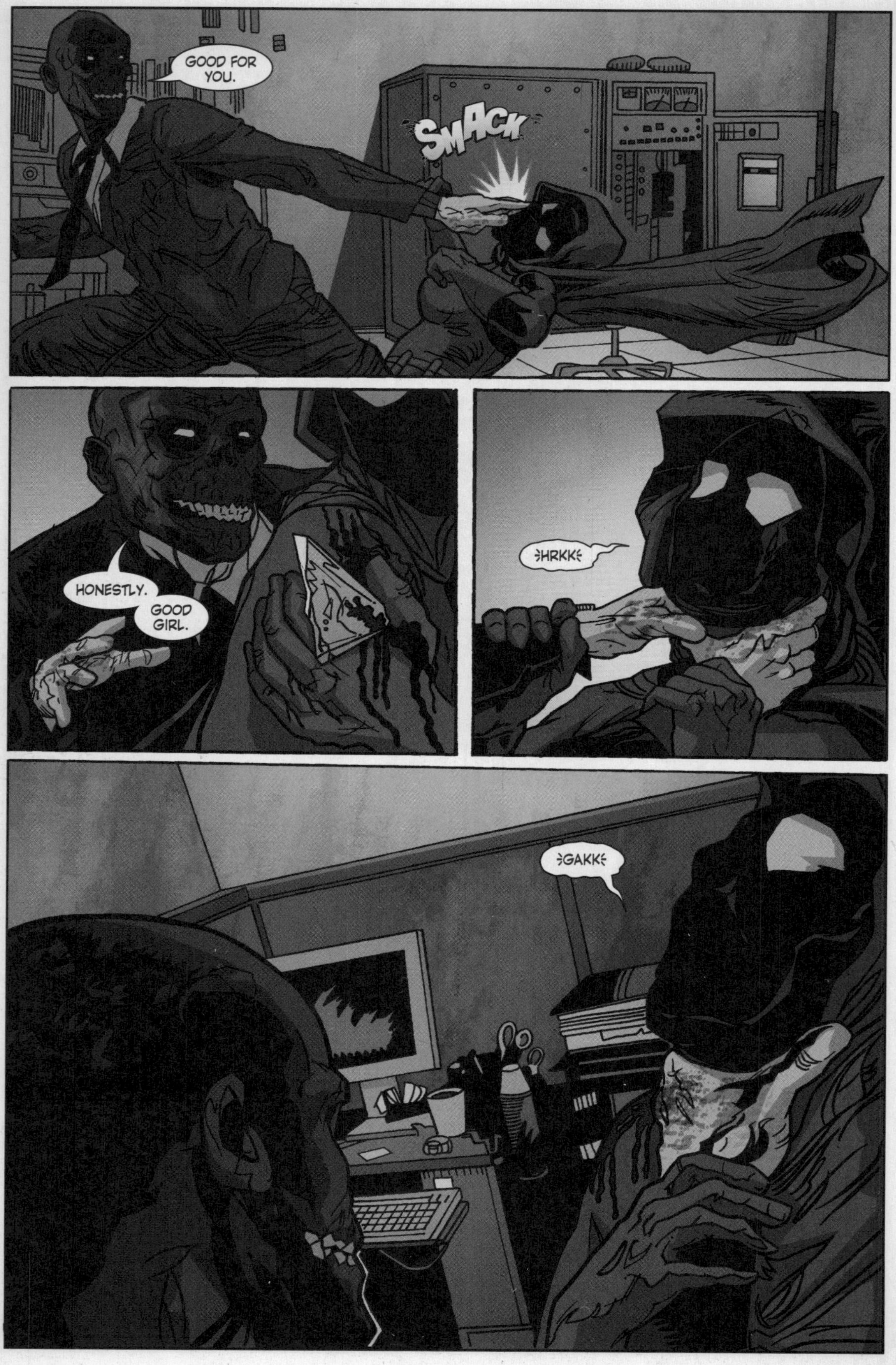
GOOD FOR YOU.
SMACK
HONESTLY.
GOOD GIRL.
HRKK
GAKK

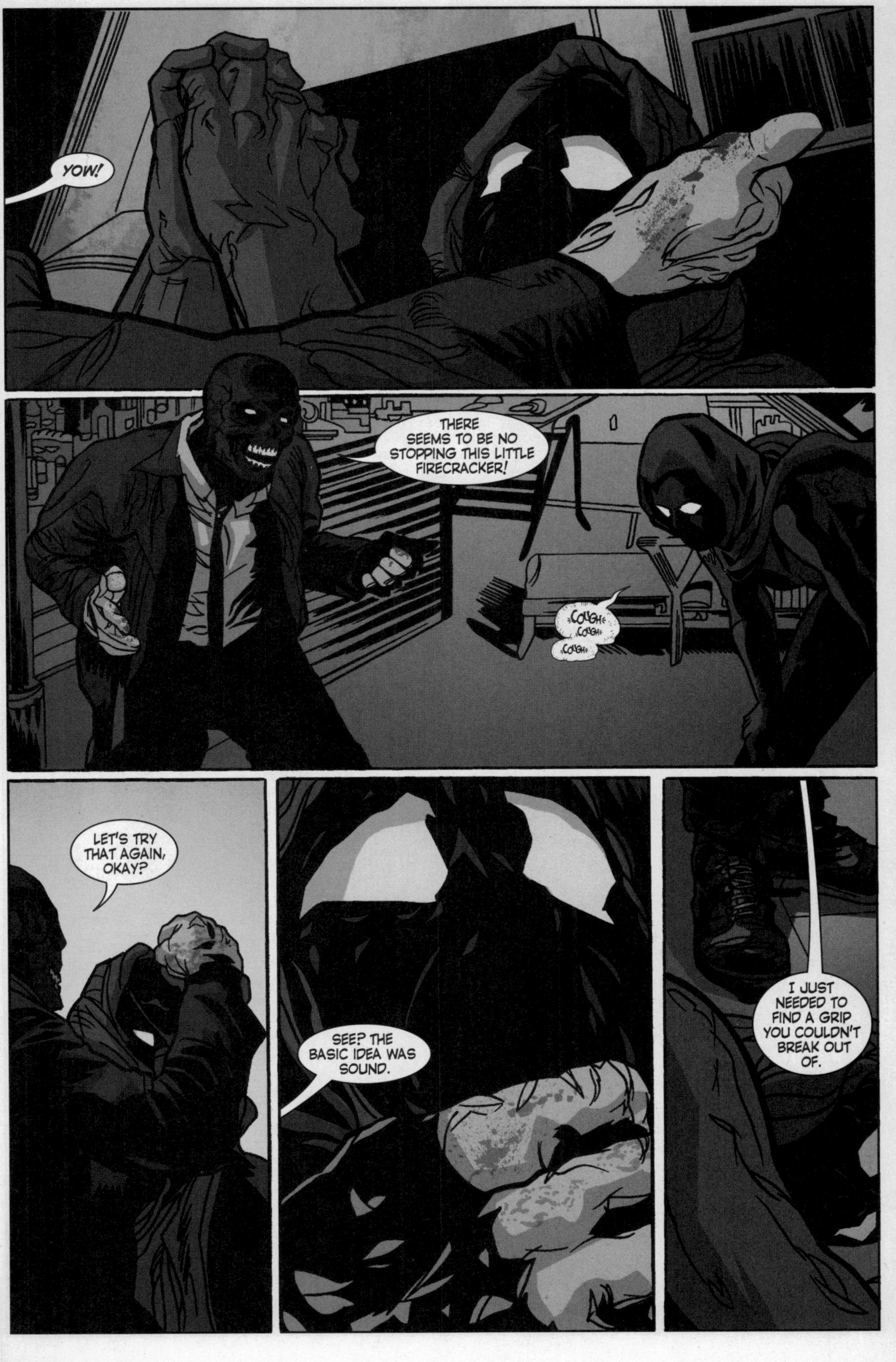
YOW!
THERE SEEMS TO BE NO STOPPING THIS LITTLE FIRECRACKER!
COUGH COUGH COUGH
LET'S TRY THAT AGAIN, OKAY?
SEE? THE BASIC IDEA WAS SOUND.
I JUST NEEDED TO FIND A GRIP YOU COULDN'T BREAK OUT OF.

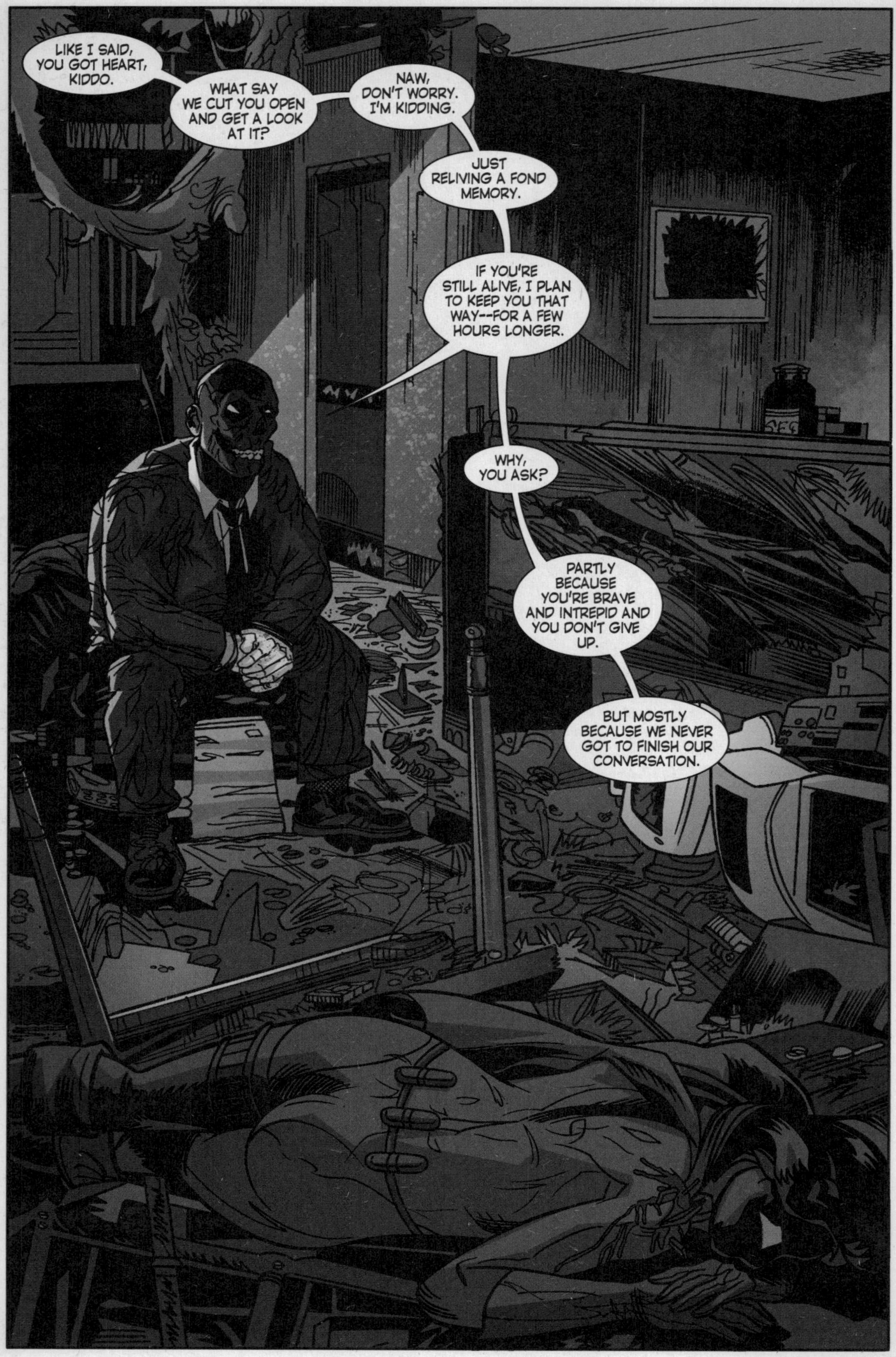
LIKE I SAID, YOU GOT HEART, KIDDO.
WHAT SAY WE CUT YOU OPEN AND GET A LOOK AT IT?
NAW, DON'T WORRY. I'M KIDDING.
JUST RELIVING A FOND MEMORY.
IF YOU'RE STILL ALIVE, I PLAN TO KEEP YOU THAT WAY--FOR A FEW HOURS LONGER.
WHY, YOU ASK?
PARTLY BECAUSE YOU'RE BRAVE AND INTREPID AND YOU DON'T GIVE UP.
BUT MOSTLY BECAUSE WE NEVER GOT TO FINISH OUR CONVERSATION.

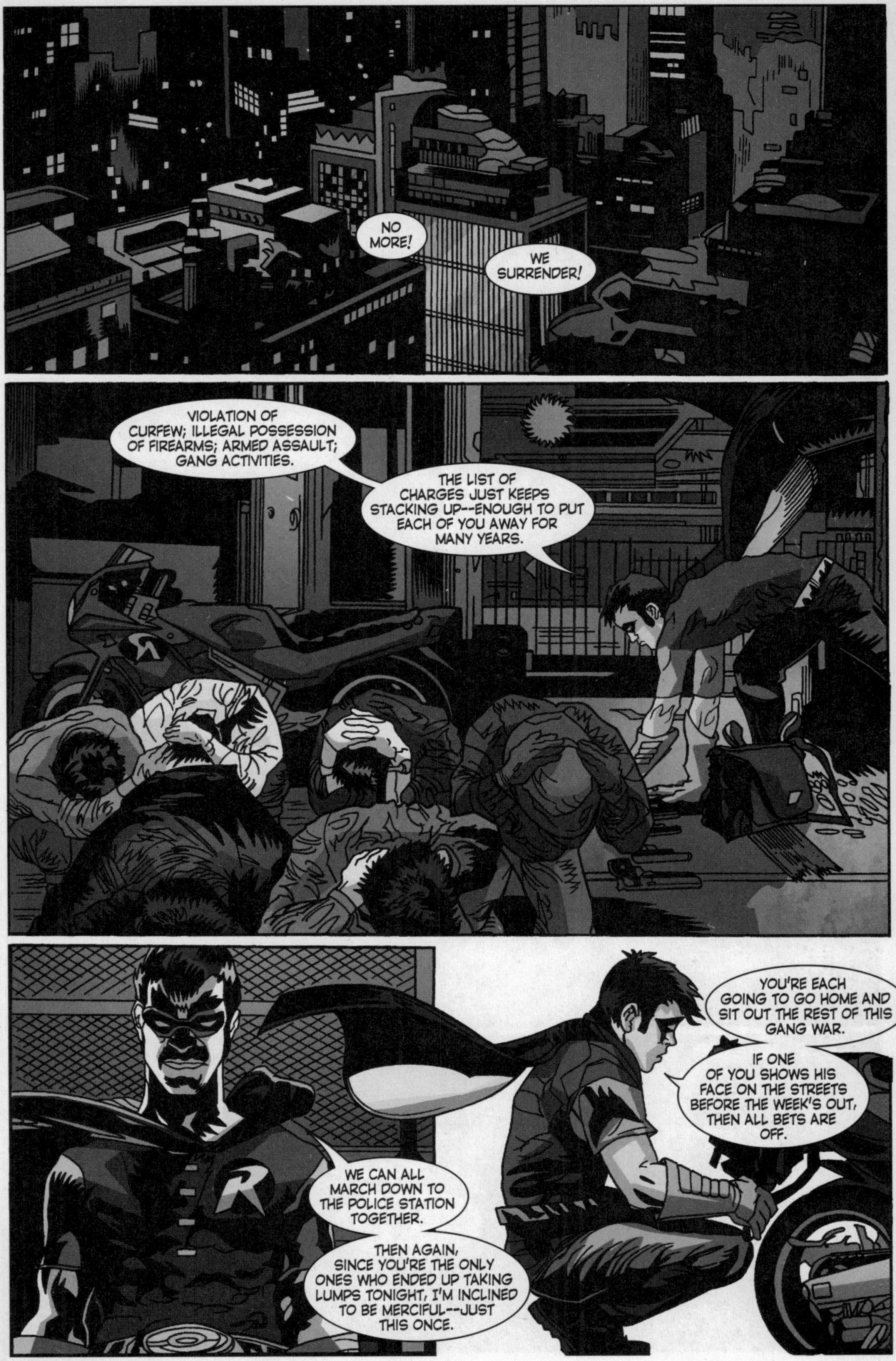
NO MORE!
WE SURRENDER!
VIOLATION OF CURFEW; ILLEGAL POSSESSION OF FIREARMS; ARMED ASSAULT; GANG ACTIVITIES.
THE LIST OF CHARGES JUST KEEPS STACKING UP--ENOUGH TO PUT EACH OF YOU AWAY FOR MANY YEARS.
WE CAN ALL MARCH DOWN TO THE POLICE STATION TOGETHER.
THEN AGAIN, SINCE YOU'RE THE ONLY ONES WHO ENDED UP TAKING LUMPS TONIGHT, I'M INCLINED TO BE MERCIFUL--JUST THIS ONCE.
YOU'RE EACH GOING TO GO HOME AND SIT OUT THE REST OF THIS GANG WAR.
IF ONE OF YOU SHOWS HIS FACE ON THE STREETS BEFORE THE WEEK'S OUT, THEN ALL BETS ARE OFF.

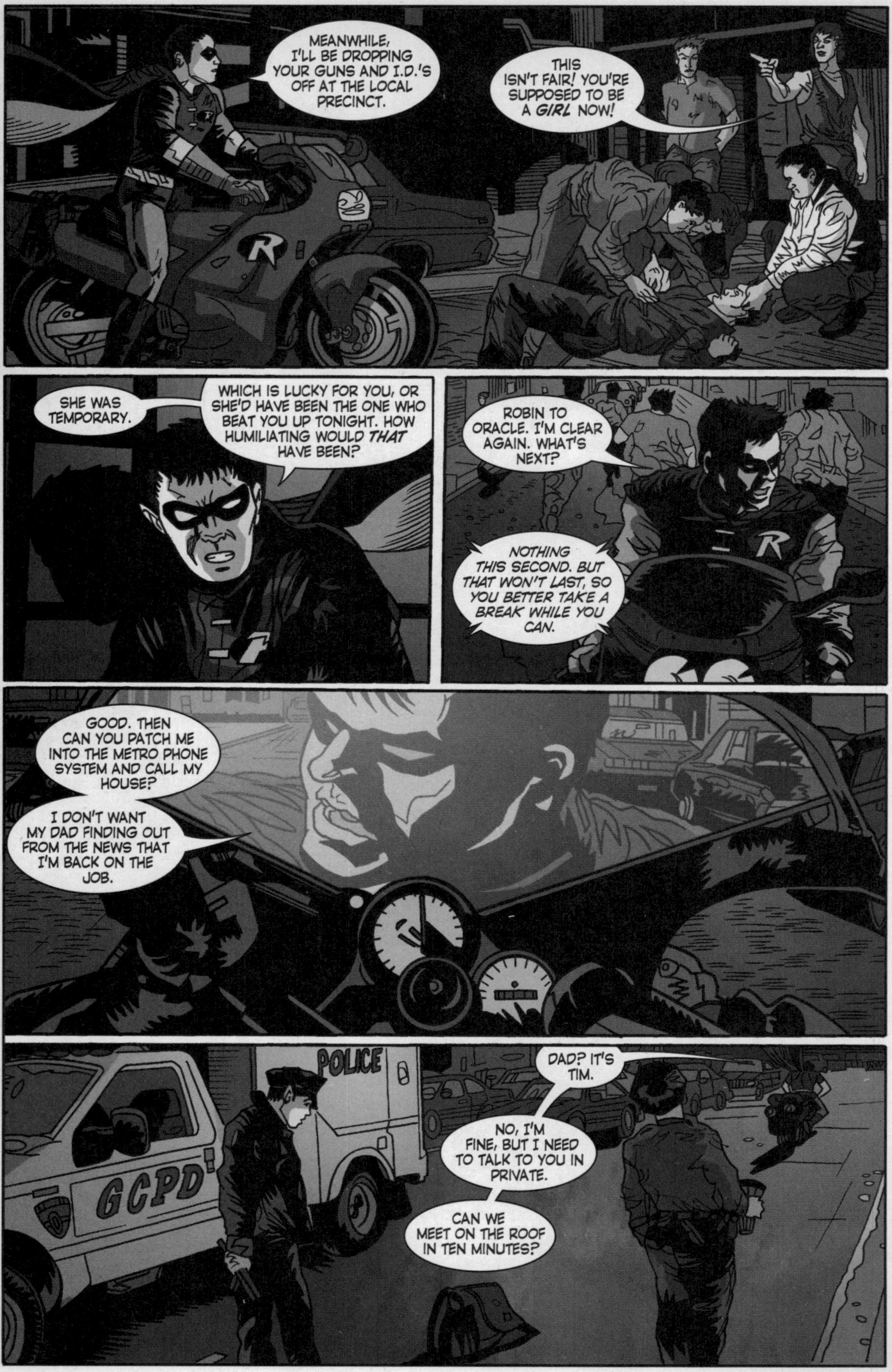
MEANWHILE, I'LL BE DROPPING YOUR GUNS AND I.D.'S OFF AT THE LOCAL PRECINCT.
THIS ISN'T FAIR! YOU'RE SUPPOSED TO BE A *GIRL* NOW!
SHE WAS TEMPORARY.
WHICH IS LUCKY FOR YOU, OR SHE'D HAVE BEEN THE ONE WHO BEAT YOU UP TONIGHT. HOW HUMILIATING WOULD *THAT* HAVE BEEN?
ROBIN TO ORACLE. I'M CLEAR AGAIN. WHAT'S NEXT?
NOTHING THIS SECOND. BUT THAT WON'T LAST, SO YOU BETTER TAKE A BREAK WHILE YOU CAN.
GOOD. THEN CAN YOU PATCH ME INTO THE METRO PHONE SYSTEM AND CALL MY HOUSE?
I DON'T WANT MY DAD FINDING OUT FROM THE NEWS THAT I'M BACK ON THE JOB.
POLICE
GCPD
DAD? IT'S TIM.
NO, I'M FINE, BUT I NEED TO TALK TO YOU IN PRIVATE.
CAN WE MEET ON THE ROOF IN TEN MINUTES?

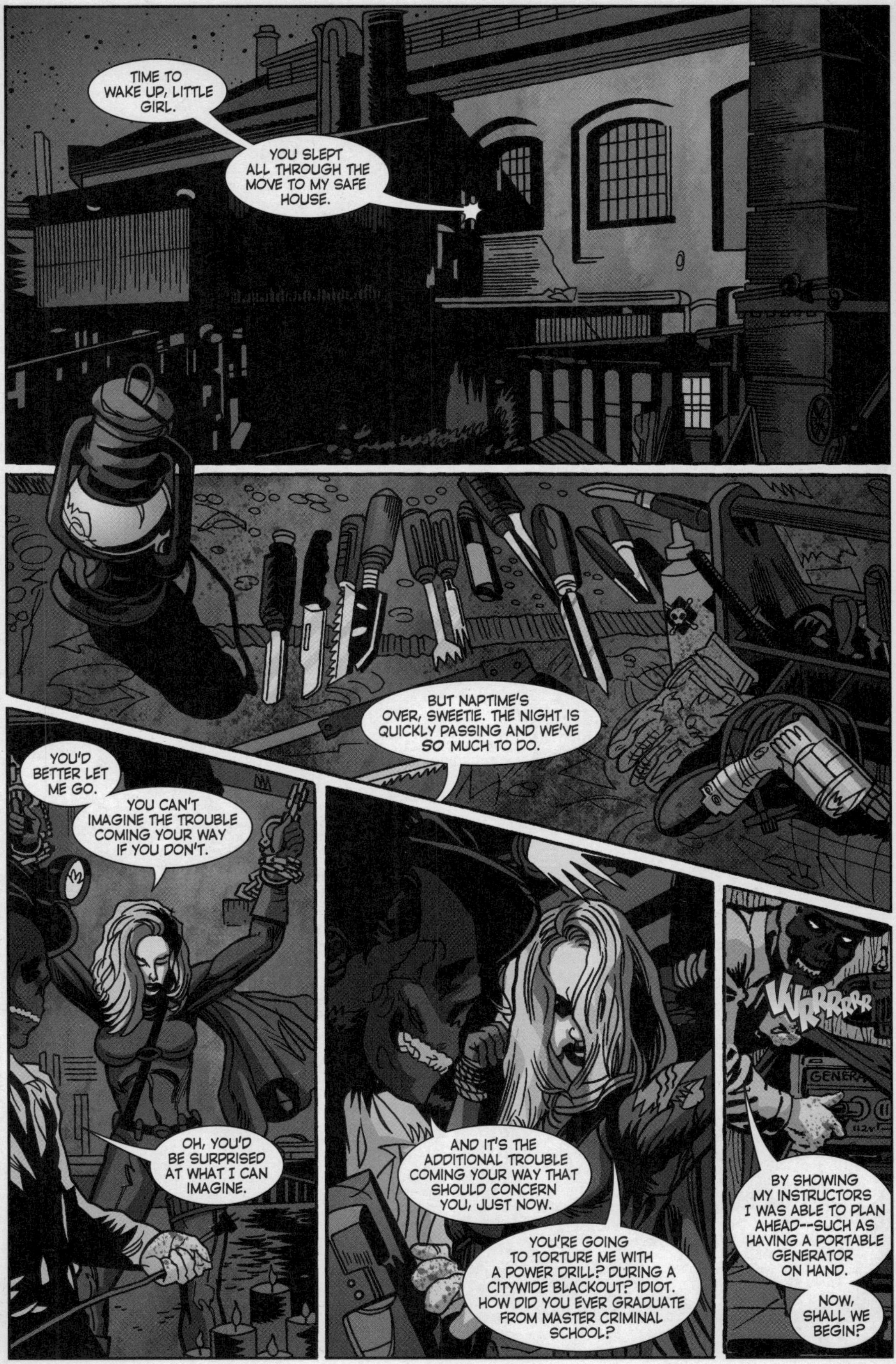
TIME TO WAKE UP, LITTLE GIRL.
YOU SLEPT ALL THROUGH THE MOVE TO MY SAFE HOUSE.
BUT NAPTIME'S OVER, SWEETIE. THE NIGHT IS QUICKLY PASSING AND WE'VE SO MUCH TO DO.
YOU'D BETTER LET ME GO.
YOU CAN'T IMAGINE THE TROUBLE COMING YOUR WAY IF YOU DON'T.
OH, YOU'D BE SURPRISED AT WHAT I CAN IMAGINE.
AND IT'S THE ADDITIONAL TROUBLE COMING YOUR WAY THAT SHOULD CONCERN YOU, JUST NOW.
YOU'RE GOING TO TORTURE ME WITH A POWER DRILL? DURING A CITYWIDE BLACKOUT? IDIOT. HOW DID YOU EVER GRADUATE FROM MASTER CRIMINAL SCHOOL?
WRRRRRR
GENERA
BY SHOWING MY INSTRUCTORS I WAS ABLE TO PLAN AHEAD--SUCH AS HAVING A PORTABLE GENERATOR ON HAND.
NOW, SHALL WE BEGIN?

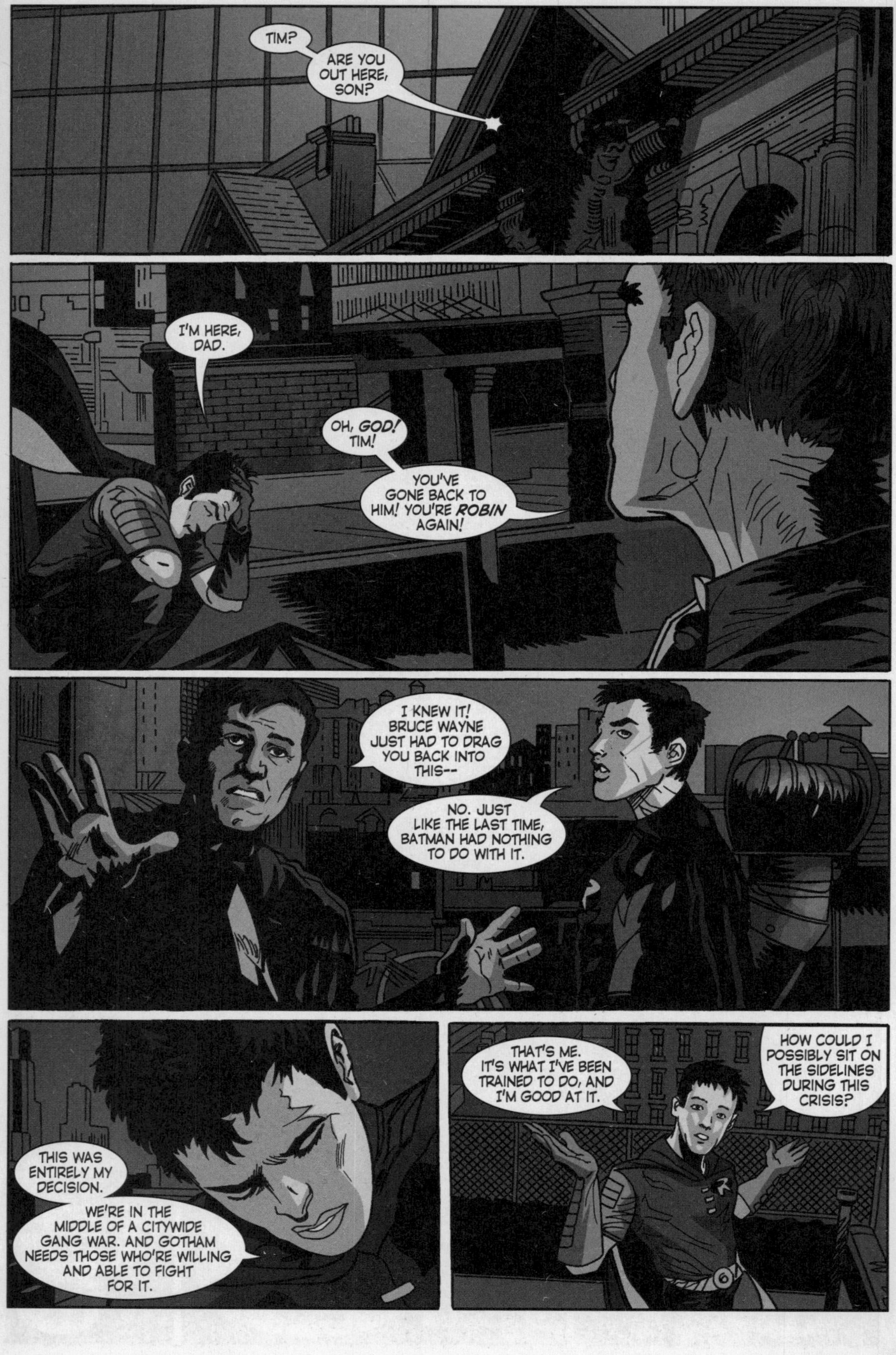
TIM?
ARE YOU OUT HERE, SON?
I'M HERE, DAD.
OH, *GOD!* TIM!
YOU'VE GONE BACK TO HIM! YOU'RE *ROBIN* AGAIN!
I KNEW IT! BRUCE WAYNE JUST HAD TO DRAG YOU BACK INTO THIS--
NO. JUST LIKE THE LAST TIME, BATMAN HAD NOTHING TO DO WITH IT.
THIS WAS ENTIRELY MY DECISION.
WE'RE IN THE MIDDLE OF A CITYWIDE GANG WAR. AND GOTHAM NEEDS THOSE WHO'RE WILLING AND ABLE TO FIGHT FOR IT.
THAT'S ME. IT'S WHAT I'VE BEEN TRAINED TO DO, AND I'M GOOD AT IT.
HOW COULD I POSSIBLY SIT ON THE SIDELINES DURING THIS CRISIS?

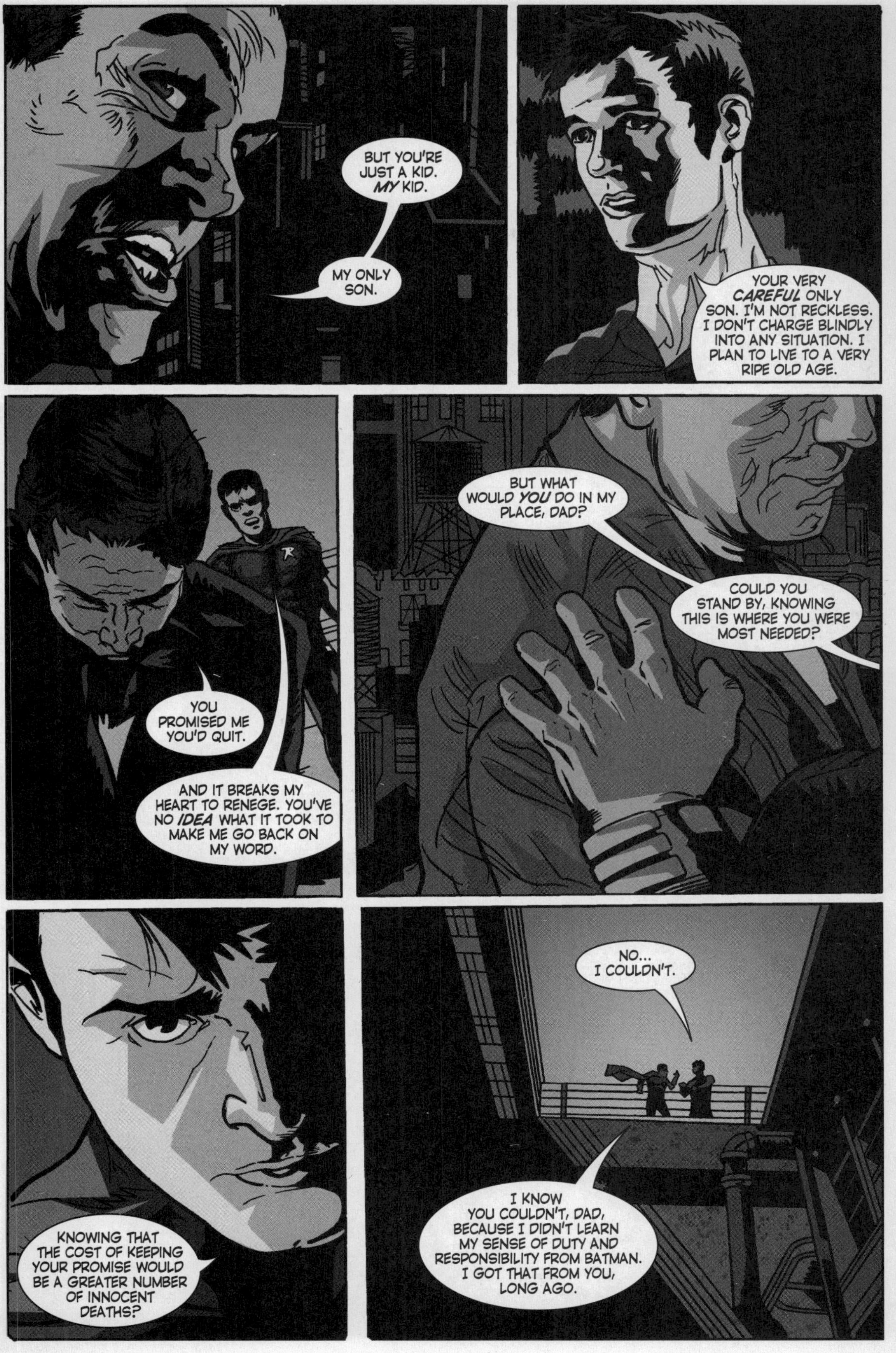
BUT YOU'RE JUST A KID. *MY* KID.
MY ONLY SON.
YOUR VERY *CAREFUL* ONLY SON. I'M NOT RECKLESS. I DON'T CHARGE BLINDLY INTO ANY SITUATION. I PLAN TO LIVE TO A VERY RIPE OLD AGE.
YOU PROMISED ME YOU'D QUIT.
AND IT BREAKS MY HEART TO RENEGE. YOU'VE NO *IDEA* WHAT IT TOOK TO MAKE ME GO BACK ON MY WORD.
BUT WHAT WOULD *YOU* DO IN MY PLACE, DAD?
COULD YOU STAND BY, KNOWING THIS IS WHERE YOU WERE MOST NEEDED?
KNOWING THAT THE COST OF KEEPING YOUR PROMISE WOULD BE A GREATER NUMBER OF INNOCENT DEATHS?
NO... I COULDN'T.
I KNOW YOU COULDN'T, DAD, BECAUSE I DIDN'T LEARN MY SENSE OF DUTY AND RESPONSIBILITY FROM BATMAN. I GOT THAT FROM YOU, LONG AGO.

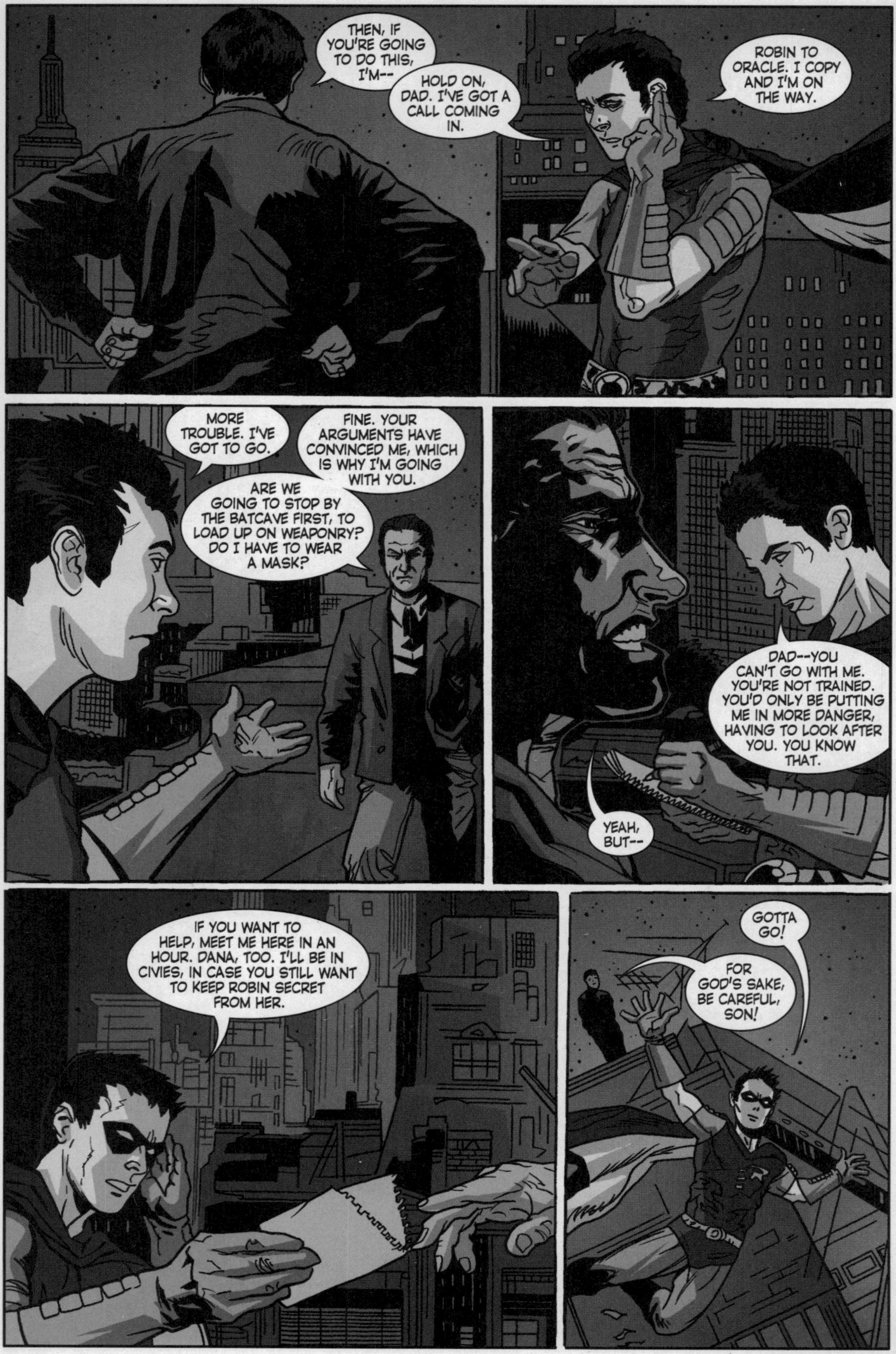
THEN, IF YOU'RE GOING TO DO THIS, I'M--
HOLD ON, DAD. I'VE GOT A CALL COMING IN.
ROBIN TO ORACLE. I COPY AND I'M ON THE WAY.
MORE TROUBLE. I'VE GOT TO GO.
FINE. YOUR ARGUMENTS HAVE CONVINCED ME, WHICH IS WHY I'M GOING WITH YOU.
ARE WE GOING TO STOP BY THE BATCAVE FIRST, TO LOAD UP ON WEAPONRY? DO I HAVE TO WEAR A MASK?
DAD--YOU CAN'T GO WITH ME. YOU'RE NOT TRAINED. YOU'D ONLY BE PUTTING ME IN MORE DANGER, HAVING TO LOOK AFTER YOU. YOU KNOW THAT.
YEAH, BUT--
IF YOU WANT TO HELP, MEET ME HERE IN AN HOUR. DANA, TOO. I'LL BE IN CIVIES, IN CASE YOU STILL WANT TO KEEP ROBIN SECRET FROM HER.
GOTTA GO!
FOR GOD'S SAKE, BE CAREFUL, SON!

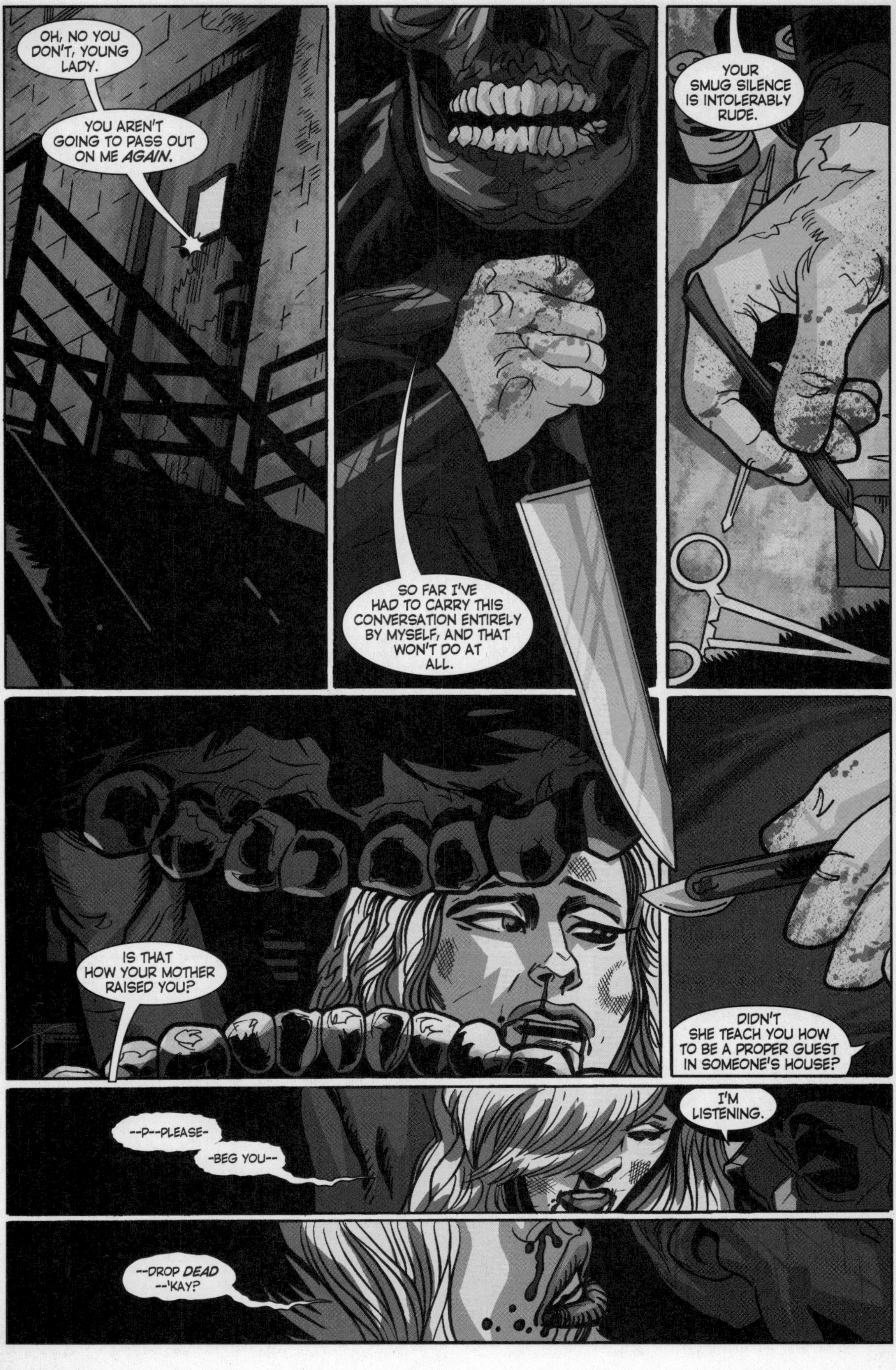
OH, NO YOU DON'T, YOUNG LADY.
YOU AREN'T GOING TO PASS OUT ON ME *AGAIN*.
SO FAR I'VE HAD TO CARRY THIS CONVERSATION ENTIRELY BY MYSELF, AND THAT WON'T DO AT ALL.
YOUR SMUG SILENCE IS INTOLERABLY RUDE.
IS THAT HOW YOUR MOTHER RAISED YOU?
DIDN'T SHE TEACH YOU HOW TO BE A PROPER GUEST IN SOMEONE'S HOUSE?
--P--PLEASE-
-BEG YOU--
I'M LISTENING.
--DROP *DEAD* --'KAY?

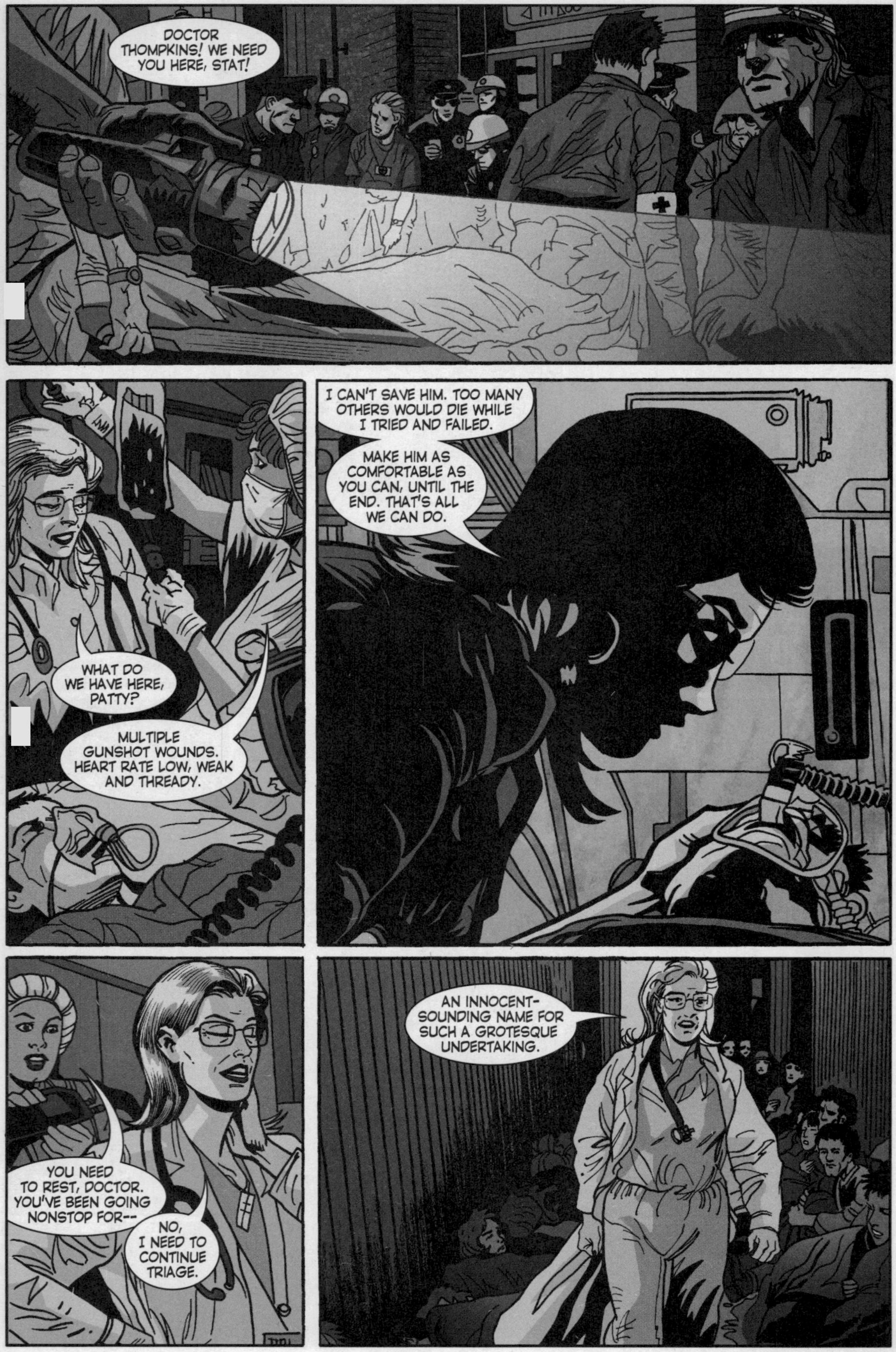
DOCTOR THOMPKINS! WE NEED YOU HERE, STAT!
WHAT DO WE HAVE HERE, PATTY?
MULTIPLE GUNSHOT WOUNDS. HEART RATE LOW, WEAK AND THREADY.
I CAN'T SAVE HIM. TOO MANY OTHERS WOULD DIE WHILE I TRIED AND FAILED.
MAKE HIM AS COMFORTABLE AS YOU CAN, UNTIL THE END. THAT'S ALL WE CAN DO.
YOU NEED TO REST, DOCTOR. YOU'VE BEEN GOING NONSTOP FOR--
NO, I NEED TO CONTINUE TRIAGE.
AN INNOCENT-SOUNDING NAME FOR SUCH A GROTESQUE UNDERTAKING.

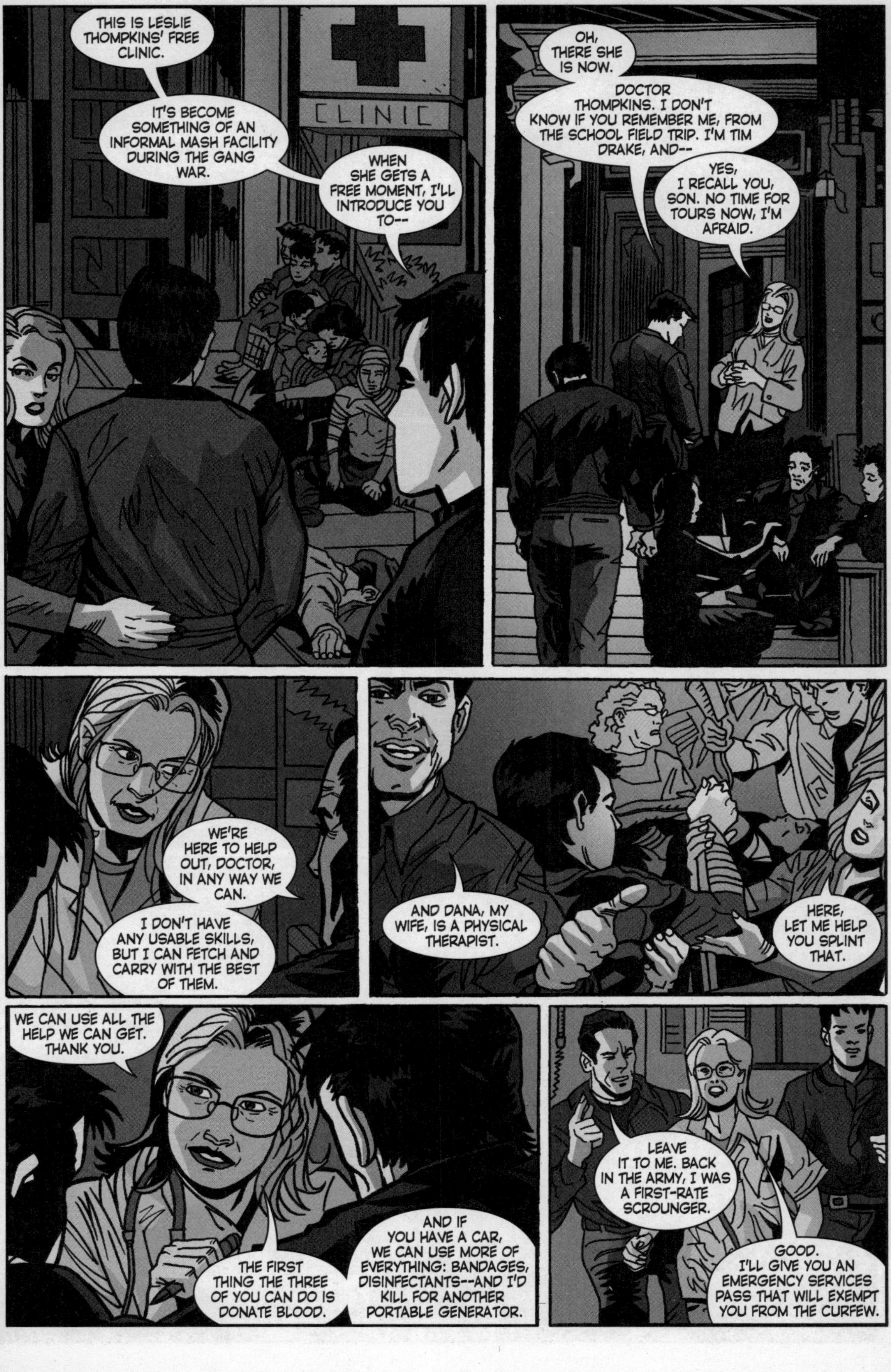
THIS IS LESLIE THOMPKINS' FREE CLINIC.
IT'S BECOME SOMETHING OF AN INFORMAL MASH FACILITY DURING THE GANG WAR.
WHEN SHE GETS A FREE MOMENT, I'LL INTRODUCE YOU TO--
CLINIC
OH, THERE SHE IS NOW.
DOCTOR THOMPKINS. I DON'T KNOW IF YOU REMEMBER ME, FROM THE SCHOOL FIELD TRIP. I'M TIM DRAKE, AND--
YES, I RECALL YOU, SON. NO TIME FOR TOURS NOW, I'M AFRAID.
WE'RE HERE TO HELP OUT, DOCTOR, IN ANY WAY WE CAN.
I DON'T HAVE ANY USABLE SKILLS, BUT I CAN FETCH AND CARRY WITH THE BEST OF THEM.
AND DANA, MY WIFE, IS A PHYSICAL THERAPIST.
HERE, LET ME HELP YOU SPLINT THAT.
WE CAN USE ALL THE HELP WE CAN GET. THANK YOU.
THE FIRST THING THE THREE OF YOU CAN DO IS DONATE BLOOD.
AND IF YOU HAVE A CAR, WE CAN USE MORE OF EVERYTHING: BANDAGES, DISINFECTANTS--AND I'D KILL FOR ANOTHER PORTABLE GENERATOR.
LEAVE IT TO ME. BACK IN THE ARMY, I WAS A FIRST-RATE SCROUNGER.
GOOD. I'LL GIVE YOU AN EMERGENCY SERVICES PASS THAT WILL EXEMPT YOU FROM THE CURFEW.

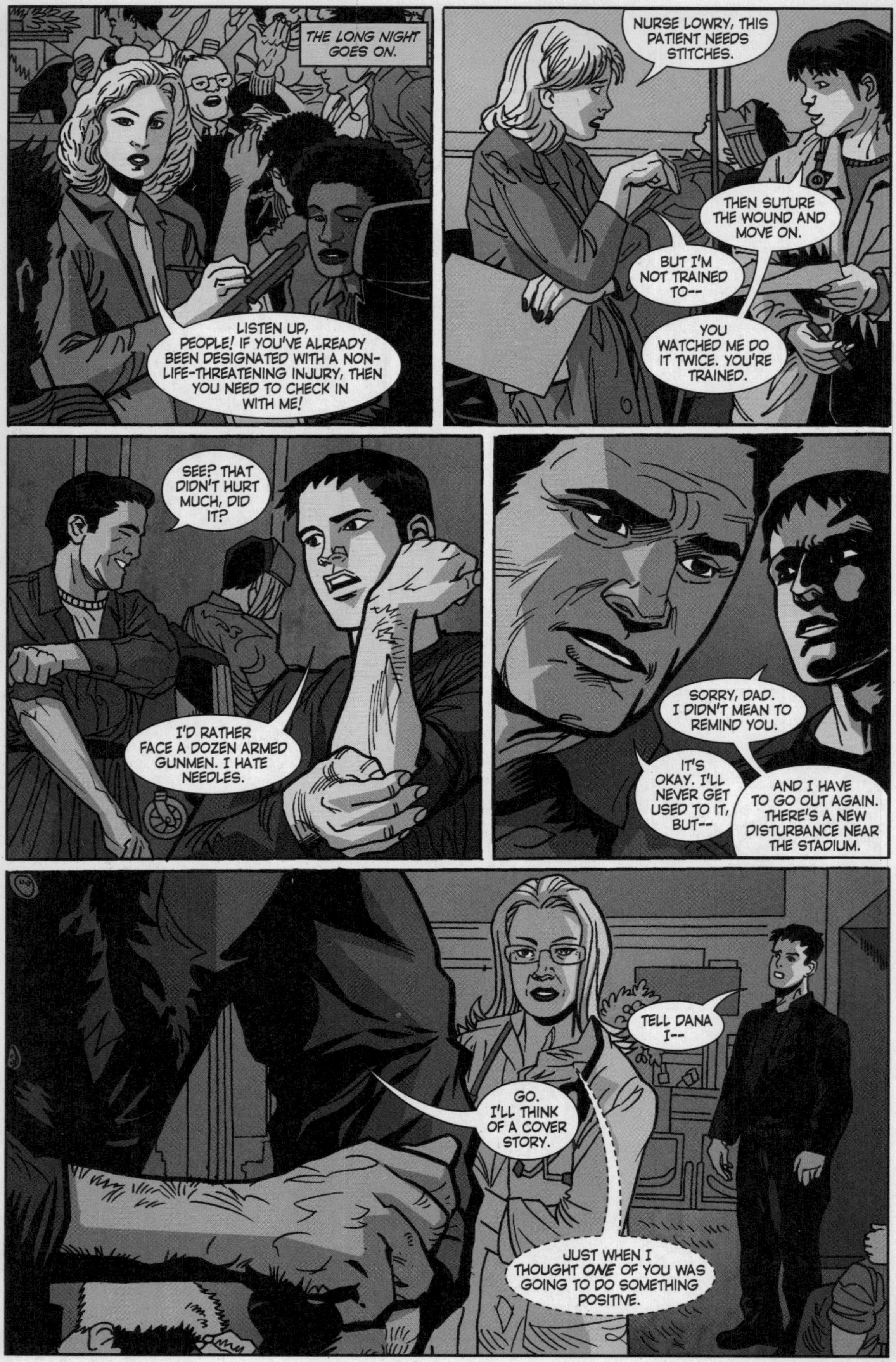
THE LONG NIGHT GOES ON.
LISTEN UP, PEOPLE! IF YOU'VE ALREADY BEEN DESIGNATED WITH A NON-LIFE-THREATENING INJURY, THEN YOU NEED TO CHECK IN WITH ME!
NURSE LOWRY, THIS PATIENT NEEDS STITCHES.
THEN SUTURE THE WOUND AND MOVE ON.
BUT I'M NOT TRAINED TO--
YOU WATCHED ME DO IT TWICE. YOU'RE TRAINED.
SEE? THAT DIDN'T HURT MUCH, DID IT?
I'D RATHER FACE A DOZEN ARMED GUNMEN. I HATE NEEDLES.
SORRY, DAD. I DIDN'T MEAN TO REMIND YOU.
IT'S OKAY. I'LL NEVER GET USED TO IT, BUT--
AND I HAVE TO GO OUT AGAIN. THERE'S A NEW DISTURBANCE NEAR THE STADIUM.
TELL DANA I--
GO. I'LL THINK OF A COVER STORY.
JUST WHEN I THOUGHT *ONE* OF YOU WAS GOING TO DO SOMETHING POSITIVE.

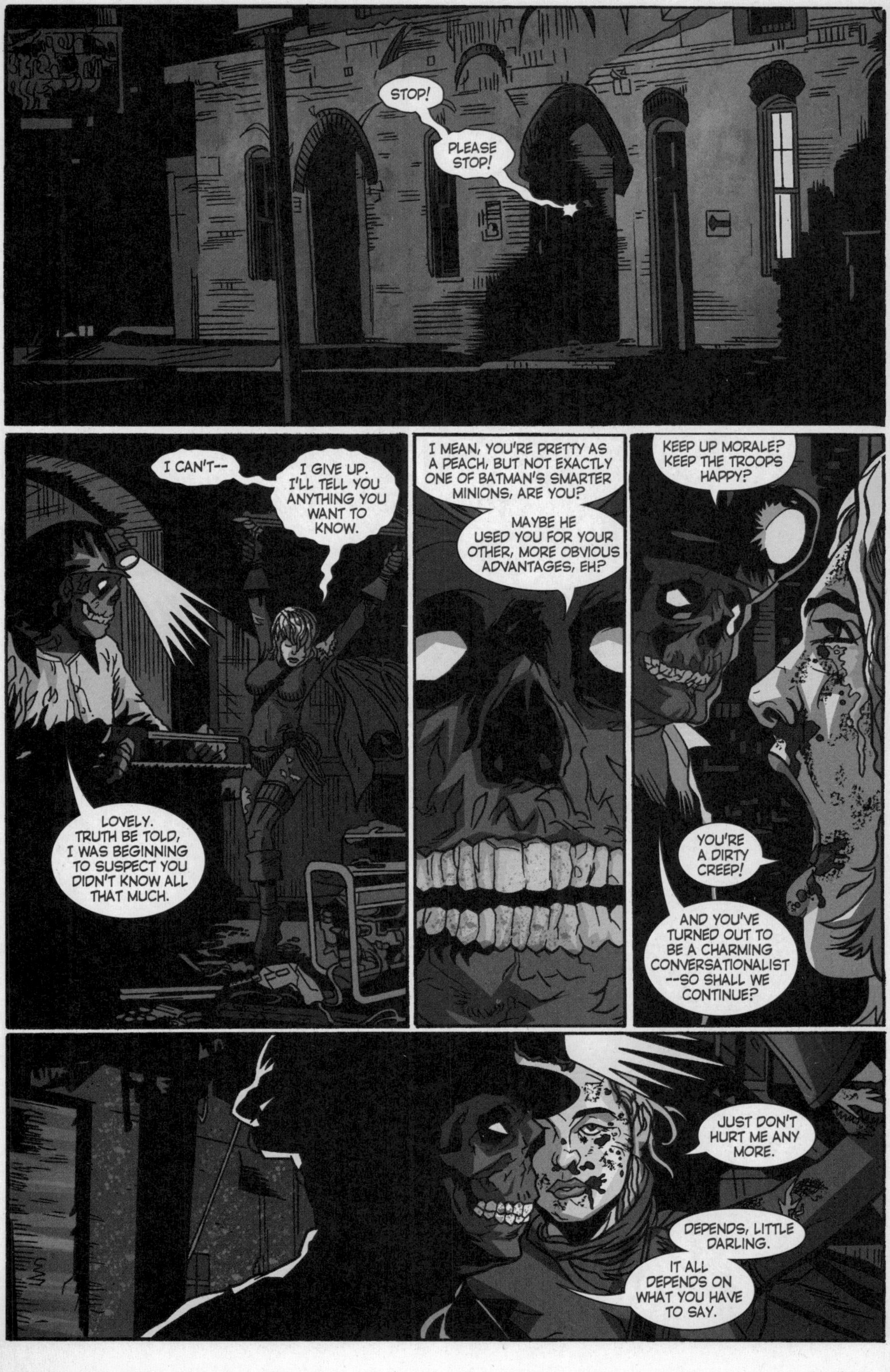
STOP!
PLEASE STOP!
I CAN'T--
I GIVE UP. I'LL TELL YOU ANYTHING YOU WANT TO KNOW.
LOVELY. TRUTH BE TOLD, I WAS BEGINNING TO SUSPECT YOU DIDN'T KNOW ALL THAT MUCH.
I MEAN, YOU'RE PRETTY AS A PEACH, BUT NOT EXACTLY ONE OF BATMAN'S SMARTER MINIONS, ARE YOU?
MAYBE HE USED YOU FOR YOUR OTHER, MORE OBVIOUS ADVANTAGES, EH?
KEEP UP MORALE? KEEP THE TROOPS HAPPY?
YOU'RE A DIRTY CREEP!
AND YOU'VE TURNED OUT TO BE A CHARMING CONVERSATIONALIST --SO SHALL WE CONTINUE?
JUST DON'T HURT ME ANY MORE.
DEPENDS, LITTLE DARLING.
IT ALL DEPENDS ON WHAT YOU HAVE TO SAY.

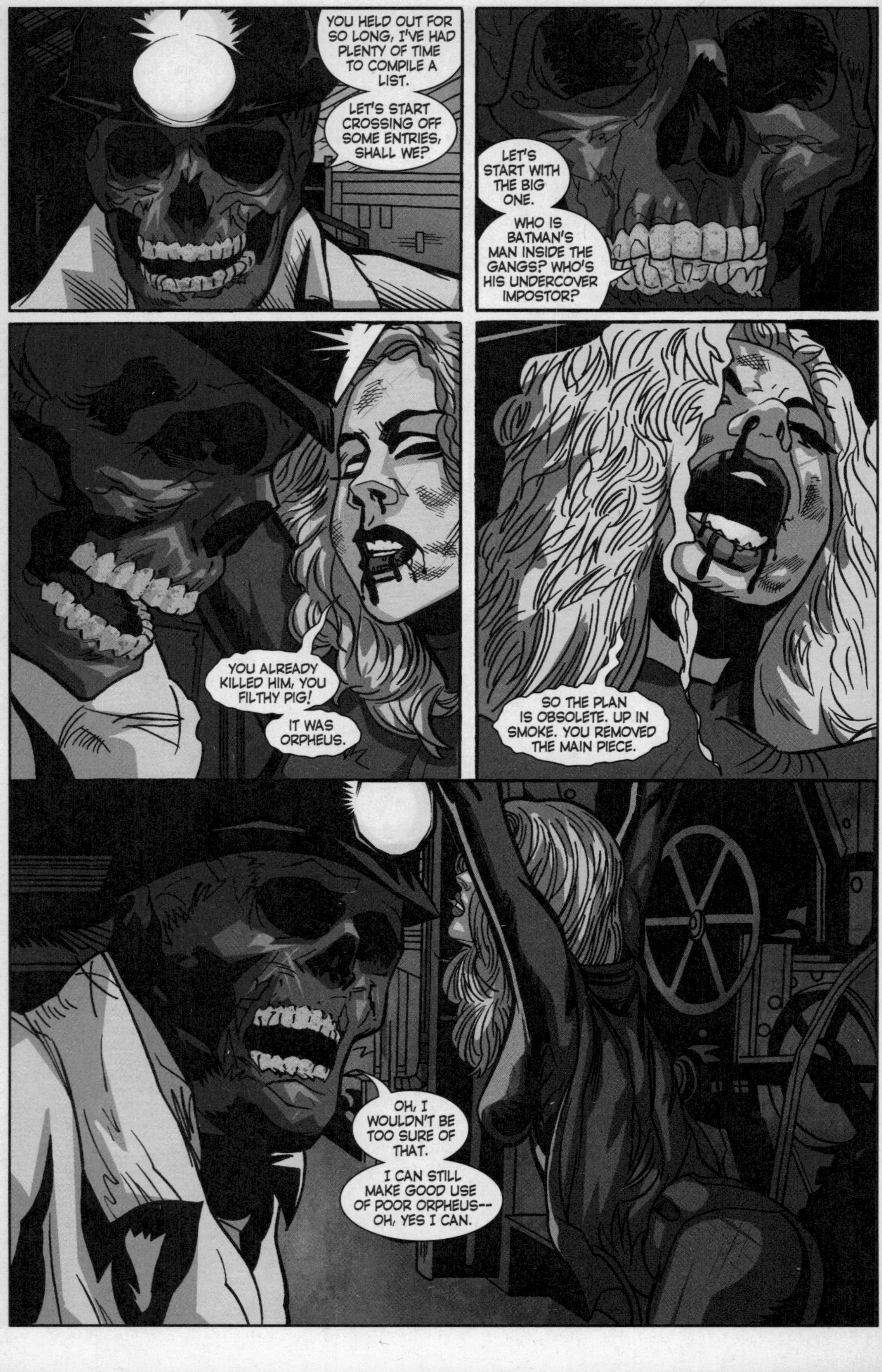
YOU HELD OUT FOR SO LONG, I'VE HAD PLENTY OF TIME TO COMPILE A LIST.
LET'S START CROSSING OFF SOME ENTRIES, SHALL WE?
LET'S START WITH THE BIG ONE.
WHO IS BATMAN'S MAN INSIDE THE GANGS? WHO'S HIS UNDERCOVER IMPOSTOR?
YOU ALREADY KILLED HIM, YOU FILTHY PIG!
IT WAS ORPHEUS.
SO THE PLAN IS OBSOLETE. UP IN SMOKE. YOU REMOVED THE MAIN PIECE.
OH, I WOULDN'T BE TOO SURE OF THAT.
I CAN STILL MAKE GOOD USE OF POOR ORPHEUS-- OH, YES I CAN.

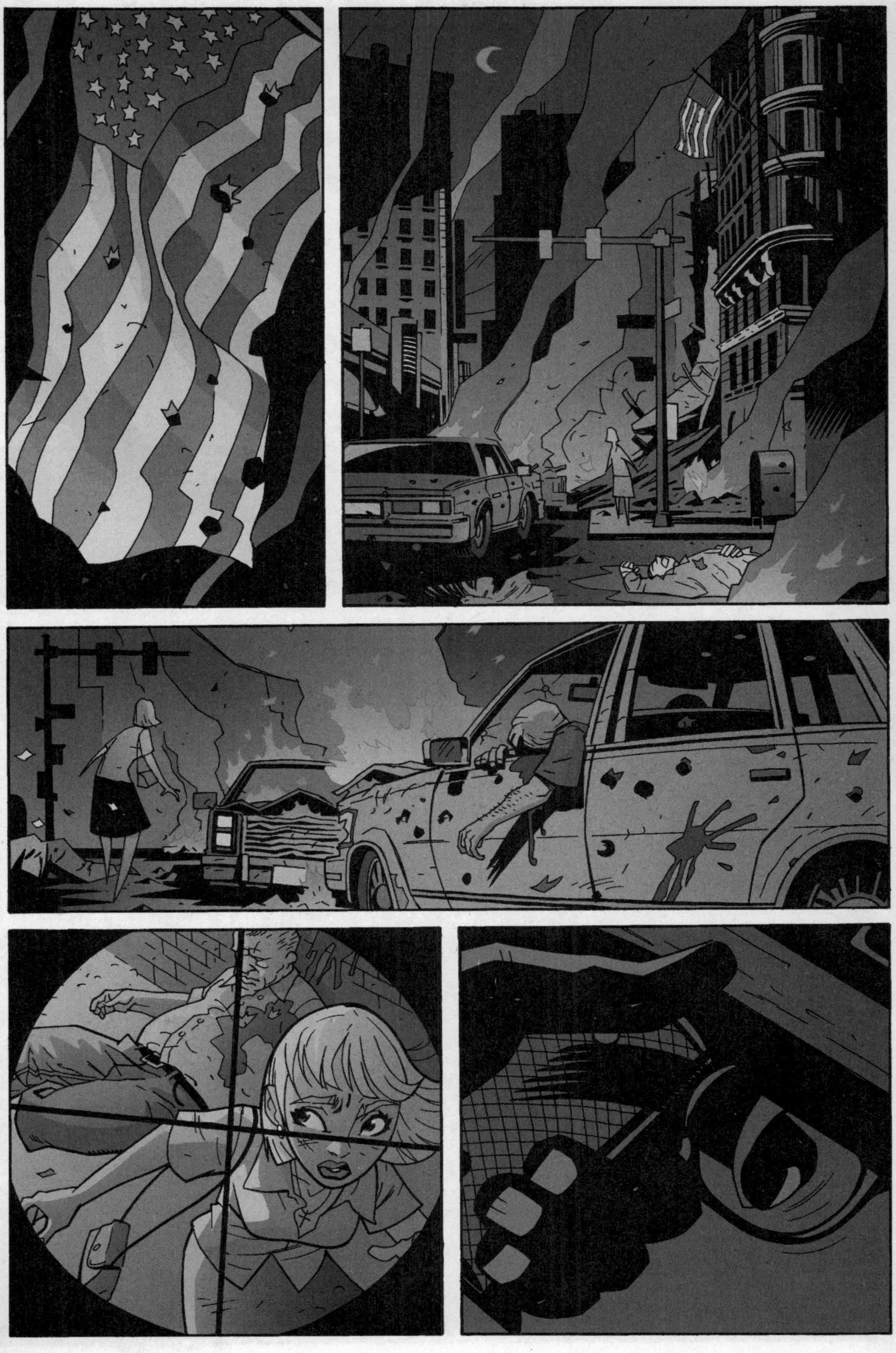

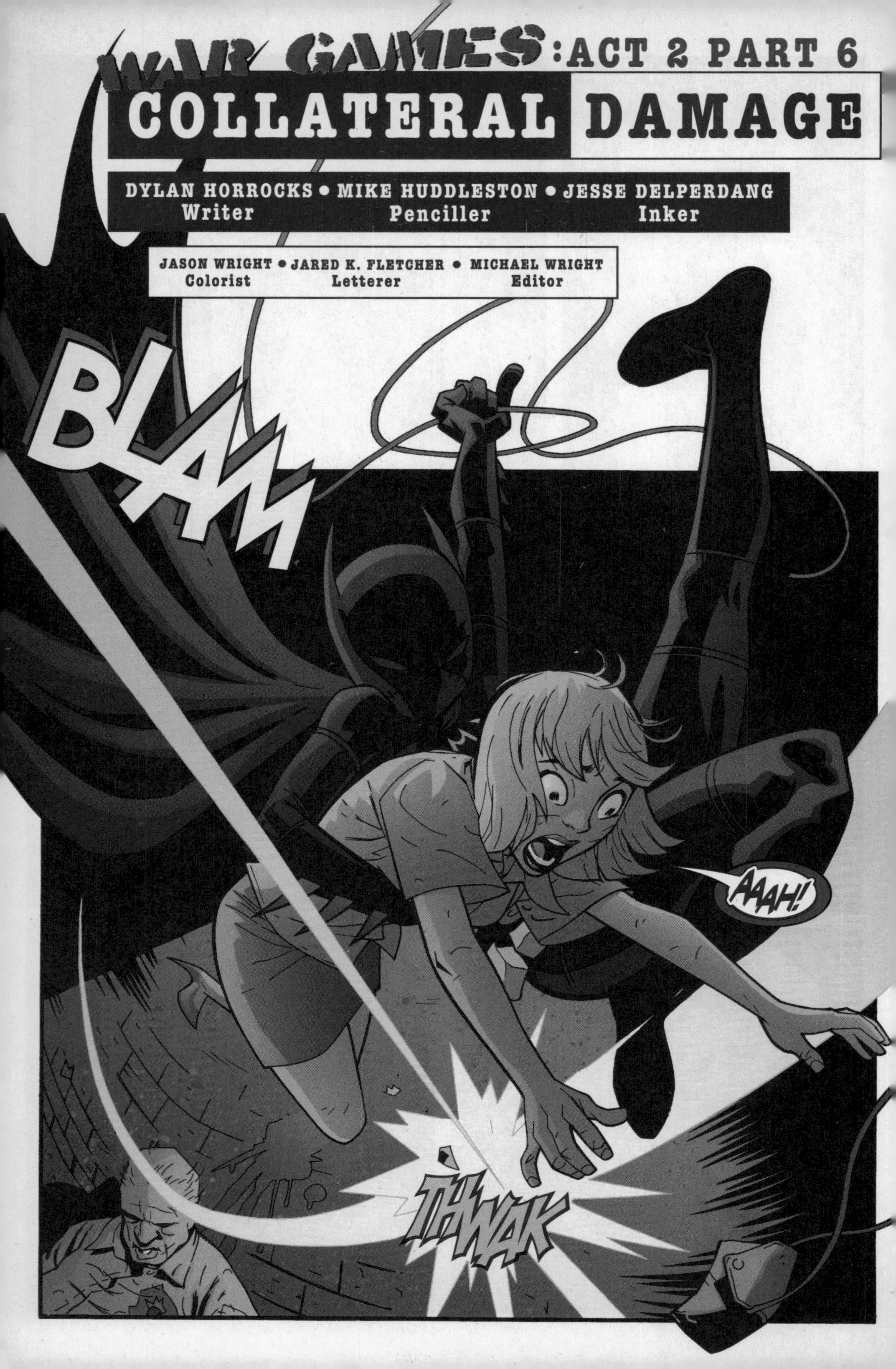
WAR GAMES: ACT 2 PART 6
COLLATERAL DAMAGE
DYLAN HORROCKS • MIKE HUDDLESTON • JESSE DELPERDANG
Writer Penciller Inker
JASON WRIGHT • JARED K. FLETCHER • MICHAEL WRIGHT
Colorist Letterer Editor
BLAM
AAAH!
THWAK

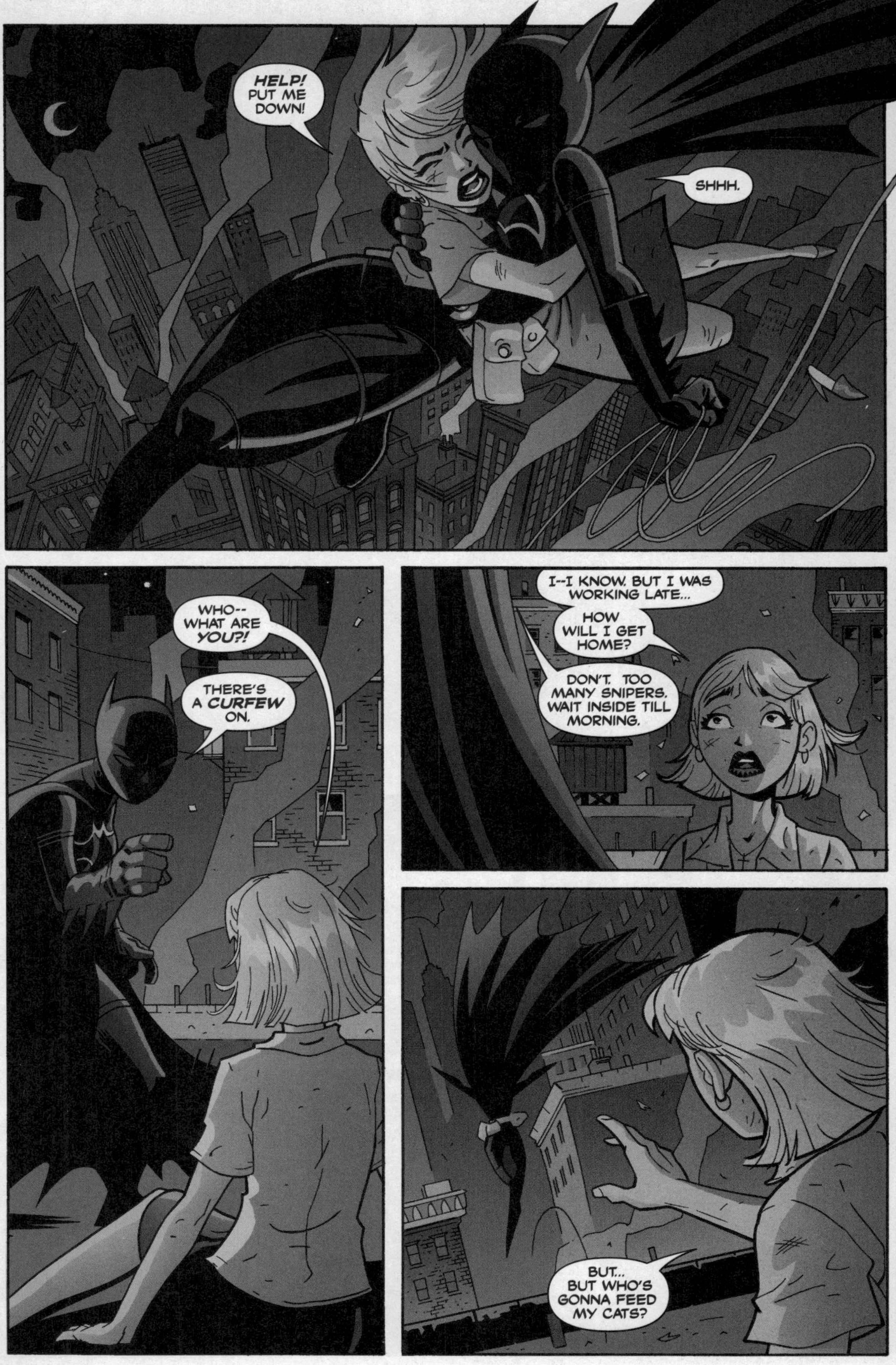
HELP! PUT ME DOWN!
SHHH.
WHO-- WHAT ARE YOU?!
THERE'S A CURFEW ON.
I--I KNOW. BUT I WAS WORKING LATE...
HOW WILL I GET HOME?
DON'T. TOO MANY SNIPERS. WAIT INSIDE TILL MORNING.
BUT... BUT WHO'S GONNA FEED MY CATS?

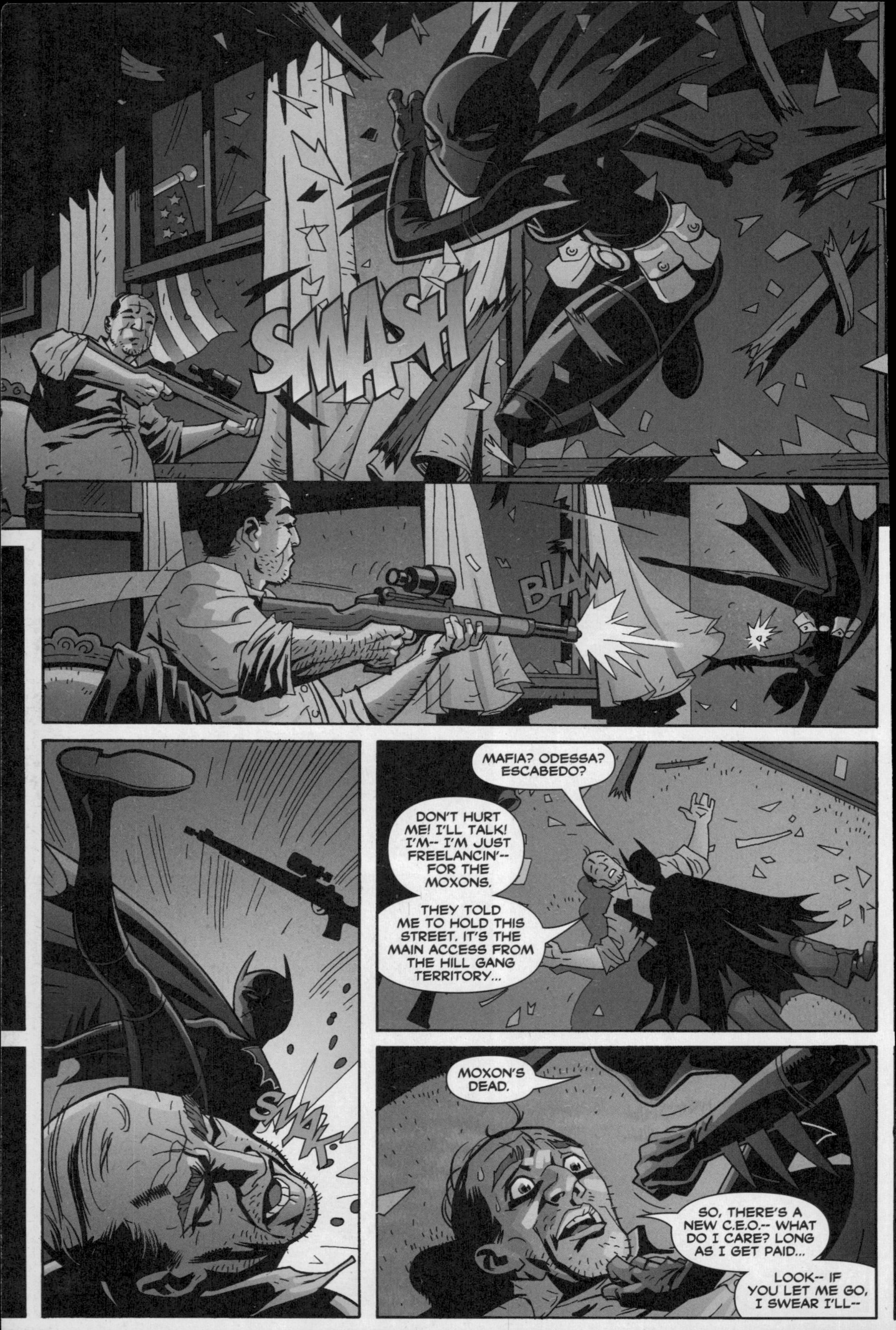
SMASH
BLAM
SMAK
MAFIA? ODESSA? ESCABEDO?
DON'T HURT ME! I'LL TALK! I'M-- I'M JUST FREELANCIN'-- FOR THE MOXONS.
THEY TOLD ME TO HOLD THIS STREET. IT'S THE MAIN ACCESS FROM THE HILL GANG TERRITORY...
MOXON'S DEAD.
SO, THERE'S A NEW C.E.O.-- WHAT DO I CARE? LONG AS I GET PAID...
LOOK-- IF YOU LET ME GO, I SWEAR I'LL--

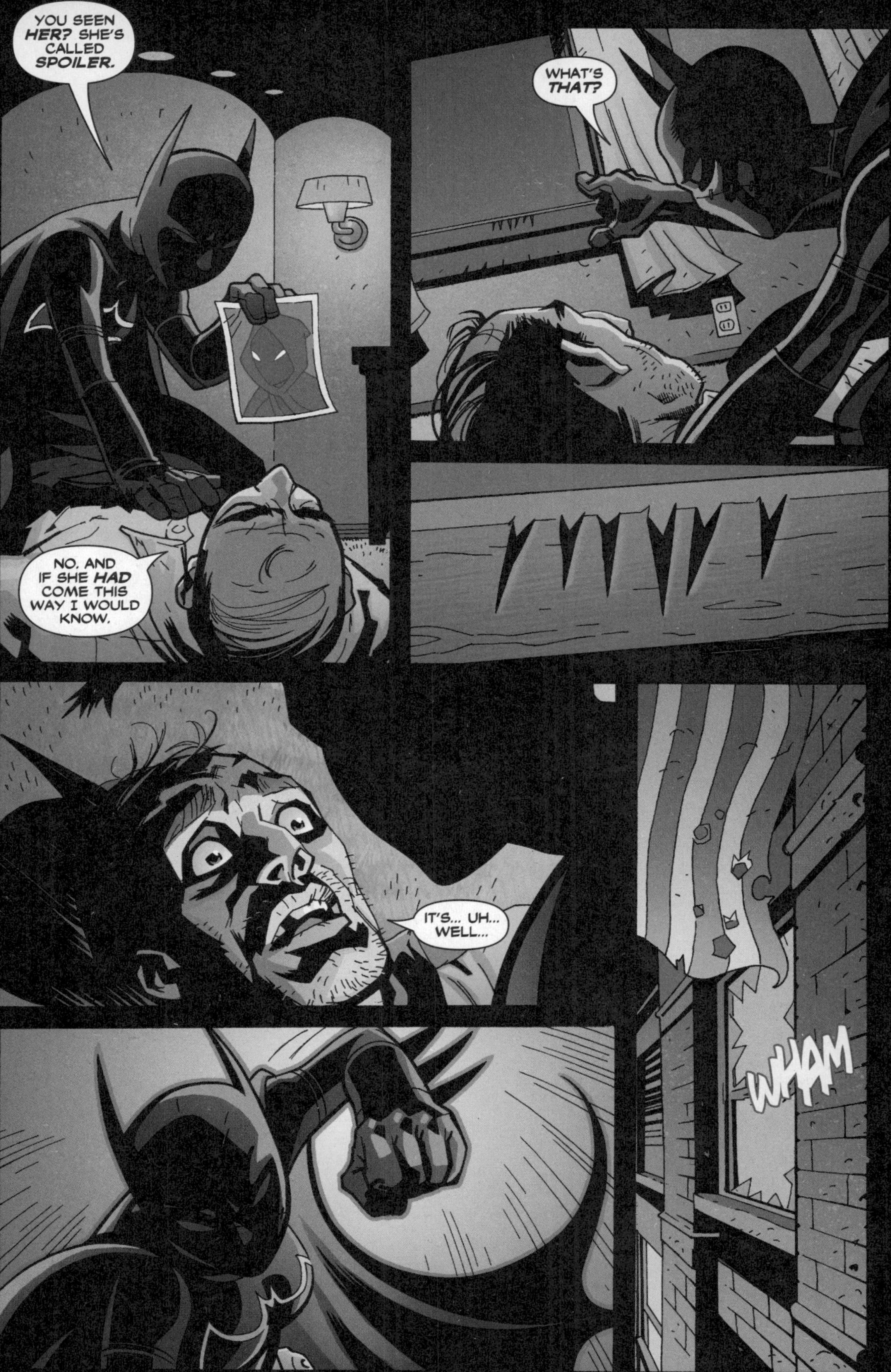
YOU SEEN HER? SHE'S CALLED SPOILER.
NO. AND IF SHE HAD COME THIS WAY I WOULD KNOW.
WHAT'S THAT?
IT'S... UH... WELL...
WHAM

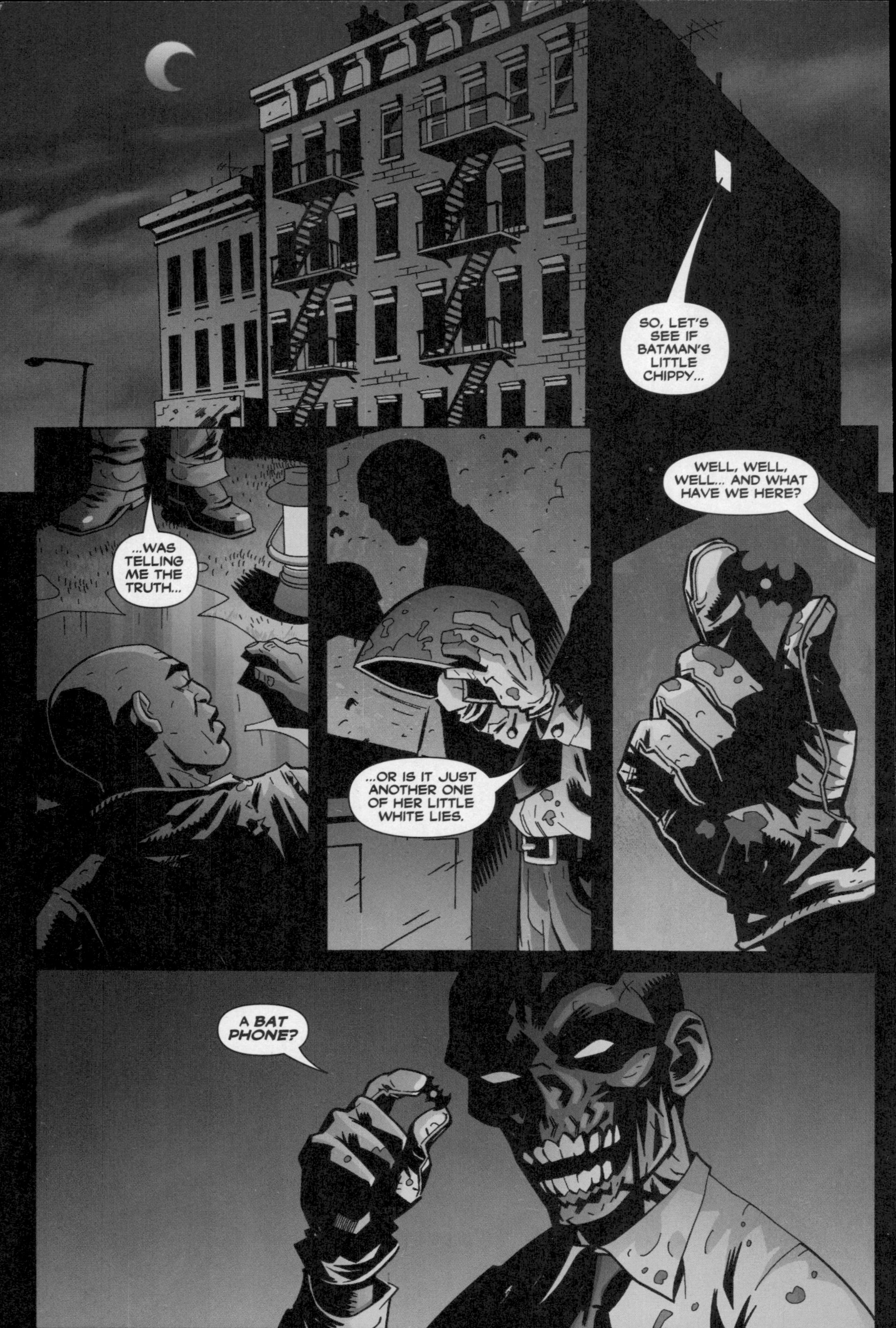
SO, LET'S SEE IF BATMAN'S LITTLE CHIPPY...
...WAS TELLING ME THE TRUTH...
...OR IS IT JUST ANOTHER ONE OF HER LITTLE WHITE LIES.
WELL, WELL, WELL... AND WHAT HAVE WE HERE?
A BAT PHONE?

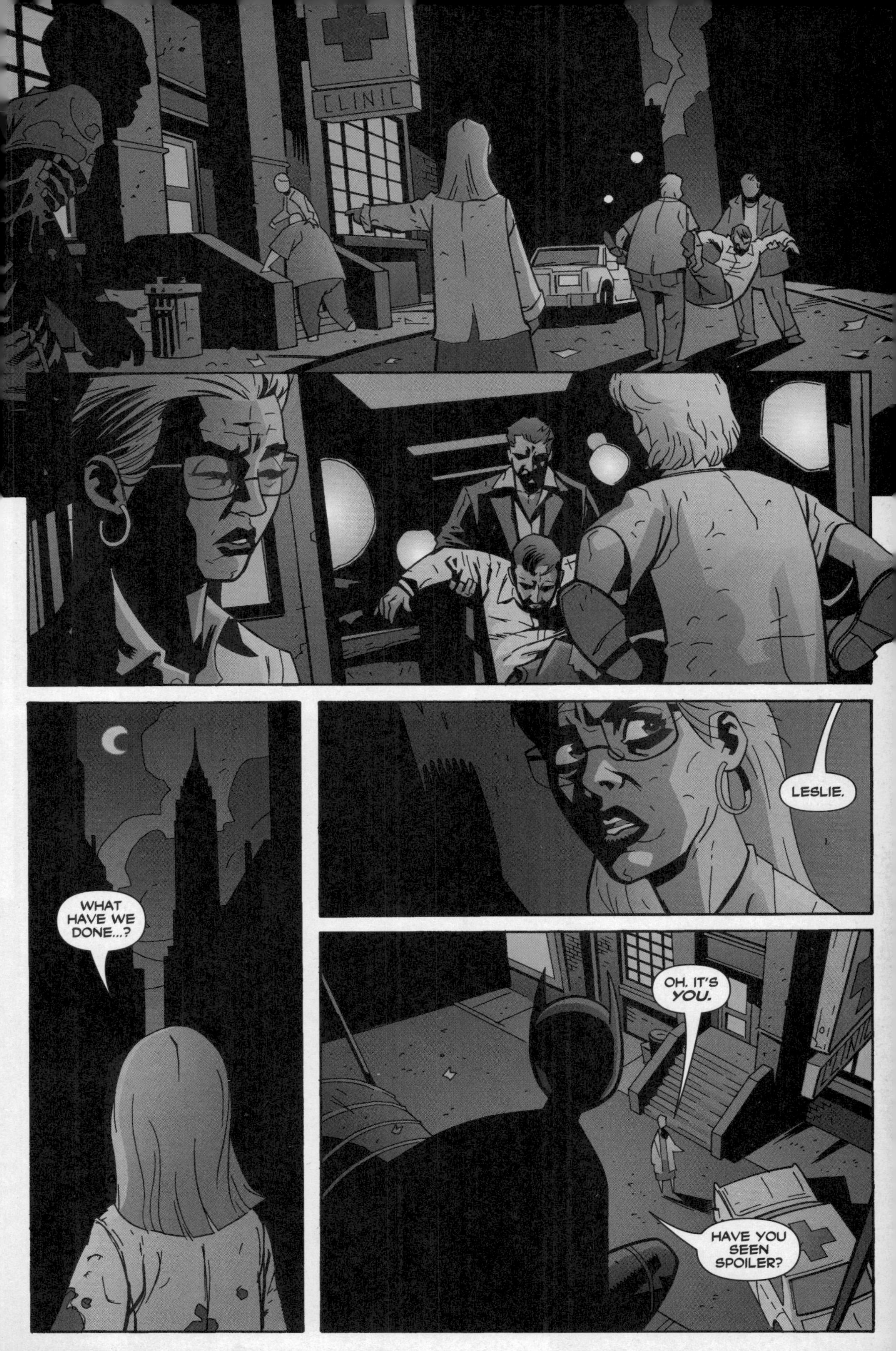
CLINIC
LESLIE.
WHAT HAVE WE DONE...?
OH. IT'S YOU.
HAVE YOU SEEN SPOILER?
CLINIC

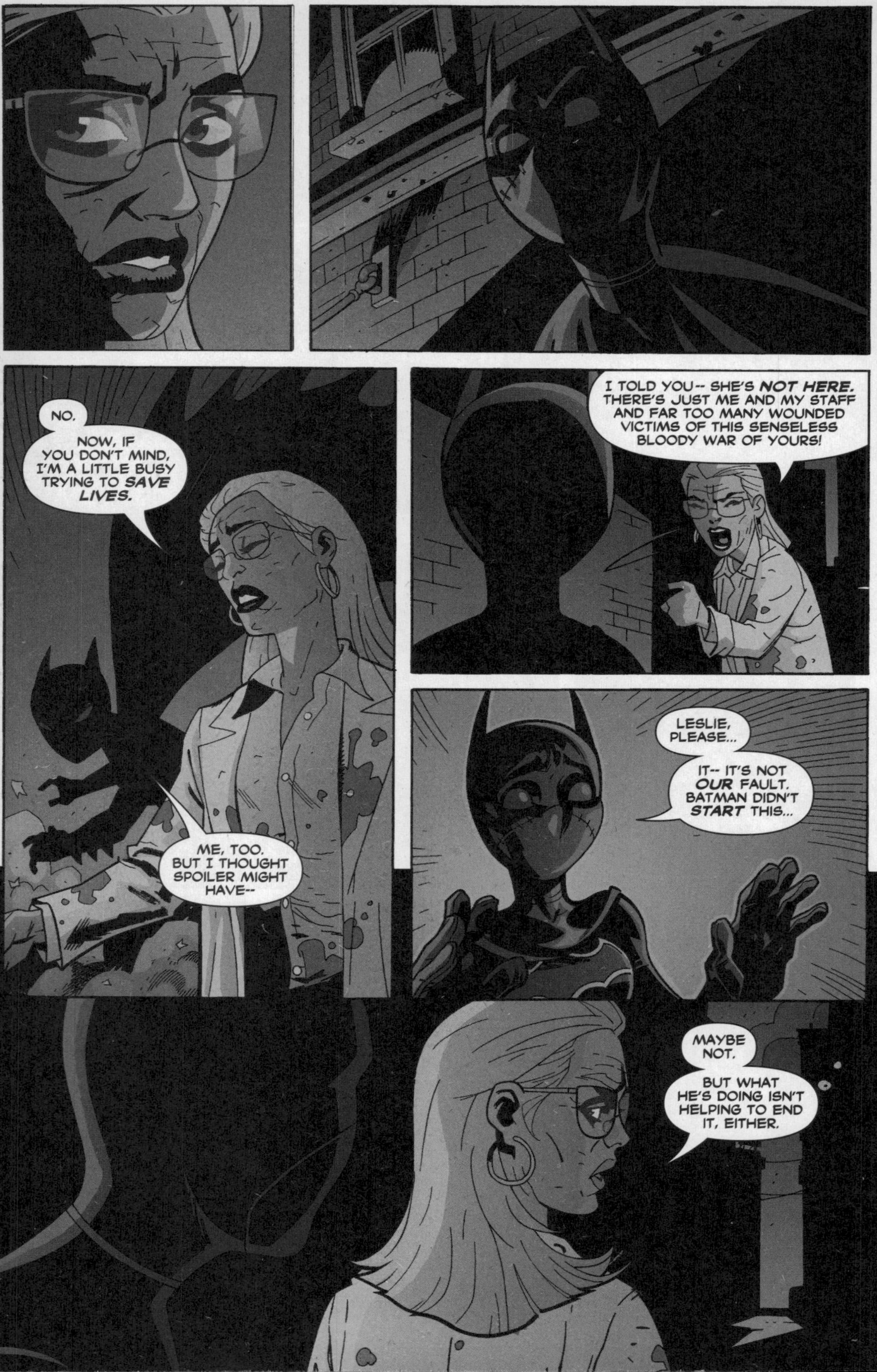
NO.
NOW, IF YOU DON'T MIND, I'M A LITTLE BUSY TRYING TO *SAVE LIVES.*
ME, TOO. BUT I THOUGHT SPOILER MIGHT HAVE--
I TOLD YOU-- SHE'S *NOT HERE.* THERE'S JUST ME AND MY STAFF AND FAR TOO MANY WOUNDED VICTIMS OF THIS SENSELESS BLOODY WAR OF YOURS!
LESLIE, PLEASE...
IT-- IT'S NOT *OUR* FAULT. BATMAN DIDN'T *START* THIS...
MAYBE NOT.
BUT WHAT HE'S DOING ISN'T HELPING TO END IT, EITHER.

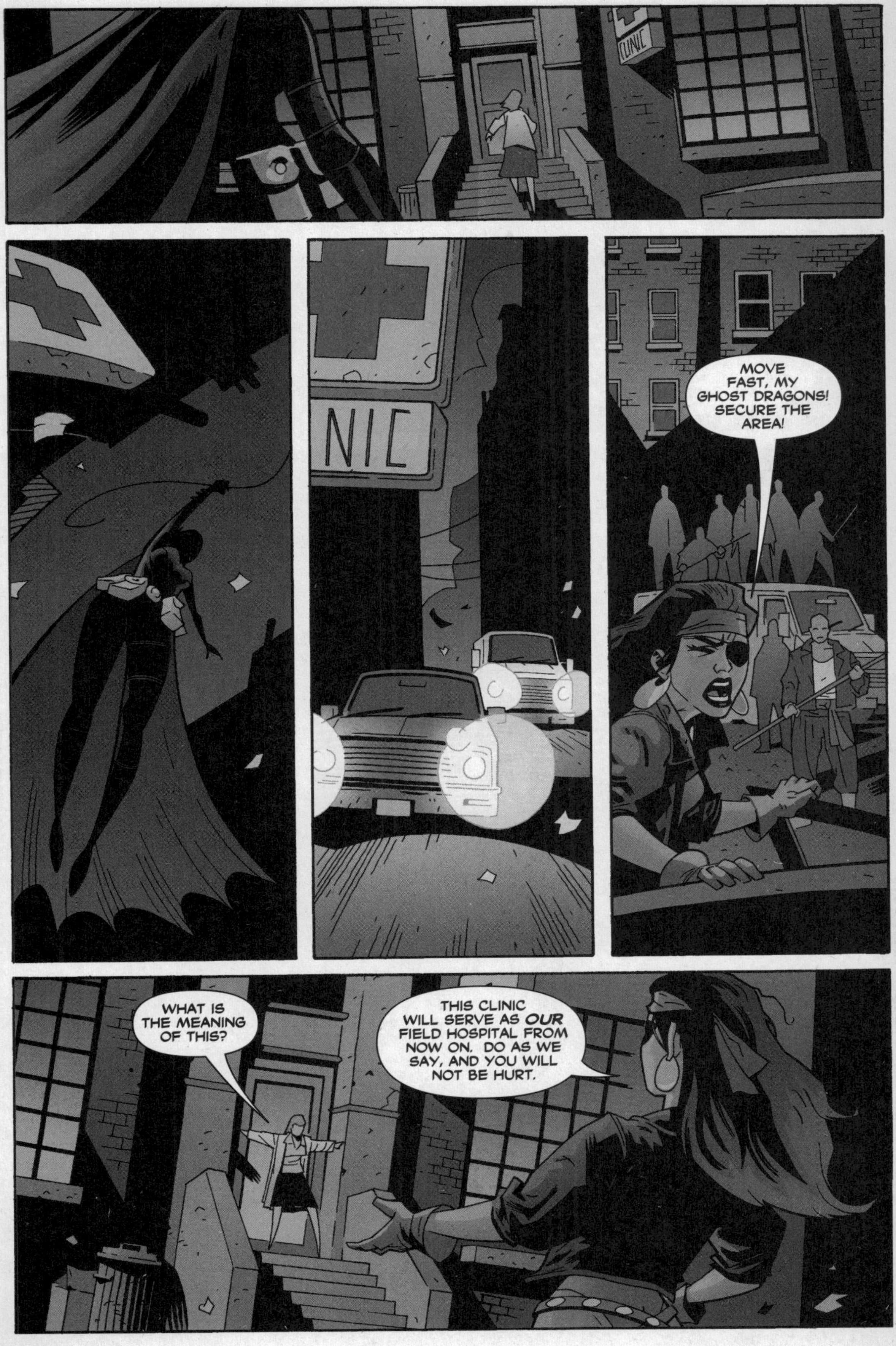
CLINIC
NIC
MOVE FAST, MY GHOST DRAGONS! SECURE THE AREA!
WHAT IS THE MEANING OF THIS?
THIS CLINIC WILL SERVE AS *OUR* FIELD HOSPITAL FROM NOW ON. DO AS WE SAY, AND YOU WILL NOT BE HURT.

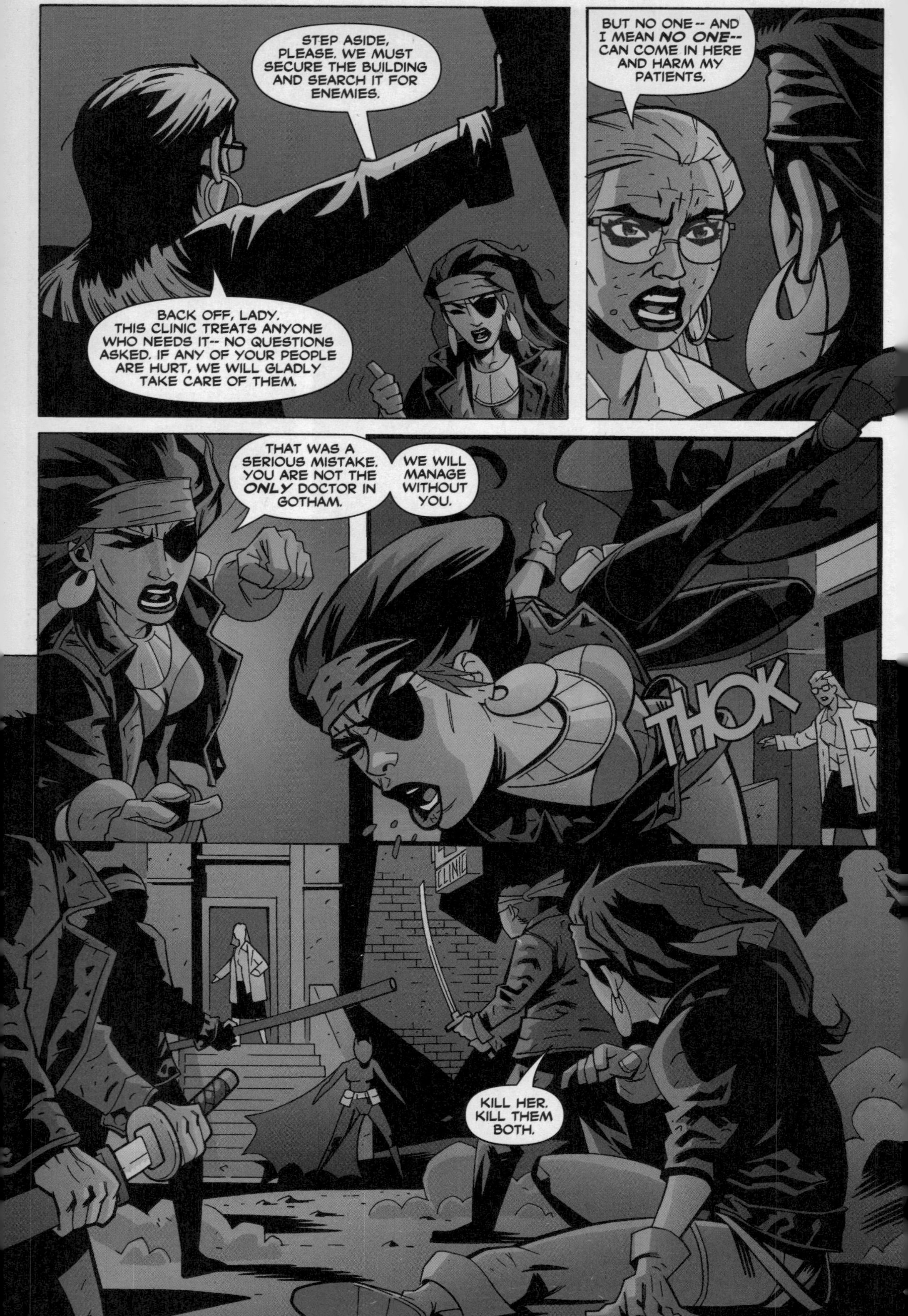
STEP ASIDE, PLEASE. WE MUST SECURE THE BUILDING AND SEARCH IT FOR ENEMIES.
BACK OFF, LADY. THIS CLINIC TREATS ANYONE WHO NEEDS IT-- NO QUESTIONS ASKED. IF ANY OF YOUR PEOPLE ARE HURT, WE WILL GLADLY TAKE CARE OF THEM.
BUT NO ONE-- AND I MEAN NO ONE-- CAN COME IN HERE AND HARM MY PATIENTS.
THAT WAS A SERIOUS MISTAKE. YOU ARE NOT THE ONLY DOCTOR IN GOTHAM.
WE WILL MANAGE WITHOUT YOU.
THOK
CLINIC
KILL HER. KILL THEM BOTH.

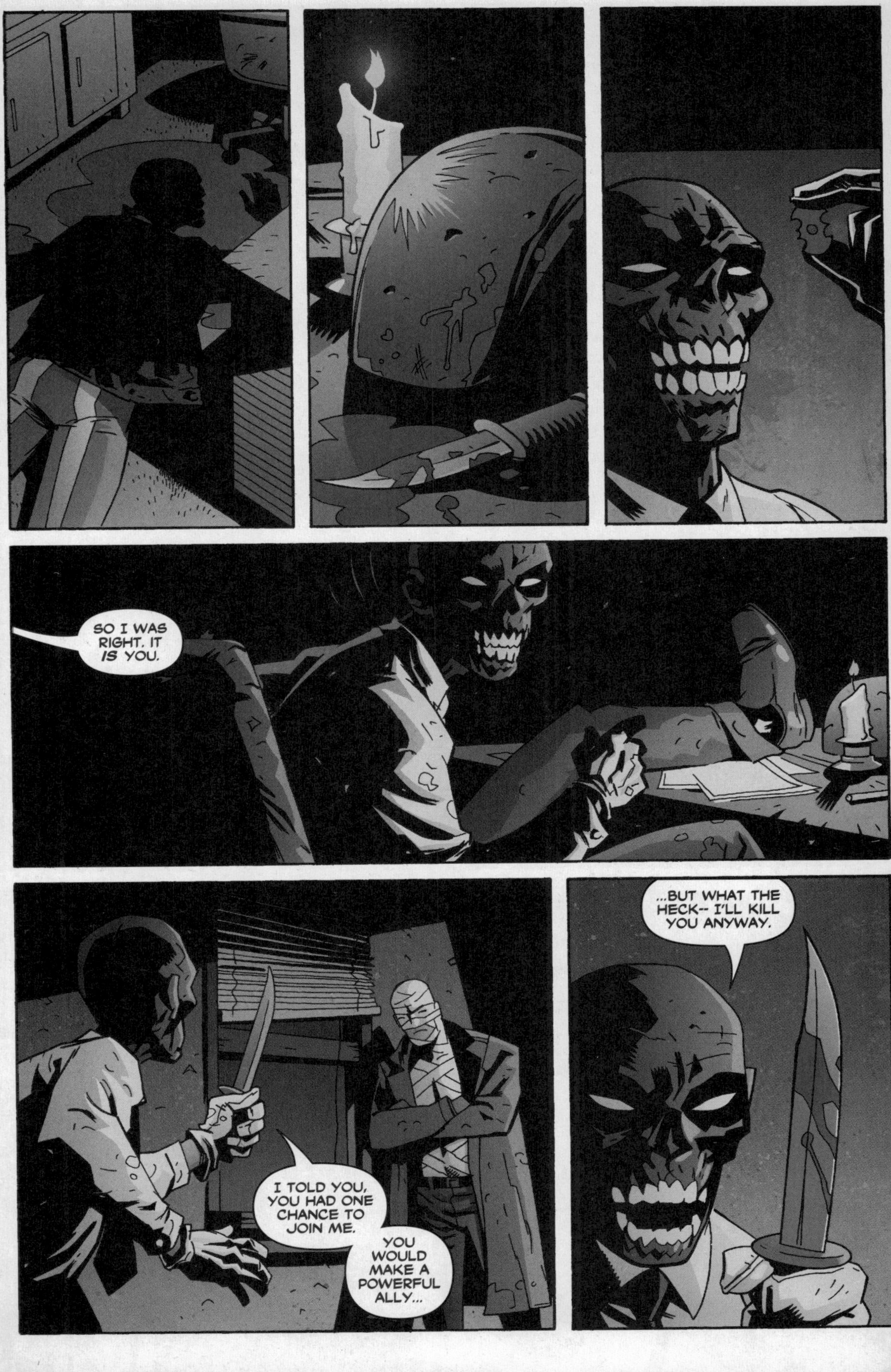
SO I WAS RIGHT. IT *IS* YOU.
I TOLD YOU, YOU HAD ONE CHANCE TO JOIN ME.
YOU WOULD MAKE A POWERFUL ALLY...
...BUT WHAT THE HECK-- I'LL KILL YOU ANYWAY.

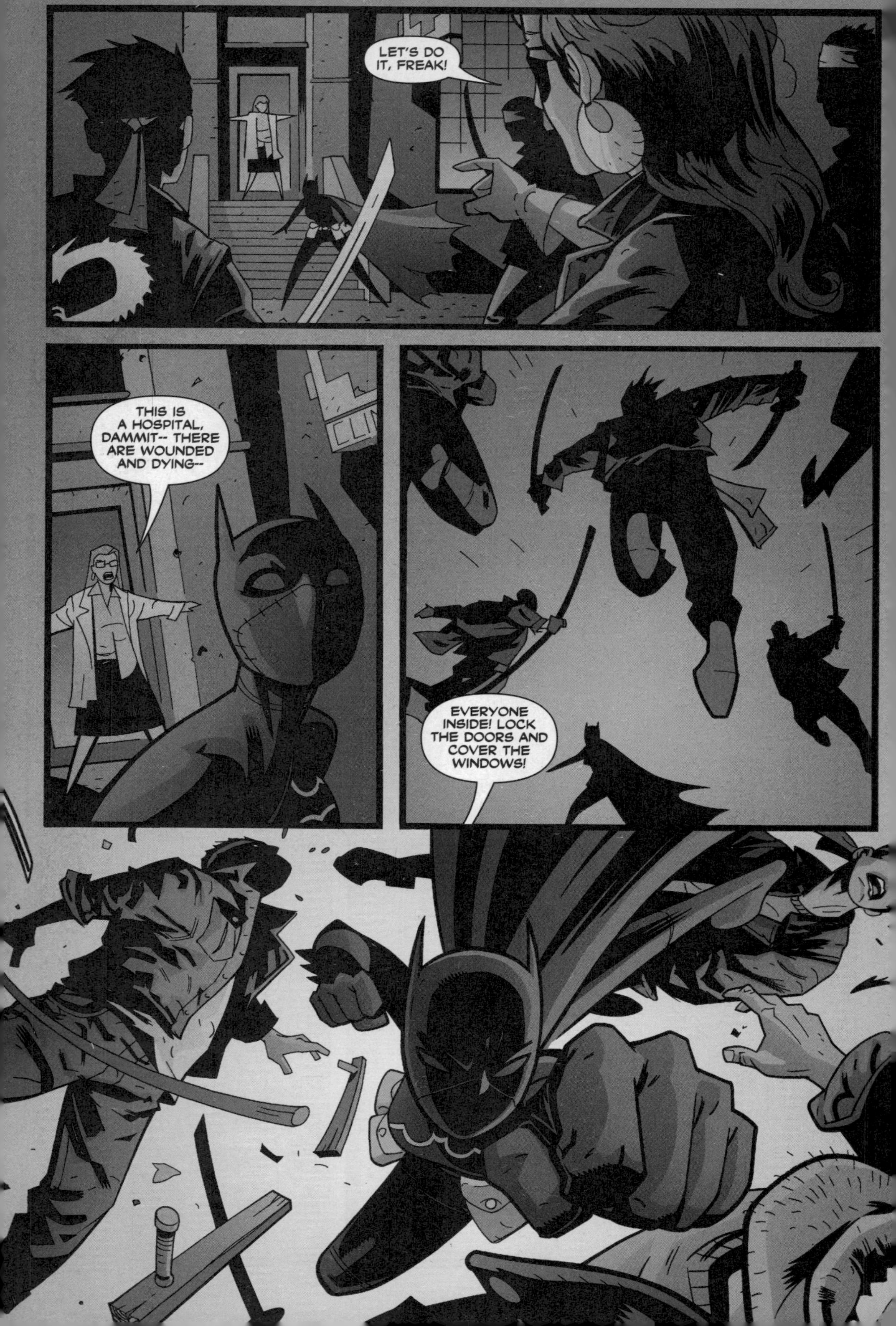
LET'S DO IT, FREAK!
THIS IS A HOSPITAL, DAMMIT-- THERE ARE WOUNDED AND DYING--
EVERYONE INSIDE! LOCK THE DOORS AND COVER THE WINDOWS!

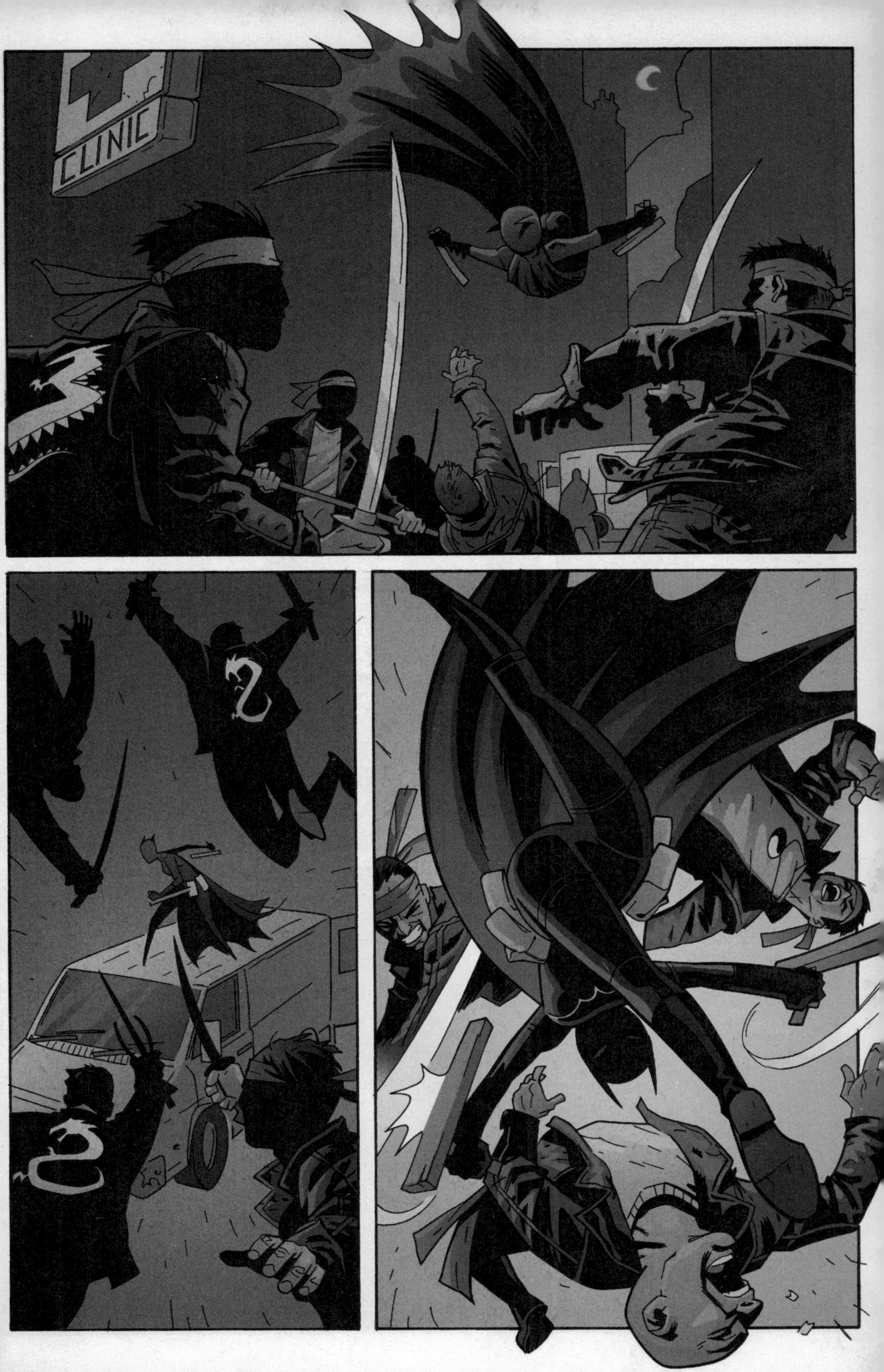
CLINIC

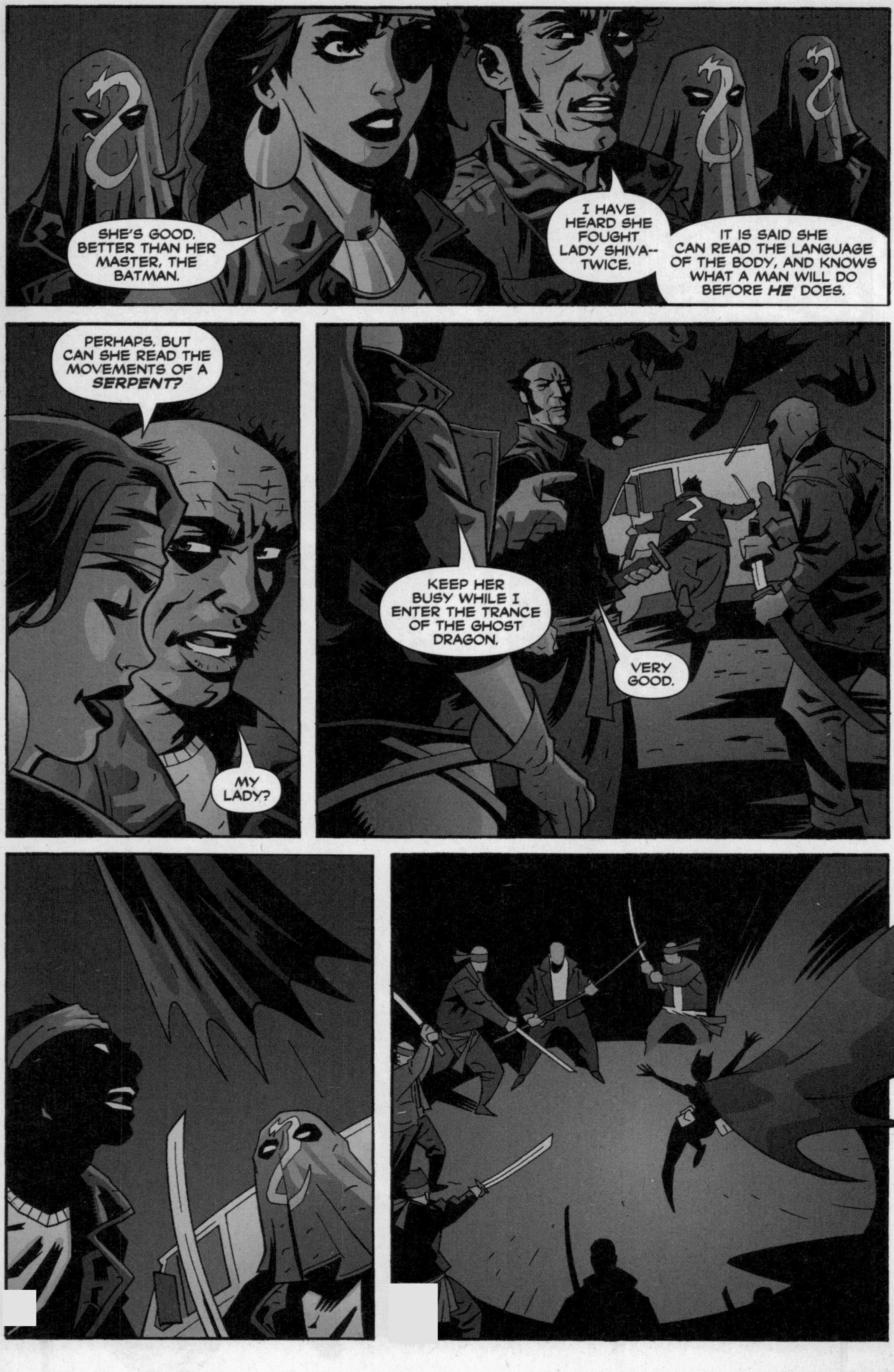
SHE'S GOOD. BETTER THAN HER MASTER, THE BATMAN.
I HAVE HEARD SHE FOUGHT LADY SHIVA--TWICE.
IT IS SAID SHE CAN READ THE LANGUAGE OF THE BODY, AND KNOWS WHAT A MAN WILL DO BEFORE HE DOES.
PERHAPS. BUT CAN SHE READ THE MOVEMENTS OF A SERPENT?
MY LADY?
KEEP HER BUSY WHILE I ENTER THE TRANCE OF THE GHOST DRAGON.
VERY GOOD.

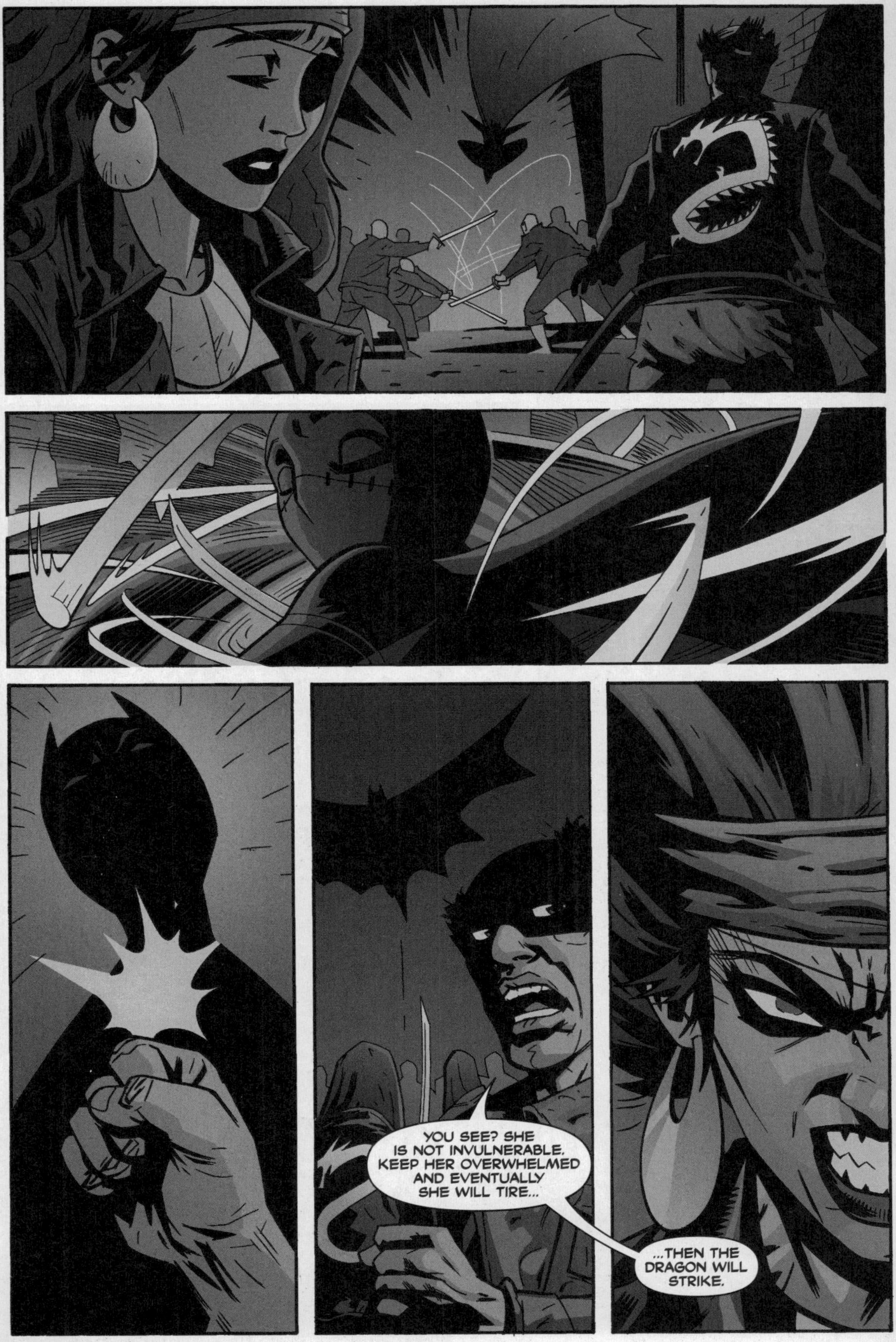
YOU SEE? SHE IS NOT INVULNERABLE. KEEP HER OVERWHELMED AND EVENTUALLY SHE WILL TIRE...
...THEN THE DRAGON WILL STRIKE.

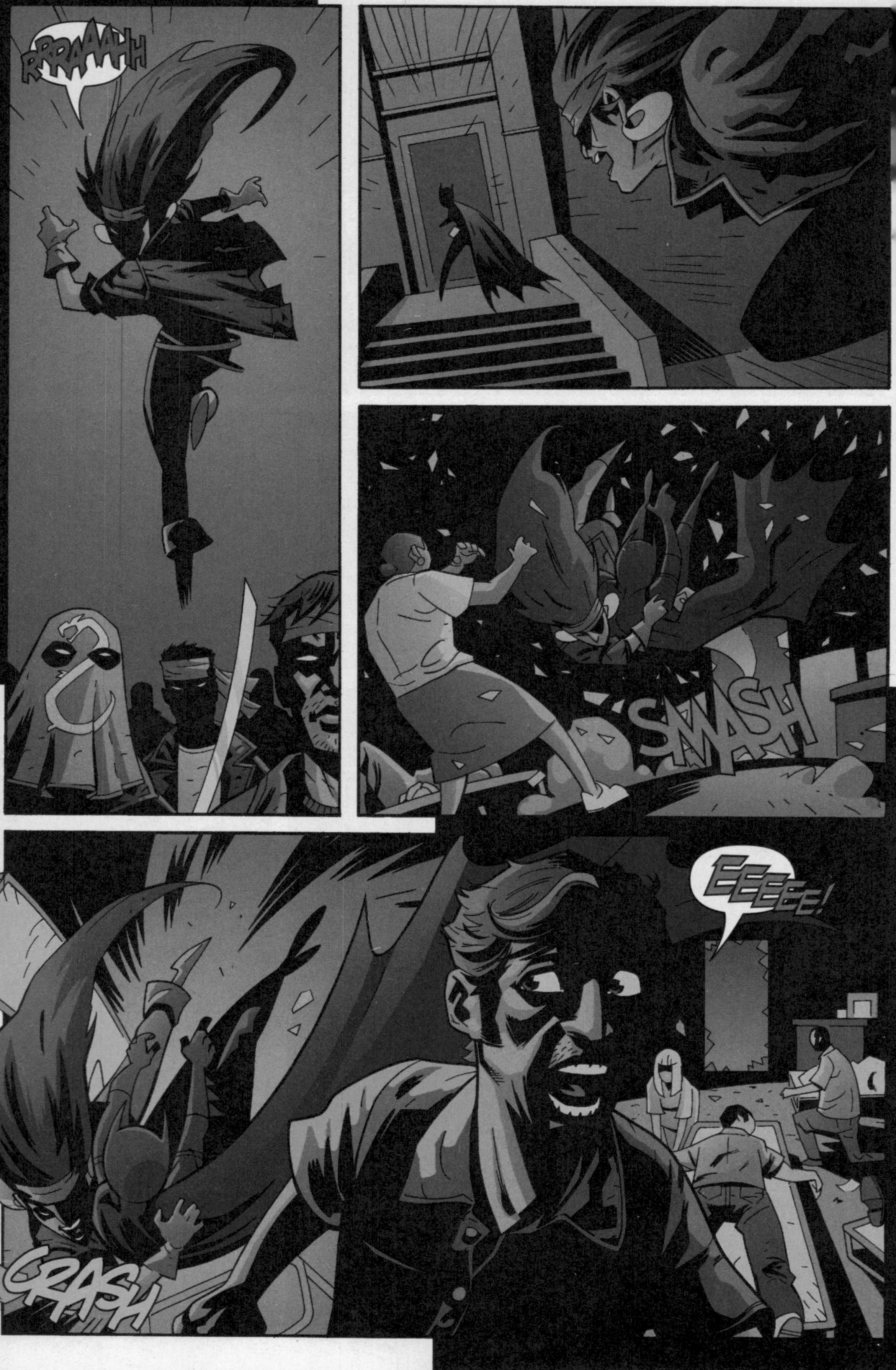
RRRAAAHH
SMASH
EEEEEE!
CRASH

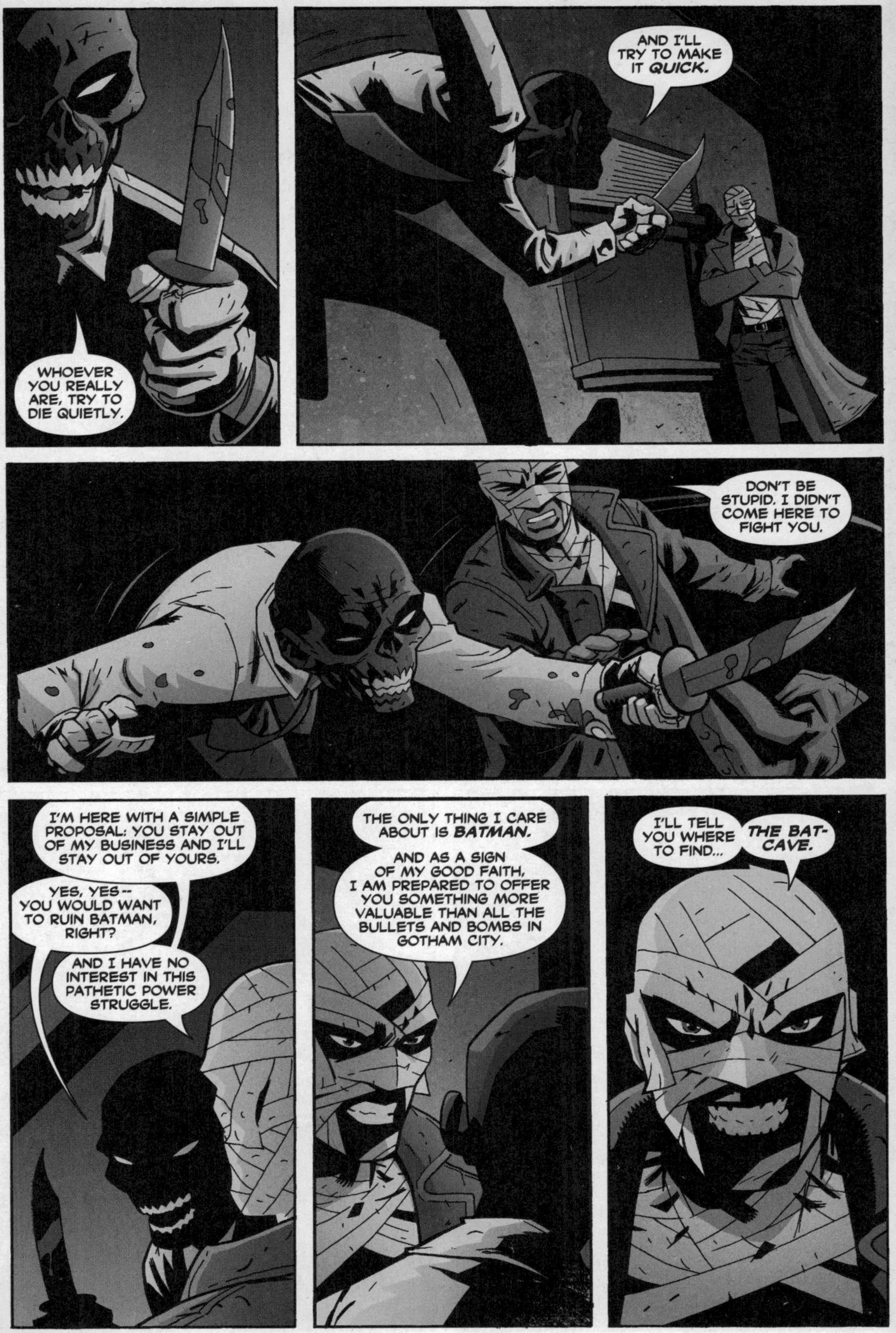
WHOEVER YOU REALLY ARE, TRY TO DIE QUIETLY.
AND I'LL TRY TO MAKE IT QUICK.
DON'T BE STUPID. I DIDN'T COME HERE TO FIGHT YOU.
I'M HERE WITH A SIMPLE PROPOSAL: YOU STAY OUT OF MY BUSINESS AND I'LL STAY OUT OF YOURS.
YES, YES-- YOU WOULD WANT TO RUIN BATMAN, RIGHT?
AND I HAVE NO INTEREST IN THIS PATHETIC POWER STRUGGLE.
THE ONLY THING I CARE ABOUT IS BATMAN.
AND AS A SIGN OF MY GOOD FAITH, I AM PREPARED TO OFFER YOU SOMETHING MORE VALUABLE THAN ALL THE BULLETS AND BOMBS IN GOTHAM CITY.
I'LL TELL YOU WHERE TO FIND...
THE BAT-CAVE.

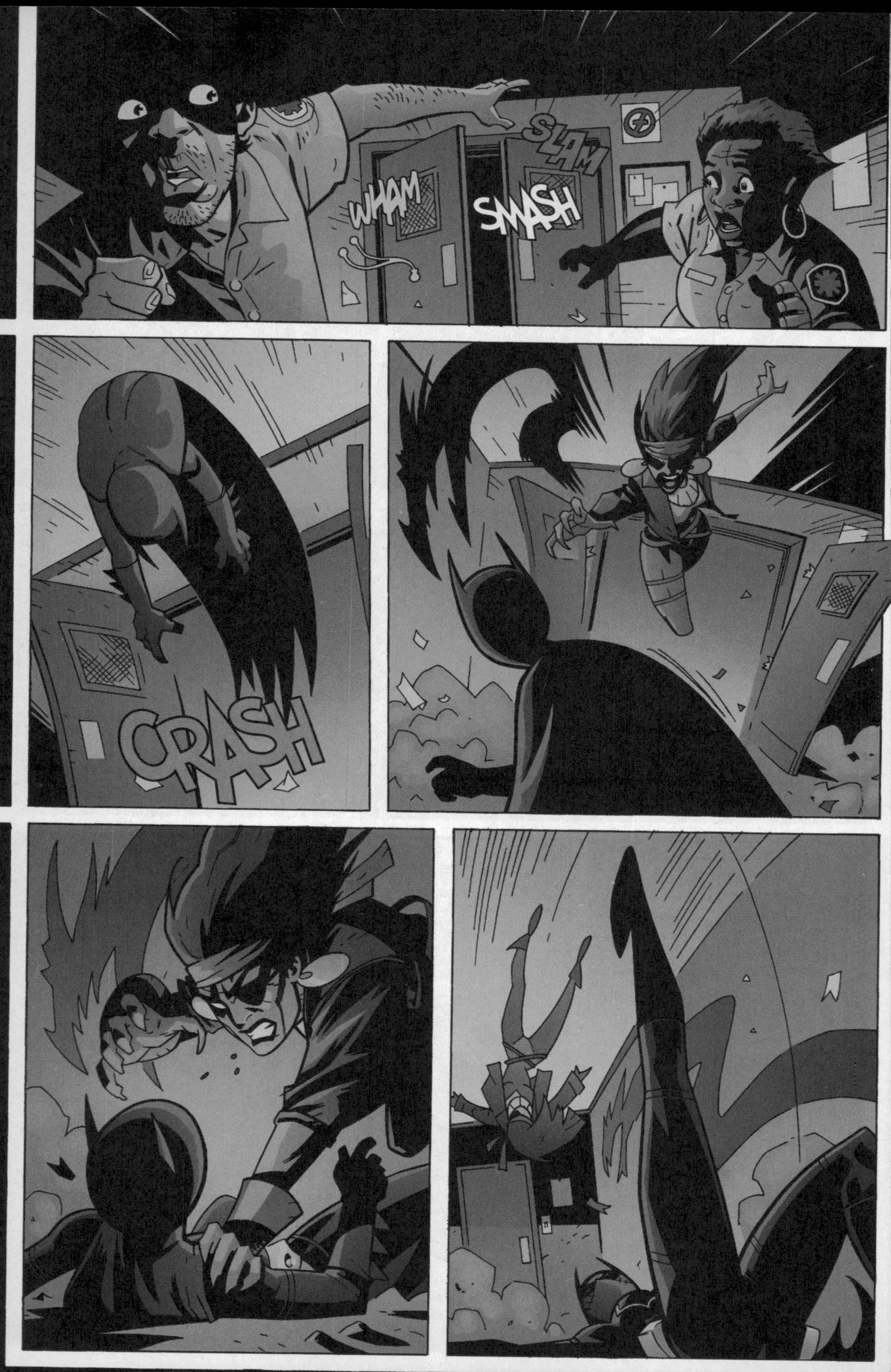
SLAM
WHAM
SMASH
CRASH

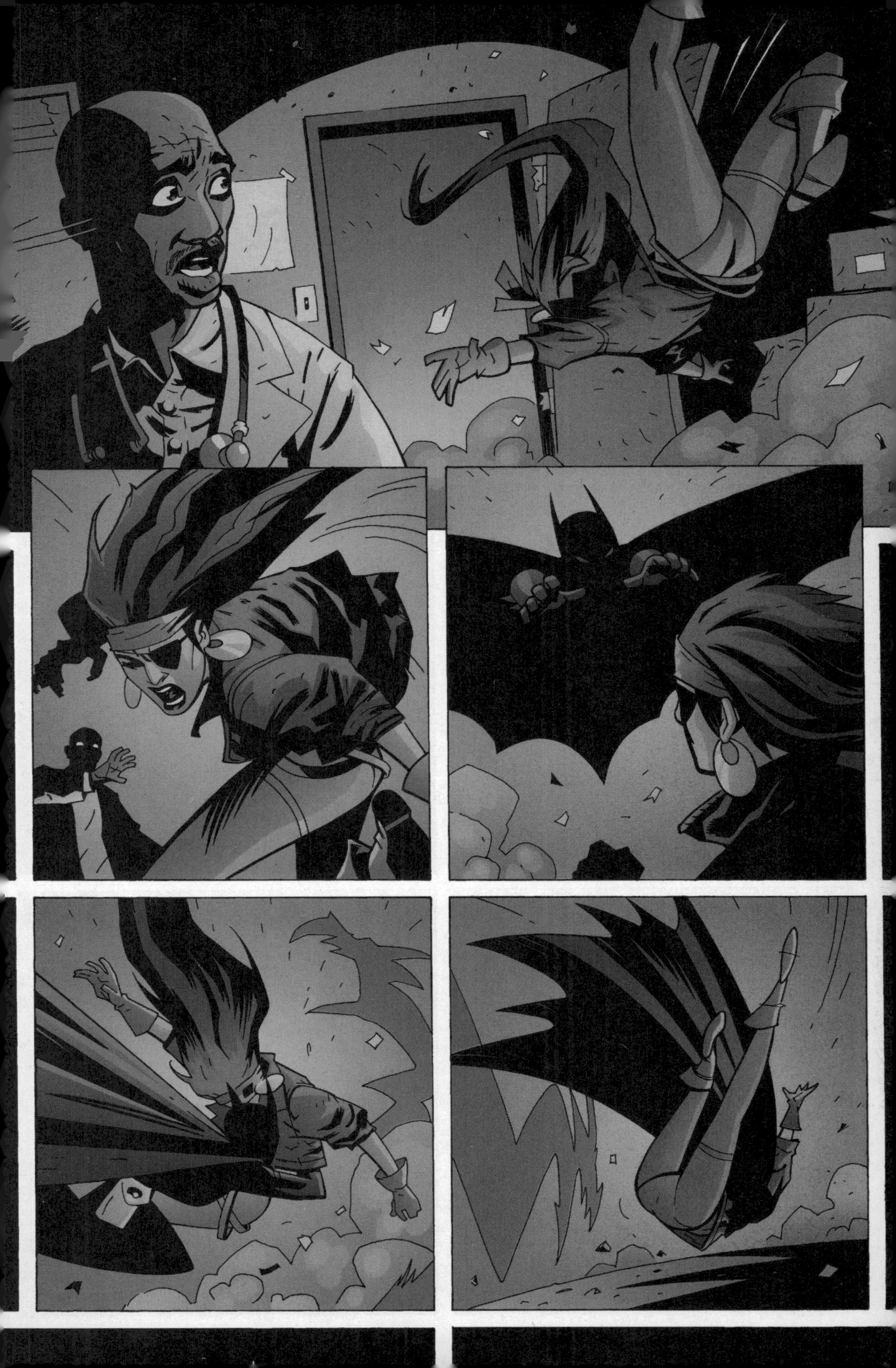

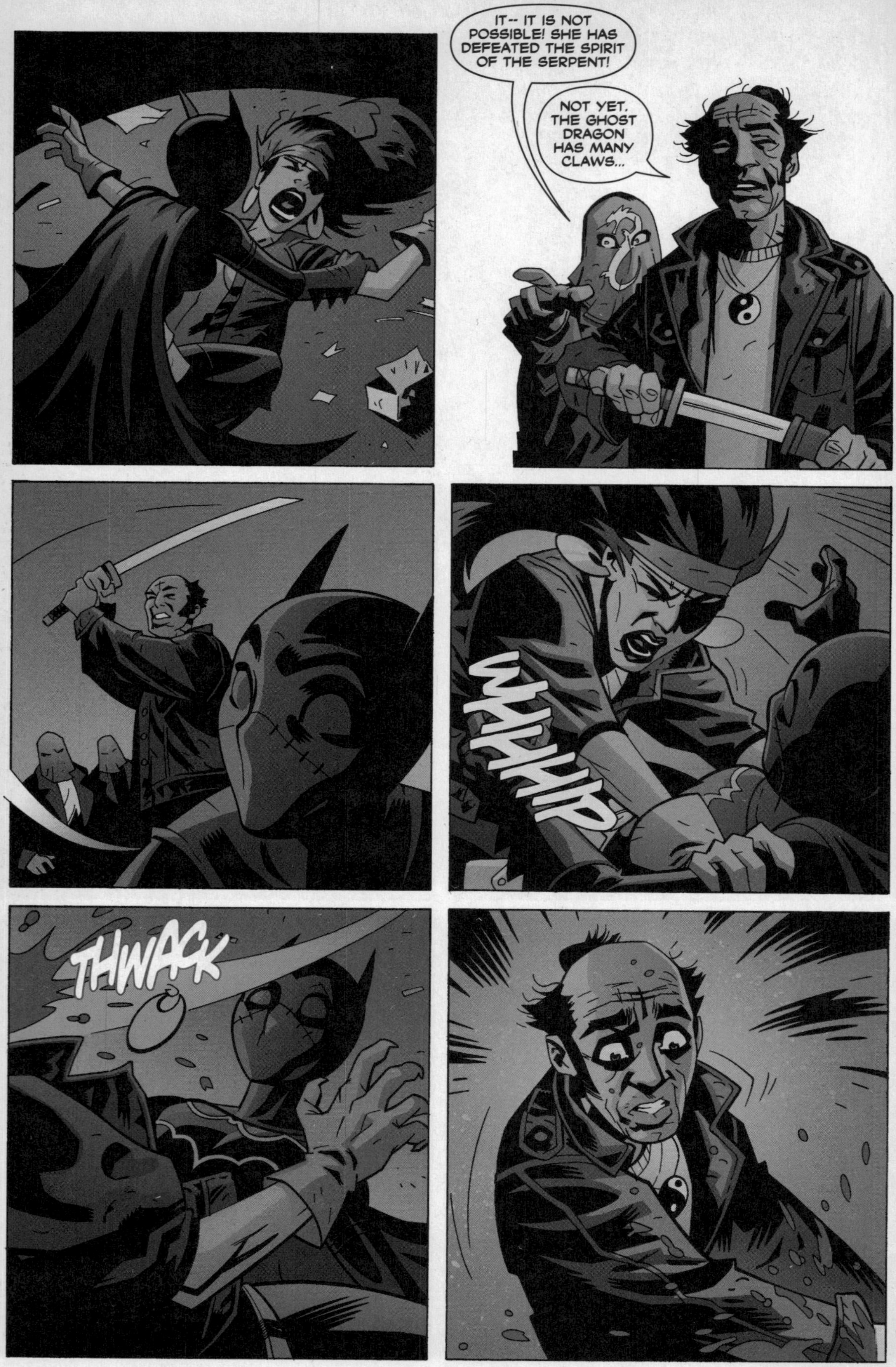
IT-- IT IS NOT POSSIBLE! SHE HAS DEFEATED THE SPIRIT OF THE SERPENT!
NOT YET. THE GHOST DRAGON HAS MANY CLAWS...
WHHHIP
THWACK

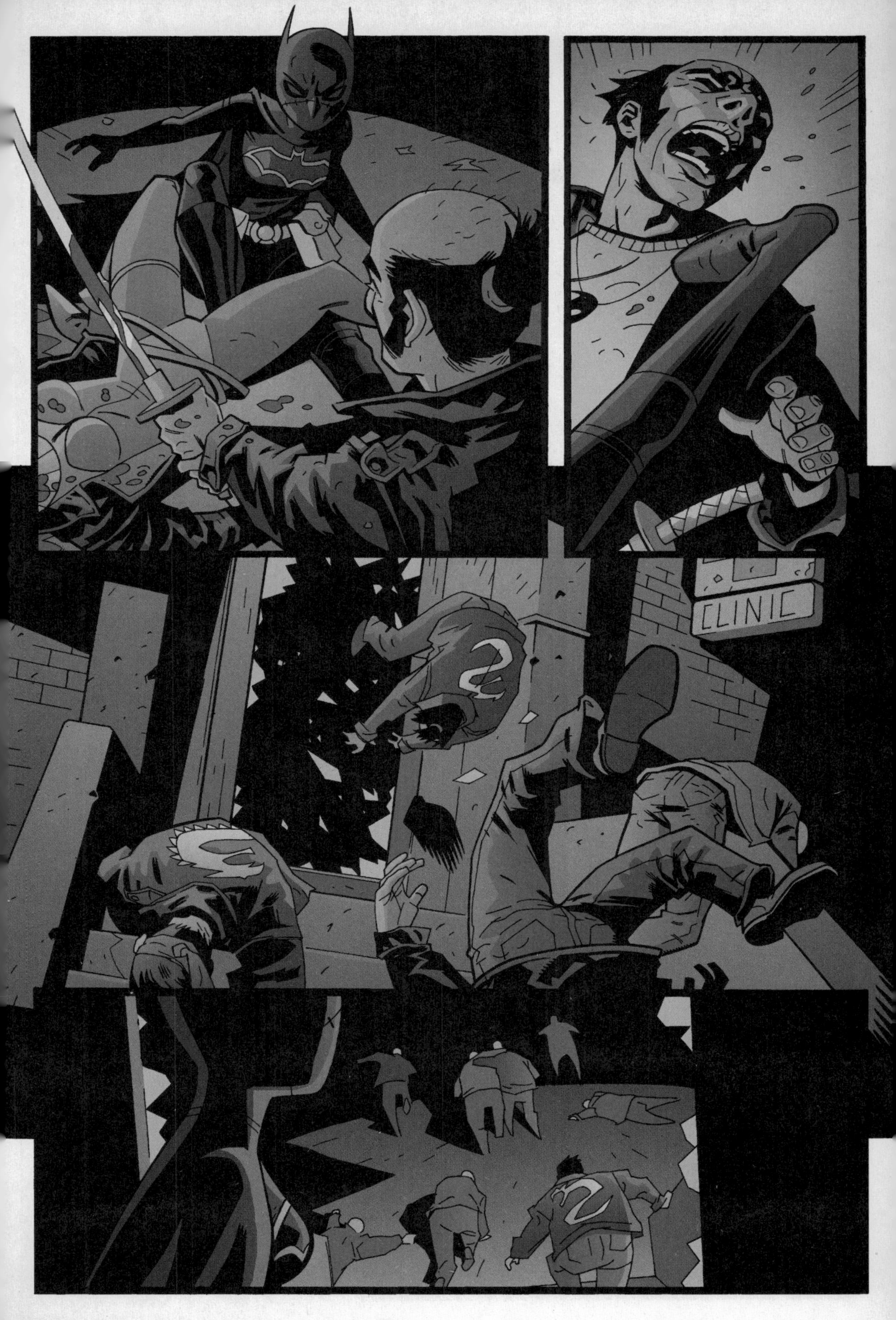
CLINIC

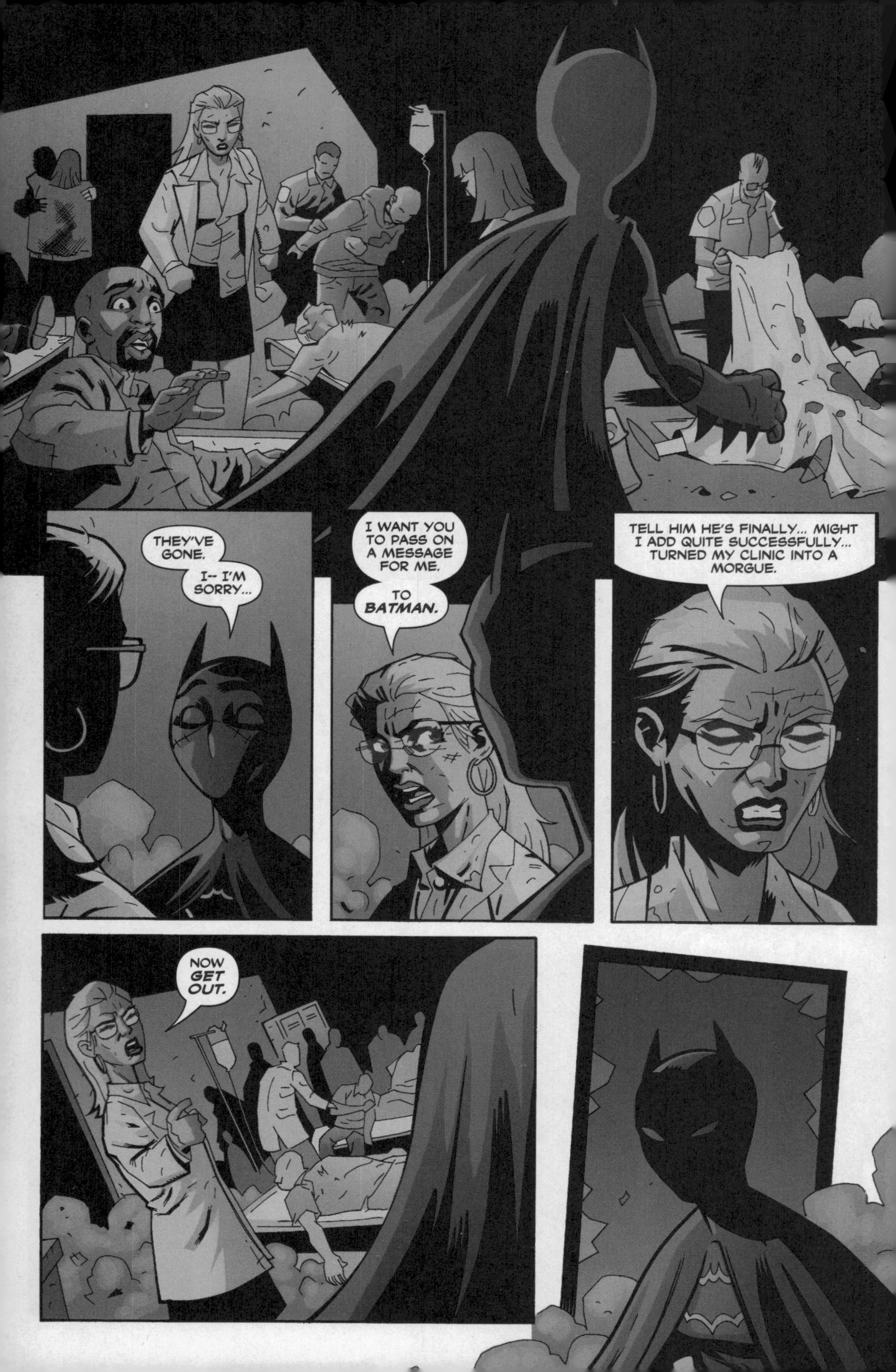
THEY'VE GONE.
I-- I'M SORRY...
I WANT YOU TO PASS ON A MESSAGE FOR ME.
TO BATMAN.
TELL HIM HE'S FINALLY... MIGHT I ADD QUITE SUCCESSFULLY... TURNED MY CLINIC INTO A MORGUE.
NOW GET OUT.

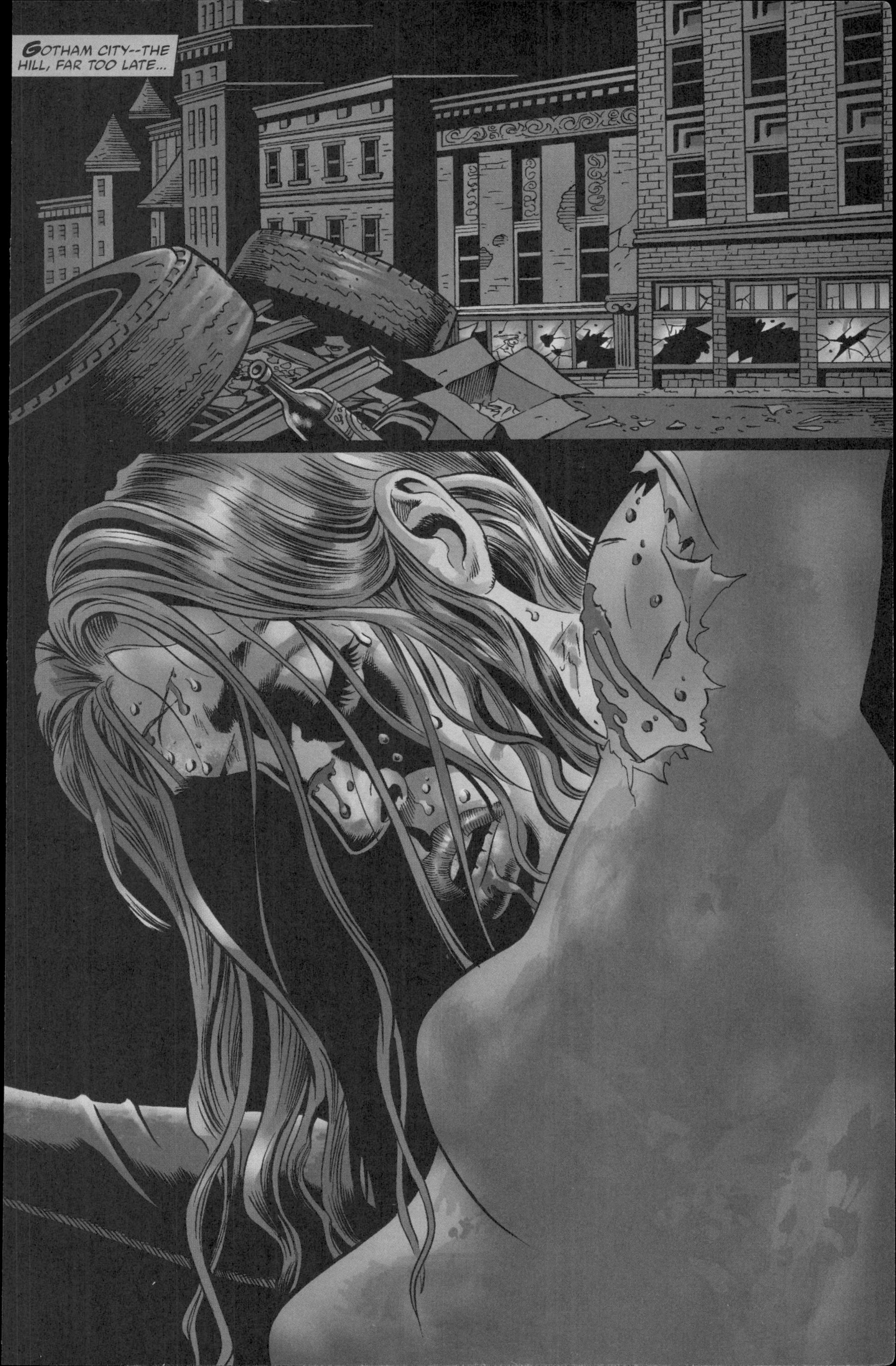
GOTHAM CITY--THE HILL, FAR TOO LATE...

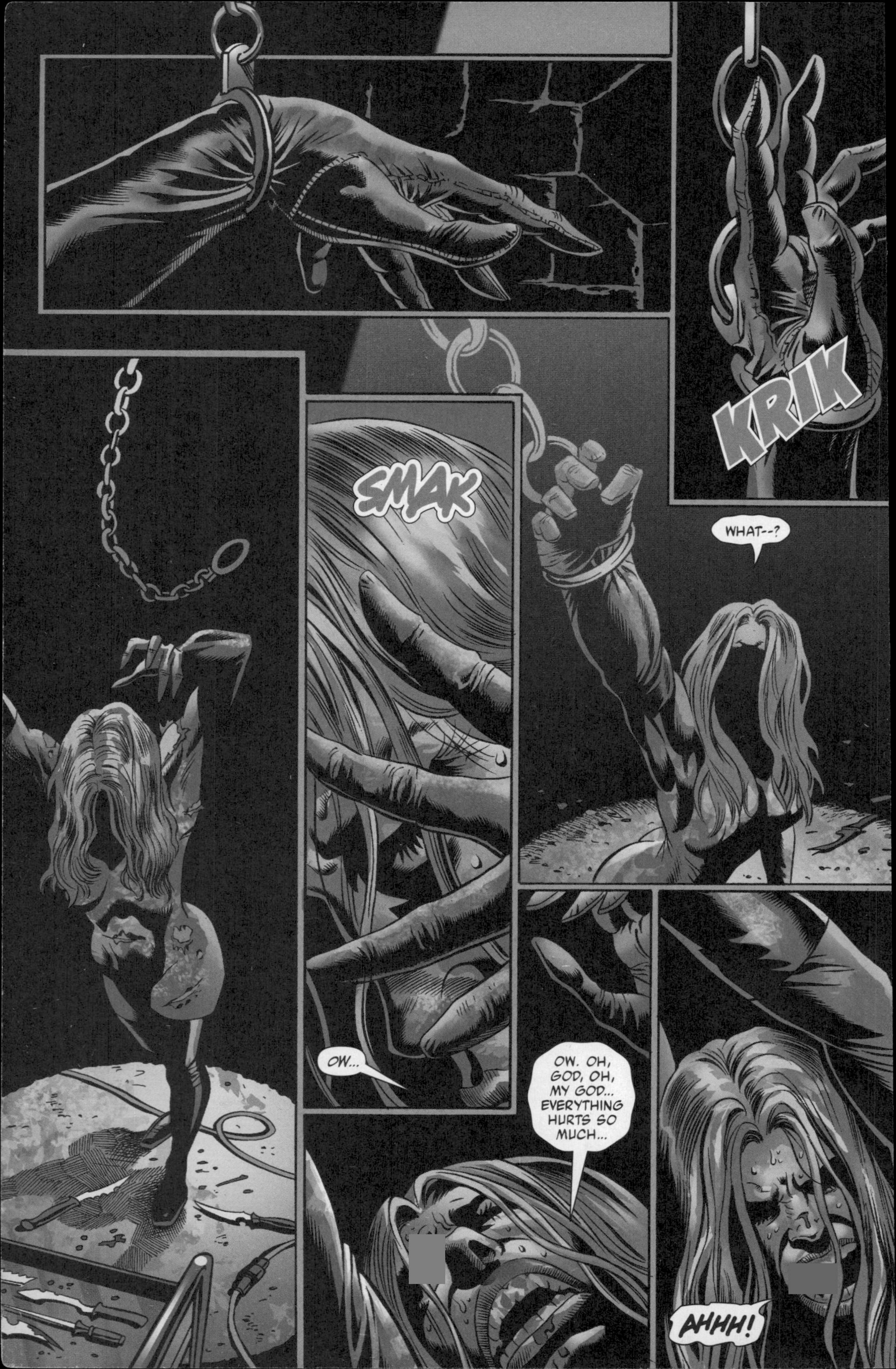
KRIK
SMAK
WHAT--?
OW...
OW. OH, GOD, OH, MY GOD... EVERYTHING HURTS SO MUCH...
AHHH!

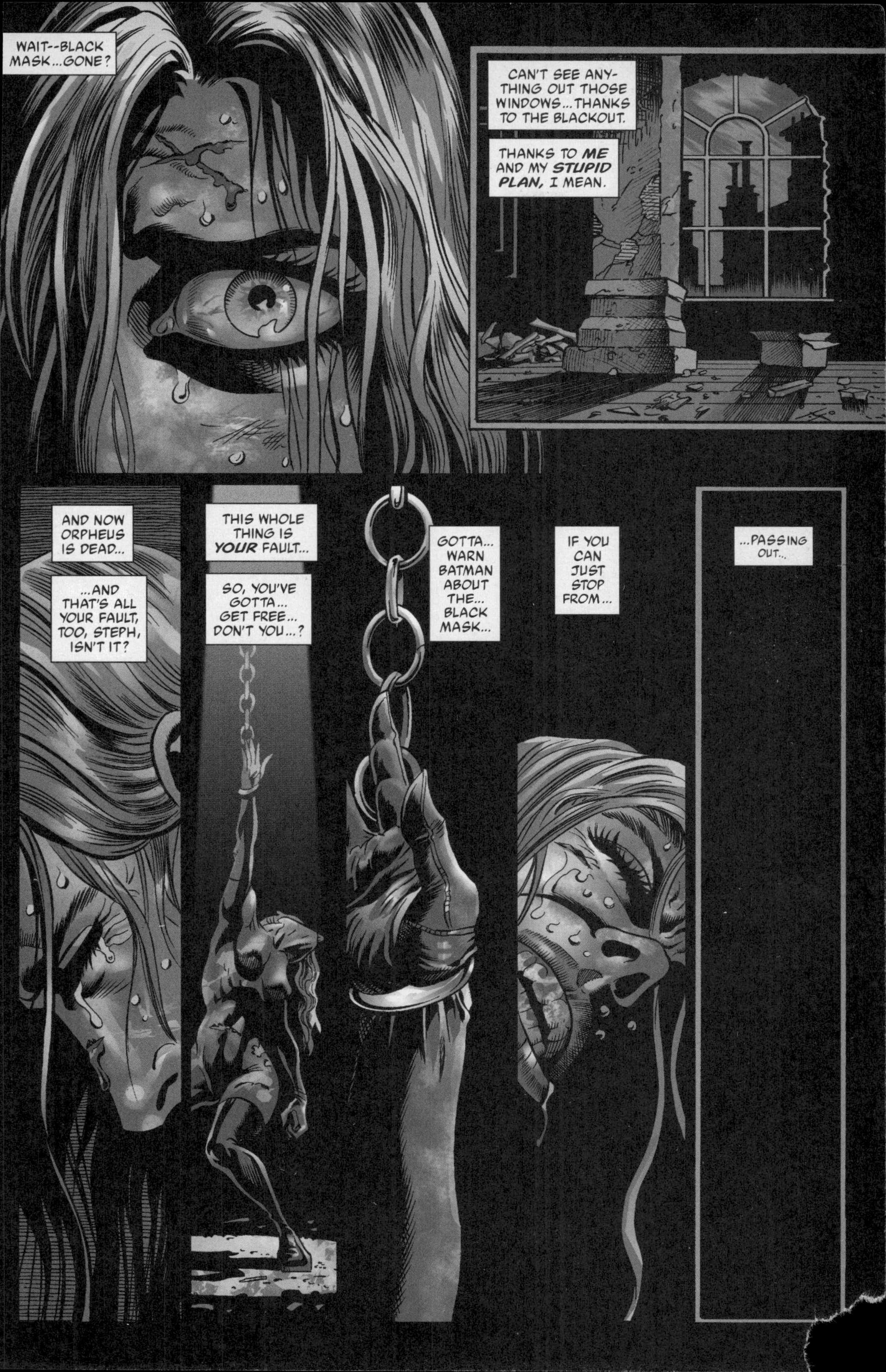
WAIT--BLACK MASK...GONE?
CAN'T SEE ANYTHING OUT THOSE WINDOWS...THANKS TO THE BLACKOUT.
THANKS TO ME AND MY STUPID PLAN, I MEAN.
AND NOW ORPHEUS IS DEAD...
...AND THAT'S ALL YOUR FAULT, TOO, STEPH, ISN'T IT?
THIS WHOLE THING IS YOUR FAULT...
SO, YOU'VE GOTTA... GET FREE... DON'T YOU...?
GOTTA... WARN BATMAN ABOUT THE... BLACK MASK...
IF YOU CAN JUST STOP FROM...
...PASSING OUT...

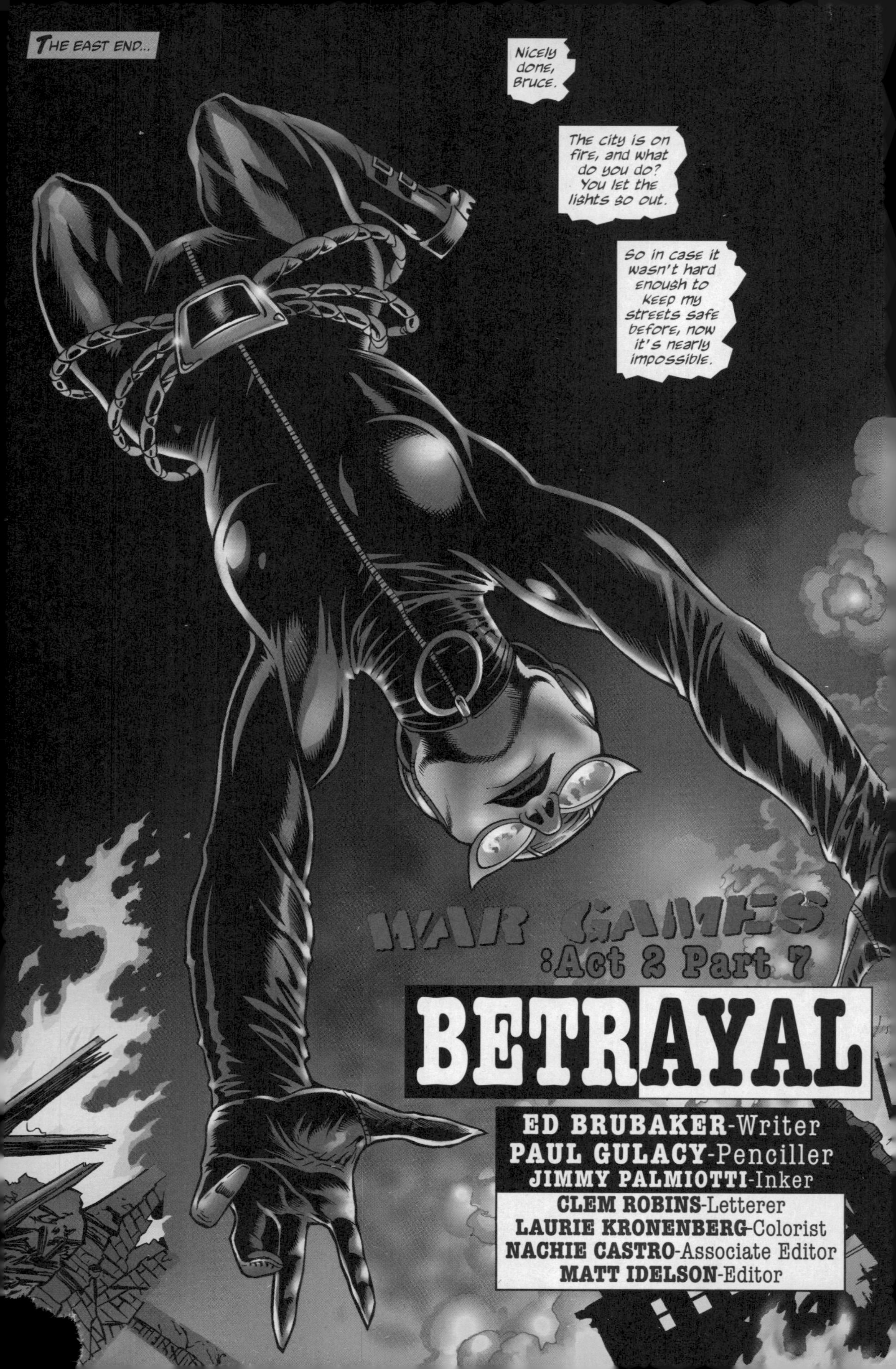
THE EAST END...
Nicely done, Bruce.
The city is on fire, and what do you do? You let the lights go out.
So in case it wasn't hard enough to keep my streets safe before, now it's nearly impossible.
WAR GAMES
:Act 2 Part 7
BETRAYAL
ED BRUBAKER-Writer
PAUL GULACY-Penciller
JIMMY PALMIOTTI-Inker
CLEM ROBINS-Letterer
LAURIE KRONENBERG-Colorist
NACHIE CASTRO-Associate Editor
MATT IDELSON-Editor

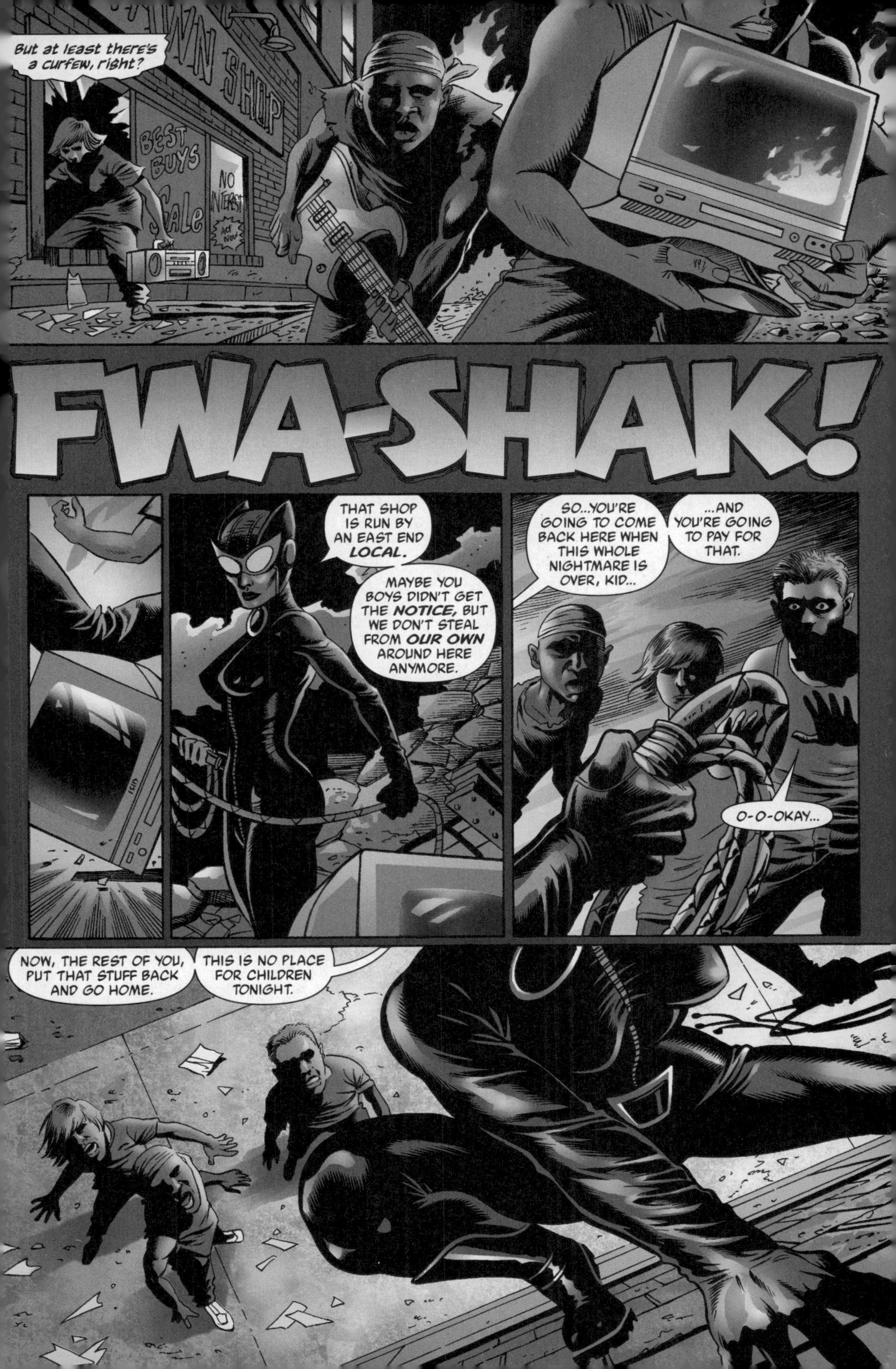
But at least there's a curfew, right?
PAWN SHOP
BEST BUYS Sale
NO INTEREST
ACT NOW
FWA-SHAK!
THAT SHOP IS RUN BY AN EAST END LOCAL.
MAYBE YOU BOYS DIDN'T GET THE NOTICE, BUT WE DON'T STEAL FROM OUR OWN AROUND HERE ANYMORE.
SO...YOU'RE GOING TO COME BACK HERE WHEN THIS WHOLE NIGHTMARE IS OVER, KID...
...AND YOU'RE GOING TO PAY FOR THAT.
O-O-OKAY...
NOW, THE REST OF YOU, PUT THAT STUFF BACK AND GO HOME.
THIS IS NO PLACE FOR CHILDREN TONIGHT.

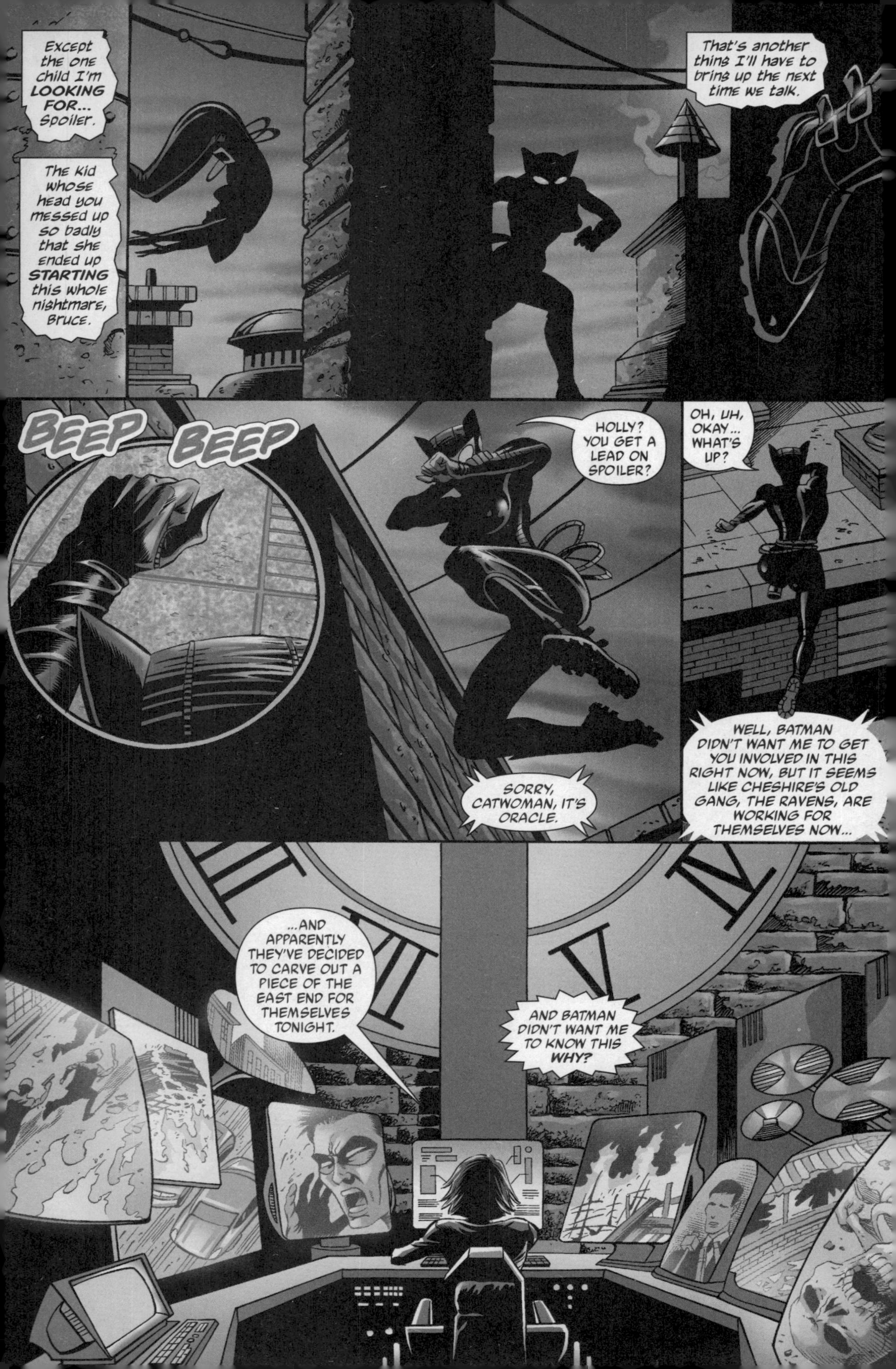

Except the one child I'm LOOKING FOR... Spoiler.
The kid whose head you messed up so badly that she ended up STARTING this whole nightmare, Bruce.
That's another thing I'll have to bring up the next time we talk.
BEEP BEEP
HOLLY? YOU GET A LEAD ON SPOILER?
SORRY, CATWOMAN, IT'S ORACLE.
OH, UH, OKAY... WHAT'S UP?
WELL, BATMAN DIDN'T WANT ME TO GET YOU INVOLVED IN THIS RIGHT NOW, BUT IT SEEMS LIKE CHESHIRE'S OLD GANG, THE RAVENS, ARE WORKING FOR THEMSELVES NOW...
...AND APPARENTLY THEY'VE DECIDED TO CARVE OUT A PIECE OF THE EAST END FOR THEMSELVES TONIGHT.
AND BATMAN DIDN'T WANT ME TO KNOW THIS WHY?

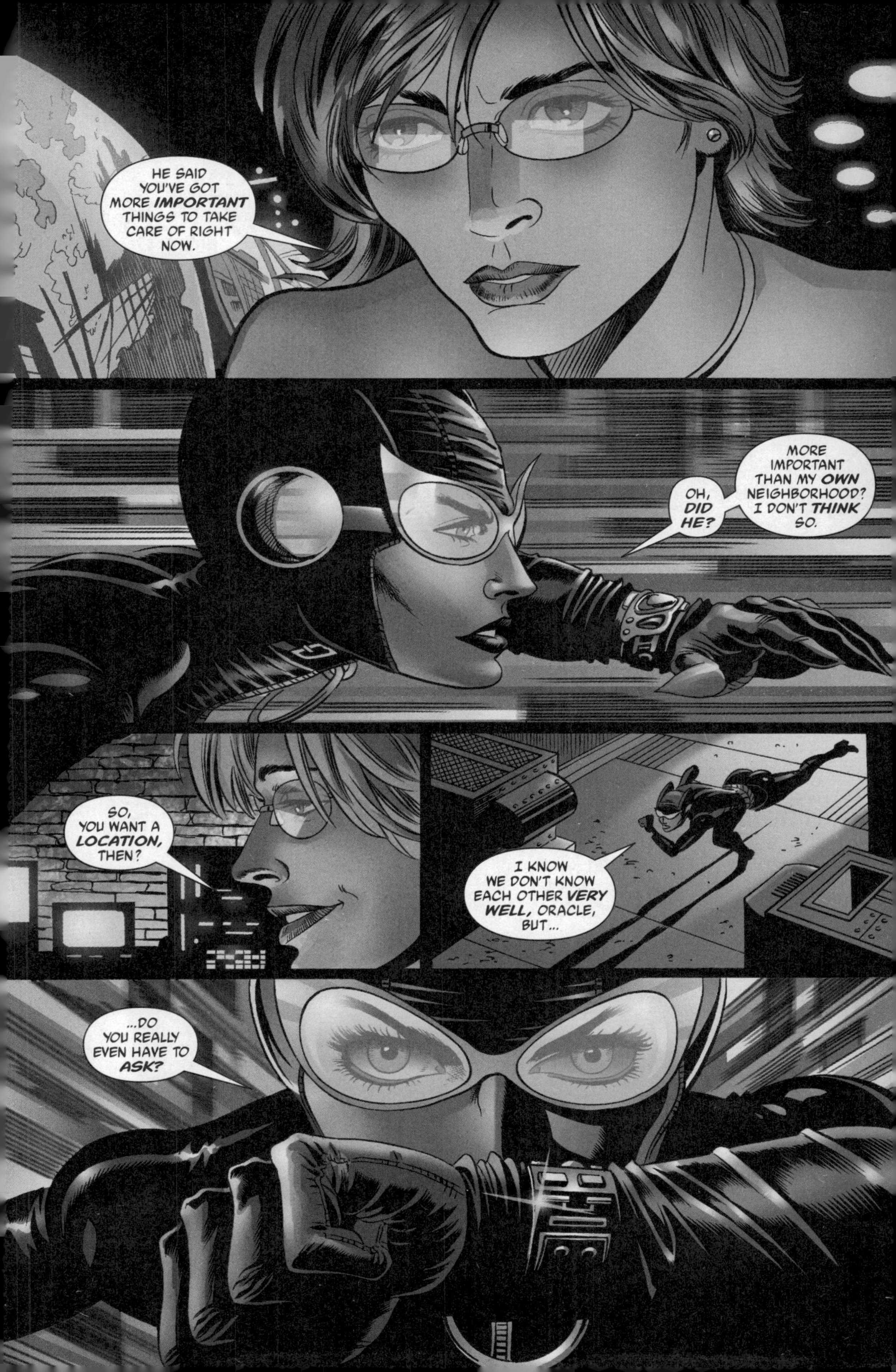
HE SAID YOU'VE GOT MORE IMPORTANT THINGS TO TAKE CARE OF RIGHT NOW.
OH, DID HE?
MORE IMPORTANT THAN MY OWN NEIGHBORHOOD? I DON'T THINK SO.
SO, YOU WANT A LOCATION, THEN?
I KNOW WE DON'T KNOW EACH OTHER VERY WELL, ORACLE, BUT...
...DO YOU REALLY EVEN HAVE TO ASK?

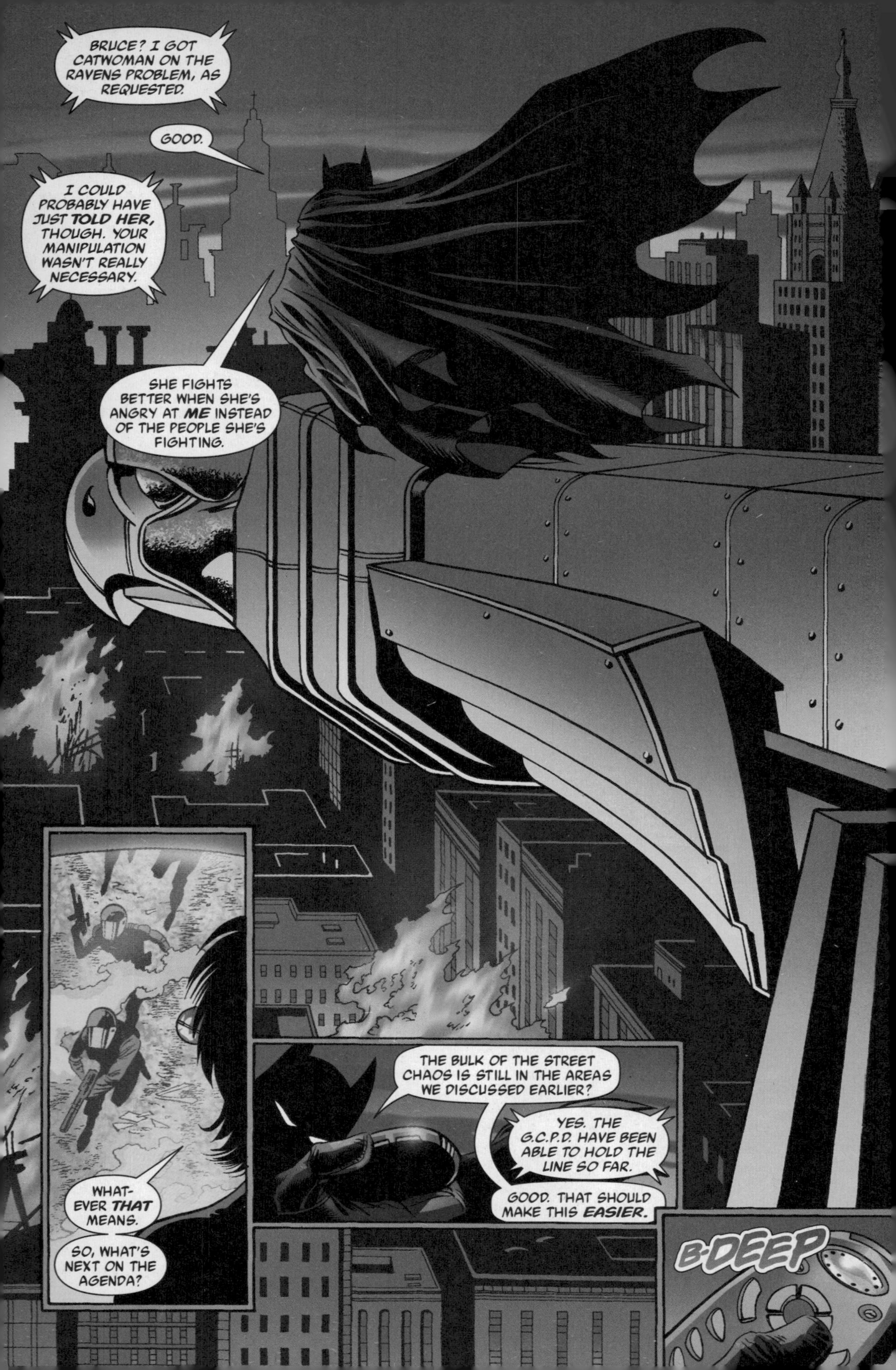
BRUCE? I GOT CATWOMAN ON THE RAVENS PROBLEM, AS REQUESTED.
GOOD.
I COULD PROBABLY HAVE JUST TOLD HER, THOUGH. YOUR MANIPULATION WASN'T REALLY NECESSARY.
SHE FIGHTS BETTER WHEN SHE'S ANGRY AT ME INSTEAD OF THE PEOPLE SHE'S FIGHTING.
WHAT-EVER THAT MEANS.
SO, WHAT'S NEXT ON THE AGENDA?
THE BULK OF THE STREET CHAOS IS STILL IN THE AREAS WE DISCUSSED EARLIER?
YES. THE G.C.P.D. HAVE BEEN ABLE TO HOLD THE LINE SO FAR.
GOOD. THAT SHOULD MAKE THIS EASIER.
B-DEEP

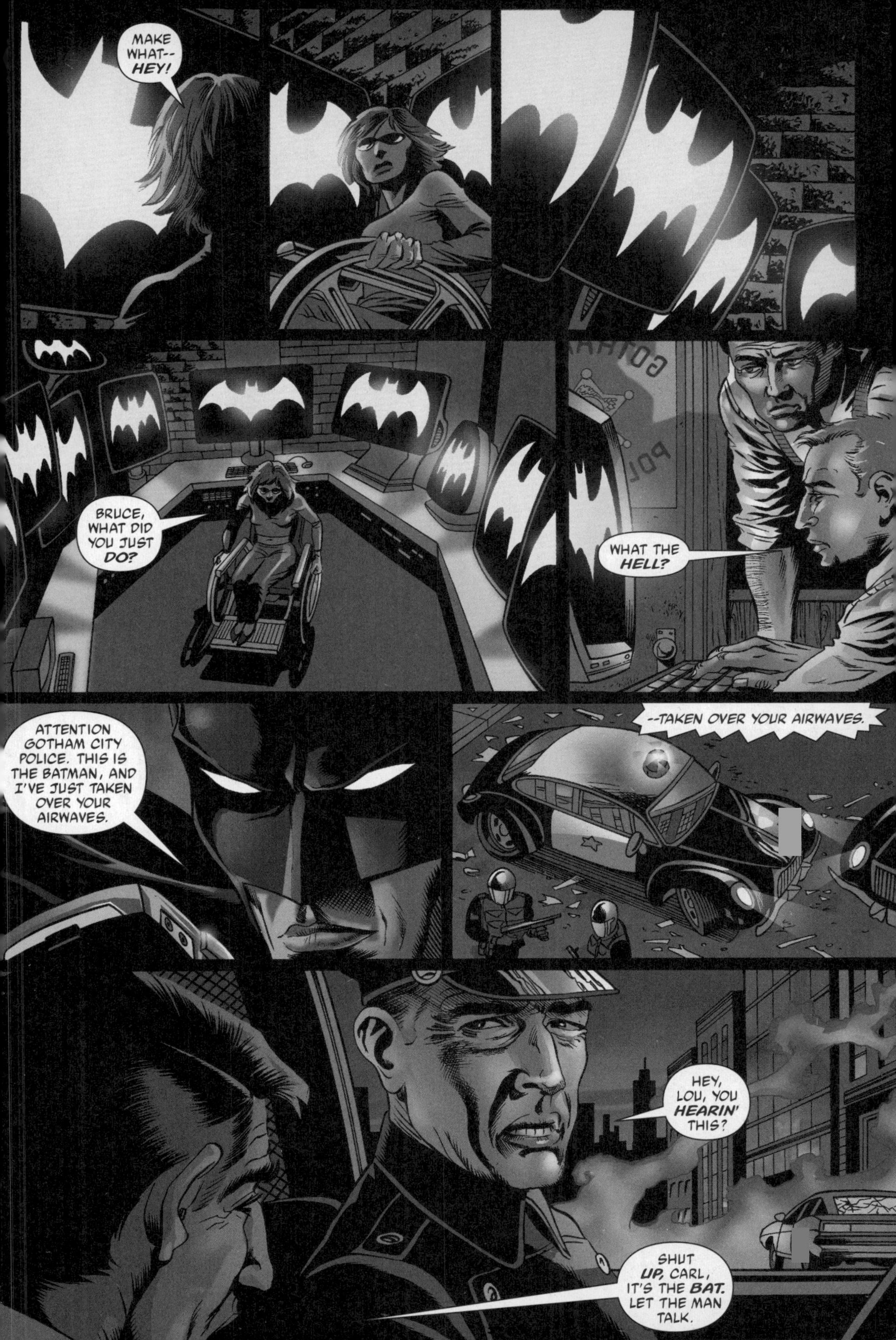
MAKE WHAT-- HEY!
BRUCE, WHAT DID YOU JUST DO?
WHAT THE HELL?
ATTENTION GOTHAM CITY POLICE. THIS IS THE BATMAN, AND I'VE JUST TAKEN OVER YOUR AIRWAVES.
--TAKEN OVER YOUR AIRWAVES.
HEY, LOU, YOU HEARIN' THIS?
SHUT UP, CARL, IT'S THE BAT. LET THE MAN TALK.

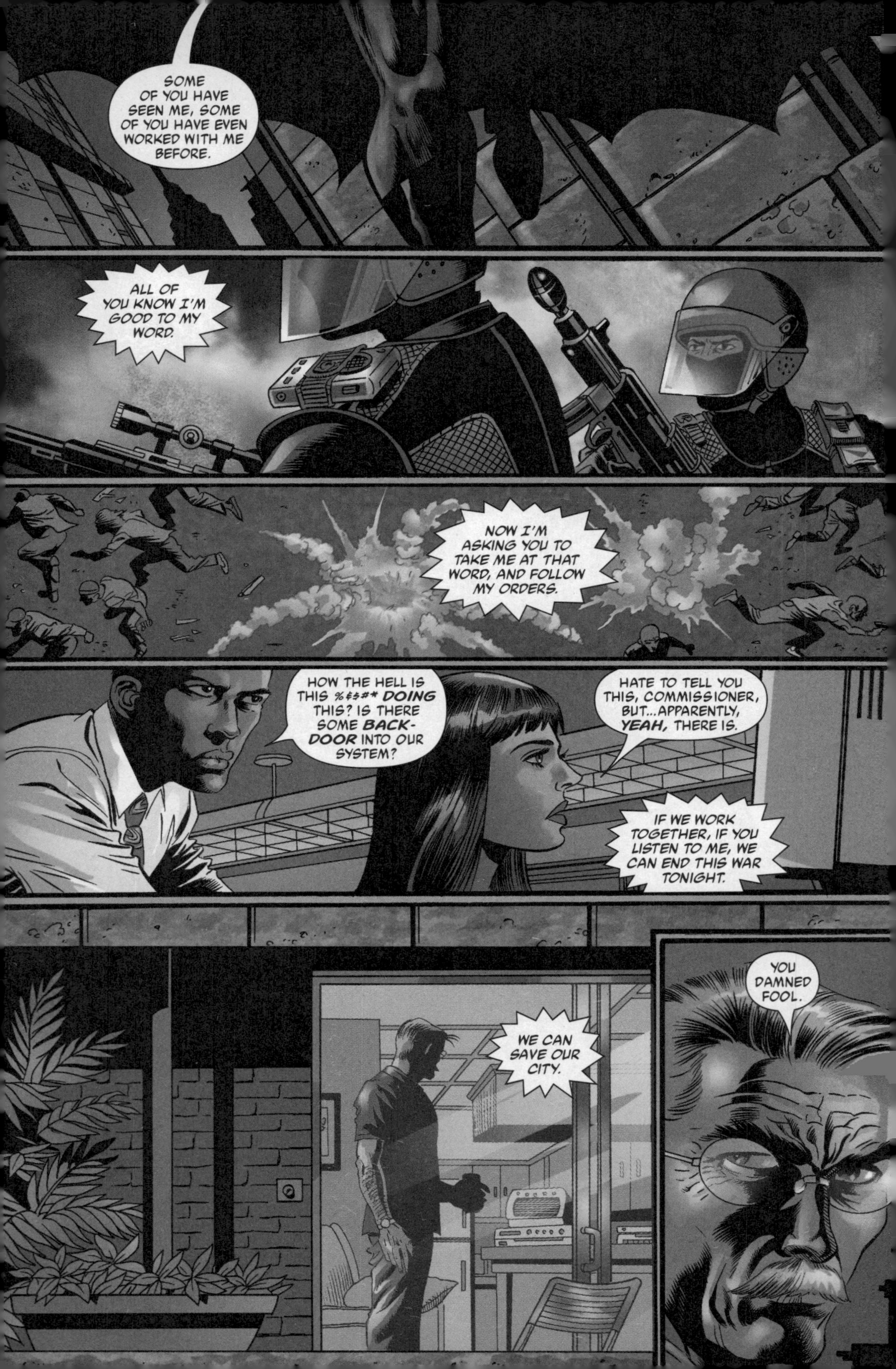
SOME OF YOU HAVE SEEN ME, SOME OF YOU HAVE EVEN WORKED WITH ME BEFORE.
ALL OF YOU KNOW I'M GOOD TO MY WORD.
NOW I'M ASKING YOU TO TAKE ME AT THAT WORD, AND FOLLOW MY ORDERS.
HOW THE HELL IS THIS %$$#* DOING THIS? IS THERE SOME BACK-DOOR INTO OUR SYSTEM?
HATE TO TELL YOU THIS, COMMISSIONER, BUT...APPARENTLY, YEAH, THERE IS.
IF WE WORK TOGETHER, IF YOU LISTEN TO ME, WE CAN END THIS WAR TONIGHT.
WE CAN SAVE OUR CITY.
YOU DAMNED FOOL.

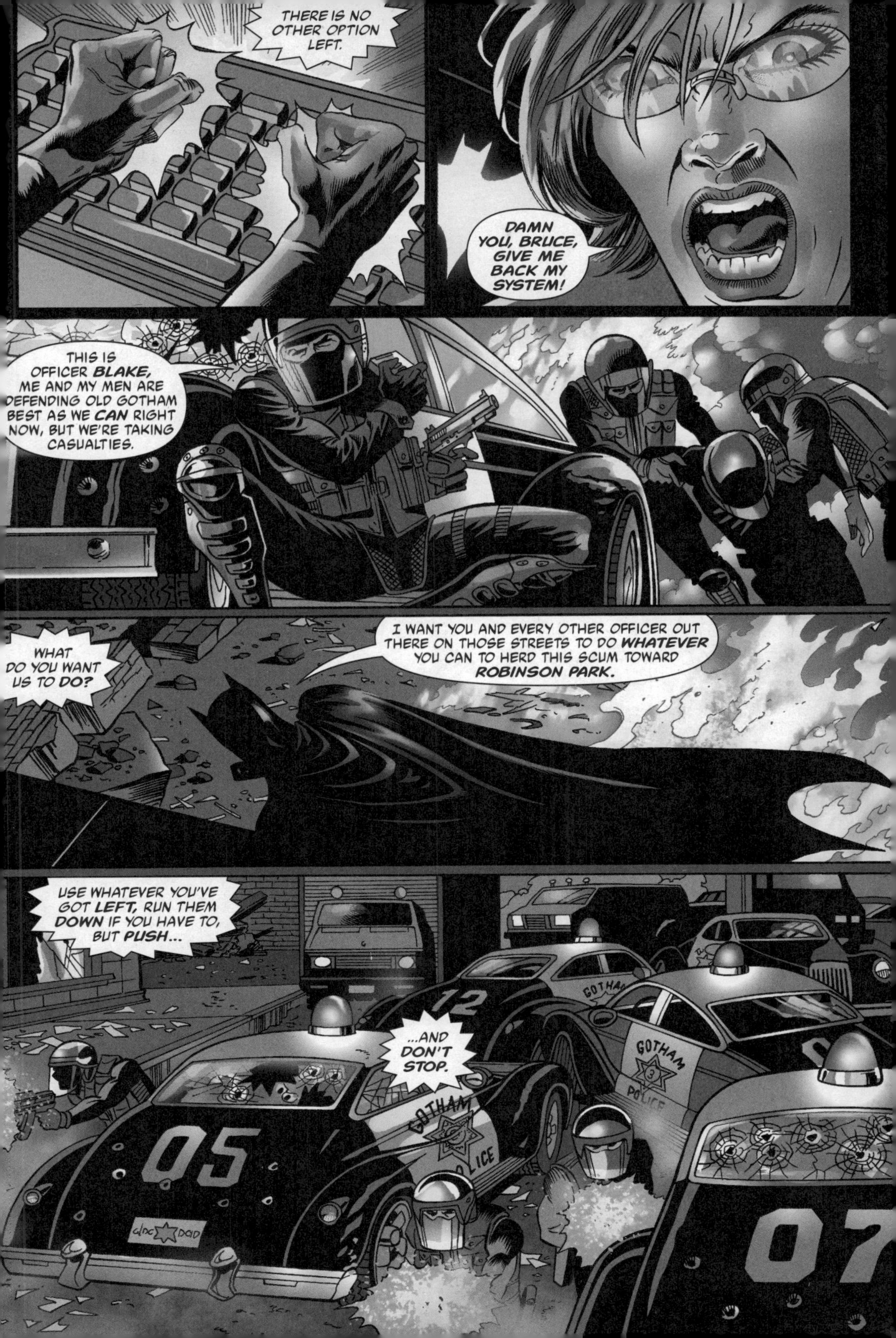
THERE IS NO OTHER OPTION LEFT.
DAMN YOU, BRUCE, GIVE ME BACK MY SYSTEM!
THIS IS OFFICER BLAKE, ME AND MY MEN ARE DEFENDING OLD GOTHAM BEST AS WE CAN RIGHT NOW, BUT WE'RE TAKING CASUALTIES.
WHAT DO YOU WANT US TO DO?
I WANT YOU AND EVERY OTHER OFFICER OUT THERE ON THOSE STREETS TO DO WHATEVER YOU CAN TO HERD THIS SCUM TOWARD ROBINSON PARK.
USE WHATEVER YOU'VE GOT LEFT, RUN THEM DOWN IF YOU HAVE TO, BUT PUSH...
...AND DON'T STOP.
12
GOTHAM
GOTHAM 3 POLICE
05
GOTHAM POLICE
07

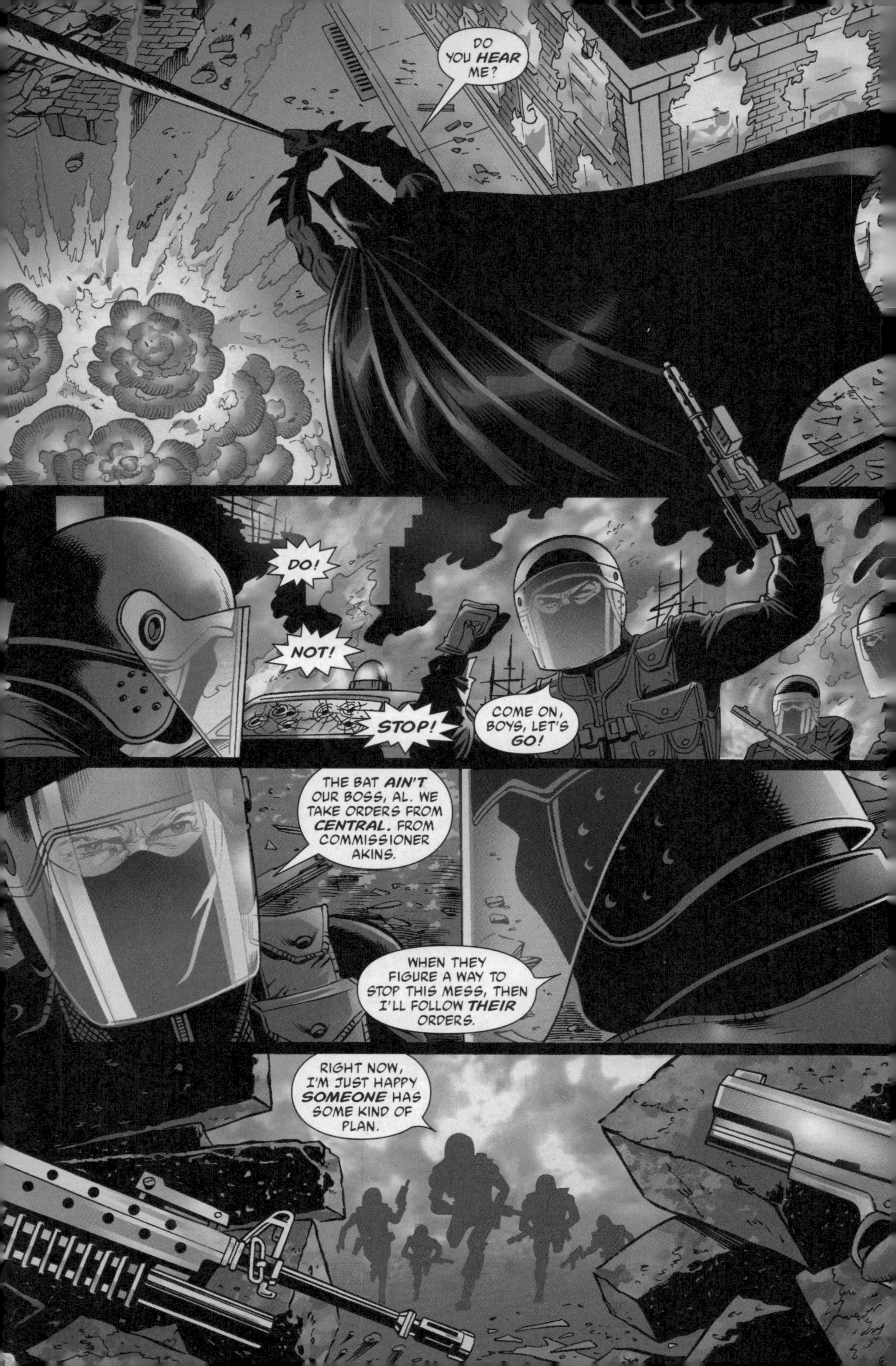
DO YOU HEAR ME?
DO!
NOT!
STOP!
COME ON, BOYS, LET'S GO!
THE BAT AIN'T OUR BOSS, AL. WE TAKE ORDERS FROM CENTRAL. FROM COMMISSIONER AKINS.
WHEN THEY FIGURE A WAY TO STOP THIS MESS, THEN I'LL FOLLOW THEIR ORDERS.
RIGHT NOW, I'M JUST HAPPY SOMEONE HAS SOME KIND OF PLAN.

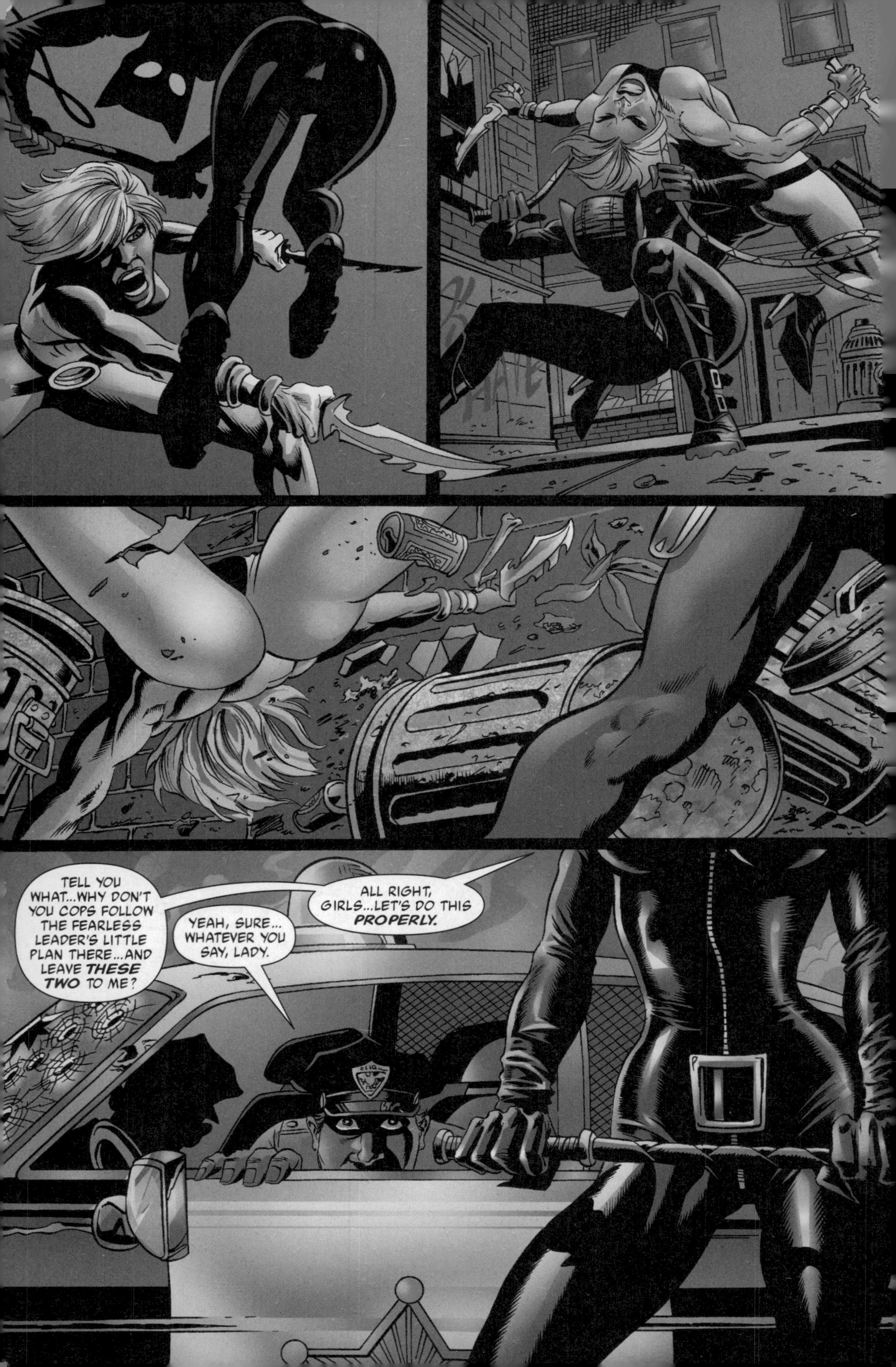
ALL RIGHT, GIRLS...LET'S DO THIS PROPERLY.
TELL YOU WHAT...WHY DON'T YOU COPS FOLLOW THE FEARLESS LEADER'S LITTLE PLAN THERE...AND LEAVE THESE TWO TO ME?
YEAH, SURE... WHATEVER YOU SAY, LADY.

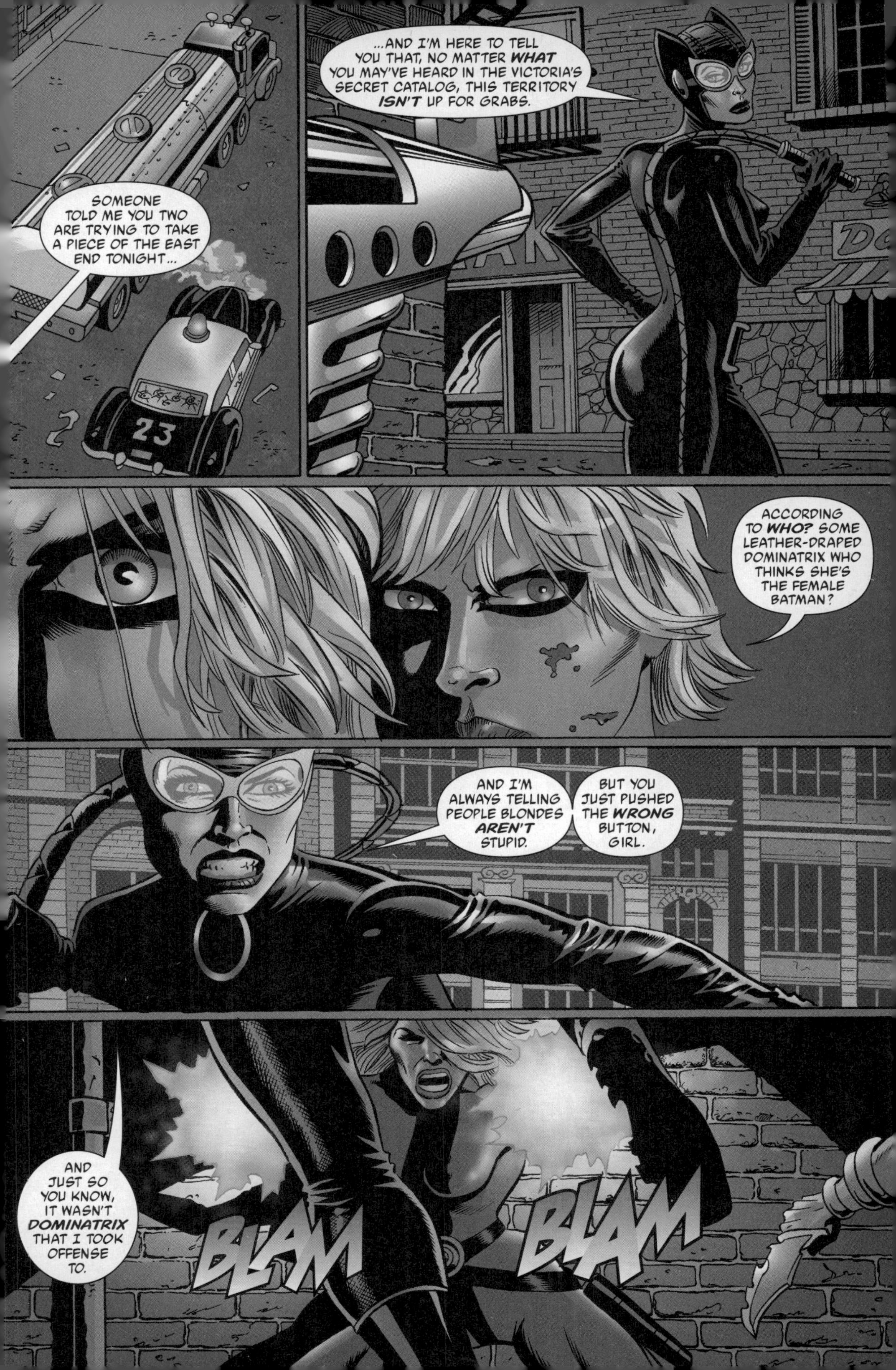

SOMEONE TOLD ME YOU TWO ARE TRYING TO TAKE A PIECE OF THE EAST END TONIGHT...
...AND I'M HERE TO TELL YOU THAT, NO MATTER **WHAT** YOU MAY'VE HEARD IN THE VICTORIA'S SECRET CATALOG, THIS TERRITORY **ISN'T** UP FOR GRABS.
23
ACCORDING TO **WHO?** SOME LEATHER-DRAPED DOMINATRIX WHO THINKS SHE'S THE FEMALE BATMAN?
AND I'M ALWAYS TELLING PEOPLE BLONDES **AREN'T** STUPID.
BUT YOU JUST PUSHED THE **WRONG** BUTTON, GIRL.
AND JUST SO YOU KNOW, IT WASN'T **DOMINATRIX** THAT I TOOK OFFENSE TO.
BLAM
BLAM

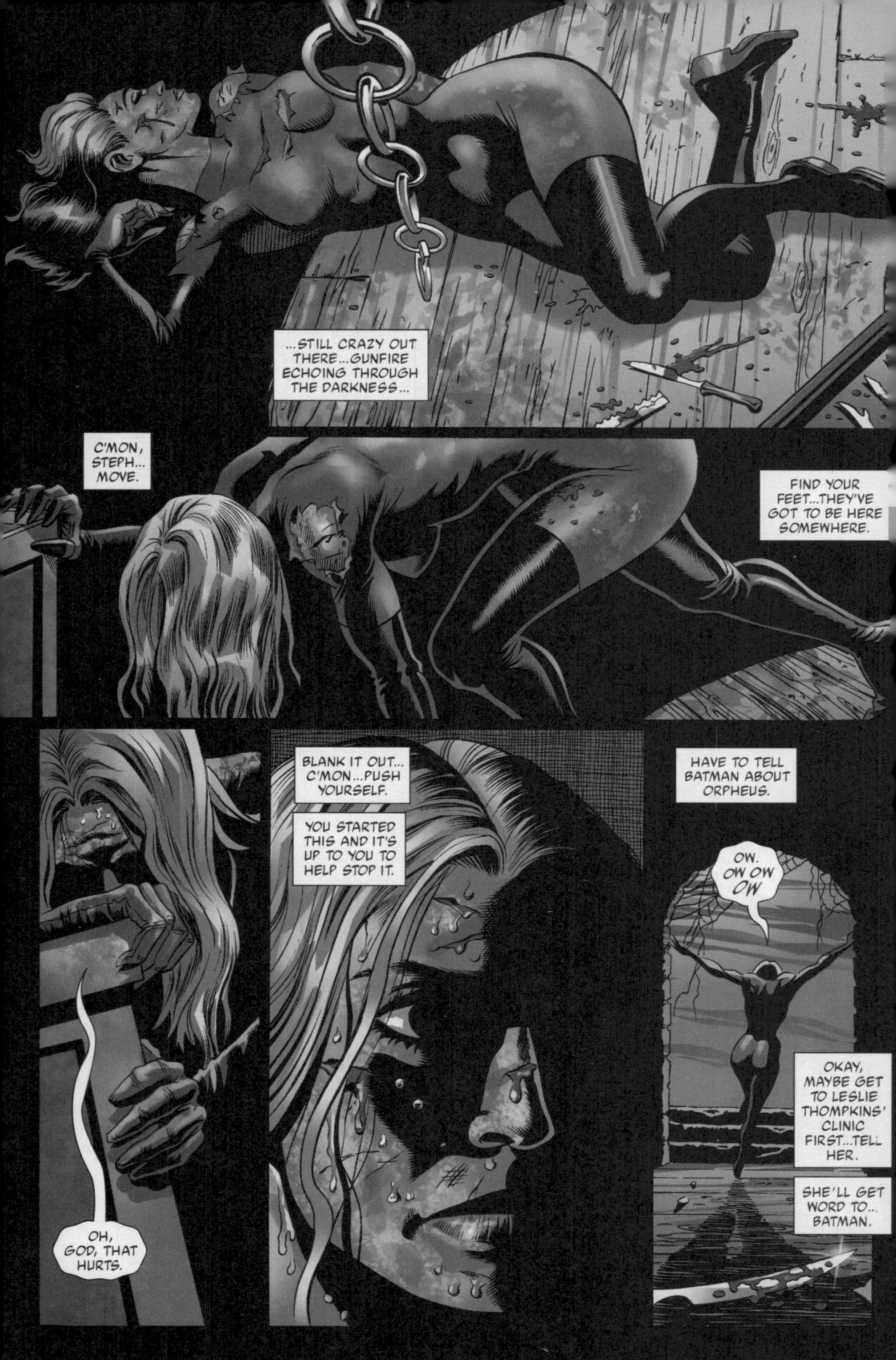
...STILL CRAZY OUT THERE...GUNFIRE ECHOING THROUGH THE DARKNESS...
C'MON, STEPH... MOVE.
FIND YOUR FEET...THEY'VE GOT TO BE HERE SOMEWHERE.
OH, GOD, THAT HURTS.
BLANK IT OUT... C'MON...PUSH YOURSELF.
YOU STARTED THIS AND IT'S UP TO YOU TO HELP STOP IT.
HAVE TO TELL BATMAN ABOUT ORPHEUS.
OW. OW OW OW
OKAY, MAYBE GET TO LESLIE THOMPKINS' CLINIC FIRST...TELL HER.
SHE'LL GET WORD TO... BATMAN.

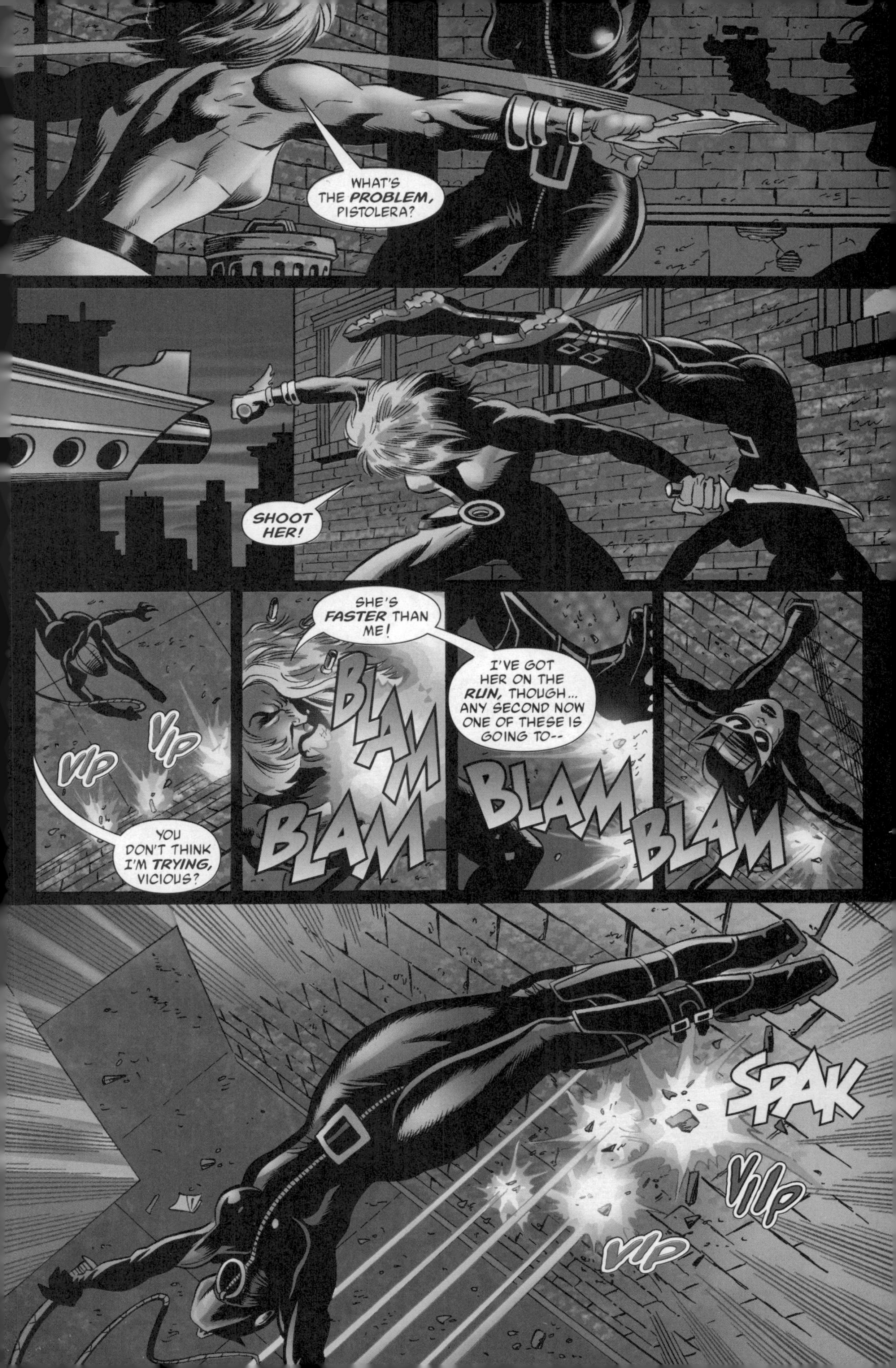
WHAT'S THE PROBLEM, PISTOLERA?
SHOOT HER!
VIP
VIP
YOU DON'T THINK I'M TRYING, VICIOUS?
SHE'S FASTER THAN ME!
BLAM
BLAM
I'VE GOT HER ON THE RUN, THOUGH... ANY SECOND NOW ONE OF THESE IS GOING TO--
BLAM
BLAM
SPAK
VIP
VIP

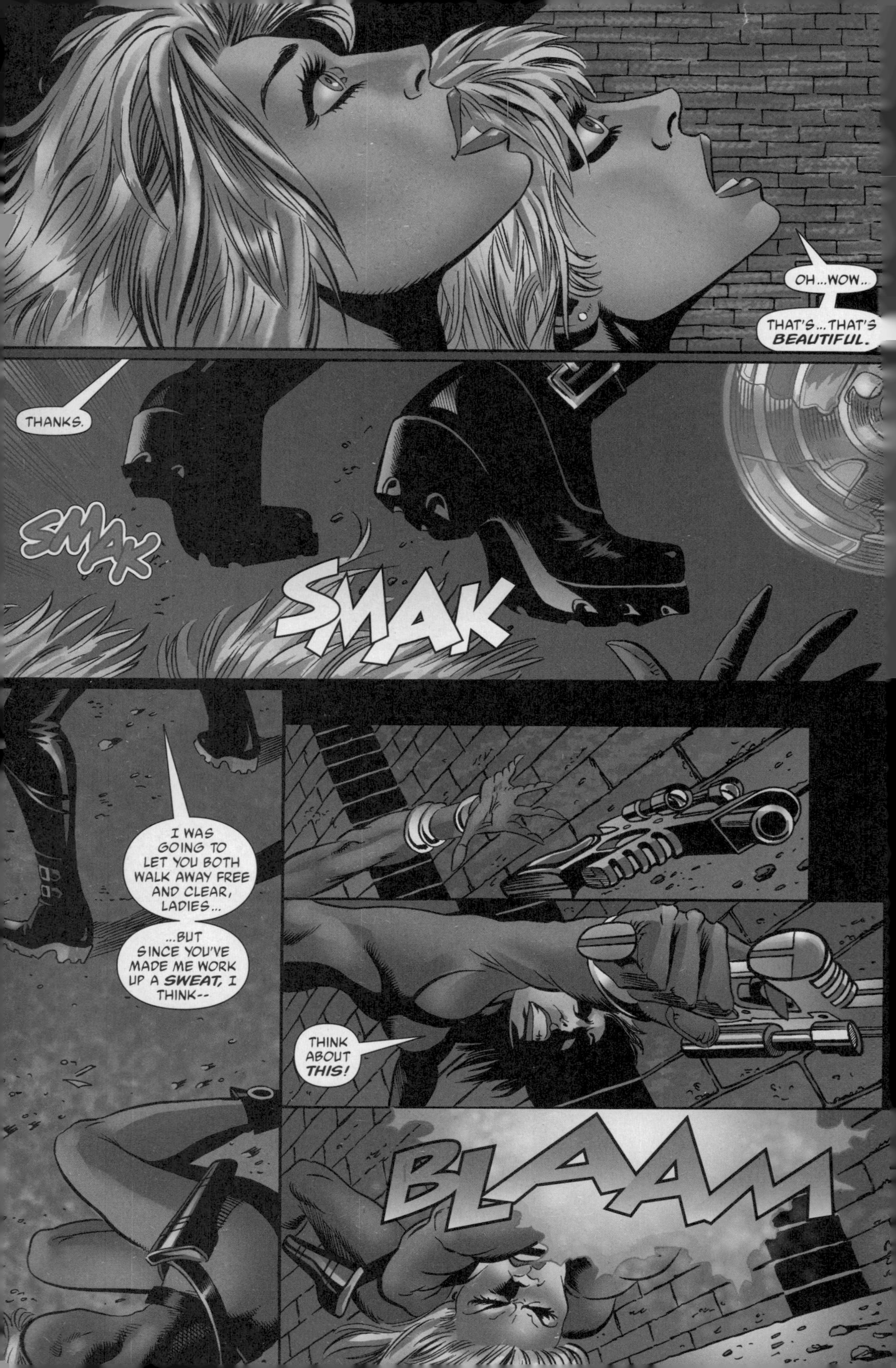
OH...WOW..
THAT'S...THAT'S BEAUTIFUL.
THANKS.
SMAK
SMAK
I WAS GOING TO LET YOU BOTH WALK AWAY FREE AND CLEAR, LADIES...
...BUT SINCE YOU'VE MADE ME WORK UP A SWEAT, I THINK--
THINK ABOUT THIS!
BLAAM

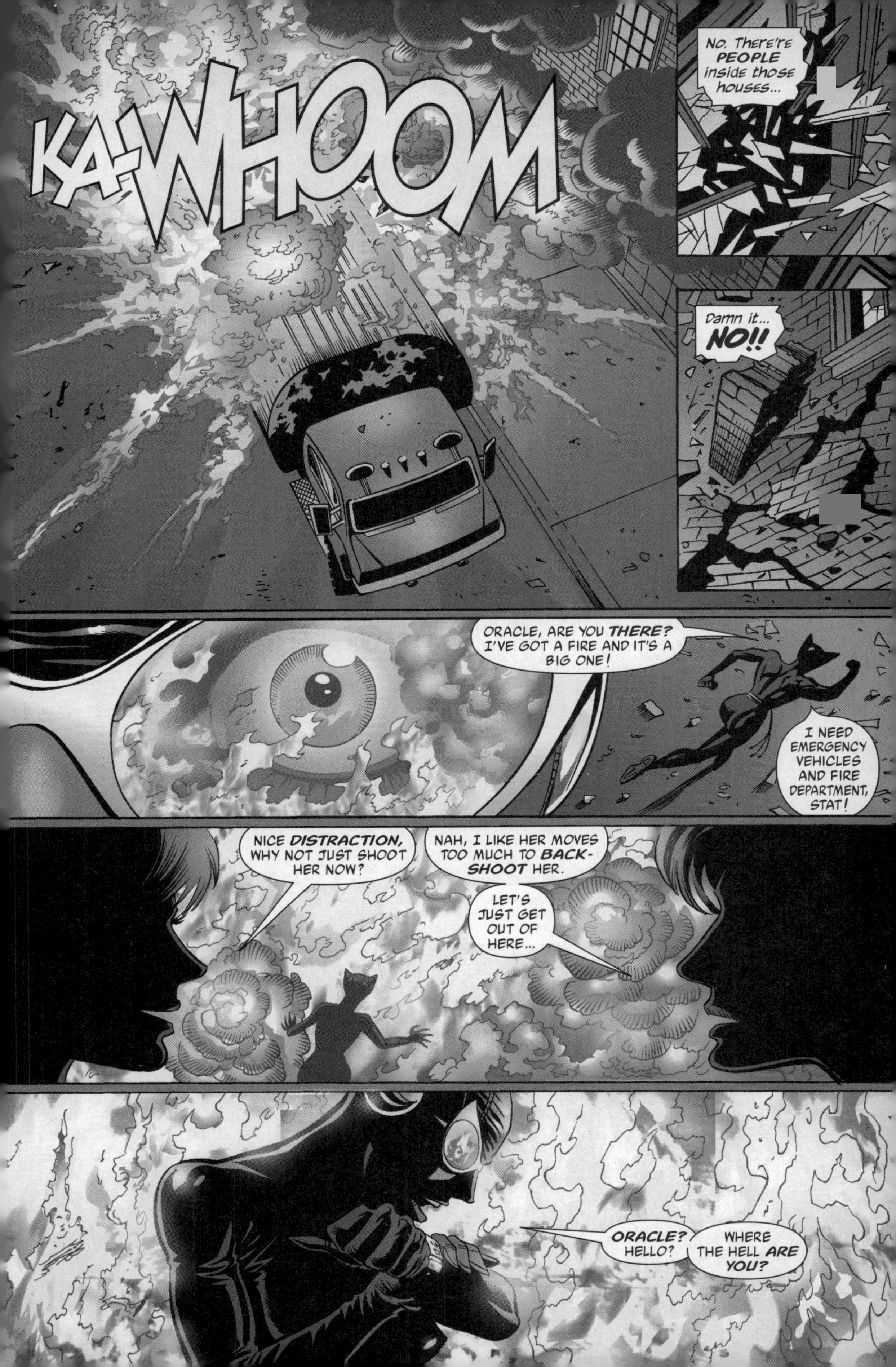
KA-WHOOM
No. There're PEOPLE inside those houses...
Damn it... NO!!
ORACLE, ARE YOU THERE? I'VE GOT A FIRE AND IT'S A BIG ONE!
I NEED EMERGENCY VEHICLES AND FIRE DEPARTMENT, STAT!
NICE DISTRACTION, WHY NOT JUST SHOOT HER NOW?
NAH, I LIKE HER MOVES TOO MUCH TO BACK-SHOOT HER.
LET'S JUST GET OUT OF HERE...
ORACLE? HELLO?
WHERE THE HELL ARE YOU?

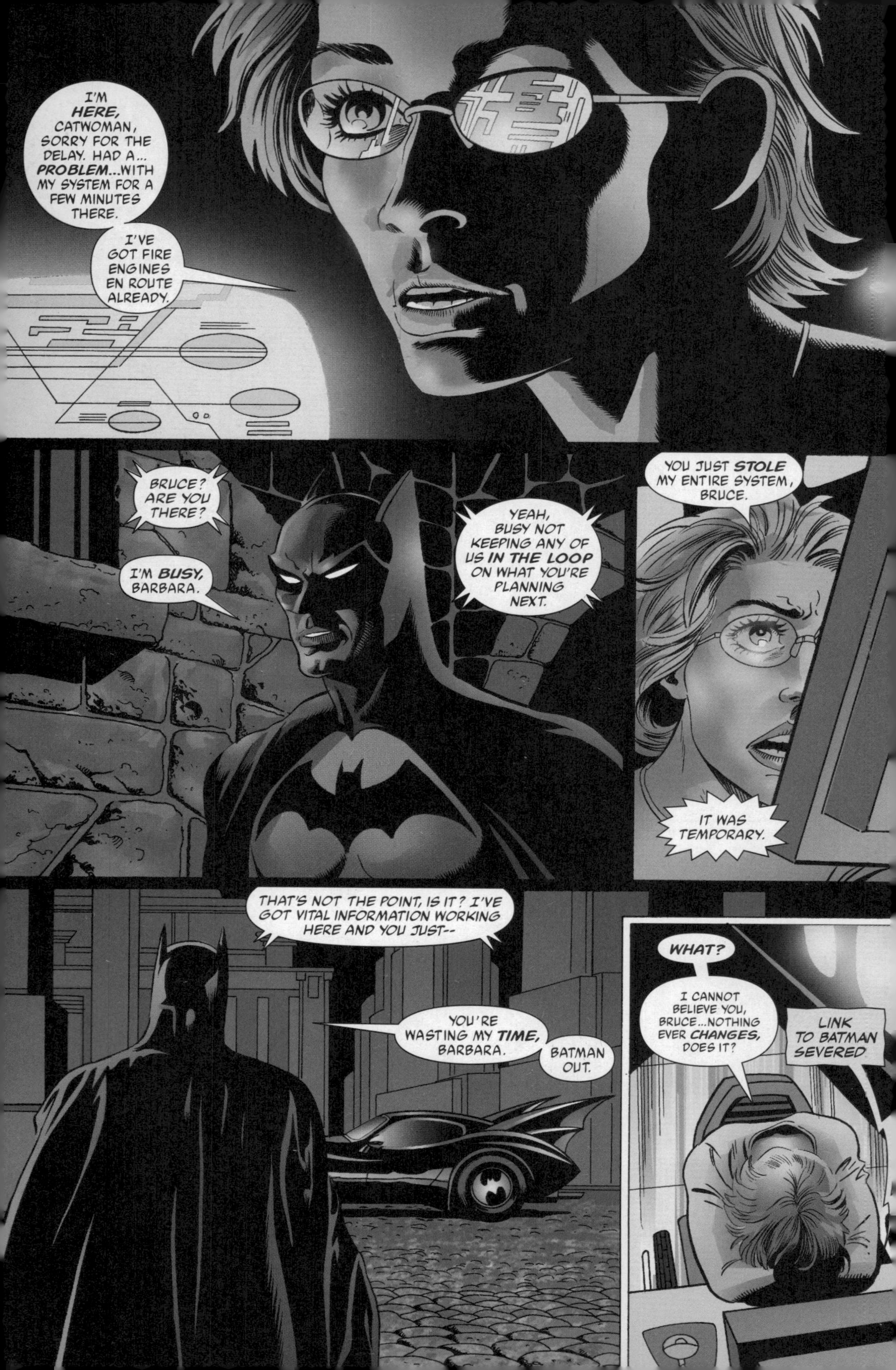
I'M HERE, CATWOMAN, SORRY FOR THE DELAY. HAD A... PROBLEM...WITH MY SYSTEM FOR A FEW MINUTES THERE.
I'VE GOT FIRE ENGINES EN ROUTE ALREADY.
BRUCE? ARE YOU THERE?
I'M BUSY, BARBARA.
YEAH, BUSY NOT KEEPING ANY OF US IN THE LOOP ON WHAT YOU'RE PLANNING NEXT.
YOU JUST STOLE MY ENTIRE SYSTEM, BRUCE.
IT WAS TEMPORARY.
THAT'S NOT THE POINT, IS IT? I'VE GOT VITAL INFORMATION WORKING HERE AND YOU JUST--
YOU'RE WASTING MY TIME, BARBARA.
BATMAN OUT.
WHAT?
I CANNOT BELIEVE YOU, BRUCE...NOTHING EVER CHANGES, DOES IT?
LINK TO BATMAN SEVERED

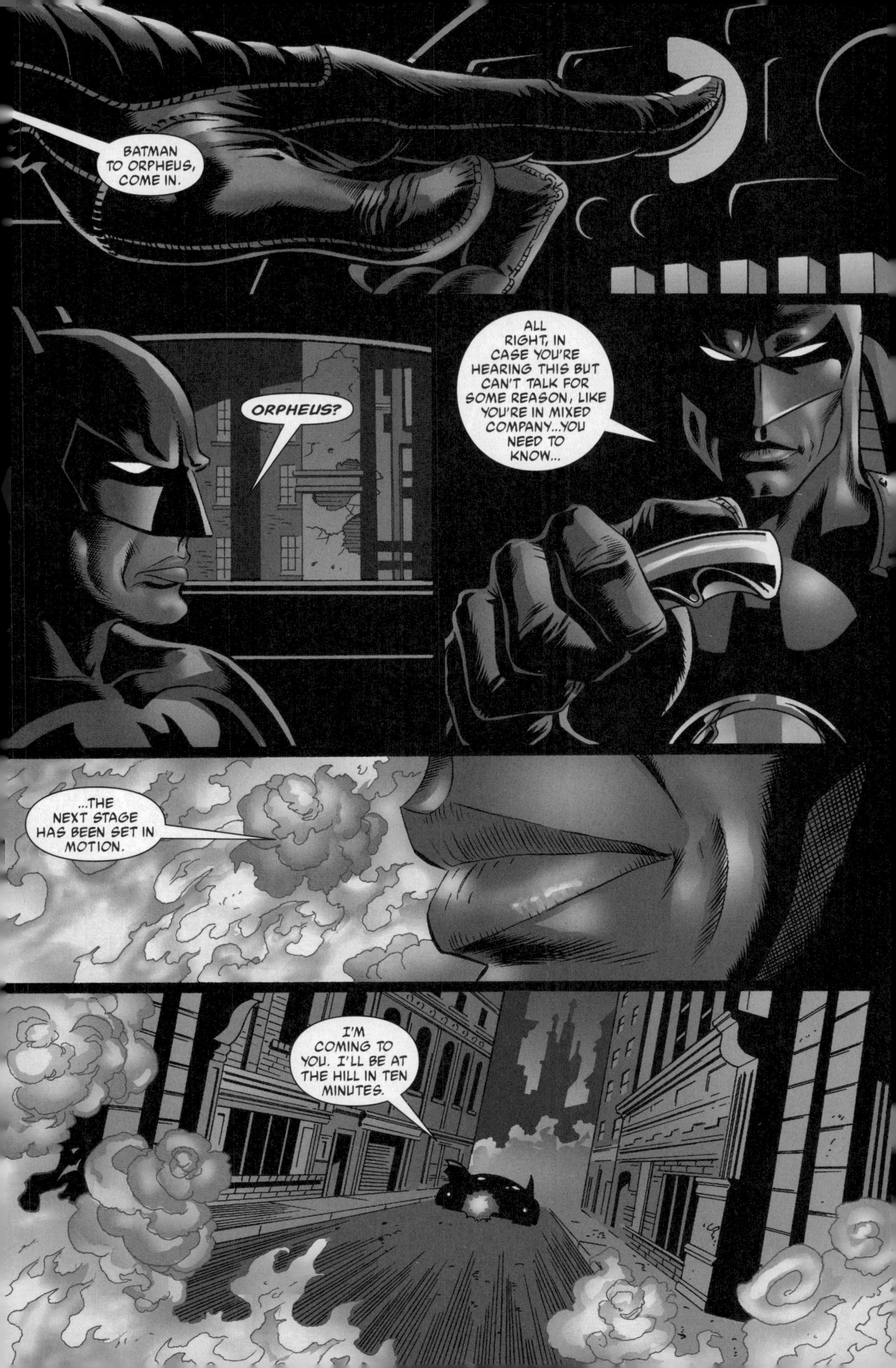
BATMAN TO ORPHEUS, COME IN.
ORPHEUS?
ALL RIGHT, IN CASE YOU'RE HEARING THIS BUT CAN'T TALK FOR SOME REASON, LIKE YOU'RE IN MIXED COMPANY...YOU NEED TO KNOW...
...THE NEXT STAGE HAS BEEN SET IN MOTION.
I'M COMING TO YOU. I'LL BE AT THE HILL IN TEN MINUTES.

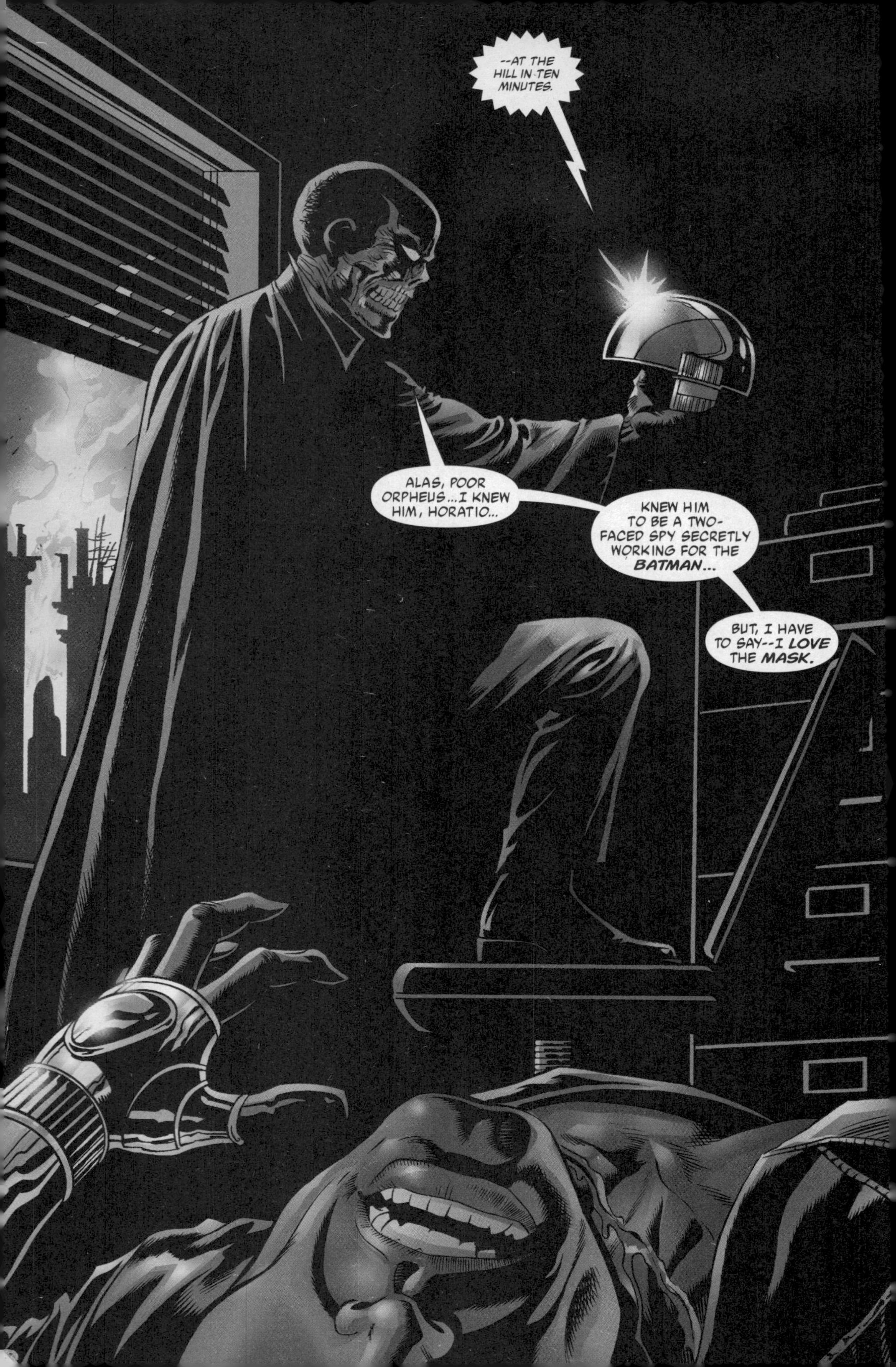
--AT THE HILL IN TEN MINUTES.
ALAS, POOR ORPHEUS...I KNEW HIM, HORATIO...
KNEW HIM TO BE A TWO-FACED SPY SECRETLY WORKING FOR THE BATMAN...
BUT, I HAVE TO SAY--I LOVE THE MASK.

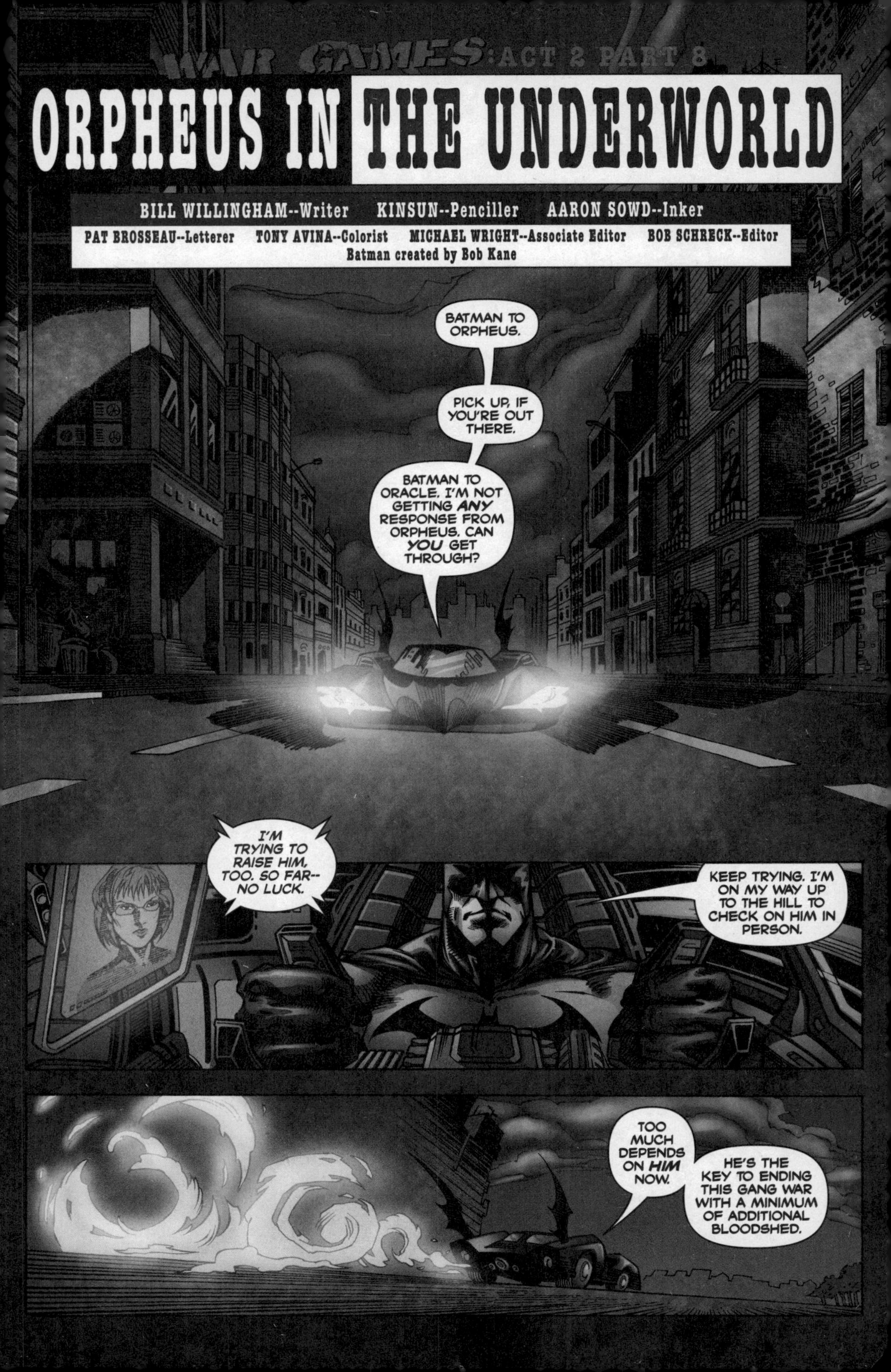
WAR GAMES: ACT 2 PART 8
ORPHEUS IN THE UNDERWORLD
BILL WILLINGHAM--Writer KINSUN--Penciller AARON SOWD--Inker
PAT BROSSEAU--Letterer TONY AVINA--Colorist MICHAEL WRIGHT--Associate Editor BOB SCHRECK--Editor
Batman created by Bob Kane
BATMAN TO ORPHEUS.
PICK UP, IF YOU'RE OUT THERE.
BATMAN TO ORACLE. I'M NOT GETTING ANY RESPONSE FROM ORPHEUS. CAN YOU GET THROUGH?
I'M TRYING TO RAISE HIM, TOO. SO FAR-- NO LUCK.
KEEP TRYING. I'M ON MY WAY UP TO THE HILL TO CHECK ON HIM IN PERSON.
TOO MUCH DEPENDS ON HIM NOW.
HE'S THE KEY TO ENDING THIS GANG WAR WITH A MINIMUM OF ADDITIONAL BLOODSHED.

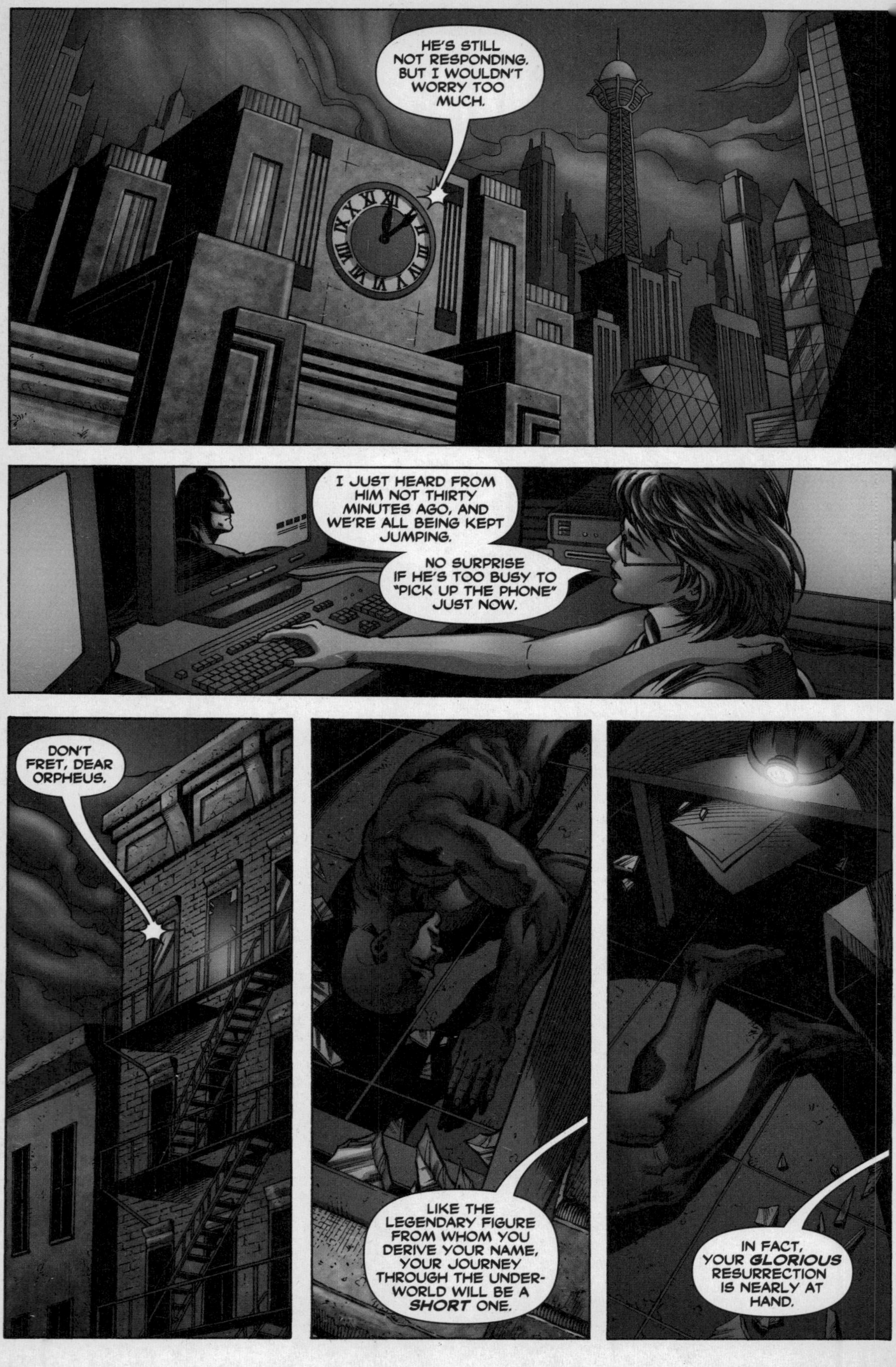
HE'S STILL NOT RESPONDING. BUT I WOULDN'T WORRY TOO MUCH.
I JUST HEARD FROM HIM NOT THIRTY MINUTES AGO, AND WE'RE ALL BEING KEPT JUMPING.
NO SURPRISE IF HE'S TOO BUSY TO "PICK UP THE PHONE" JUST NOW.
DON'T FRET, DEAR ORPHEUS.
LIKE THE LEGENDARY FIGURE FROM WHOM YOU DERIVE YOUR NAME, YOUR JOURNEY THROUGH THE UNDER-WORLD WILL BE A SHORT ONE.
IN FACT, YOUR GLORIOUS RESURRECTION IS NEARLY AT HAND.

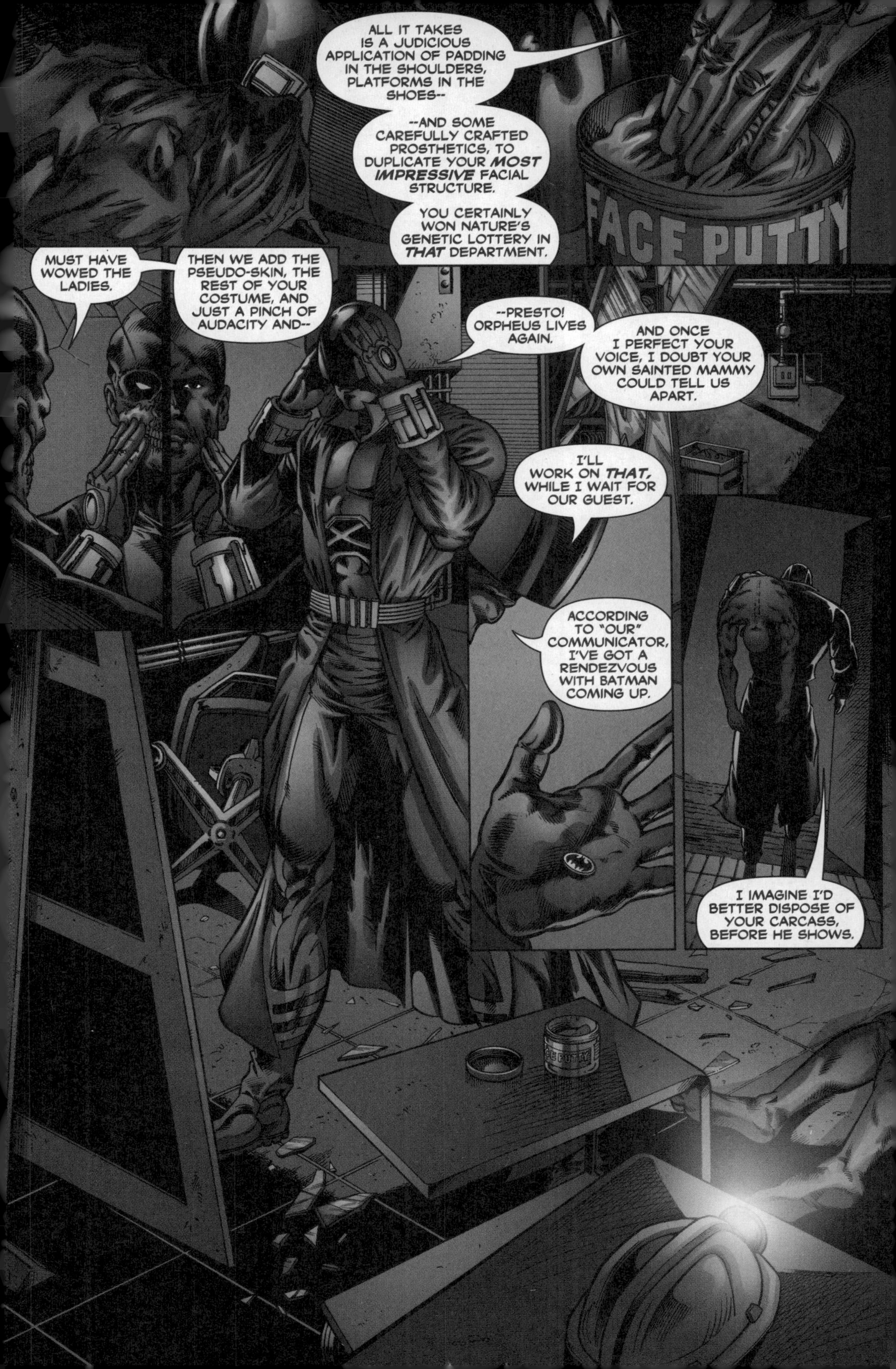
ALL IT TAKES IS A JUDICIOUS APPLICATION OF PADDING IN THE SHOULDERS, PLATFORMS IN THE SHOES--
--AND SOME CAREFULLY CRAFTED PROSTHETICS, TO DUPLICATE YOUR *MOST IMPRESSIVE* FACIAL STRUCTURE.
YOU CERTAINLY WON NATURE'S GENETIC LOTTERY IN *THAT* DEPARTMENT.
FACE PUTTY
MUST HAVE WOWED THE LADIES.
THEN WE ADD THE PSEUDO-SKIN, THE REST OF YOUR COSTUME, AND JUST A PINCH OF AUDACITY AND--
--PRESTO! ORPHEUS LIVES AGAIN.
AND ONCE I PERFECT YOUR VOICE, I DOUBT YOUR OWN SAINTED MAMMY COULD TELL US APART.
I'LL WORK ON *THAT,* WHILE I WAIT FOR OUR GUEST.
ACCORDING TO "OUR" COMMUNICATOR, I'VE GOT A RENDEZVOUS WITH BATMAN COMING UP.
I IMAGINE I'D BETTER DISPOSE OF YOUR CARCASS, BEFORE HE SHOWS.

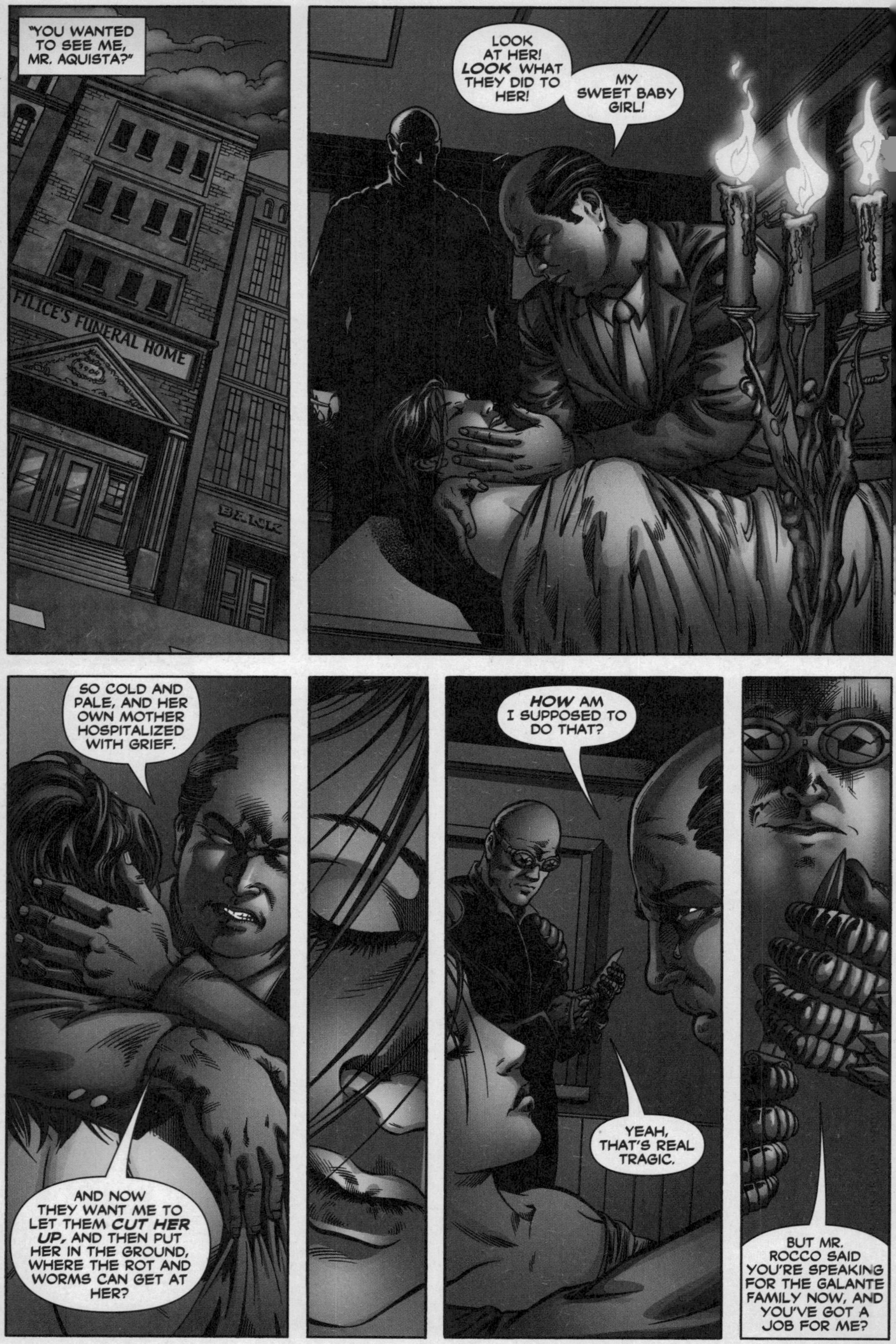
"YOU WANTED TO SEE ME, MR. AQUISTA?"
FILICE'S FUNERAL HOME
LOOK AT HER! LOOK WHAT THEY DID TO HER!
MY SWEET BABY GIRL!
SO COLD AND PALE, AND HER OWN MOTHER HOSPITALIZED WITH GRIEF.
AND NOW THEY WANT ME TO LET THEM CUT HER UP, AND THEN PUT HER IN THE GROUND, WHERE THE ROT AND WORMS CAN GET AT HER?
HOW AM I SUPPOSED TO DO THAT?
YEAH, THAT'S REAL TRAGIC.
BUT MR. ROCCO SAID YOU'RE SPEAKING FOR THE GALANTE FAMILY NOW, AND YOU'VE GOT A JOB FOR ME?

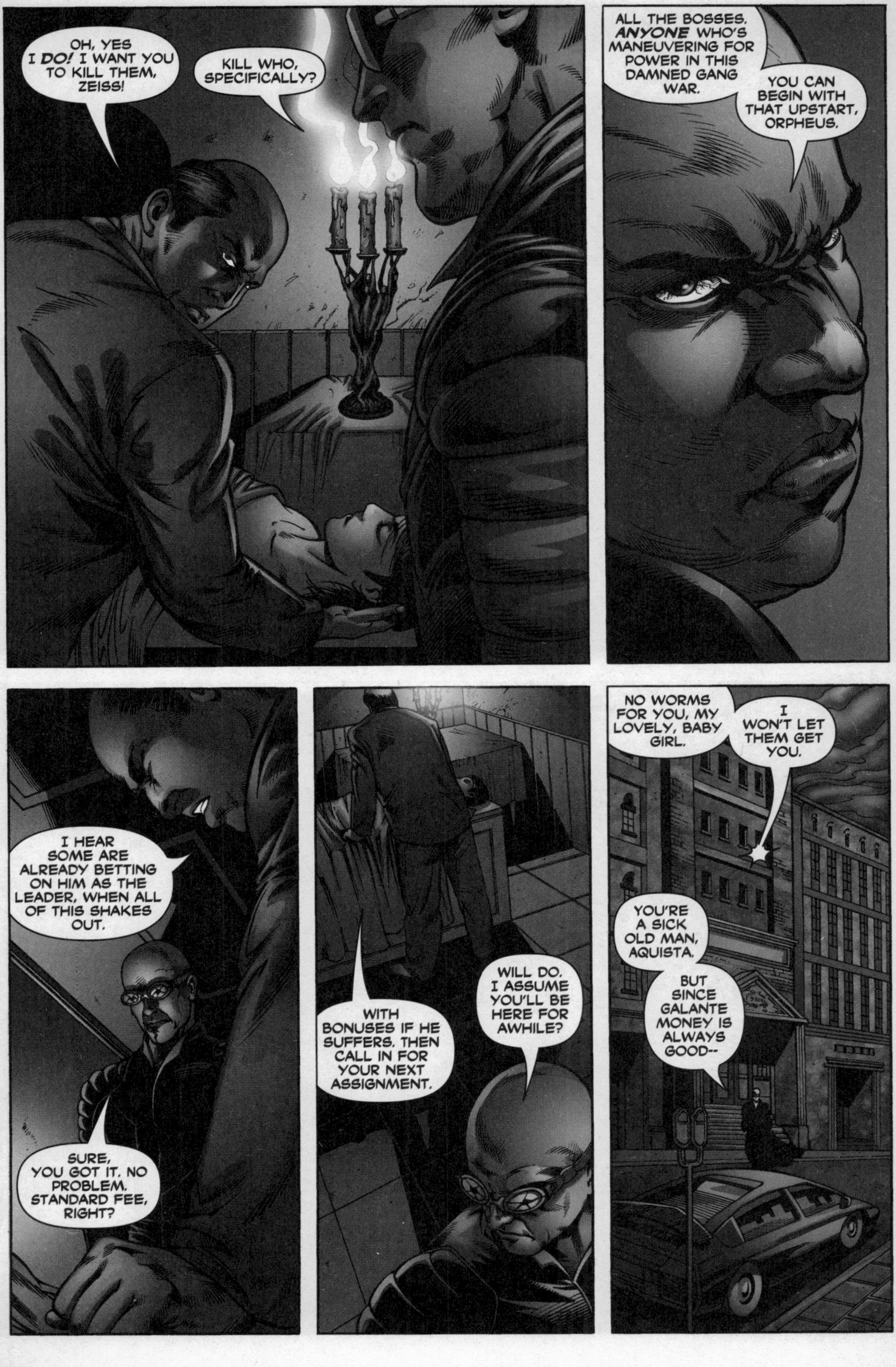
OH, YES I DO! I WANT YOU TO KILL THEM, ZEISS!
KILL WHO, SPECIFICALLY?
ALL THE BOSSES. ANYONE WHO'S MANEUVERING FOR POWER IN THIS DAMNED GANG WAR.
YOU CAN BEGIN WITH THAT UPSTART, ORPHEUS.
I HEAR SOME ARE ALREADY BETTING ON HIM AS THE LEADER, WHEN ALL OF THIS SHAKES OUT.
SURE, YOU GOT IT. NO PROBLEM. STANDARD FEE, RIGHT?
WITH BONUSES IF HE SUFFERS. THEN CALL IN FOR YOUR NEXT ASSIGNMENT.
WILL DO. I ASSUME YOU'LL BE HERE FOR AWHILE?
NO WORMS FOR YOU, MY LOVELY, BABY GIRL.
I WON'T LET THEM GET YOU.
YOU'RE A SICK OLD MAN, AQUISTA.
BUT SINCE GALANTE MONEY IS ALWAYS GOOD--

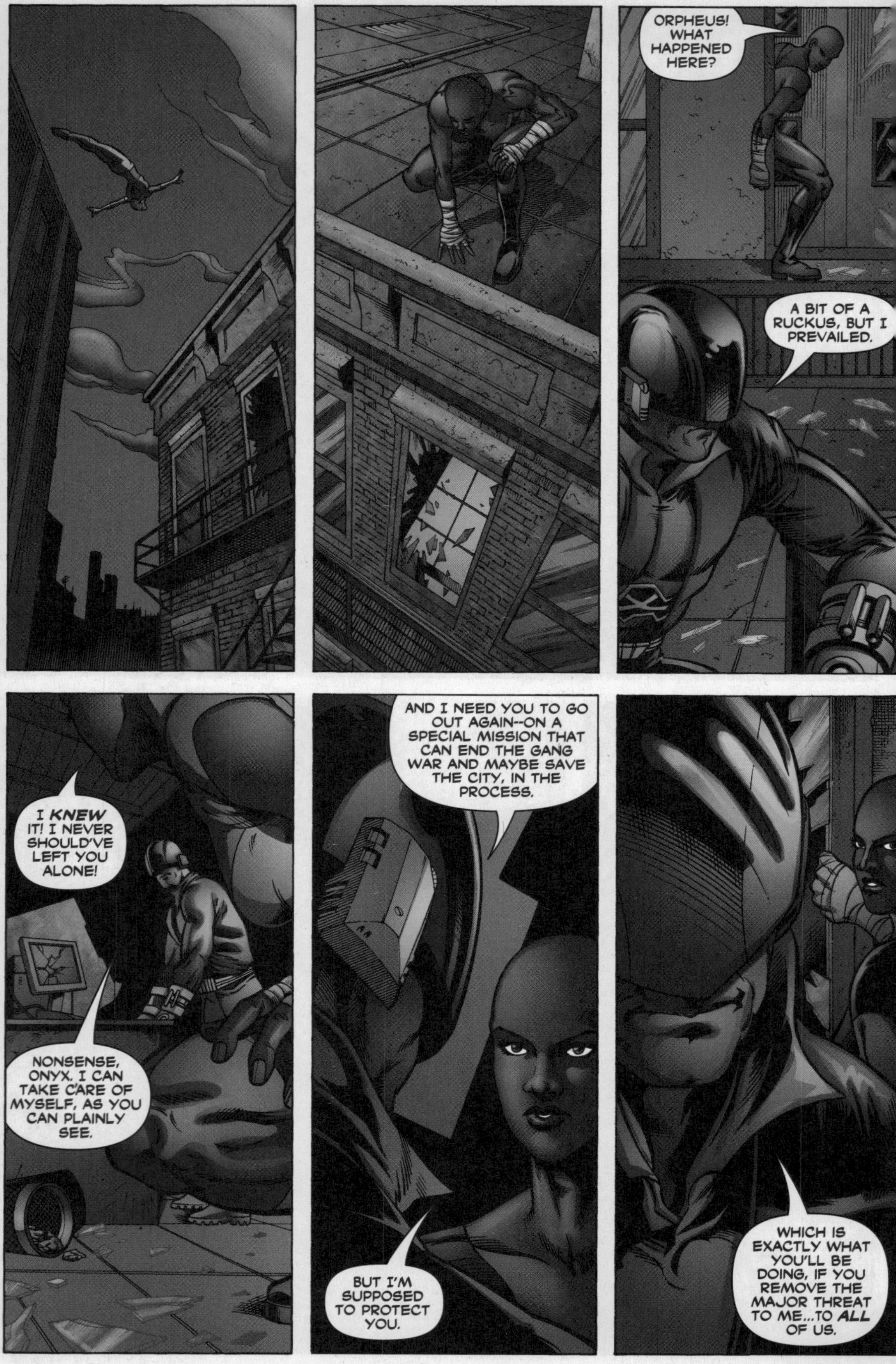
ORPHEUS! WHAT HAPPENED HERE?
A BIT OF A RUCKUS, BUT I PREVAILED.
I KNEW IT! I NEVER SHOULD'VE LEFT YOU ALONE!
NONSENSE, ONYX. I CAN TAKE CARE OF MYSELF, AS YOU CAN PLAINLY SEE.
BUT I'M SUPPOSED TO PROTECT YOU.
AND I NEED YOU TO GO OUT AGAIN--ON A SPECIAL MISSION THAT CAN END THE GANG WAR AND MAYBE SAVE THE CITY, IN THE PROCESS.
WHICH IS EXACTLY WHAT YOU'LL BE DOING, IF YOU REMOVE THE MAJOR THREAT TO ME...TO ALL OF US.

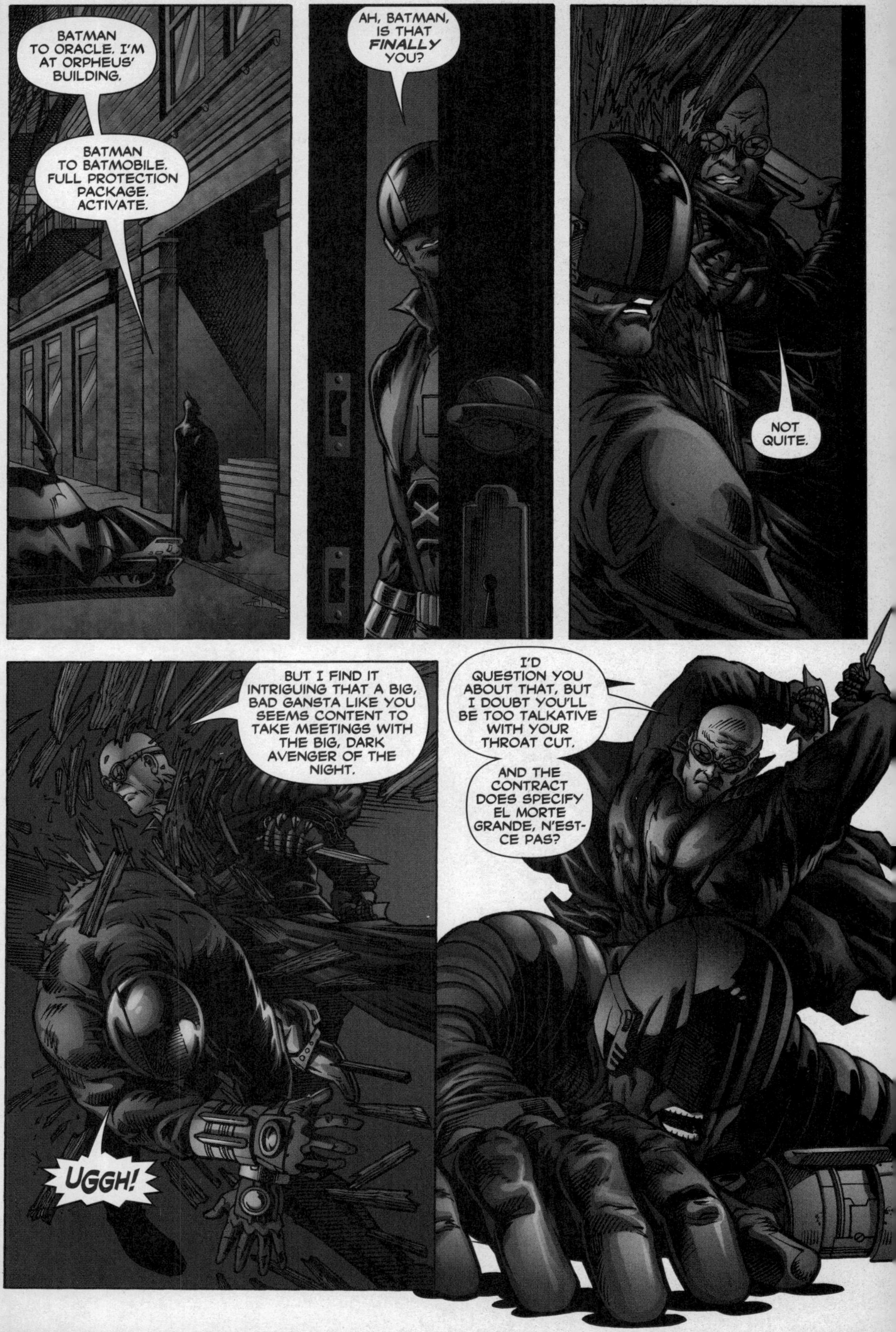
BATMAN TO ORACLE. I'M AT ORPHEUS' BUILDING.
BATMAN TO BATMOBILE. FULL PROTECTION PACKAGE. ACTIVATE.
AH, BATMAN, IS THAT FINALLY YOU?
NOT QUITE.
BUT I FIND IT INTRIGUING THAT A BIG, BAD GANSTA LIKE YOU SEEMS CONTENT TO TAKE MEETINGS WITH THE BIG, DARK AVENGER OF THE NIGHT.
UGGH!
I'D QUESTION YOU ABOUT THAT, BUT I DOUBT YOU'LL BE TOO TALKATIVE WITH YOUR THROAT CUT.
AND THE CONTRACT DOES SPECIFY EL MORTE GRANDE, N'EST-CE PAS?

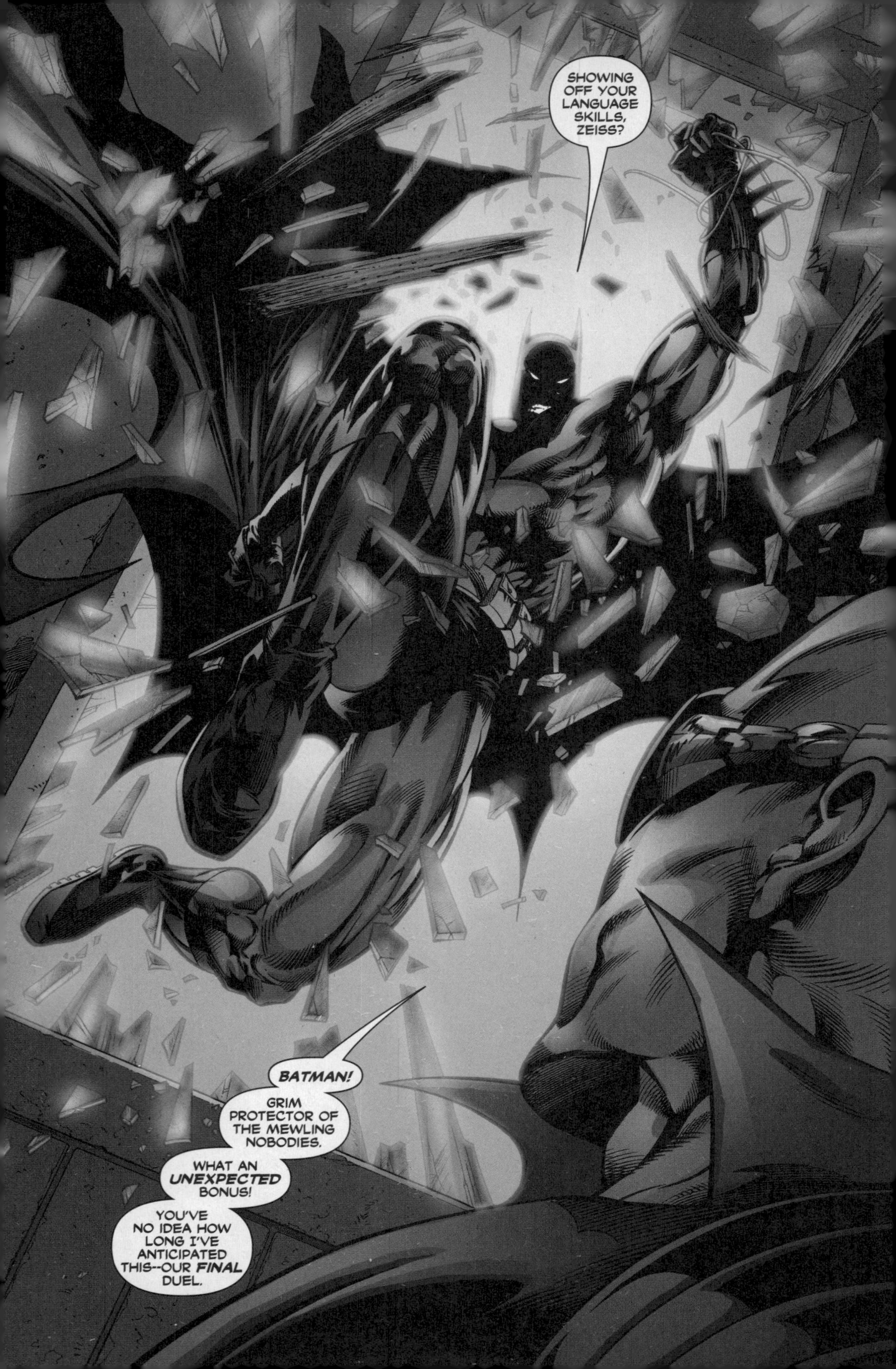
SHOWING OFF YOUR LANGUAGE SKILLS, ZEISS?
BATMAN!
GRIM PROTECTOR OF THE MEWLING NOBODIES.
WHAT AN UNEXPECTED BONUS!
YOU'VE NO IDEA HOW LONG I'VE ANTICIPATED THIS--OUR FINAL DUEL.

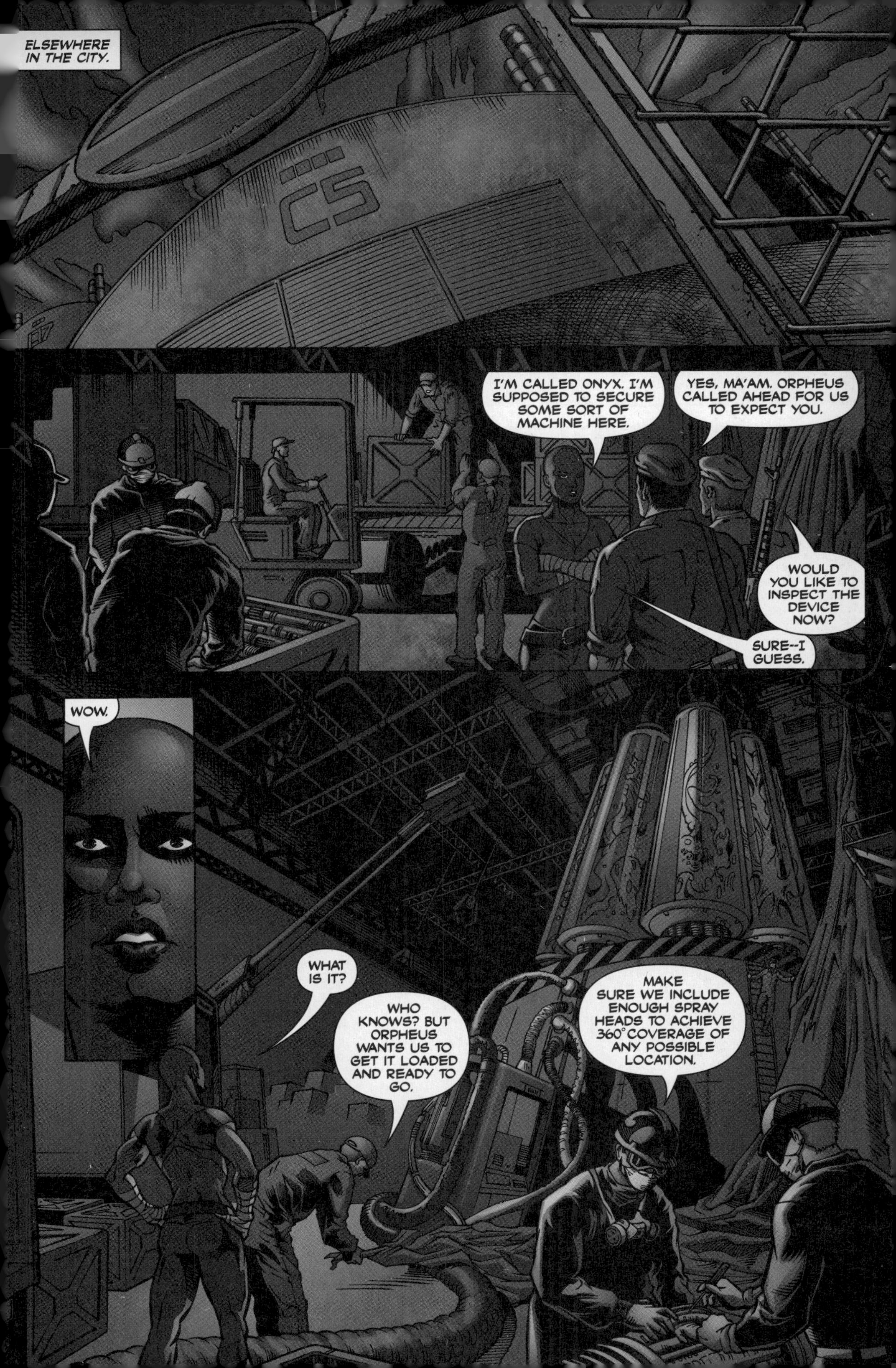
ELSEWHERE IN THE CITY.
CS
I'M CALLED ONYX. I'M SUPPOSED TO SECURE SOME SORT OF MACHINE HERE.
YES, MA'AM. ORPHEUS CALLED AHEAD FOR US TO EXPECT YOU.
WOULD YOU LIKE TO INSPECT THE DEVICE NOW?
SURE--I GUESS.
WOW.
WHAT IS IT?
WHO KNOWS? BUT ORPHEUS WANTS US TO GET IT LOADED AND READY TO GO.
MAKE SURE WE INCLUDE ENOUGH SPRAY HEADS TO ACHIEVE 360° COVERAGE OF ANY POSSIBLE LOCATION.

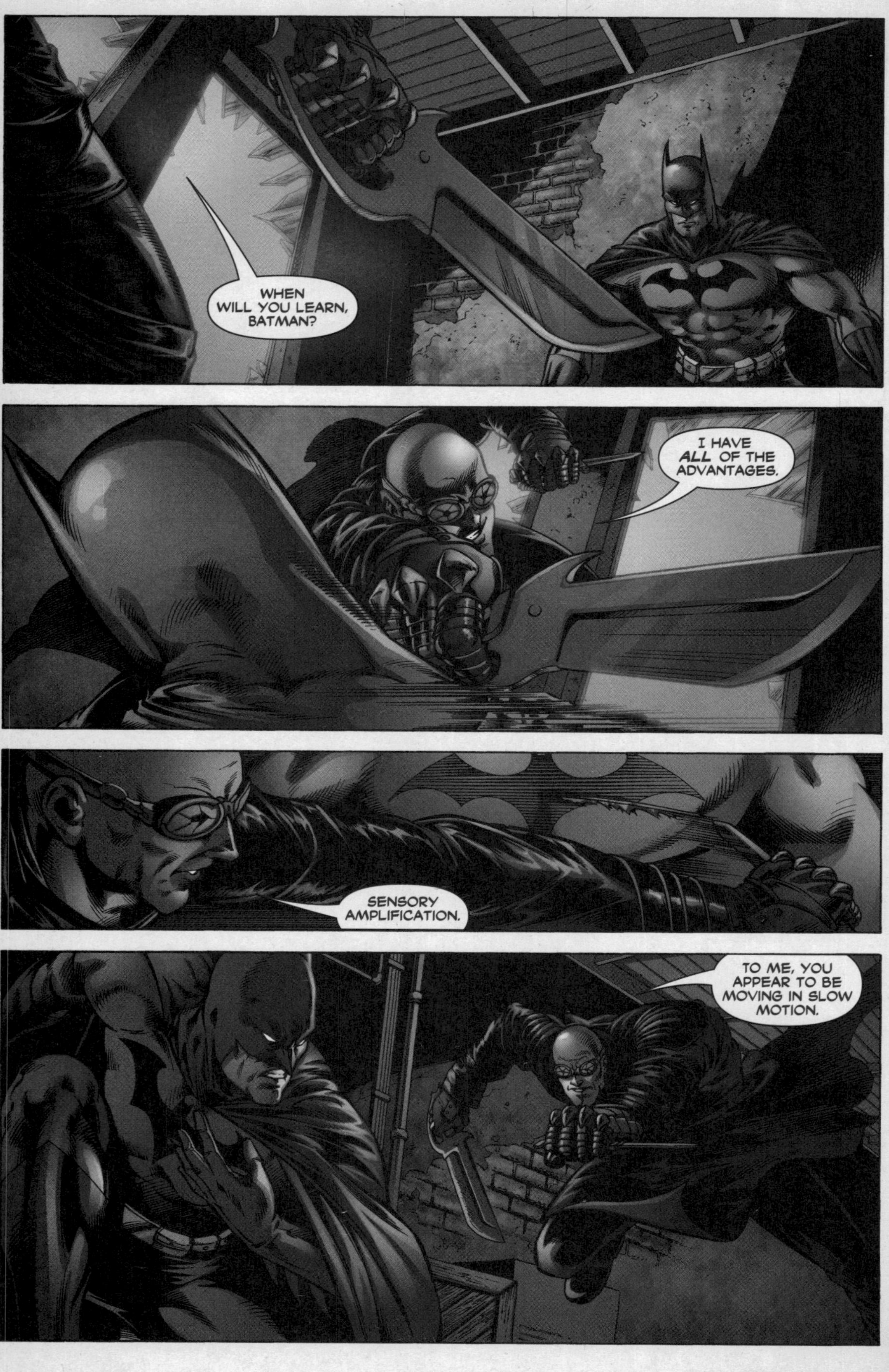
WHEN WILL YOU LEARN, BATMAN?
I HAVE ALL OF THE ADVANTAGES.
SENSORY AMPLIFICATION.
TO ME, YOU APPEAR TO BE MOVING IN SLOW MOTION.

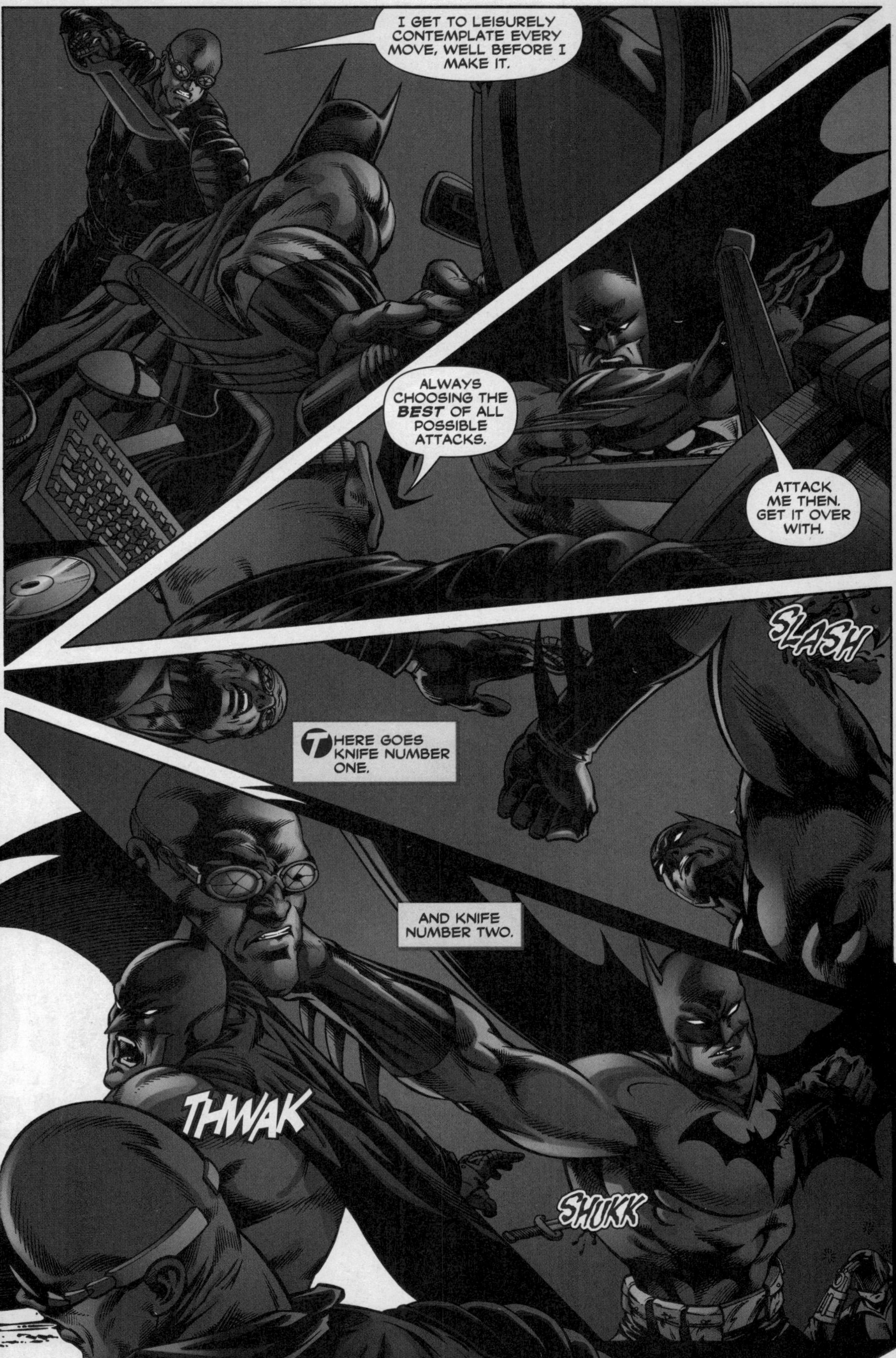

I GET TO LEISURELY CONTEMPLATE EVERY MOVE, WELL BEFORE I MAKE IT.
ALWAYS CHOOSING THE BEST OF ALL POSSIBLE ATTACKS.
ATTACK ME THEN. GET IT OVER WITH.
SLASH
THERE GOES KNIFE NUMBER ONE.
AND KNIFE NUMBER TWO.
THWAK
SHUKK

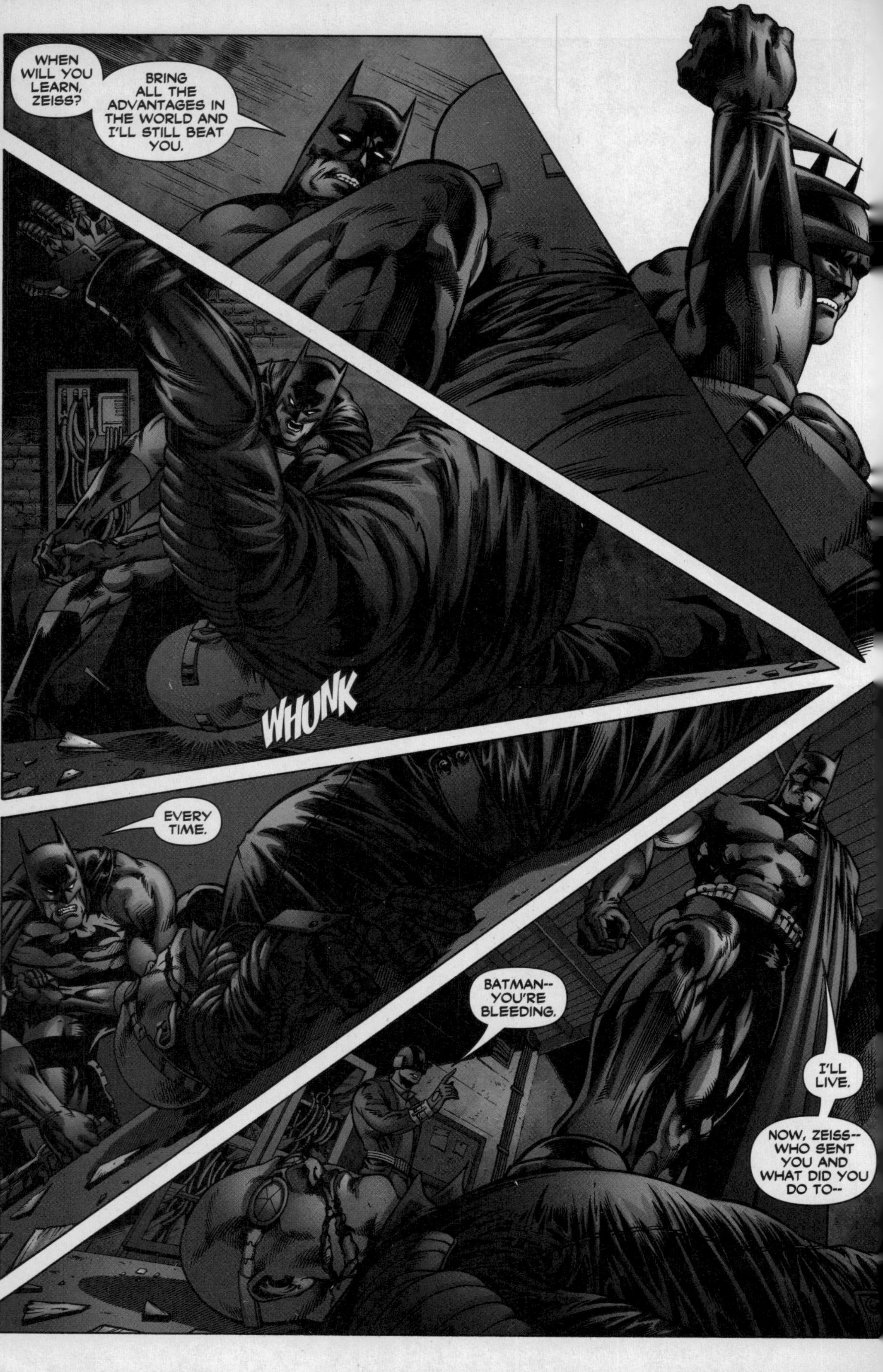
WHEN WILL YOU LEARN, ZEISS?
BRING ALL THE ADVANTAGES IN THE WORLD AND I'LL STILL BEAT YOU.
WHUNK
EVERY TIME.
BATMAN-- YOU'RE BLEEDING.
I'LL LIVE.
NOW, ZEISS-- WHO SENT YOU AND WHAT DID YOU DO TO--

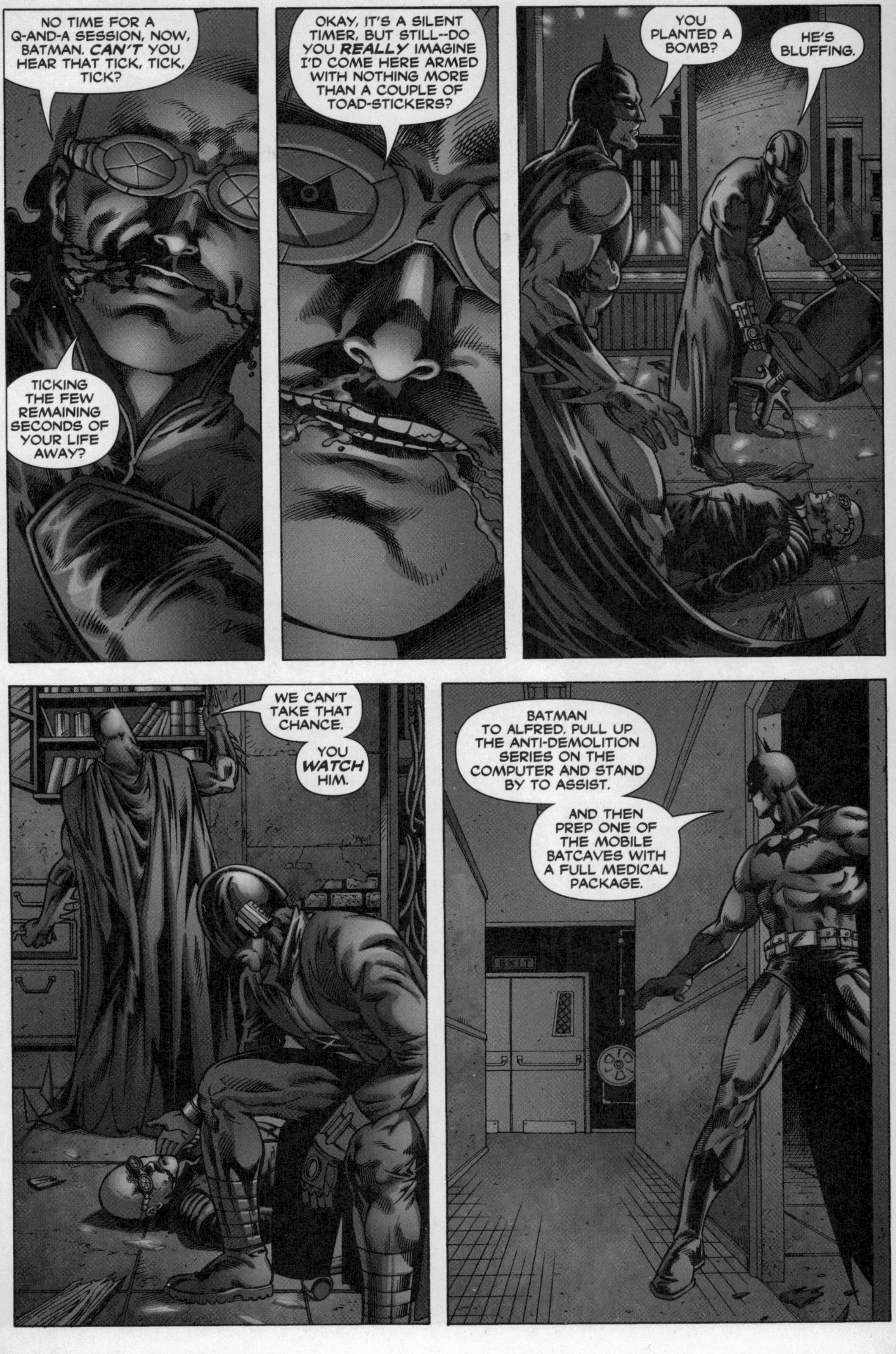
NO TIME FOR A Q-AND-A SESSION, NOW, BATMAN. CAN'T YOU HEAR THAT TICK, TICK, TICK?
TICKING THE FEW REMAINING SECONDS OF YOUR LIFE AWAY?
OKAY, IT'S A SILENT TIMER, BUT STILL--DO YOU REALLY IMAGINE I'D COME HERE ARMED WITH NOTHING MORE THAN A COUPLE OF TOAD-STICKERS?
YOU PLANTED A BOMB?
HE'S BLUFFING.
WE CAN'T TAKE THAT CHANCE.
YOU WATCH HIM.
BATMAN TO ALFRED. PULL UP THE ANTI-DEMOLITION SERIES ON THE COMPUTER AND STAND BY TO ASSIST.
AND THEN PREP ONE OF THE MOBILE BATCAVES WITH A FULL MEDICAL PACKAGE.
EXIT

YOU CAN HOME IN ON MY LOCATION, WHEN-- HOLD IT! HERE IT IS!

ENOUGH PLASTIC EXPLOSIVE TO DECAPITATE THE TOP THREE FLOORS OF THIS PLACE.

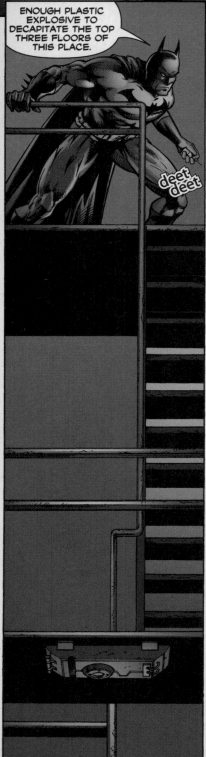

deet deet

WHAT CAN I DO TO HELP?

WATCH OUR PRISONER.

I'LL DO THIS.

CLEVER JOB, ZEISS.

I DIDN'T CATCH THAT, SIR.

MULTIPLE INTERDEPENDENT FAIL-SAFES.

REDUNDANT IGNITION SWITCHES.

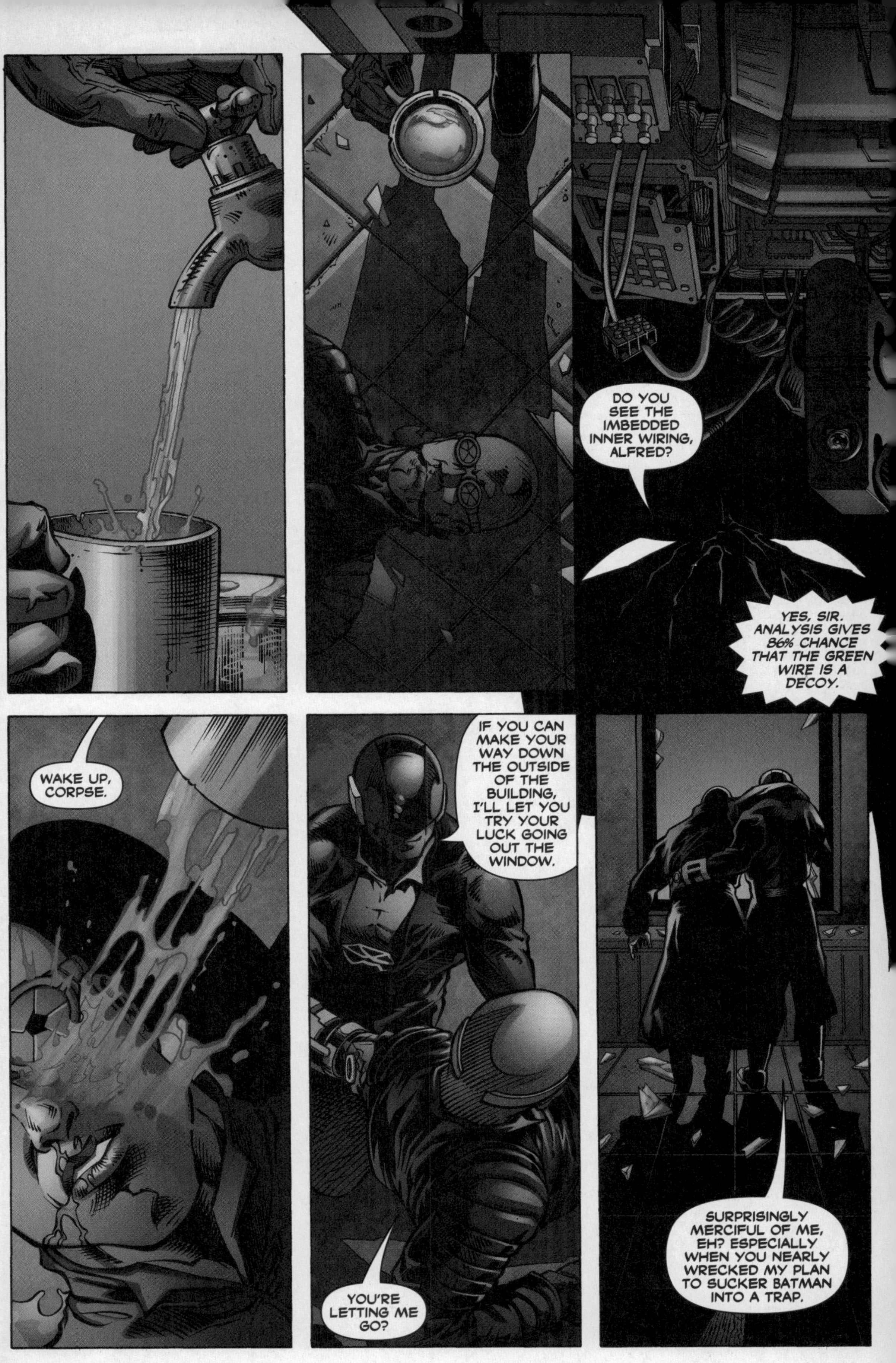
DO YOU SEE THE IMBEDDED INNER WIRING, ALFRED?
YES, SIR. ANALYSIS GIVES 86% CHANCE THAT THE GREEN WIRE IS A DECOY.
WAKE UP, CORPSE.
IF YOU CAN MAKE YOUR WAY DOWN THE OUTSIDE OF THE BUILDING, I'LL LET YOU TRY YOUR LUCK GOING OUT THE WINDOW.
YOU'RE LETTING ME GO?
SURPRISINGLY MERCIFUL OF ME, EH? ESPECIALLY WHEN YOU NEARLY WRECKED MY PLAN TO SUCKER BATMAN INTO A TRAP.

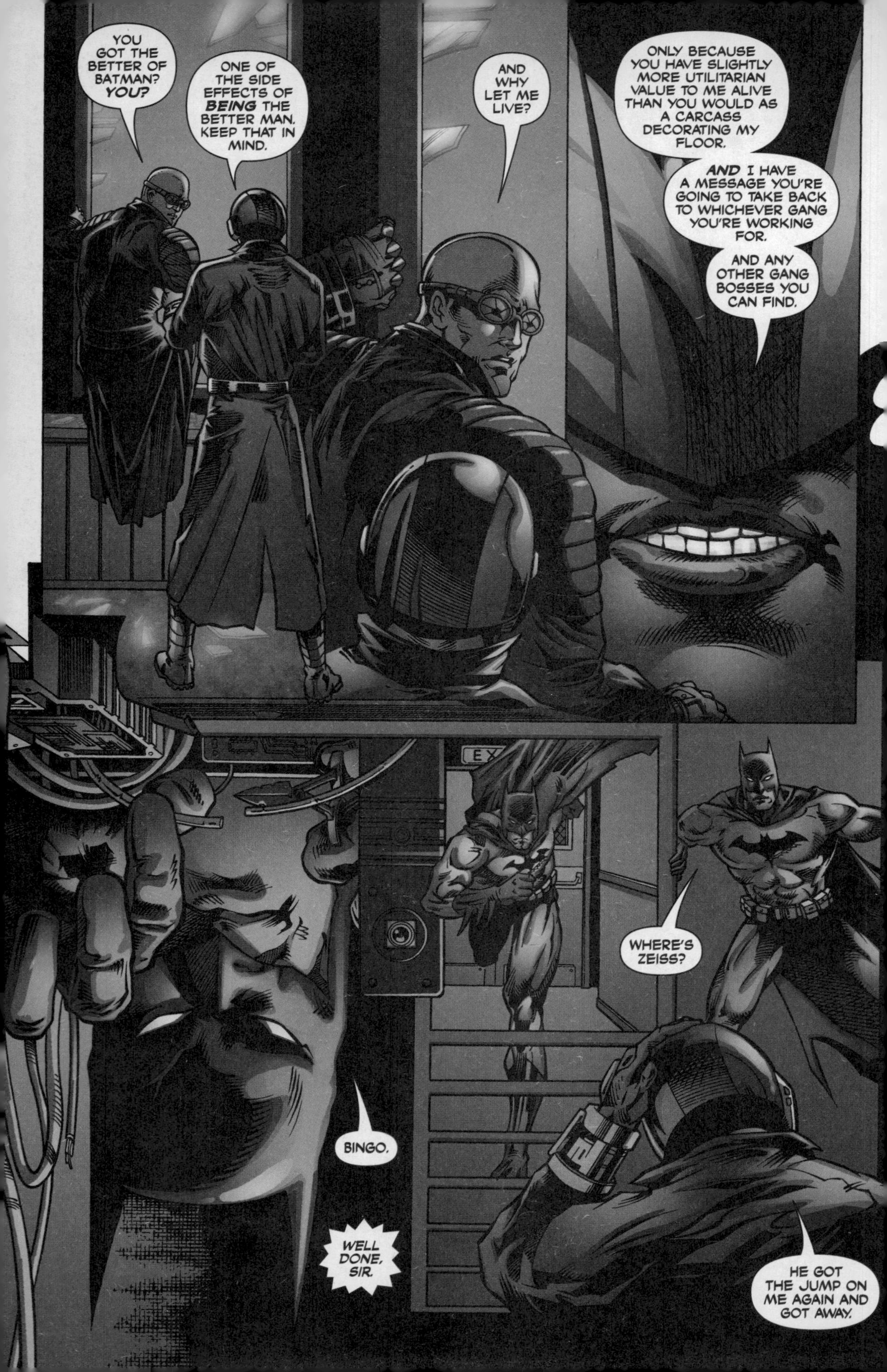
YOU GOT THE BETTER OF BATMAN? *YOU?*
ONE OF THE SIDE EFFECTS OF ***BEING*** THE BETTER MAN. KEEP THAT IN MIND.
AND WHY LET ME LIVE?
ONLY BECAUSE YOU HAVE SLIGHTLY MORE UTILITARIAN VALUE TO ME ALIVE THAN YOU WOULD AS A CARCASS DECORATING MY FLOOR.
AND I HAVE A MESSAGE YOU'RE GOING TO TAKE BACK TO WHICHEVER GANG YOU'RE WORKING FOR.
AND ANY OTHER GANG BOSSES YOU CAN FIND.
WHERE'S ZEISS?
HE GOT THE JUMP ON ME AGAIN AND GOT AWAY.
BINGO.
WELL DONE, SIR.

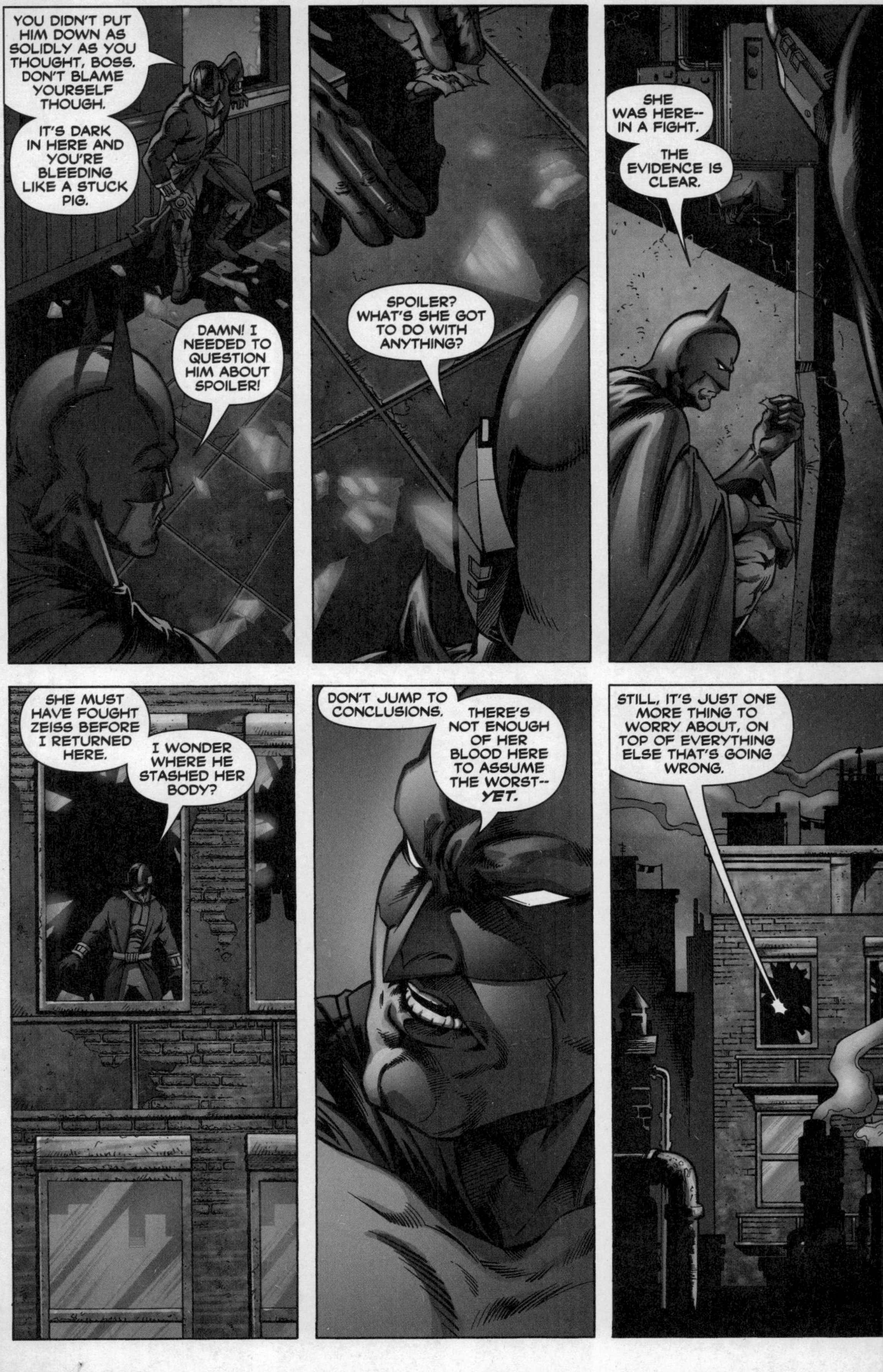
YOU DIDN'T PUT HIM DOWN AS SOLIDLY AS YOU THOUGHT, BOSS. DON'T BLAME YOURSELF THOUGH.
IT'S DARK IN HERE AND YOU'RE BLEEDING LIKE A STUCK PIG.
DAMN! I NEEDED TO QUESTION HIM ABOUT SPOILER!
SPOILER? WHAT'S SHE GOT TO DO WITH ANYTHING?
SHE WAS HERE-- IN A FIGHT.
THE EVIDENCE IS CLEAR.
SHE MUST HAVE FOUGHT ZEISS BEFORE I RETURNED HERE.
I WONDER WHERE HE STASHED HER BODY?
DON'T JUMP TO CONCLUSIONS.
THERE'S NOT ENOUGH OF HER BLOOD HERE TO ASSUME THE WORST-- *YET.*
STILL, IT'S JUST ONE MORE THING TO WORRY ABOUT, ON TOP OF EVERYTHING ELSE THAT'S GOING WRONG.

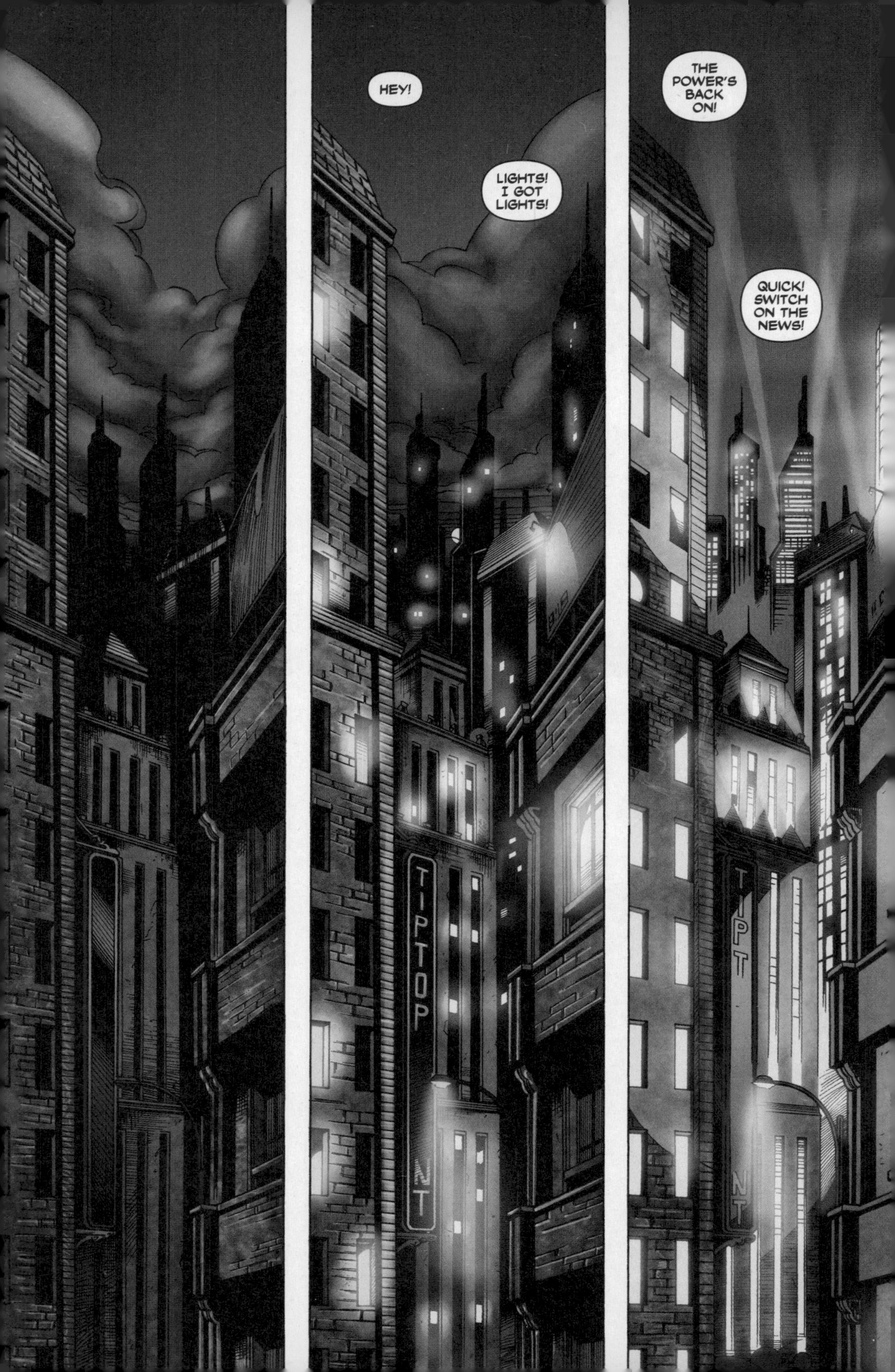
HEY!
LIGHTS! I GOT LIGHTS!
THE POWER'S BACK ON!
QUICK! SWITCH ON THE NEWS!
TIPTOP
NT
TIPT
NT

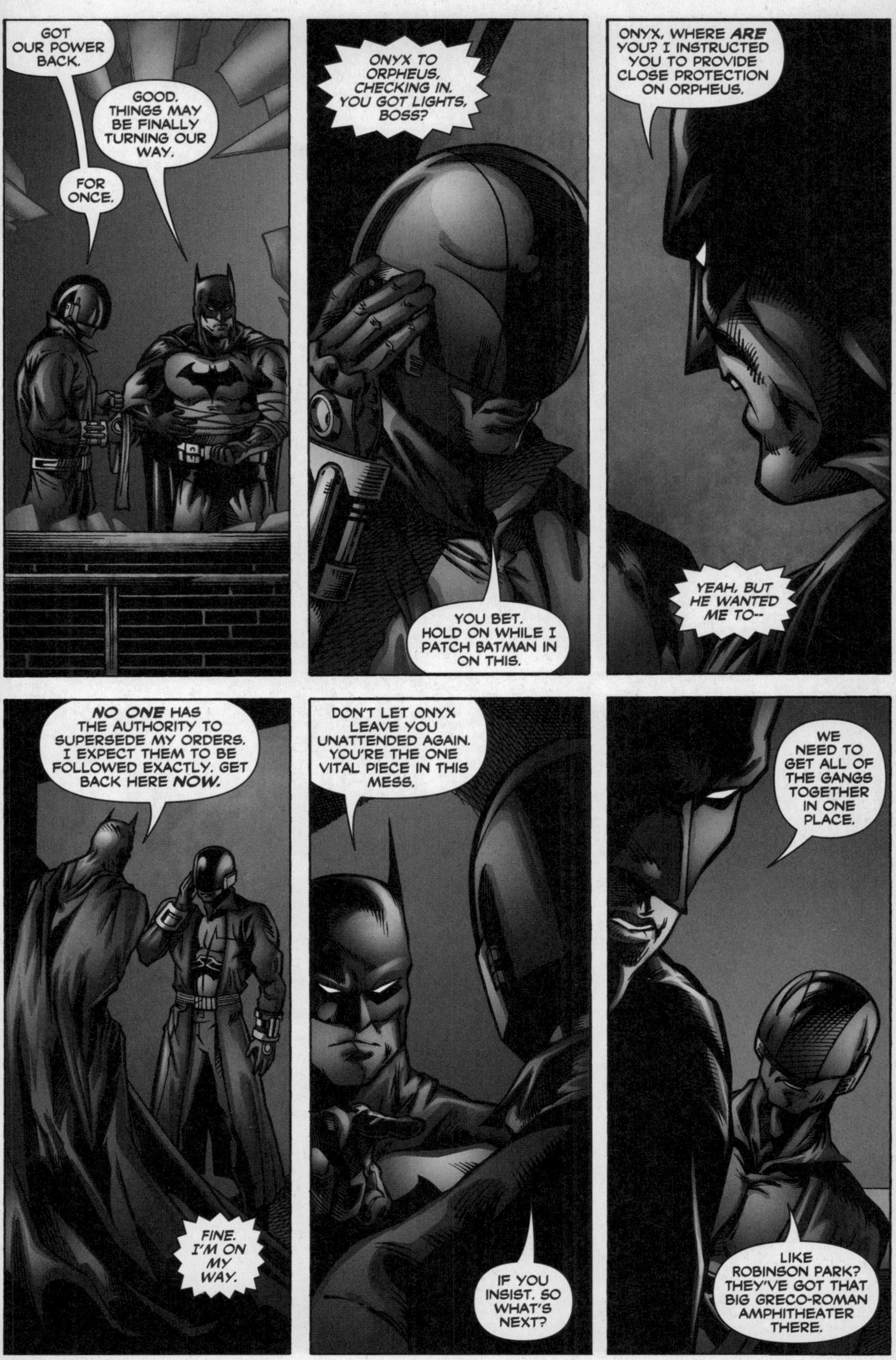
GOT OUR POWER BACK.
GOOD. THINGS MAY BE FINALLY TURNING OUR WAY.
FOR ONCE.
ONYX TO ORPHEUS, CHECKING IN. YOU GOT LIGHTS, BOSS?
YOU BET. HOLD ON WHILE I PATCH BATMAN IN ON THIS.
ONYX, WHERE ARE YOU? I INSTRUCTED YOU TO PROVIDE CLOSE PROTECTION ON ORPHEUS.
YEAH, BUT HE WANTED ME TO--
NO ONE HAS THE AUTHORITY TO SUPERSEDE MY ORDERS. I EXPECT THEM TO BE FOLLOWED EXACTLY. GET BACK HERE NOW.
FINE. I'M ON MY WAY.
DON'T LET ONYX LEAVE YOU UNATTENDED AGAIN. YOU'RE THE ONE VITAL PIECE IN THIS MESS.
IF YOU INSIST. SO WHAT'S NEXT?
WE NEED TO GET ALL OF THE GANGS TOGETHER IN ONE PLACE.
LIKE ROBINSON PARK? THEY'VE GOT THAT BIG GRECO-ROMAN AMPHITHEATER THERE.

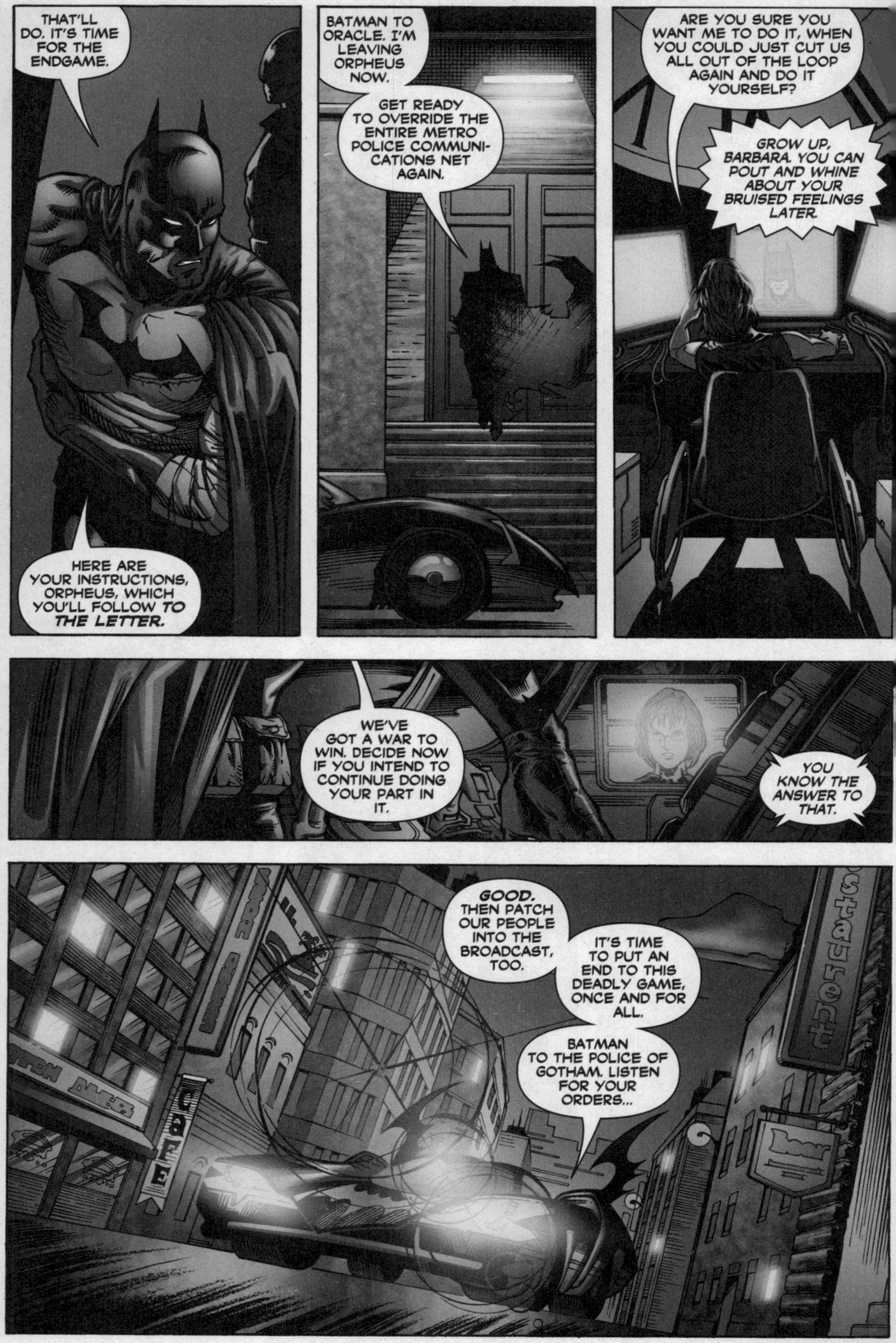
THAT'LL DO. IT'S TIME FOR THE ENDGAME.
HERE ARE YOUR INSTRUCTIONS, ORPHEUS, WHICH YOU'LL FOLLOW TO THE LETTER.
BATMAN TO ORACLE. I'M LEAVING ORPHEUS NOW.
GET READY TO OVERRIDE THE ENTIRE METRO POLICE COMMUNI-CATIONS NET AGAIN.
ARE YOU SURE YOU WANT ME TO DO IT, WHEN YOU COULD JUST CUT US ALL OUT OF THE LOOP AGAIN AND DO IT YOURSELF?
GROW UP, BARBARA. YOU CAN POUT AND WHINE ABOUT YOUR BRUISED FEELINGS LATER.
WE'VE GOT A WAR TO WIN. DECIDE NOW IF YOU INTEND TO CONTINUE DOING YOUR PART IN IT.
YOU KNOW THE ANSWER TO THAT.
GOOD. THEN PATCH OUR PEOPLE INTO THE BROADCAST, TOO.
IT'S TIME TO PUT AN END TO THIS DEADLY GAME, ONCE AND FOR ALL.
BATMAN TO THE POLICE OF GOTHAM. LISTEN FOR YOUR ORDERS...

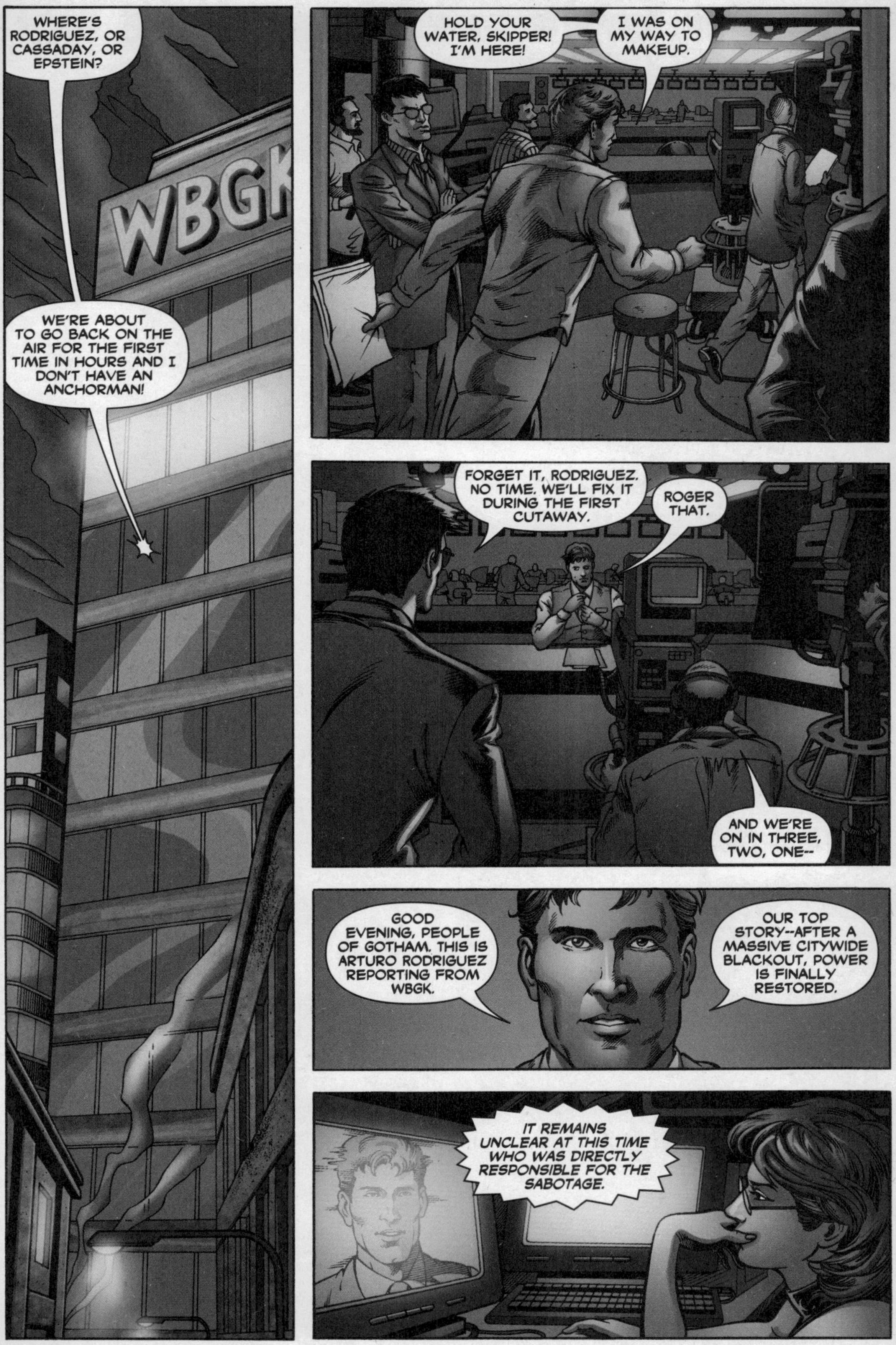
WHERE'S RODRIGUEZ, OR CASSADAY, OR EPSTEIN?
WE'RE ABOUT TO GO BACK ON THE AIR FOR THE FIRST TIME IN HOURS AND I DON'T HAVE AN ANCHORMAN!
WBGK
HOLD YOUR WATER, SKIPPER! I'M HERE!
I WAS ON MY WAY TO MAKEUP.
FORGET IT, RODRIGUEZ. NO TIME. WE'LL FIX IT DURING THE FIRST CUTAWAY.
ROGER THAT.
AND WE'RE ON IN THREE, TWO, ONE--
GOOD EVENING, PEOPLE OF GOTHAM. THIS IS ARTURO RODRIGUEZ REPORTING FROM WBGK.
OUR TOP STORY--AFTER A MASSIVE CITYWIDE BLACKOUT, POWER IS FINALLY RESTORED.
IT REMAINS UNCLEAR AT THIS TIME WHO WAS DIRECTLY RESPONSIBLE FOR THE SABOTAGE.

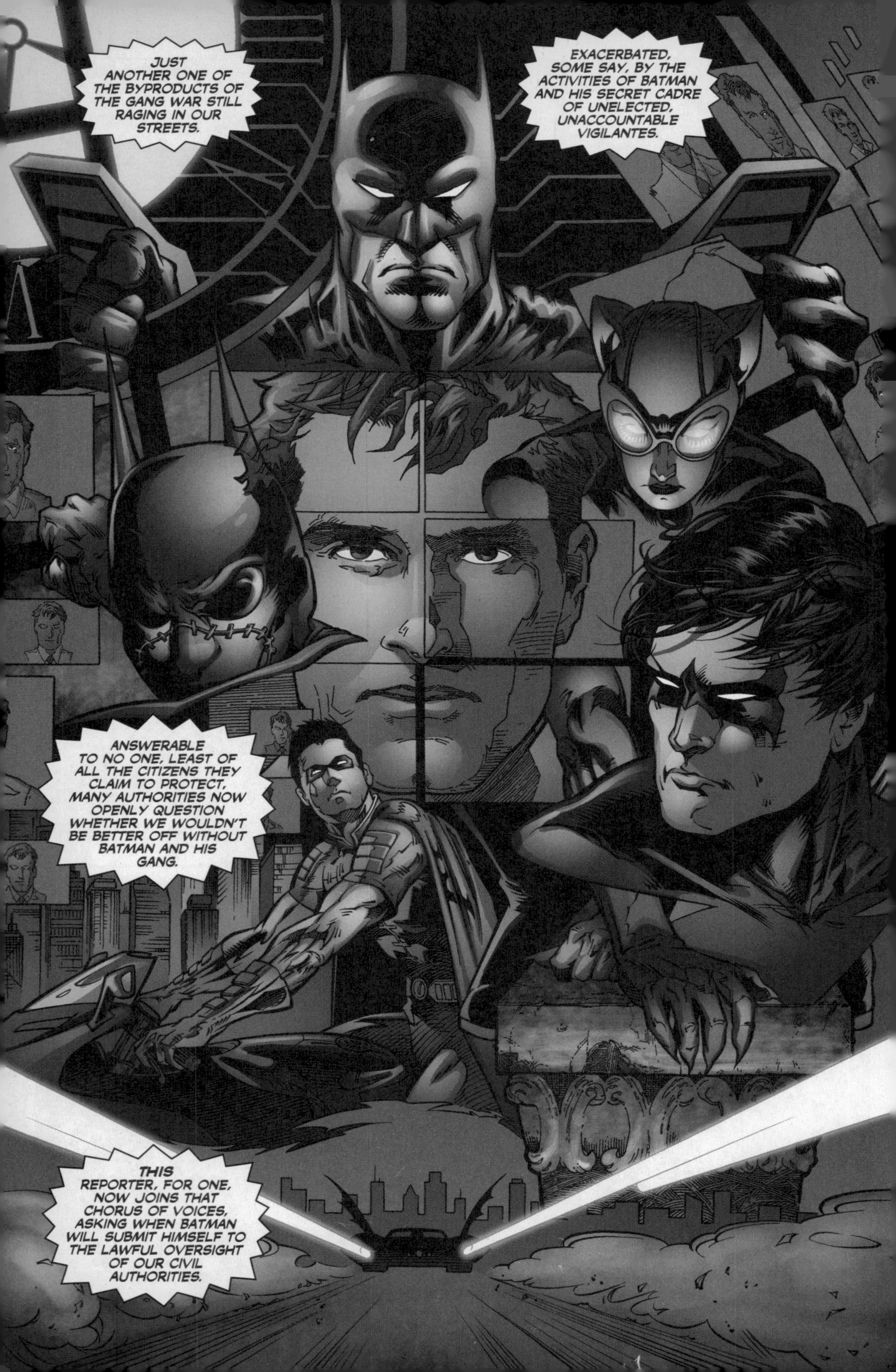
JUST ANOTHER ONE OF THE BYPRODUCTS OF THE GANG WAR STILL RAGING IN OUR STREETS.
EXACERBATED, SOME SAY, BY THE ACTIVITIES OF BATMAN AND HIS SECRET CADRE OF UNELECTED, UNACCOUNTABLE VIGILANTES.
ANSWERABLE TO NO ONE, LEAST OF ALL THE CITIZENS THEY CLAIM TO PROTECT, MANY AUTHORITIES NOW OPENLY QUESTION WHETHER WE WOULDN'T BE BETTER OFF WITHOUT BATMAN AND HIS GANG.
THIS REPORTER, FOR ONE, NOW JOINS THAT CHORUS OF VOICES, ASKING WHEN BATMAN WILL SUBMIT HIMSELF TO THE LAWFUL OVERSIGHT OF OUR CIVIL AUTHORITIES.

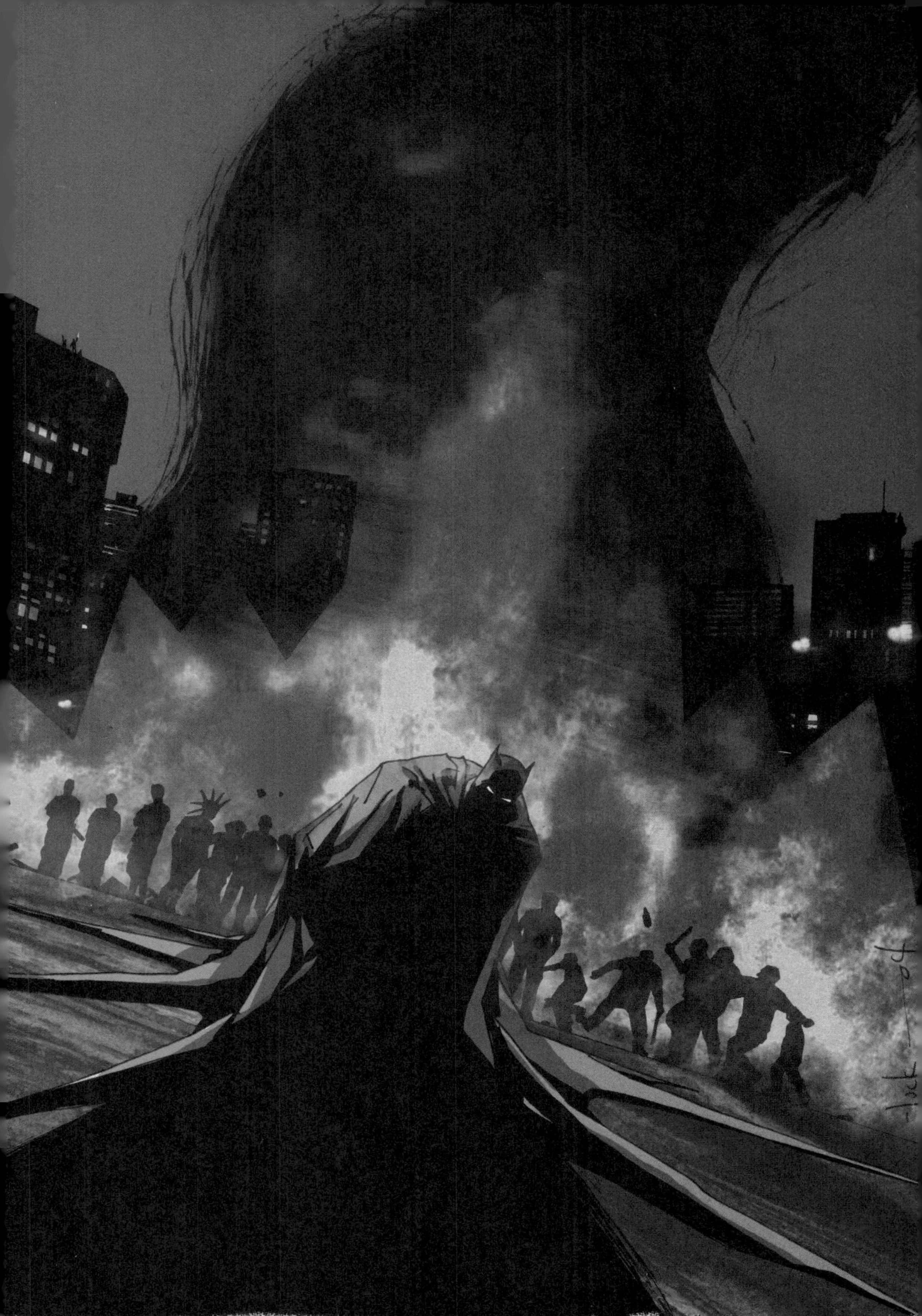

COVER GALLERY

DETECTIVE COMICS #798 Cover by Jock

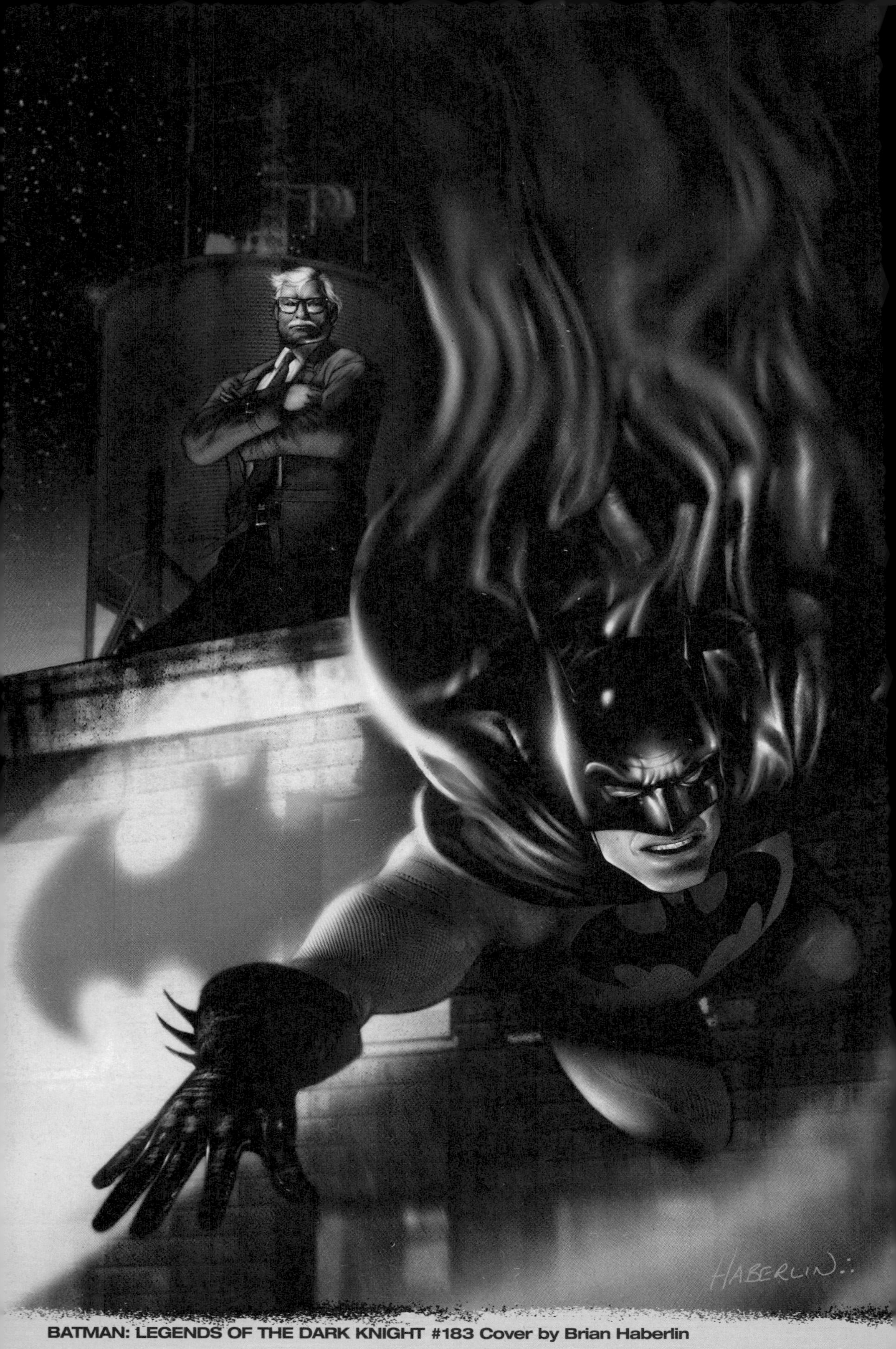
HABERLIN

BATMAN: LEGENDS OF THE DARK KNIGHT #183 Cover by Brian Haberlin

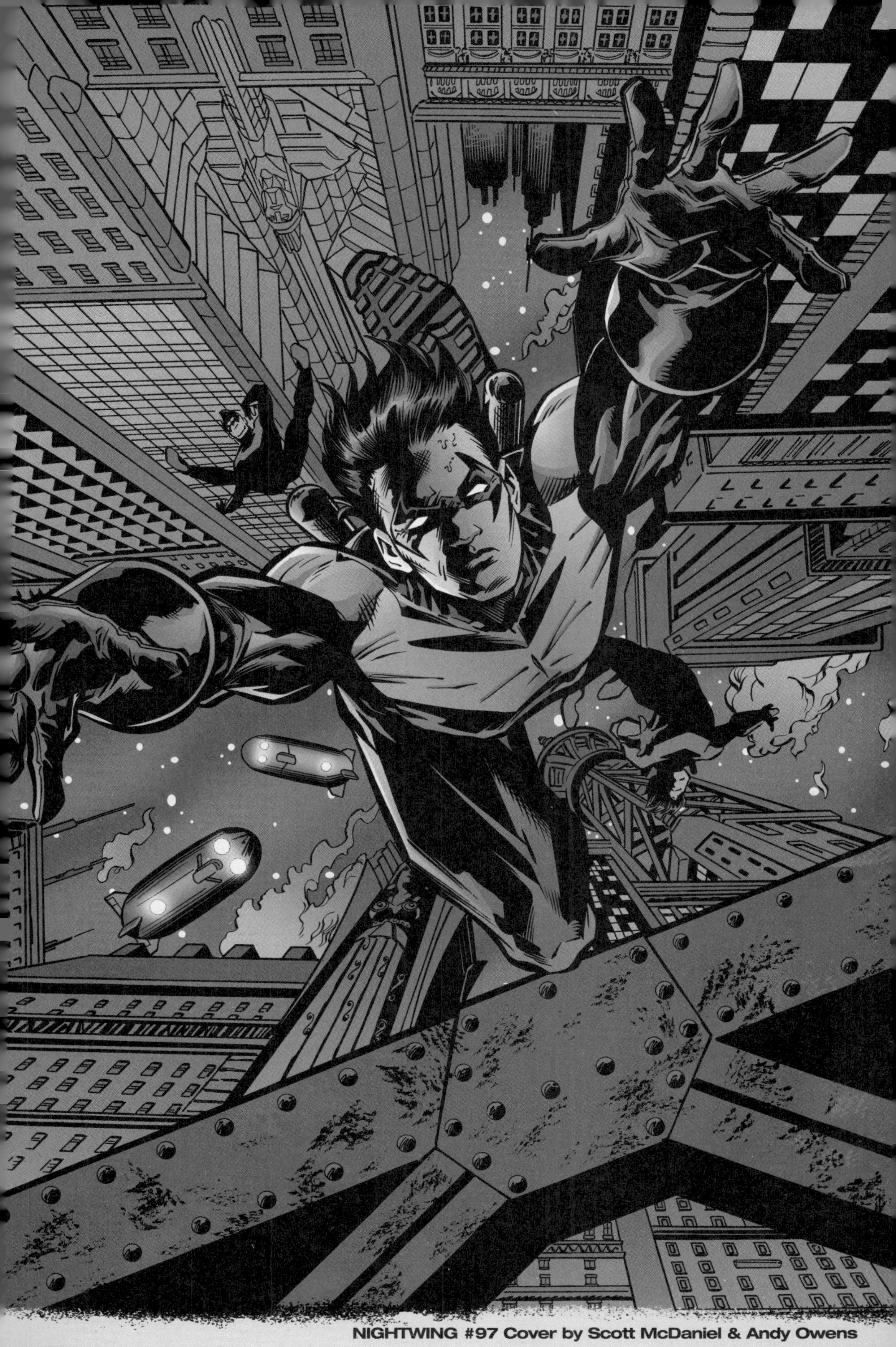

NIGHTWING #97 Cover by Scott McDaniel & Andy Owens

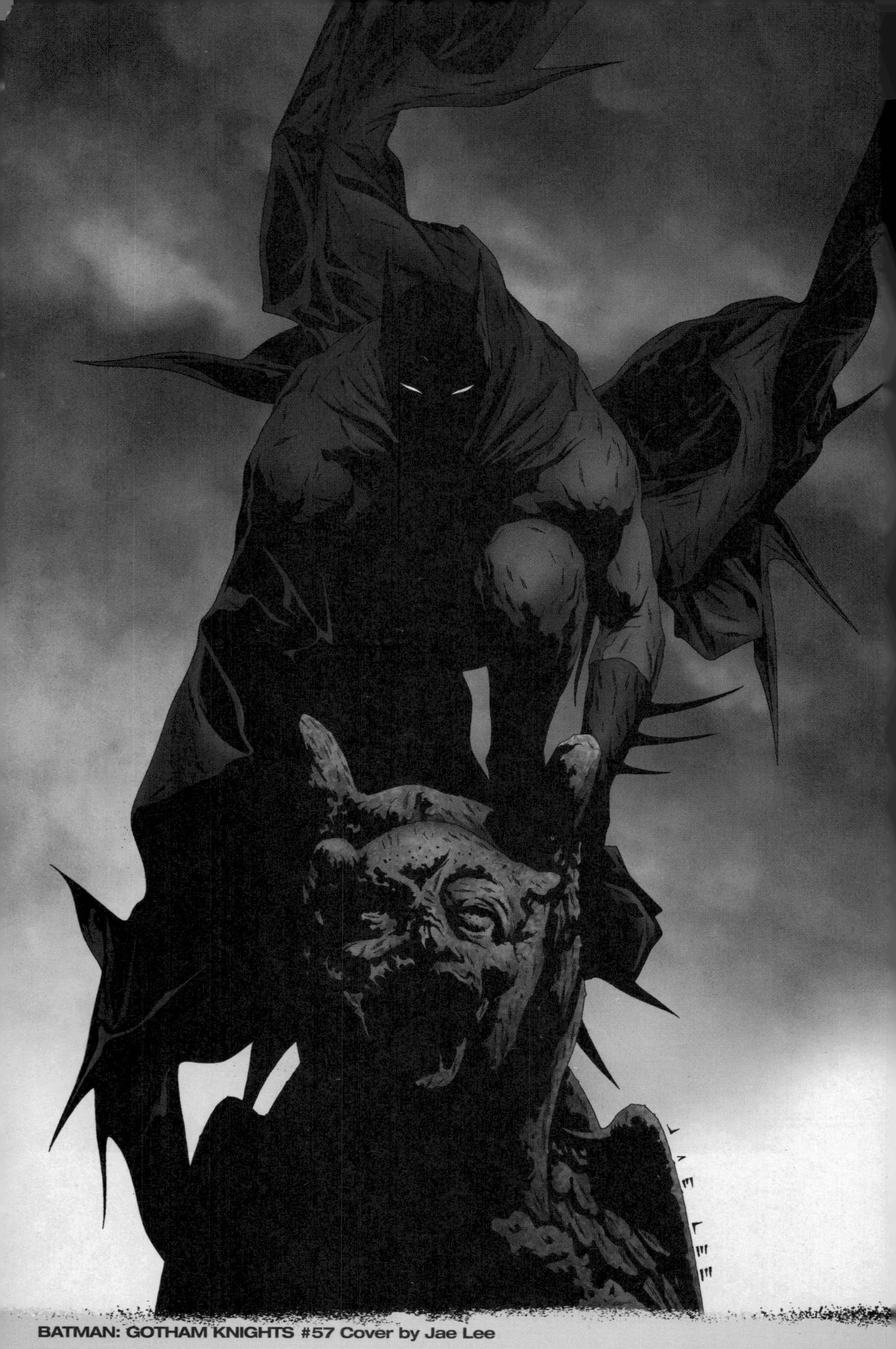

BATMAN: GOTHAM KNIGHTS #57 Cover by Jae Lee

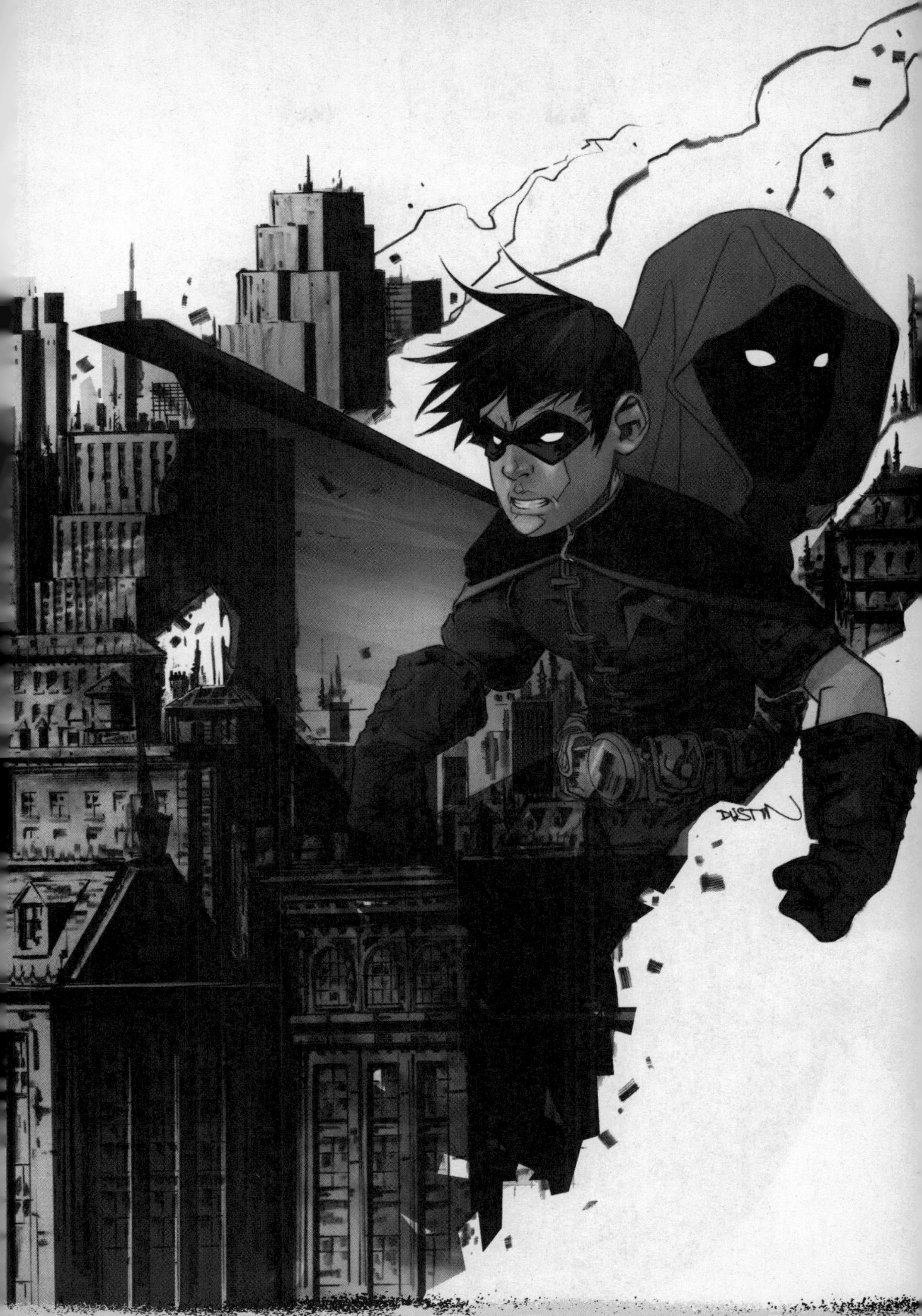
DUSTIN

ROBIN #130 Cover by Dustin Nguyen

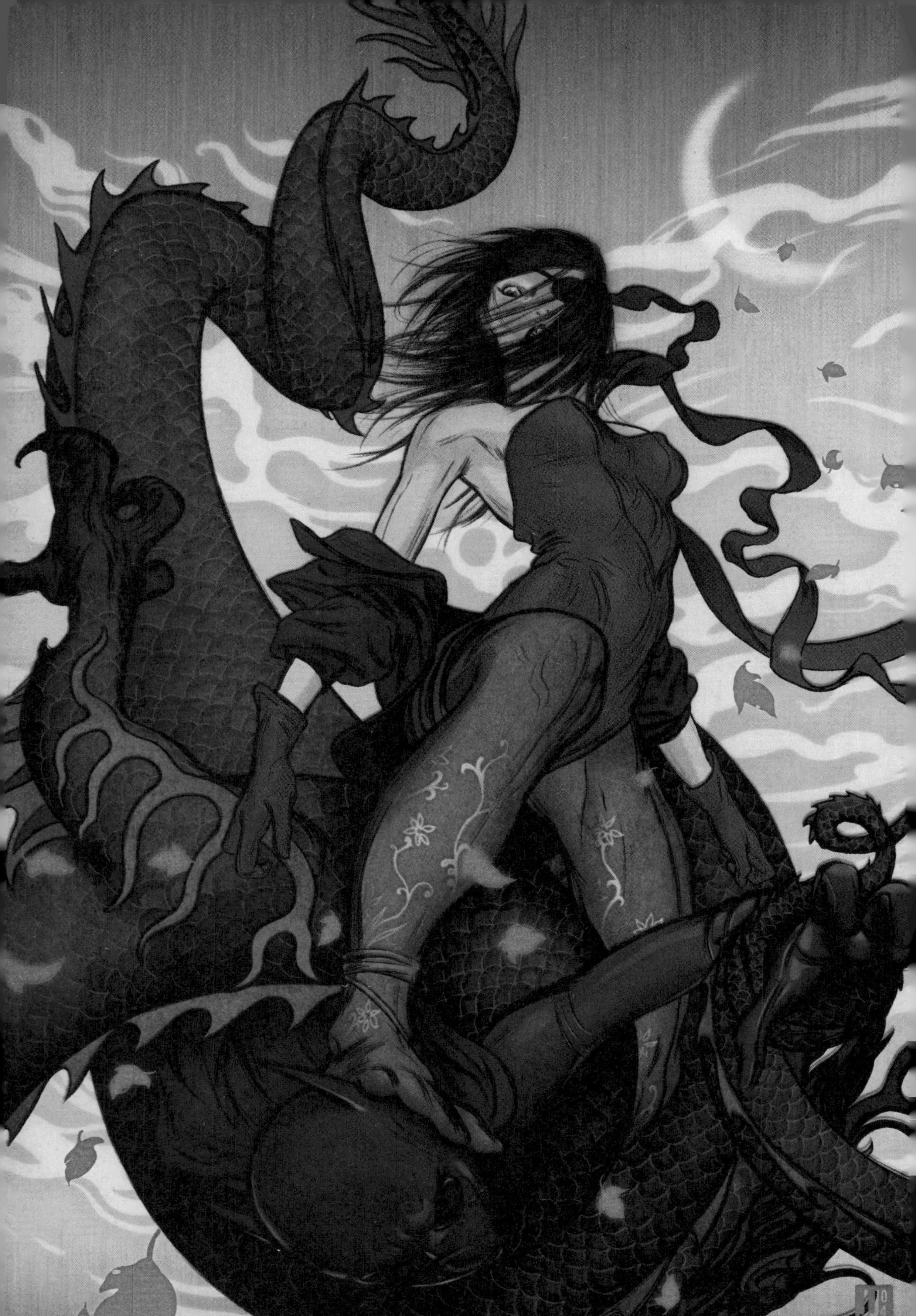

BATGIRL #56 Cover by James Jean

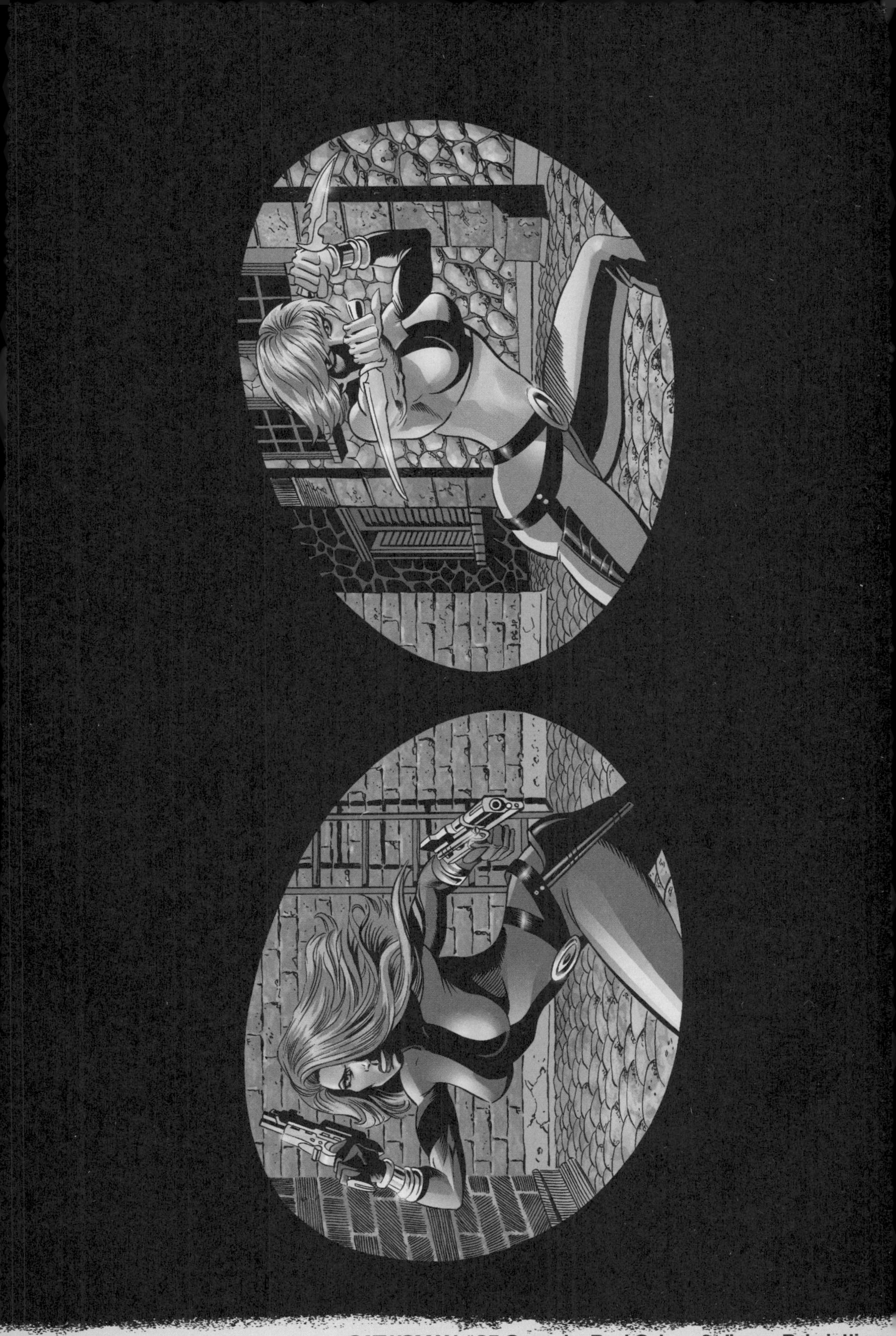

CATWOMAN #35 Cover by Paul Gulacy & Jimmy Palmiotti

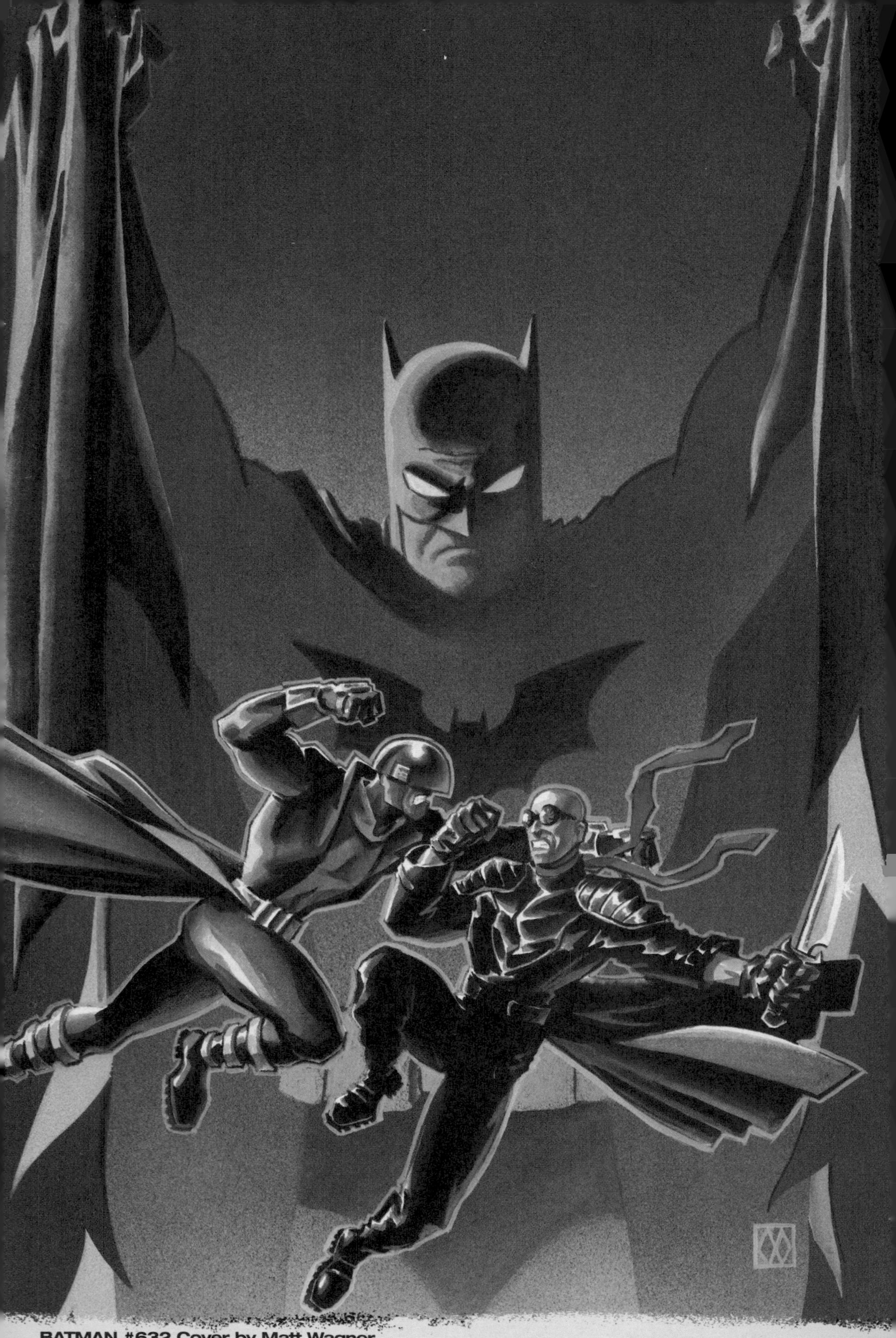

BATMAN #632 Cover by Matt Wagner

Preliminary sketch, BATMAN: WAR DRUMS

Early on it was decided one artist should handle the covers for the WAR GAMES collections, and James Jean was the first choice. Here, he discusses his approach to all covers along with a look at the step-by-step process.

Exactly how do you begin work on a cover (be it BATGIRL, FABLES or WAR GAMES)?

I love reading the script and thinking about the story. Sometimes it's the little, incidental details rather than the big, explosive plot elements that make the covers fun to put together.

Do you prefer getting input from the editors and talent before starting?

Definitely. The process is best when it's collaborative.

Do you prefer covers that are story specific or more impressionistic?

The strongest covers tell a story and work on a more universal level at the same time. I like to manipulate the hierarchy of detail and incidents in the cover so that it's instantly appealing but has a longer "read."

For WAR GAMES, editor Matt Idelson suggested a checkerboard approach for the first cover. What happened then?

The checkerboard idea for the first cover was a great springboard for the conception of all three covers. It was interesting to see how the motif was transformed through each cover — the first cover showed all the major players in place, the second cover zoomed in on the action and echoed a street map, and on the last cover I broke and skewed the checkerboard to reflect the turmoil in the story.

COVERING WAR GAMES
A CHAT WITH JAMES JEAN

After submitting a sketch, do you appreciate a certain amount of give and take with the editor? When does it become too much?

I'm a refiner when it comes to sketches, so after doing bunch of thumbnails I usually come up with one solid sketch. It always helps to have an editor or art director take a fresh look at the drawing and send comments. But the process becomes stilted when an art director comes at me with their own sketch and expects me to be a pair of hands to execute his/her idea.

When doing a series such as WAR GAMES, do you prefer linking the covers thematically? What was the thinking after the first one?

I've tried to link story arcs thematically, but it doesn't always work out. With FABLES, each cover of a story arc would take on its own distinct "look" despite the design conventions I would try to use to link them together. In the end, I'm more interested in thwarting convention than anything else.

What happens once you've received sketch approval?

It's difficult to replicate the energy of the sketch in a final drawing or painting, so I blow up the sketch and transfer it with a light box or with blue transfer paper. After the final drawing/painting is finished, I scan it in and finish it in Photoshop. During the process, I will also scan in a bunch of textures or other elements that I've painted to flesh things out.

You've used a few different styles with your artwork. What's the thinking behind that?

It's not so much deliberate as an intuitive response to the material. Each cover tells its own story, and the unique elements in each composition affect the how the picture is resolved.

How quickly can you do a cover after receiving sketch approval?

Two days is as fast as I'm able to go at the moment, but three to four days is enough time to craft something really nice.

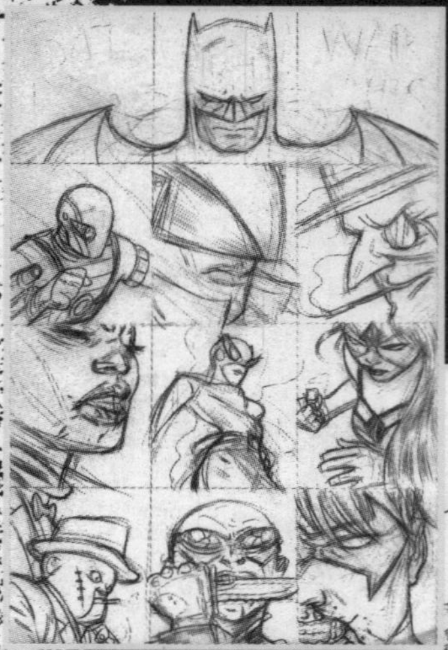

Preliminary sketches, BATMAN: WAR GAMES volume 1

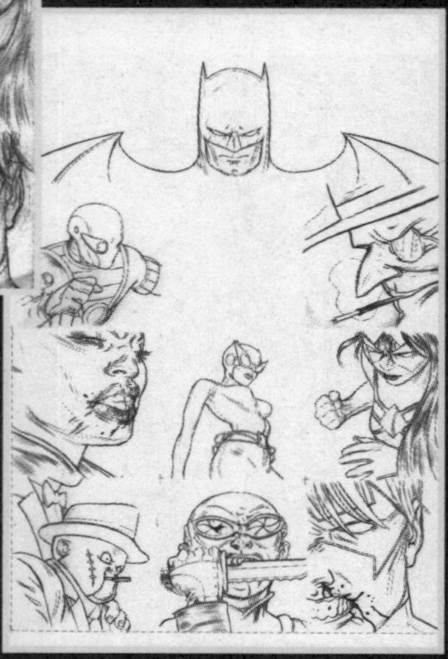

Final color sketch, BATMAN: WAR GAMES volume 1

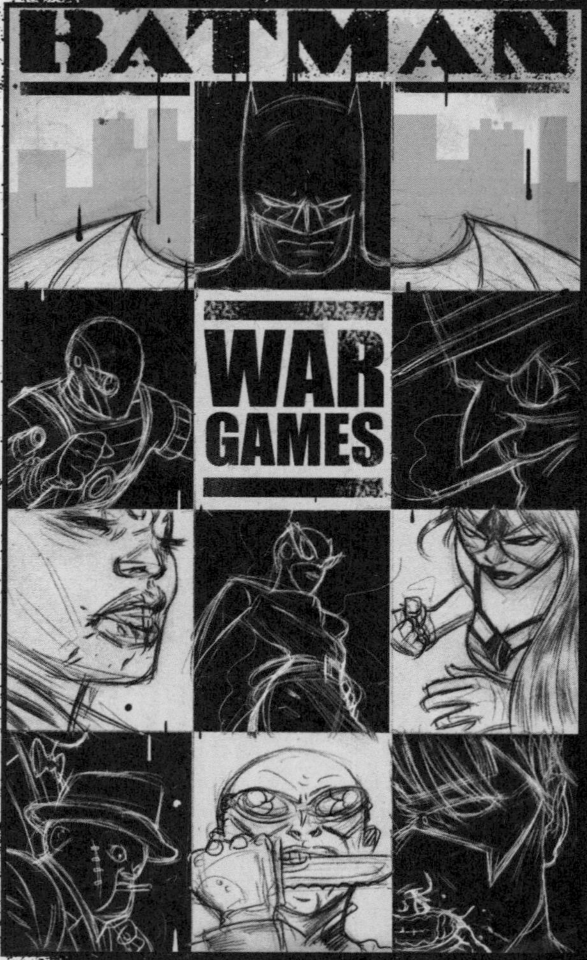
BATMAN
WAR GAMES

Do you often have to make changes after the cover is submitted?

Almost never.

Cover copy can make or break covers. Do you prefer knowing the amount of copy expected when sketching?

Sure — I also love incorporating and manipulating the cover copy and logo into the composition of the cover. I don't always get the opportunity, though.

What else goes into the process we should know about?

Lots of love.

Are you satisfied seeing the printed book?

Yes!

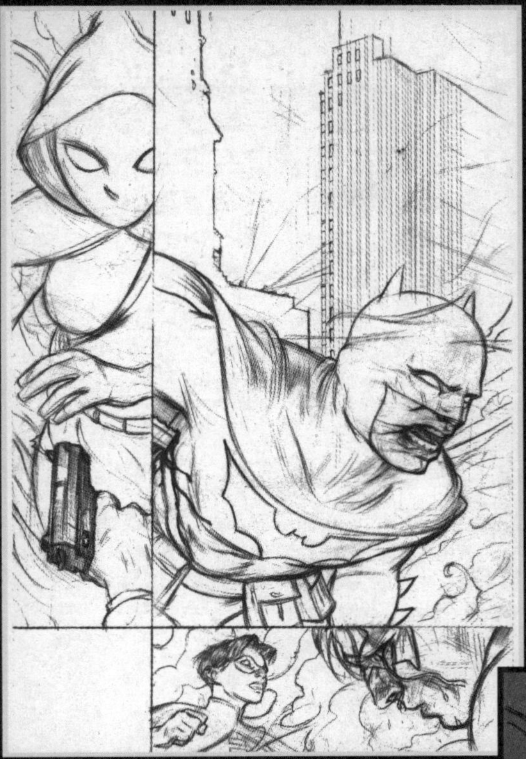

Preliminary sketch, BATMAN: WAR GAMES volume 2

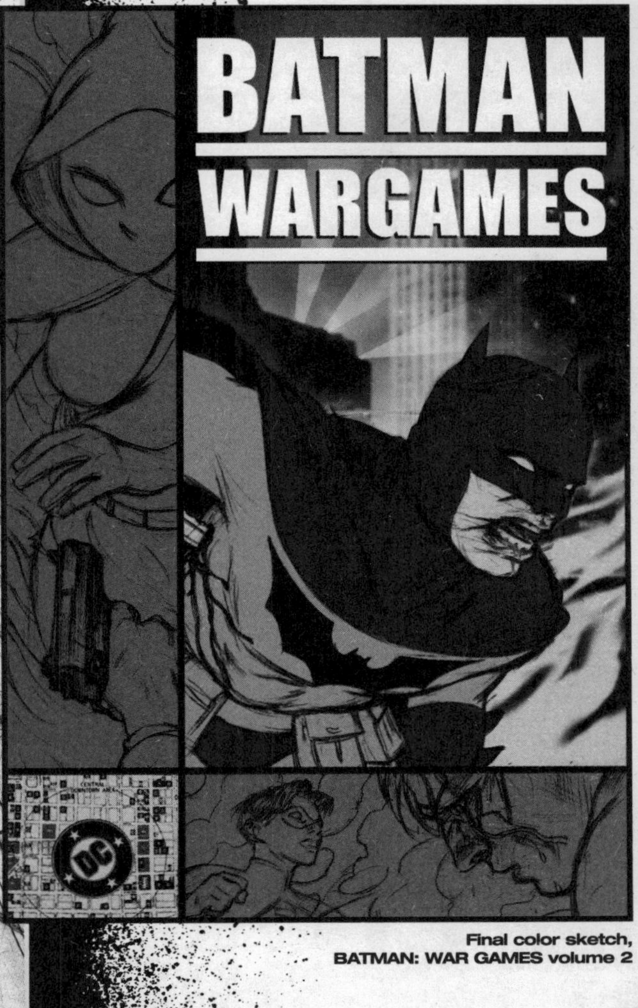
BATMAN
WARGAMES

Final color sketch, BATMAN: WAR GAMES volume 2

Preliminary sketch, BATMAN: WAR GAMES volume 3

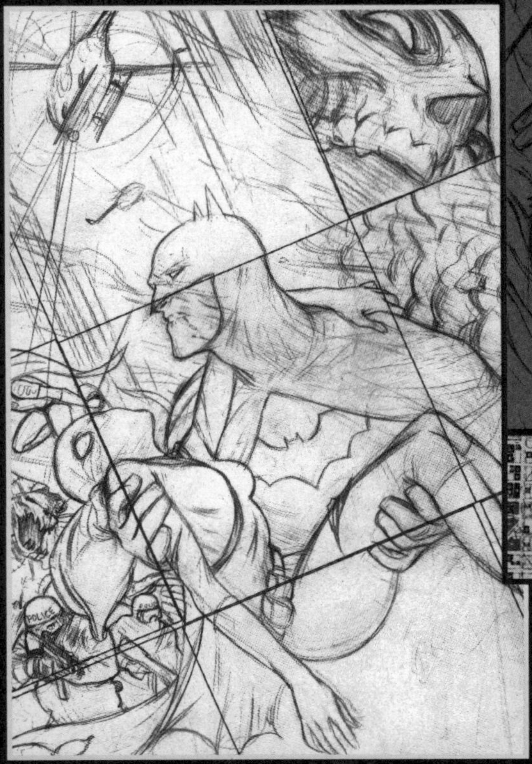

B A T M A N
THE QUEST FOR JUSTICE CONTINUES IN THESE BOOKS FROM DC:

TO FIND MORE COLLECTED EDITIONS AND MONTHLY COMIC BOOKS FROM DC COMICS,
CALL 1-888-COMIC BOOK FOR THE NEAREST COMICS SHOP OR GO TO YOUR LOCAL BOOK STORE.

Visit us at www.dccomics.com

BM0012